D1526812

LEADERS
OF THE
VICTORIAN REVOLUTION

Leaders of the
Victorian Revolution

By

JOHN W. *William* CUNLIFFE

D. LIT. (UNIVERSITY OF LONDON), LITT. D. (COLUMBIA UNIVERSITY)

*Professor of English and Director Emeritus of the
School of Journalism of Columbia University
in the City of New York*

KENNIKAT PRESS, INC.
PORT WASHINGTON, N. Y.

LEADERS OF THE VICTORIAN REVOLUTION

First published 1934
Reissued 1969 by Kennikat Press

Library of Congress Catalog Card No: 69-16481
SBN 8046-0521-1
Manufactured in the United States of America

ESSAY AND GENERAL LITERATURE INDEX REPRINT SERIES

PREFACE

The prevailing conflict and confusion of opinion as to the literary and spiritual achievements of Victorian England are partly due to the fact that many of the issues then raised are still live issues, on which people differ according to natural temperament, material interests, and inherited prejudices. But the Victorian Era is now sufficiently remote for some of its issues to be judged with detachment on a basis of adequate acquaintance with what the Victorians thought, said, and wrote. They wrote (and printed) a great deal; and naturally they did not all think the same thing. Then (as now) there were those who looked back to a Golden Age in the past; those who were entirely occupied with material concerns of the immediate present; and those who pressed forward to a millennium to be reached in a not too distant future. By choice, and almost by necessity, it is with the last class that we are mainly concerned. In any age the men advocating movement, and more especially movement over ground not hitherto traversed, will have more things and more interesting things to say than the admirers of a romantic past or the mere defenders of things as they are.

In the Victorian Age there was a good deal of moving of ancient landmarks; and though there was doubtless a good deal left unmoved, it seems more profitable from our point of view to consider what the Victorians accomplished than what they left undone. If we realize how much they had to do, and how much they did, we shall have a sounder basis for consideration of what is still to do; and from an acquaintance with what they attempted and accomplished, we may gain a clearer conception of what it is possible to achieve in the immediate future.

During the Victorian Era the English developed the industrial, democratic, and humanitarian civilization, dependent upon the application of science to agriculture, manufacture, and transportation, which has become characteristic of the modern world; and their writers had a major share in the conflict between the authoritative spokesmen of revealed religion and the protagonists of scientific research which has revolutionized modern thought. The movements thus set on foot are still going on, and no man yet knows their ultimate achievements in thought and practice; but

v

it is well worth while to study by what steps, with what searchings of heart, and with what literary reverberations, these changes in the mind of man and his organization of his industrial, social, and political life were accomplished within the limits of the Victorian period.

CONTENTS

vii

LEADERS
OF THE
VICTORIAN REVOLUTION

CHAPTER I

INTRODUCTORY

THE VICTORIAN ERA saw the accomplishment of a revolution which was more significant for England than that of 1688 and hardly less important for the world than the French Revolution, of which indeed it was a far-off echo. But while the French Revolution was political in its earlier manifestations, and in its later Napoleonic developments patriotically belligerent, the Victorian Revolution was in the main industrial, and extended its influence by the peaceful arts of manufacture, transhipment, communication, trade, and commerce. At the beginning of the Victorian Era, England was still mainly an agricultural country, able to provide food for its population out of its own resources; at the end of the period, it was mainly industrial, and paid by its manufactured goods for the food supplies which it imported in large quantities from abroad. But if the change were merely in material things, it would hardly be worth while to attempt to illustrate its development from literary sources. The change from agriculture to organized mechanical industry was an obvious and potent element in the situation; but it brought with it—or at any rate was accompanied by—changes in political, intellectual, and spiritual conditions which were of even greater importance and influence.

FROM ARISTOCRACY TO DEMOCRACY

Revolutions take place in the minds of men before the accomplishment of those overt acts which constitute the material for history. The Parliamentary Reform Act of 1832 marks the first step in a series of statutes which changed the form of government in England from a landed aristocracy to an industrial democracy. The political leaders of the nation, instead of being typical aristocrats, such as the Duke of Wellington and Lord Palmerston, became members of the mercantile middle class like Sir Robert Peel and Gladstone, to be succeeded in their turn by men sprung from the manual workers, such as Snowden and Macdonald. Political control passed first from the landed nobility to a House of Commons dependent upon a restricted franchise, and at a later stage from the House of Commons to millions of men and women

3

responsive to party tradition, trade union organization, the shallow sensationalism of cheap newspapers, and the appeals to popular prejudice and enthusiasm broadcast over the radio. The immediate impulses to the first step in this political revolution appeared to be the breaking of the Duke of Wellington's windows by the London mob; riots at Birmingham, Derby, Nottingham, and Bristol; the Liberal enthusiasm of Lord John Russell; the willingness of William IV to overcome the opposition of the reactionary majority of the House of Lords by the creation of Whig peers. But these were only outward and visible signs of a vaster change in the national temper which went back for two centuries and more. The political leaven of Hampden, Cromwell, and Milton had, at long last, permeated English life and thought. During the intervening centuries the spirit of freedom which beat at the heart of Puritanism had found expression in the development of the English Colonies into the United States of America, with the further republican repercussion of the French Revolution and all that its ideas meant for the world. But while the American and French Revolutions were preluded by political agitation and established by the appeal to arms, the similar change in England from government by a privileged aristocracy to government by a democratic electorate was brought about peacefully through repeated extensions of the parliamentary franchise, enforced by the growth of the manufacturing towns and the powers of organization developed by the manufacturers, merchants, and artisans who lived in them.

INFLUENCE OF THE PURITAN MIDDLE CLASS

The aristocratic system of government fell because the supports on which it rested were undermined. Its long continuance before its fall was not merely a matter of constitutional precedent and parliamentary statute; it had the sanction of centuries of tribal tradition and the supposed authority of Holy Scripture. Maxims such as 'Fear God—Honor the King,' 'The Powers that be are ordained of God,' 'Render unto Cæsar the things that are Cæsar's' hardened in the Catechism of the Established Church, taught to all young children within its fold, into injunctions to obey their spiritual pastors and masters, to order themselves lowly and reverently to all their betters, and to do their duty in that state of life unto which it should please God to call them. In the middle and working classes who came into power through the industrial developments of the nineteenth century, Puritanism, from the very beginning of its history, had a strong and increasing hold, which was re-inforced by the Methodist revival and the growth of evangelicalism, not only in the new denominations organized after John Wesley's death, but within the Church of England itself. This serious and rather limited view of life, as it happened, was held, not only by Queen Victoria, but by her Lutheran husband, Prince Albert. Their approval strengthened and concentrated the middle-class ideals and authority, which had deep roots in English history and English character. Unlike the Queen, however, the Puritan middle class rejected the older ideal of a static society divided by Providence into upper and lower classes (the latter ordained to serve the former). In their minds, and in those of the new industrial working-class, this gave place to the Calvinistic view that it was the duty of every man to labor in his vocation and by diligence in business to win that measure of material success which was the divine recognition of his industry. Both views of life claimed the support of Scripture, but the older, more conservative view was essentially aristocratic, as the modern, Puritan view was essentially democratic.

The Puritan ideal, however, covered very much more than any political system or mode of government. It was fundamentally moral rather than political, and, whether in Geneva or in New England, claimed and exercised authority over standards of morals and manners. When it came into political supremacy in England, it came also into the exercise of a moral authority which had been unknown since the time of the Commonwealth. There was no need to put this authority into legislative form and to provide for the administration of its decrees by policeman and magistrate; it exercised itself quietly and effectively through social pressure and public opinion, silently controlling political decisions and parliamentary enactments, government appointments, the choice of bishops and of parliamentary representatives, national policy, news and comment in newspapers and periodicals, the fiction that could be read and therefore the kind of books and magazines that could be published. This controlling spirit was imaginatively incarnated in the fearsome figure of 'Mrs. Grundy,' who prescribed not only many things to be done but a great many more things that must not be done, if one wished to lead a life of respectability and responsible activity for which the approval of the community was necessary. Most of the minions who assisted in the enforcement of Mrs. Grundy's demands were unaware of the tyranny they were helping to exercise and did their work with a spontaneous conviction of rectitude; the others either protested (and for the most part submitted) or submitted without protestation.

INDUSTRY AND SCIENCE

From a psychological point of view, the new industrialism found its motive force in the Puritan conception of life; but the practical, operative secret of its power lay in modern science and invention. How far industry owed its development to the progress of science, or how far the progress of science was indebted to the stimulus of mechanical invention, it is difficult to say; all the inventions were not made by scientists, and there were many scientists of great influence who made no inventions; but undoubtedly science and mechanical invention were helpful to each other. The workman who watched the operation of physical laws in the complicated machines by which he earned his daily bread was the more inclined to give an attentive ear to scientific theory; and the manufacturer who needed the help of scientific experts in his business could not but be impressed by the advantages of a knowledge of chemistry and physics. The great Exhibition of 1851, over the organization of which the Prince Consort presided with a wholehearted devotion, was an impressive demonstration of the indebtedness of British industry to modern science, and one of its most important results was the foundation of scholarships to promote scientific research. The new colleges which were founded at Manchester and Leeds gave an impetus to technical and scientific investigation, especially in the chemical, textile, and engineering trades, and the establishment of technical schools, with night classes for the workers, gave them an opportunity not only to understand the processes of their crafts but to contribute to their improvement and sometimes to make important inventions. The substitution of electric lighting for gas, the use of electric power in industry, the introduction of the telephone and the gramophone and many other appliances and inventions not only contributed to the amenities and resources of civilized life, but created a multitude of opportunities for skilled artisans, who by their economic importance and general intelligence became an influential element in their local communities and in the nation at large.

SCIENCE AND RELIGION

Beside the historic conflicts between Puritanism and Anglicanism, Liberalism and Conservatism, industry and agriculture, there were new issues of a more profound significance. Not only sectarian dogmas and methods of government in church and state, but Christian beliefs and Christian morals which had been accepted for a thousand years were called in question. To reconcile the demands of a scientific and industrial age with the claims of a religion which embodied primitive traditions of the origin of man and of his purpose in the world here or hereafter was indeed a problem which mankind could not be expected to solve in a single generation. Many of the solutions attempted were merely palliatives, recognized as necessary to meet the demands of an immediate situation.

At first, at any rate, traditional beliefs offered more resistance to change and held their ground more firmly than traditional institutions. This was partly because Puritan and Anglican, however bitterly opposed on other issues, were at one in their defense of what Gladstone called 'The Impregnable Rock of Holy Scripture.' The scientists, for their part, were at first disinclined to encumber their investigations and theories by provoking an unnecessary attack from the embattled hierarchy, whether Anglican or Noncomformist, or both combined. The publication of Sir Charles Lyell's *Principles of Geology* in 1830–33 really indicated the abandonment by science of the attempt to adapt its teaching to a literal interpretation of the account of the Creation and Fall of Man in the first chapters of *Genesis;* Lyell gave up the 'catastrophic' theory (founded on the Biblical Deluge) and suggested that the changes in the earth's surface had probably been much the same in pre-historic as in historic time—'uniformitarian' instead of 'catastrophic.' But the great geologist, himself a sincere believer, was tactful enough to avoid an open break with the theologians, and his epoch-marking *Principles* passed without serious opposition. The foundation of the Association for the Advancement of Science a few years later provoked a clerical protest in fear that it would contest the authority of the Church, but it was not until the publication of Darwin's *Origin of Species* in 1859 that the storm really broke. At the next meeting of the Association, held in Oxford, Bishop Wilberforce was put up by the reactionary party to ridicule the new theory, which was defended by the young and then little known professor of zoölogy, Thomas H. Huxley. As Darwin preferred to stay quietly in the background, continuing his researches in his country home at Downe in Kent (now the property of the nation), Huxley became the popular champion of the new theory in a bitter conflict which ended in the complete rout of the clerical opposition.

Even if the clergy had not gone out of their way to challenge the supporters of the new theory of evolution to decide the issue by open controversy, the exercise of patriarchal authority, in political and social matters by the squire and in religion and intellectual matters by the parson, would hardly have continued. Science and the machine, depending upon expert knowledge and manual skill, are inevitably antagonists of aristocratic privilege and ecclesiastical authority. The ecclesiastical opposition to the evolution theory was also embarrassed by the development of scientific criticism in its own ranks, undermining from within that impregnable rock of Scriptural authority upon which the churches, both Anglican and Nonconformist, so confidently relied. On the other hand, there was a steady movement forward in the acceptance of facts established by modern scientific investigation and in the recognition of the duty of the community to rescue from ignorance, disease, and material degradation the submerged classes whose poverty prevented them from living a life of reasonable or even tolerable comfort and refinement.

HUMANITARIANISM AND EDUCATION

In spite of the decay of religious belief, the humanitarian movement, which had often been associated with religious leaders and religious organizations, continued in full force. John Howard and Elizabeth Fry, the advocates of prison reform in the eighteenth century; William Wilberforce, the leader of the movement for the suppression of the slave trade, and Zachary Macaulay (father of Lord Macaulay) who devoted his means and energy to the abolition of slavery in the British Colonies; Lord Shaftesbury, who introduced legislation for the protection of women and children in factories; and Florence Nightingale, who revolutionized hospital nursing, were all deeply religious. But Jeremy Bentham, the apostle of utilitarianism and legal reform, and his followers, James Mill and John Stuart Mill, were no less devoted to the public welfare without professing any form of orthodox religious belief. Robert Raikes, who established the first Sunday School at Gloucester in 1780, set out to teach the elements of secular education— the three R's, in fact—but the new institution was speedily seized upon by the Evangelicals as a means of propaganda and even set up as a test of partisanship. In Anthony Trollope's *Barchester Towers* Bishop Proudie's domineering wife makes 'Sabbath Schools' an issue to divide the evangelical sheep among the clergy from the latitudinarian goats. On the whole, the intrusion of religious and especially of dogmatic issues into elementary education was a misfortune, as a great deal of energy was spent upon attacking or defending the educational fortresses of traditional belief which might have been directed, with much greater advantage, to improving the means and methods of elementary education, but it is well to remember that what little had been done up to the beginning of the Victorian Era for the education of the poor had been done almost entirely by members, first of the Catholic Church, and then of the Anglican. It is true that the Nonconformists were subjected to educational as well as other disabilities; they were hampered in the education of their children, who were excluded from the leading educational institutions of the country. The foundation of the University of London in 1828 showed the division of educational effort prevailing at that time. The institution was originally organized to provide higher education in London on a liberal basis without denominational distinctions, but its first college (University) was promptly duplicated by the erection less than a mile away of King's College, intended to protect Anglican interests. It was not until 1871 that the religious tests imposed upon students and fellows of the Universities of Oxford and Cambridge were abolished, and when, about the same time, a system of compulsory education was organized for the whole country, care was taken to protect the vested interests of the denominational and parochial schools previously established. This division between denominational and educational aims was continued when provision was made, about the end of the century, for secondary education.

THE POSITION OF WOMEN

The lack of educational opportunity was an important element in the grievances set forth by John Stuart Mill in his important treatise *On the Subjection of Women* (1869). Girls were of course included in the scheme of 1870 for compulsory elementary education, but the older grammar schools, the endowed public schools and colleges were for men only, and it was impossible for a woman, at the beginning of the Victorian Era, to obtain a University degree in England or an education qualifying her to practise law or medicine or to take Holy Orders. Women were admitted to degrees at the University of London in 1880, and the new provincial universities founded during Victoria's reign offered the same privileges to women as to men; but up to the end of the century, while women could be educated by College dons in Oxford or

Cambridge, they could not obtain a degree at either university. Admission to the learned professions came equally slowly. Meanwhile provision was made by voluntary effort or by government action to provide high schools and boarding schools which would prepare women to pass the necessary examinations.

Next to the lack of educational opportunities stood the grievance of economic dependence. At the beginning of the Victorian Era, an English girl could become a domestic servant, a factory worker, a school teacher, or a governess; that was about all. By a strange inconsistency, Queen Victoria herself was strongly opposed to the removal of female disabilities. She wrote to the Prime Minister (Mr. Gladstone) in 1870: 'The circumstances respecting the Bill to give women the same position as men with respect to Parliamentary franchise gives her an opportunity to observe that she had for some time past wished to call Mr. Gladstone's attention to the mad and utterly demoralizing movement of the present day to place women in the same position as to professions—as men;—and amongst others, in the Medical Line. . . . And she is most anxious that it should be known how she not only disapproves but abhors the attempts to destroy all propriety and womanly feeling which will inevitably be the result of what has been proposed. The Queen is a woman herself—and knows what an anomaly her own position is:—but that can be reconciled with reason and propriety though it is a terribly difficult and trying one. But to tear away all the barriers which surround a woman, and to propose that they should study with men—things which could not be named before them—certainly not—in a mixed audience—would be to introduce a total disregard of what must be considered as belonging to the rules and principles of morality. . . . Let women be what God intended; a helpmate for man—but with totally different duties and vocations.—She wishes Mr. Gladstone would send for and see Sir William Jenner who can tell him what an awful idea this is—of allowing young girls and young men to enter the dissecting room together.'

In spite of the opposition of the Queen and other old ladies, one by one these disabilities were removed. Legislation and new interpretations of existing law gave married women the right to control their own property and their own persons. Custom no longer required women to wear clothes and hair that unfitted them for any active exercise except hunting. Probably the popularity of bicycling, lawn tennis and other outdoor games did more to win freedom for women than any legal enactment. But the long fight for the suffrage, which was not entirely won till 1928, served by long argument and agitation to draw attention to other rights and wrongs of women when their position was considered from a reasonable instead of a traditional point of view.

THE CONDITION OF THE PEOPLE

In the main, however, as a recent historian of the period (E. Wingfield-Stratford) observes, the Victorians 'concentrated on material progress, in the faith that every increase of human power over blind matter must be a good thing in itself.' In spite of a great increase in population (from 13,896,797 in 1831 to 32,527,843 in 1901) there was also a great increase in material prosperity, in which all classes shared; this brought with it a marked progress in material comfort, cleanliness, processes of sanitation, surgical methods, medical treatment, hospital equipment, and in fact almost everything affecting the health of the community, as was shown in the decrease of infectious diseases and a lowering of the death rate. Popular amusements, if they still left much to be desired in point of intelligence, became more wholesome, more decent, less brutal. An English Cabinet minister, joining with a Labor Member of Parliament in a survey of social conditions at the first Victorian Jubilee (1887) could write with a sense of elation: 'The people are better paid, they work fewer hours, they are better fed, clothed, and housed; they are better educated; their habits and customs are improved; their sports and pastimes are no longer brutal and demoralizing. The children and women are better cared for and better treated. The wheels of progress have gone on and on with accelerated speed.' Even so pessimistic an observer as George Gissing saw in the second Jubilee 'a legitimate triumph of the average man. Look back for threescore years, and who shall affect to doubt that the time has been marked by many improvements in the material life of the English people. Often have they been at logger-heads among themselves, but they have never flown at each other's throats, and from every grave dispute has resulted some substantial gain. They are a cleaner people and a more sober; in every class there is a diminution of brutality; education—stand for what it may—has notably extended; certain forms of tyranny have been abolished; certain forms of suffering, due to heedlessness or ignorance, have been abated.'

Through trade unions and co-operative associations the workpeople did a great deal to achieve their own salvation by their own efforts and organization. As the working-class toward the end of the century acquired greater political influence, and Labor members began to appear in Parliament, measures to limit working hours for men as well as for women and children, to secure compensation for accident or ill health, to provide pensions for old age and payment for lack of employment, received increased attention, though in the latter cases these privileges did not become legal rights till after the turn of the century. Universal elementary education was enforced by law in 1870, and later legislation opened opportunities for secondary and university education to young students of the working-class; university extension and other organizations for adult education were established. In all respects, especially in the vital point of higher wages, the workers were far better off at the end of Victoria's reign than they had been at the beginning; they were better housed, fed, and clothed; better educated, more intelligent, more independent.

The improvement in economic conditions brought with it inevitable changes in social and spiritual conditions, especially for the oppressed or neglected. The control of the children by the parents, of the wife by the husband, of woman by man, was called in question, and gradually, at any rate in part, discarded or mitigated. All kinds of prescriptive rights and traditional authorities which had hitherto passed unquestioned were challenged; many ancient landmarks were swept away, or their original significance and purpose entirely changed. Even the rights of property were no longer treated with unquestioned respect, but called upon to justify themselves from the point of view of social advantage.

Evidently changes as far-reaching and deep-seated as are outlined above could not be accomplished without violent controversy and bitter opposition. The general temper of the people at the beginning of the Victorian Era, while favorable to moderate reform, was against revolution. Sir Walter Scott, the most popular writer of the preceding generation, had been distinctly conservative in spirit, and Wordsworth, Coleridge, and Southey, spokesmen of revolt at the beginning of the century, had long ago succumbed to reaction. Byron and Shelley were notorious rebels whose opinions were execrated, however fervently their poetry might be admired. It was by a series of gradual changes that the aristocratic and agricultural England, which had saved Europe from Napoleon, became the very different industrial and democratic England of the nineteenth century.

SUMMARY

It will be seen that the Victorian Revolution involved changes much more profound and far-reaching than the constitutional reforms and parliamentary enactments beginning with the Act of 1832 and completed by the Act of 1928 which established universal suffrage for adult men and women on equal terms. It affected not merely the machinery of government but the prevailing conceptions of the end of life, of what it was right to do and to say, and what might be expected of English people and what might be imposed upon them. These ideas were worked out gradually and they are still being worked out. They were at first the ideas of a few—perhaps of a solitary philosopher or man of letters; they were communicated partly by word of mouth but more by the written word, which the spread of popular education and cheap books and newspapers made increasingly powerful. It is the purpose of this volume to trace the development of these ideas in the works of their principal exponents, to set forth what manner of men they were and what were the conditions and circumstances that led them to the expression of opinions which, from being the views of a small minority, came to be universally accepted, not only in Great Britain, but throughout and even beyond the English-speaking world.

If a formula should be sought which would sum up the essence of these changes in the briefest possible space it might be found in the words *Industrialism* and *Science*—and if Industrialism be defined as the application of Science to manufacture, transportation, and communication by means of mechanical invention and industrial organization, the single word *Science* might be accepted as the main element in the transformation of the England of agriculture and commerce of the earlier centuries into the modern England whose development began in the eighteenth century and is still going on. It was the fate of Victorian England to be faced with problems of belief and of industrial organization which afterwards became world problems and which have not yet been found capable of satisfactory solution. The Victorian contributions towards a solution were in the English manner—adjustments in the shape of compromises which were in their nature temporary and had to be superseded, revised, or rejected as the situation became clearer and developed in a different direction from what had been expected. But the general movement was forward and secured manifest gains for the common good.

A TENTATIVE DIVISION

The problem of the Victorians was to find a compromise—or a succession of compromises—among contending interests and influences; life for the vast majority must be lived rather than theorized about, and it need not surprise us that the successive answers to the various problems were neither unanimous, nor consecutive, nor consistent. The new conditions were inextricably involved with what had gone before, and the continuous movement of opinion, political, social, or religious, does not submit to be put neatly into pigeon holes. But some tentative classification, founded mainly on chronological considerations, will be of advantage to the student, and our survey will therefore be based upon a division of the principal writers into three main groups:—

(1) Early Victorians, including those writers whose main literary activities began before 1860.

(2) Middle Victorians, who began to attract public attention between 1860 and 1880.

(3) Later Victorians, who did not exert any considerable influence till after 1880.

It is obvious that this classification must be approximate rather than exact, and its value consists mainly in helping the student to fix in his own mind a clear outline of the chronological succession of the more important Victorian authors, their relations to each other and to the formative period of their literary development. A young writer growing up in the generation before 1860 was under very different intellectual influences from those prevailing during the period 1860–80; and from 1880 on to the end of the century there were further changes which will, it is hoped, be made clear when that period comes under review. For the sake of convenience, the period up to 1860 may be regarded as pre-evolutionary; that of 1860–80 as the period of the controversy about evolution; and that between 1880 and the end of the century as the period of general acceptance of the evolutionary theory and of scientific ascendancy. Other important issues were, of course, being discussed at the same time, but the evolution controversy appears to offer the greatest advantages as a clue for what the young twentieth century reader may regard as the labyrinth of Victorian opinion.

PART I
EARLY VICTORIANS
(*1832–1860*)

CHAPTER II

THE EARLY VICTORIANS

(*1832–1860*)

ALTHOUGH Queen Victoria actually came to the throne in 1837, the year 1832 is generally accepted as the beginning of the Victorian Era, mainly because the First Reform Bill became law in that year. This date is convenient for literary reasons: Sir Walter Scott died in 1832, and his death marks a break with the period of the Romantic Revival; Goethe died in the same year; Coleridge and Lamb two years later. The Oxford Movement was making a definite beginning with the publication of the first *Tracts for the Times*, Tennyson and Browning were giving their first poems to an inattentive public, Dickens was scoring his earliest successes—all before Queen Victoria's accession. Macaulay's precocious genius had long been recognized, and Carlyle, though he had not yet caught public attention, had settled in London, resolutely launched on a literary career.

Our upward limit for the period of the Early Victorians (1860) is—it must be confessed—arbitrarily fixed at that date as a matter of convenience for the student of literature; the main reasons underlying the choice are the significant works that appeared about that time—Darwin's *Origin of Species*, *Essays and Reviews*, George Eliot's *Adam Bede*, and Meredith's *Ordeal of Richard Feverel*, which seem to indicate a new phase of Victorian development.

THE REFORM ACT

The Reform Act which gives us a chronological starting point was noteworthy rather for what it signified than for what it actually did. As we examine its provisions with the detached view of a century later, it seems a very moderate instalment of reform. In a country with a population of fourteen millions it admitted to the franchise 450,000 additional voters, thus creating a new electorate of less than half a million, all connected with property. No borough containing less than 2,000 inhabitants was to send a member to Parliament, and those containing less than 4,000 inhabitants were to send only one; this disfranchised sixty little boroughs, each returning two members, and reduced the representation of forty-seven others from two members to one each. Seven great towns, including Manchester, Birmingham, and Leeds, as yet unrepresented in the House of Commons, were allotted two members each; twenty other towns and eight London areas received one. The right to vote rested upon a property qualification of £10 a year. In introducing the Bill Lord John Russell appealed to the members of the unreformed House of Commons not to resent the infusion of a new popular spirit, but to show that they were determined 'not to be representatives of a small class, or of a particular interest, but to form a body who, representing the people, springing from the people, and sympathizing with the people, can fairly call on the people to support the future burdens of the country.'

At that time, records the London Observer of March 3, 1831, 'the new plan took all parties by surprise. It surpassed the expectations of the Radicals, and alarmed the Tory and Aristocratical Party beyond all description.' The privileged classes were right in supposing that the principle of popular representation, once accepted, meant ultimately the loss of their privileges; they were needlessly alarmed if they thought the passing of the Reform Bill would be immediately destructive of their power and influence. A whole generation was to elapse before a Conservative leader, Benjamin Disraeli, afterwards the Earl of Beaconsfield, carried the Second Reform Act of 1867, which extended the suffrage to the artisans of the manufacturing towns. The noble families lost their 'pocket' boroughs, but they continued to exercise a very great political influence; the Whitmores continued to represent Bridgenorth in the House of Commons as they had done since 1660, and when the Marlboroughs of Blenheim wanted a seat in Parliament for a younger son, Lord Randolph Churchill, they sought it—and found it—in the neighboring borough of Woodstock. In the end, as has been noted, the Prime Ministers, from being almost inevitably peers, became necessarily Commoners, and a hereditary seat in the House of Lords, instead of being a political asset, became a political misfortune; but nearly a century had rolled round before this became a maxim of political expediency.

At the first election under the new suffrage, the voters very naturally returned to power the Whig party who had carried the Reform Act, and the first Reform Government passed some useful legislation of a moderate character. The system of administering poor law relief was re-organized, and grants were made in support of voluntary education for the children of the working people.

The Municipal Corporations Act of 1835 gave the great manufacturing towns power to manage their own affairs and to provide
for their inhabitants air, light, water, and the sanitary conditions
necessary for a large community concentrated in a small space
owing to the requirements of trade and manufacture.   But the
Whig Government soon lost the impetus to reform, and when
Victoria came to the throne it had settled down to a do-nothing
policy under Lord Melbourne, whose usual attitude to a follower
burning to remedy some public grievance or notorious abuse was
'Why not let it alone?'   The simple folk who had regarded the
passing of the Reform Act as the inauguration of the Millennium
were naturally disappointed, and the Conservatives came back
into power under Sir Robert Peel.   Peel was described by his bitterest adversary, Disraeli, as 'a transcendant administrator of public
business and a matchless master of debate'; Gladstone counted
'the voice of Sir Robert Peel' as one of the two perfect things he
had known; and it was this combination of administrative ability
with oratorical genius that made Peel the inevitable leader of a
party composed mainly of country gentlemen to whose ranks he
did not really belong, for he was the son of a Lancashire manufacturer.   The times were difficult; the Chartists were pressing
for the electoral reforms which the Reform Act had not included—
Universal Suffrage, Vote by Ballot, and Annual Parliaments—
and were emphasizing these demands by dangerous riots and
monster petitions to Parliament; the Manchester School of economists, traders, and politicians, combined in the Anti-Corn Law
League, were urging by a skilfully conducted agitation that the
import tax on wheat protected the interests of the great land-
owners and their dependents at the expense of all the rest of the
population, especially the working-class and their employers.   A
potato famine in Ireland gave emphasis to the cry that 'bread
was dear, and human flesh was cheap,' and Peel yielded, first in
the provisions of the Budget, and then by the total repeal of the
Corn Laws.   The popular outcry against the taxation of food and
the economic situation gave Peel little choice, but he failed to
carry with him the country gentlemen upon whom he depended
for his majority in the House of Commons; virulently assailed by
the unscrupulous political adventurer, Benjamin Disraeli, who
had entered the House of Commons at the beginning of the Victorian Era as a 'Radical Conservative,' Peel was hurled from
power with screams and hoots as a traitor to his party, and a year
or two later (1850) died in retirement.

THE PALMERSTON ADMINISTRATION

Peel's place as the national leader was taken by Viscount Palmerston (1784–1865), who, to use the phrase of a recent biographer (Philip Guedalla) 'spoke the last word of the Eighteenth Century.' Another historian of the Victorian Era (O. F. Christie) says: 'Palmerston is the man we think of as the protagonist of England in these changeful and pregnant years; a most laborious statesman but also a man of the world; at home in society and on the Turf; of undaunted courage and inexhaustible vitality, and (it may be admitted) "touched with no ascetic gloom."' Palmerston took the cheerful and comfortable view that the Reform Act had settled the electoral situation for the time being, and there was no need to worry about it; he conducted a spirited foreign policy with Liberal tendencies, assisted in the establishment of United Italy, and made the name of England respected abroad; his aristocratic connections and moderate views commended him to the admirers of the old *régime;* his sportsmanship and somewhat domineering patriotism made him popular with the masses; educated at Harrow, one of the oldest schools of the aristocracy, and also at the more liberal University of Edinburgh, he knew how to make the best of both the world that was passing and the world that was to come. He held out one hand to the traditional past and the other to the democratic future. 'We have shown,' he said, 'that liberty is compatible with order; that individual freedom is reconcilable with obedience to the law. We have shown the example of a nation in which every class of society accepts with cheerfulness the lot which Providence has assigned to it, while at the same time every individual of every class is constantly striving to raise himself in the social scale—not by injustice and wrong, not by violence and illegality, but by persevering good conduct and by the steady and energetic exertion of the moral and intellectual faculties with which his Creator has endowed him.'

A thorough Englishman in his independence of conduct, Palmerston at first offended the Queen and the Prince Consort by his offhand manner of conducting the affairs of the Foreign Office without consulting them or even informing them of what he was doing; but they were ultimately convinced of his genuine patriotism and devotion to the national welfare, and he became one of Victoria's favorite ministers. He was popular with the masses, and formed a useful steadying influence in the time of transition in which he lived.

SOCIAL INFLUENCE OF THE COUNTY FAMILIES

While the Whig nobility and the county members kept a slowly relaxing grip on the reins of political power, the social influence of the county families was, during the period of the Early Victorians, hardly diminished. No part of the English social structure of the nineteenth century is so difficult for the young American student to realize, and English writers for English readers seldom trouble to explain it, as (though it is now disappearing) it was once a phase of English life so familiar that the average Englishman accepted it without explanation. An American observer, Wallace Notestein, Professor of English History at Yale University, may therefore be quoted in explanation of a social phenomenon of primary significance for the understanding of English life and literature, especially during the first half of Victoria's reign. The county families, he points out, formed a kind of highland of rank, above which were the peaks of the nobility, and below which were the great plains of the middle class, and the swamps of the 'lower classes.' Within this highland territory there went forward for centuries an enclosed and self-centered life which Professor Notestein describes in detail as follows: 'There is in every shire a marked group of people who are lords of the manor, that is, own estates with tenantry upon them; they live in the country house next the church or at least near the village, their wives open bazaars and do deeds of kindness; their children, when home from school, play tennis with the children of the clergy and of the neighboring nobility. Their sons go to public school, possibly to Oxford or Cambridge, and enter the Army, the Navy, the Civil Service, occasionally the Church, or stay on the land. The daughters may be presented [at Court], and by and by they will marry the men they have known at the county hunts and the county balls. Such people are hardly distinguishable from the nobility who live in the same way. A duke would of course be a more exalted person than a squire, but his daughter might marry the squire's son. If a squire has been on the land for generations, his local prestige may be greater than that of the new nobility. A Lowther in Cumberland or a Harcourt in Oxfordshire, whose family had provided justices of peace and high sheriffs of the county for six centuries, would enjoy a position to be envied by a Lloyd Georgian or even a Victorian noble family. Like good furniture, families in good condition are enhanced in value by age. At some distant date their position may have been gained by fighting; for centuries now, however, most families have risen out of those who had made money in business, and were willing to exchange some of it for a "seat" and what would sooner or later go with it, coats of arms and the visiting cards of the other landed people of the county.'

At the beginning of the nineteenth century the county families could live a self-contained life of their own, almost independent of the fashionable London world on the one hand, or the middle- and working-class population of the market towns on the other; if they were wealthy enough, they might break the monotony of country life by an occasional visit to Bath or to the metropolis; the novels of Jane Austen are almost entirely taken up with life on this plane. With the increasing facilities for transportation and communication afforded in the early years of the Victorian Era and the growing importance of the manufacturing towns, the contacts of the county families with the world outside inevitably became more frequent, though they still maintained their social privileges and kept a ring from which people engaged in 'trade' were as a rule excluded. This transition stage is admirably illustrated in George Eliot's *Middlemarch*, a masterly study of provincial life at the beginning of the Victorian Era. The county families living on their own estates on the outskirts of Middlemarch form a society apart, into which even the clerical and professional families of the town are admitted only occasionally and as it were on sufferance. The townspeople have their own social life, distinct from that of the county gentry and the farmers of the country round about; socially, the county families are still supreme and no one seems to dream of challenging their supremacy.

Of the life of the 'lower classes' at this period we have a very lively picture in the novels of Dickens, so far as London is concerned; but when, as in *Hard Times*, he attempts to deal with the manufacturing North, with which he was very little acquainted, he goes sadly astray. For the life of the Lancashire cotton operatives we must turn to the more realistic studies of Mrs. Gaskell (*Mary Barton* and *North and South*); and for that of the farmers of the Yorkshire border, to the strange romances of the Brontë sisters—*Jane Eyre*, *Shirley*, and *Wuthering Heights*. George Eliot is still our best guide for the life of the Midlands in the first half of the century, though all of her novel writing was done in the second half; *Adam Bede*, *Silas Marner*, *The Mill on the Floss* and *Felix Holt the Radical* all give us pictures of the England George Eliot remembered from her own childhood or from her childish recollections of the stories and talk of her elders. The novels of Hardy frequently go back to this earlier time, which for the Middle and Later Victorians had something of the glamour of romance, as of an England which had disappeared and was recalled to literary life with a passion of regret, or at any rate of sentimental fondness.

RAILWAYS

How gradual was the change to the new industrialism may be illustrated by the chill and even timid welcome given to the introduction of railways. Creevey, the diarist, recording his first experience ('for I cannot call it pleasure') of going at the prodigious rate of twenty miles an hour, just before the beginning of the Victorian Era, says: 'But, observe, the machine was occasionally made to put itself out or go it; and then we went at the rate of twenty-three miles an hour, and just with the same ease as to motion or absence of friction as the other reduced pace. But the quickest motion is to me frightful; it is really flying, and it is impossible to divest yourself of the notion of instant death to all upon the least accident happening. It gave me a headache that has not left me. Sefton is convinced that some damnable thing must come of it; but he and I seem more struck with such apprehension than others.'

For the first few years of their married life, Prince Albert would not allow the Queen to travel by train, though he used the new invention himself; when a train he was on attained a speed of thirty miles an hour, he uttered a gentle reproof, 'Not quite so fast next time, Mr. Conductor, if you please.' An engineer who had the audacity to get up a speed of forty-five miles an hour was promptly dismissed by the company as a reward for the achievement. It is to the Queen's credit that when she was permitted to take a ride on the train in 1842, she liked it—was, in fact, 'quite charmed with it.' Horse omnibuses, so long a feature of the streets of Victorian London, came in about the same time as the railroads, and the slower form of locomotion was much the more popular. Creevey notes in his diary: 'I have for the first time boarded an omnibus, and it is charming. I just long to go back to one in Piccadilly.'

MANNERS AND CUSTOMS

Steel pens were another invention of 1832, but old-fashioned people continued for many years to use quills, until some misguided person discovered that they commanded a readier sale as toothpicks. Looking back on early Victorian England, one is first of all impressed with a sense of its continuity with the preceding age—the Age of the Romantic Revival. Romanticism as a popular taste degenerated into sentimentalism, of which we find abundant evidence, not only in the novels of Dickens, but also in those of his great contemporary and rival, Thackeray, although in his own time the latter was regarded as cynical. In different ways, Carlyle and Newman both belong to the age of romance, and romanticism had manifest influences upon the thought of Tennyson and Browning.

Even the prudery which is so often regarded as peculiarly characteristic of the Victorian Era really dates back to an earlier period. A modern biographer of Thomas Bowdler, who undertook to improve Shakespeare's plays by the omission of 'those words and expressions which cannot with propriety be read aloud in a family,' remarks that the young girl who was the tenth and presiding muse of the Victorian Era, was 'the perfectly natural daughter of the Princess Victoria and Thomas Bowdler, Esq., F.R.S. and S.A.' The observation is just, but it must be remembered that Bowdler expurgated Shakespeare and purified Gibbon 'in the wicked world of the Regency and his Most Christian Majesty George the Fourth.' No doubt Victoria had a good deal to do with it, and it is noteworthy that in *The Ladies' Pocket Book of Etiquette*, published in the year after her accession, the anonymous author warns the Young Girl against 'the pollution of the Waltz' in the following terms: 'Ask the mother, before the demon of fashion has taken possession of her feelings, and shut her eyes to the unhallowed nature of many of its rites—could she see, without the severest self-reproach, the blush of conscious shame, of an intuitive sense of impropriety, mantling in the cheek of her child, until habit and éclat have deadened her sense of what is correct, and destroyed those first and holy and pure feelings which are the great safeguards of woman's virtue?' But all the blame for this kind of sentimental nonsense cannot be laid upon the broad back of Queen Victoria. Thackeray, in the preface to *Pendennis*, complained that he could not deal with the youthful escapades of his hero in the same spirit of realism as Fielding had dealt with the amatory adventures of Tom Jones; but as the editor of Cornhill, Thackeray refused a story by Anthony Trollope because it was about a gentleman 'who was minded to run away with a married woman.' So, when *Punch* was started in 1840, Thackeray's congratulations were upon its 'purity.' 'So many jokes and so little harm. . . . We will laugh in the company of our wives and children; we will tolerate no indecorum; we like our matrons and girls to be pure.' When Victoria's first Prime Minister, Lord Melbourne, in his eighteenth century manner indulged in a somewhat doubtful joke, the young queen remarked primly, 'We are not amused.'

THE VICTORIAN SMUGNESS

It was at once the strength and weakness of the early Victorians that they took themselves seriously. Already at the beginning of the period they were impressed by their own achievements and confident for the future. Looking forward for a century, Macaulay foresaw that 'in the year 1930 a population of fifty millions, better fed, clad, and lodged than the English of our time, will cover these islands, that Sussex and Huntingdonshire will be wealthier than the wealthiest parts of the West Riding of Yorkshire are now, that cultivation, rich as that of a flower-garden, will be carried up to the very tops of Ben Nevis and Helvellyn, that machines constructed on principles yet undiscovered will be in every house, that there will be no highways but railroads, no traveling but by steam, that our debt, vast as it seems to us, will appear to our great-grandchildren a trifling encumbrance, which might easily be paid off in a year or two.' (Essay on Southey's *Colloquies of Society*.)

In a similar prophetic dream (*Locksley Hall*), published a dozen years later, Tennyson (not yet Poet Laureate)

> dipped into the future, far as human eye could see,
> Saw the Vision of the world, and all the wonder that would be.
>
> Saw the heavens fill with commerce, argosies of magic sails,
> Pilot of the purple twilight, dropping down with costly bales;
>
> Heard the heavens fill with shouting, and there rained a ghastly dew
> From the nations' airy navies grappling in the central blue . . .
>
> Till the war-drum throbbed no longer, and the battle-flags were furled
> In the Parliament of man, the Federation of the World.
>
> There the common sense of most shall hold a fretful realm in awe,
> And the kindly earth shall slumber, lapped in universal law.

The Victorians had a sublime faith in parliamentary institutions. Mr. Odo Russell, the British Resident at Rome, gave good advice to the Pope as to the management of the Papal States: 'We derive great happiness from our free institutions and would be glad to see our neighbors in Europe as happy and prosperous as we are.' The Pope, in January 1859, refused to follow this good advice, and within two years he lost the Papal States, which became part of the Kingdom of Italy, established largely through the connivance and encouragement of the British Government. In 1851, W. E. Gladstone, in a letter addressed to the British Prime Minister, described the administration of King Ferdinand as 'the negation of God erected into a system of government,' and within ten years Garibaldi had landed at Naples, with the hardly concealed protection of British warships, and had freed Sicily and Southern Italy from Bourbon misrule. Lord Palmerston, Lord John Russell, and W. E. Gladstone were the leading members of the British Government at that time, and when Lord John Russell visited Italy in later years he found his portrait joined with those of Mazzini, Cavour, and Garibaldi as the liberators of the new kingdom.

This somewhat dictatorial policy in the cause of freedom and order abroad gave the Early Victorians a glow of enthusiasm, and perhaps distracted their attention unduly from oppression and degradation nearer home. They felt (as D. C. Somervell puts it) that they 'lived in an age of absolutely unprecedented development. Population was growing as it had never grown before, and, from the forties onward, wealth grew faster than population. . . . The Victorian Englishman felt that he was a member of the greatest nation in the world at the most important epoch of human history, and that he must rise to the occasion.' In the future of England, and of any other nation that chose to follow England's wise example, he had full confidence, and he did not expect the Government to interfere—except with foreign nations; he felt quite able to look after his own business himself. 'It is not,' said Macaulay in the Essay already quoted, 'by the intermeddling of Mr. Southey's idol, the omniscient and omnipotent State, but by the prudence and energy of the people, that England has hitherto been carried forward in civilization; and it is to the same prudence and the same energy that we now look with comfort and good hope. Our rulers will best promote the improvement of the nation by strictly confining themselves to their legitimate duties, by leaving capital to find its most lucrative course, commodities their fair price, industry and intelligence their natural reward, idleness and folly their natural punishment, by maintaining peace, by defending property, by diminishing the price of law, and by observing strict economy in every department of the state. Let the Government do this: the People will assuredly do the rest.'

BLOTS ON EARLY VICTORIAN CIVILIZATION

This self-confidence was a marked feature of Macaulay's personality, but it is also characteristic of the national temper and of the time. The scientists were beginning to plead for less dogmatism and a closer attention to the facts, but as yet they made little impression. A leading Nonconformist divine, Dr. Cummings, said in 1852: 'If there be in any instance contradiction between a clear text of the Bible, and a supposed fact or discovery made by the geologist, my inference, without hesitation, is that the geologist must have made a mistake, that Moses made none.' This seems to involve the further assumption that Dr. Cummings made none, though he did rent a house on a lease running far beyond the date he had fixed for the final judgment of mankind; but that is a date about which many others have been mistaken, before and since.

The more serious mistakes were those of the economists, politicians, landowners, and employers of labor who insisted on applying the principles of *laissez faire* to agriculture and industry in disregard of the obvious facts. The Early Victorians were generally (and sincerely) of opinion that if the restrictions on agriculture, trade, and industry were removed, and every man would take advantage of his natural gifts and opportunities, social grievances and labor troubles would adjust themselves. They were by no means unconscious of the problem of poverty; 'the poor,' they read in the Bible, 'ye have always with you,' and they were aware of the fact by experience, as well as by the reading of history and Holy Writ. They knew that there was agricultural poverty, as well as industrial poverty, and that unhealthy houses, dirt, and disease existed in small hamlets and scattered farms as well as in the slums of London and the great manufacturing towns. Agricultural poverty in England was desperate in 1832: poor law relief cost seven million pounds, or ten shillings per head of the population; in 1830 there were widespread agricultural riots and rick-burnings, and though no lives were lost (except that of one rioter), five hundred boys and men were transported to Van Diemen's Land and New South Wales. The condition of the village population was said by contemporary observers to be worse than that of West Indian slaves; Lord Carnarvon said in Parliament that the English laborer had been reduced to a plight more abject than that of any race in Europe. J. L. and Barbara Hammond, after a careful investigation (*The English Labourer, 1760–1832*), confirm Lord Carnarvon's view: 'The English laborer alone was the poorer; poorer in money, poorer in happiness, poorer in sympathy, and infinitely poorer in horizon and in hope. The riches that he had been promised by the champions of enclosure had faded into something less than a maintenance. The wages he received without land had a lower purchasing power than the wages he had received in the days when his wages were supplemented by common rights.' In 1825 the wages of agricultural laborers were generally nine shillings a week, and the price of wheat was nine shillings a bushel.

A Sussex clergyman, Thomas Robert Malthus, pointed a warning finger at the origin of the evil before the end of the eighteenth century in his famous *Essay on the Principle of Population as it affects the future Improvement of Society* (1798), in which he drew attention to the tendency of the propagative impulse of mankind to go beyond the means of subsistence; but he had no remedy to offer except a suggestion, in a later edition, that the submerged poor, who were chiefly held guilty of this excessive breeding, should exercise 'moral restraint.' This was neither a popular nor a practical remedy, and the general inclination was to accept, as a logical consequence of the reasoning of Malthus, that poverty was inevitable. When Lord Melbourne was urged by a more Radical Peer to give immediate attention to the subject of agricultural distress, Melbourne rejoined: 'I understand it perfectly, and that is my reason for saying nothing about it.' Pressed for further explanation, Melbourne merely added, 'I consider it hopeless.' 'You think with Malthus,' continued the questioner, 'that vice and misery are the only cure?' 'No,' Melbourne answered, 'but the evil is in numbers and the sort of competition that ensues.'

The situation was remedied to some extent by the Repeal of the Corn Laws, the opening up of the prairie lands of North America, the development of steam navigation, and the opportunities for employment offered by the growth of the factory towns. But the constant pressure of the poverty-stricken rural population upon the factory towns kept wages low, conditions of work bad, and living conditions still worse. The Trade Union Magazine of 1833 says: 'We eat the worst food, drink the worst drink—our raiment, our houses, our everything, bear signs of poverty, and we are gravely told that this must be our lot.' Nassau Senior, writing of a Manchester working-class suburb, says: 'In one place we found a whole street following the course of a ditch, because in this way deeper cellars would be secured without the cost of digging, cellars not for storing wares or rubbish, but for dwellings of human beings. Not one house of this street escaped the cholera. In general the streets of these suburbs are unpaved, with a dung heap or ditch in the middle; the houses are built back to back, without ventilation or drainage, and whole families are limited to a corner of a cellar or a garret.' It is no wonder that the amusements and recreations of the people were often of the lowest and most brutal description. Dr. Hawkins, giving evidence before the Factory Commission of 1833, said: 'It is impossible not to notice the total absence of public gardens, parks, and walks at Manchester: it is scarcely in the power of the factory workman to taste the breath of nature or to look upon its verdure, and this defect is a strong impediment to convalescence from disease, which is usually tedious and difficult at Manchester.' Of the neighboring factory town of Bolton a contemporary observer wrote in 1842: 'Anything like the squalid misery, the slow, moldering, putrefying death by which the weak and feeble of the working-classes are perishing here, it never befel my eyes to behold nor my imagination to conceive.'

One of the bitterest grievances of the working people was that they were denied opportunities for improving their lot by education. Count has been made of the number of men and women who were married or witnessed marriages in Lancashire and Cheshire during the years 1839, 1840, and 1841, and it is found that more than half of them were not able to sign their names. In the Factory Inspectors' Report for 1842 it is stated that in an area of thirty-two square miles comprising Oldham and Ashton, with a population of 105,000, there was not a single public day school for poor children. Lady John Russell records that when she and her husband founded a day school at Petersham in 1849, objection was made on the ground that it would 'ruin the aristocratic character of the village.'

CONTEMPORARY PROTESTS

The concentration of poverty in industrial centers had at least this advantage, that it forced itself upon public attention by means of crime, disorder, drunkenness, filth, squalor, infectious disease, and high death rates, especially among slum children. The Chartist agitation which began about 1838 seemed to produce no immediate result beyond the presentation of a monster petition to Parliament in April, 1848, and the imprisonment of a few of the leading agitators; but it gave voice to the discontent of the workers and their resentment that the Reform Bill had brought so little alleviation of their unhappy lot. A more lasting effect was produced by the efforts of the leading writers of the time. Carlyle's potent rhetoric did much to rouse the Early Victorian public to a sense of the festering sores which afflicted the body politic; and about the middle of the century his fulminations were re-inforced by the powerful voice of John Ruskin. The poets spoke no less earnestly or indignantly. Tom Hood, the popular poet of the day, not long before his death in 1845, pleaded in the columns of Punch the cause of the sweated domestic worker in the dressmaking and tailoring trades:

> With fingers weary and worn,
>   With eyelids heavy and red,
> A woman sat in unwomanly rags,
>   Plying her needle and thread—
> Stitch! stitch! stitch!
>   In poverty, hunger, and dirt,
> And still with a voice of dolorous pitch,—
> Would that its tone could reach the Rich!—
>   She sang this 'Song of the Shirt!'

Another popular poet of the time, Elizabeth Barrett, published in Blackwood's Magazine the same year *The Cry of the Children*, which may not count for much as poetry, but leaves one in no doubt as to the passionate sincerity of the speaker or as to the reality of the wrongs that called for redress:

> 'For oh,' say the children, 'we are weary
>   And we cannot run or leap;
> If we cared for any meadows, it were merely
>   To drop down in them and sleep.
> Our knees tremble sorely in the stooping,
>   We fall upon our faces trying to go;
> And underneath our heavy eyelids drooping,
>   The reddest flower would look as pale as snow:
> For, all day, we drag our burden tiring
>   Through the coal-dark, underground.—
> Or, all day, we drive the wheels of iron
>   In the factories, round and round.'

Tennyson, in the somewhat hectic accents of the hero of *Maua* (1855), drew attention to the crying evils of the time:—

Peace sitting under her olive, and slurring the days gone by,
When the poor are hoveled, and hustled together, each sex, like swine,
When only the ledger lives, and when only not all men lie;
Peace in her vineyard—yes!—but a company forges the wine.

And the vitriol madness flushes up in the ruffian's head,
Till the filthy by-lane rings to the yell of the trampled wife,
And chalk and alum and plaster are sold to the poor for bread,
And the spirit of murder works in the very means of life.

And Sleep must lie down armed, for the villainous centerbits
Grind on the wakeful ear in the hush of the moonless nights,
While another is cheating the sick of a few last gasps, as he sits
To pestle a poisoned poison behind his crimson lights.

When a Mammonite mother kills her babe for a burial fee,
And Timour-Mammon grins on a pile of children's bones,
Is it peace or war? Better war! loud war by land and by sea,
War with a thousand battles, and shaking a hundred thrones.

The prophets and the poets were only re-echoing in passionate
verse or emphatic prose the sober statements of fact contained in
Government reports. One commission after another was appointed
to receive sworn testimony as to the employment of children as
chimney-sweeps in London, and the poverty-stricken oppression
endured by the chain-workers of the Midlands, the Lancashire
cotton operatives, and the coalminers of the North. A sickening
tale, in which may be found the true source of modern Socialism.
It was in these parliamentary reports that Friedrich Engels found
the material for his *Condition of the English Working Class in 1844;*
later, he and his fellow socialist, Karl Marx, working among the
books and newspaper files of the British Museum Library, elaborated the theory of *Das Kapital*, which was in the following century to revolutionize Russia and upset the world.

REMEDIAL MEASURES

There is no need to dwell in detail upon these ancient wrongs;
their horrors are familiar to every student of early nineteenth
century history and literature. The employment of little children
to work for long hours in the Lancashire cotton mills and to climb
through the flues of London mansions was still going on at the
beginning of the Victorian Era. The Hammonds write of the
Factory Act of 1832: 'Children were left entirely unprotected,
except in the cotton industry, and in the cotton industry their

masters might work children of nine for twelve hours a day exclu-
sive of meal times. Such regulations, however, as were imposed
were academic, for no effective machinery was provided to enforce
them.' The employment of children under fourteen as chimney-
sweeps except as apprentices was prohibited in 1834, and the Act
of 1840 forbad the climbing of chimneys to all except adults; an
amendment in 1864 prevented the employment of any child under
ten by a chimney-sweep except on his own premises. The Commission Report of 1842 states that children in mines were at that date
still employed, not only as 'trappers' to open and shut the doors
of the airshafts, and as 'fillers' to load the trucks underground,
but as 'pushers,' to shove or drag the trucks to the foot of the
shaft. 'A girdle is put round the naked waist, to which a chain
from the carriage is hooked and passed between the legs, and the
boys crawl on their hands and knees, drawing the carriage after
them.' 'Very few under six or seven' are employed as 'pushers'
says the Commission Report, but the 'trappers' were boys and
girls generally from five to eight years of age.

The appointment of the Commission on the Employment of
Children and Young Persons, from which the above facts are
quoted, was brought about largely by the exertions of an Evangelical Peer, the Earl of Shaftesbury (1801–85), who had opposed
the Reform Act and later opposed the repeal of the Corn Laws,
but gave long years to the study of the condition of the wage
earners and was largely instrumental in procuring legislation for
their protection and the removal of such hideous abuses as are
outlined above. The Ten Hours Act of 1847 applied only to the
employment of women and children in factories, but as these constituted two-thirds of the employees in cotton mills, work could
not be carried on without them, and in actual practice the limitation of hours affected the men as well; provision was also made for
regular inspection to see that the law was observed, for proper
ventilation and sanitation in the mills, and for the protection of
life and limb from unfenced or dangerous machinery. Further
legislation was found necessary from time to time, but considerable
progress was made during this Early Victorian period.

To the modern observer the application of these remedies may
seem halting and inadequate, but the effective panacea for poverty
in a modern industrial state has yet to be discovered; in an ancient
agricultural state poverty was inevitable, unless population was
severely checked. The Victorians had much less faith in legislation
and government control than in individual effort, and by the

efforts of the workers themselves (individual or combined) a great deal was accomplished. From the beginning of the century almost up to the beginning of the Victorian Era, the workers were hampered and intimidated in uniting to protect their own interests by the Combination Acts. The Acts forbad combinations among the masters as well as among the men, but so far as the masters were concerned they were a dead letter; as magistrates, the employers had the administration of the law in their own hands, and they administered it to their own advantage. The repeal of the Combination Laws in 1824–25 was the workers' charter of liberty, and they proceeded to take increasing advantage of it. A Grand General Union of Spinners was formed after an unsuccessful strike in the cotton trade in 1829, and the following summer the National Association for the Protection of Labor was founded, succeeded in 1834 by the Grand National Consolidated Trades Union. They did not last very long, but the principles on which they were founded gave hints for the later organization of the General Federation of Trade Unions, which acquired great influence. Beside the Trade Unions, the already existing Friendly Societies which provided help for their members in case of sickness and death were now encouraged, and developed to very important proportions.

Next to the oppressive landlord and the tyrannical employer, the workers regarded as their principal enemies the extortionate butchers, bakers, and grocers who charged them exorbitant prices for the necessities of life and induced them to involve themselves in burdensome debts. They tried to co-operate in purchasing and distribution, but without permanent success until the formation of the Rochdale Society of Equitable Pioneers in 1844. Nothing could have been more modest than the beginnings of this organization; its principles were simple: (1) all purchases by cash payments; (2) proportional division of the profits among the members according to the amount of their purchases. Their capital was small and their members few—twenty-eight in number, each of whom put in a few shillings to make a start. The first salesman and cashier were each paid threepence an hour (equal to five cents at the present rate of exchange) for their services, which were rendered after their daily work; the first president received six shillings (equal to about one dollar) for the trouble of securing the first premises—the Toad Lane store, which has recently been rescued from oblivion and solemnly dedicated as a monument with good wishes from American, Austrian, Czecho-Slovakian, Danish, Finnish, Swedish, Swiss, and other co-operators. In the

North of England manufacturing towns the co-operative societies revolutionized retail trading within a generation, and went on to widespread undertakings in the wholesale field. Their activities in providing library and educational facilities for their members and lending them money to build their own homes were an important factor in the establishment of those features of thrift, independence, and self-reliance which soon became characteristic of the working populations of the Lancashire and Yorkshire manufacturing towns.

One other element in the liberation of the working people must be mentioned—the rise of the popular press. Up to 1836 the newspaper stamp tax was fourpence a copy, which made the purchase of a newspaper impossible for the poor. William Cobbett (1762–1835), the greatest journalist of the pre-Victorian period, evaded the tax by publishing his *Twopenny Trash* at irregular intervals, and others defied the law; in the five years before Cobbett's death five hundred people were sent to prison for publishing journals without stamps. In 1836 the stamp was reduced from fourpence to a penny, and in 1855 it was abolished.

The defects of the modern popular press are many and obvious, but it remains the greatest safeguard against oppression and corruption. If a serious grievance can be exposed to the light of day, it is on its way to being remedied by force of public opinion, if any such remedial force exists. It was to public opinion that Macaulay and Carlyle appealed in their earlier writings, for they were both journalists until they became historians, and much of their work was journalism, though it might not appear in a newspaper. The changed attitude of the Government toward the Press from the eighteenth century, when it could be cajoled, bribed, intimidated, or prosecuted, to that of the nineteenth century, when it was feared, if not respected, is amusingly recorded in the plaintive remark of Lord Liverpool, a pre-Victorian Prime Minister, to his colleague Lord Castlereagh: 'No paper of any character, and consequently an established sale, will accept money from Government; and indeed their profits are so enormous in all critical times, when their support is the most necessary, that no pecuniary assistance that Government can offer would really be worth their acceptance. The truth is they look only to their sale. They make their way like sycophants with the public, by finding out the prejudices and pre-possessions of the moment and flattering them; and the number of *soi-disant* Government or Opposition papers abound just as the Government is generally popular or unpopular.'

CHAPTER III

EARLY VICTORIAN PROSE WRITERS

THOMAS BABINGTON MACAULAY
(*1800–1859*)

BORN in the last year of the eighteenth century, Macaulay may be reckoned one of the earliest of the Great Victorians; a precocious youth, he attracted public attention, when still fresh from college, by an article ('Milton,' 1825) in the Edinburgh Review, to which he soon became a constant contributor. Entering the House of Commons in 1830, he took an active part in the debates preceding the passage of the First Reform Bill (1832) and made a considerable reputation as a parliamentary orator. Endowed with prodigious powers of memory and mental concentration, well-educated and an omnivorous reader in several languages, a convinced and consistent Whig with excellent connections, he was early admitted to public office; but he had seen his father sacrifice the interests of his family to forward the abolition of the slave trade in the British dominions, and when the Bill to effect this purpose was before the House young Macaulay twice offered his resignation to the Prime Minister rather than compromise his personal independence on that issue. A few years later, in order to re-establish the financial position of his father's family, ruined by his father's devotion to public interests, Macaulay gave up his political career to accept a lucrative position under the East India Company.

In his first essay in the Edinburgh Review Macaulay had expressed his admiration not only for the sublime works with which Milton's genius had enriched English literature but for 'the zeal with which he labored for the public good, the fortitude with which he endured every private calamity, the lofty disdain with which he looked down on temptations and dangers, the deadly hatred which he bore to bigots and tyrants, and the faith which he so sternly kept with his country and with his fame.' It is noteworthy that the two English masterpieces Macaulay undertook to reproduce from memory if all printed copies should be lost were *Paradise Lost* and *Pilgrim's Progress*—the greatest monuments of

Puritan learning and piety. His father, one of the leaders of the Protestant Evangelical party in the Church of England, came of a Scotch family which had given several ministers to the Presbyterian Church; and young Macaulay grew up in an atmosphere of Puritan morality and piety, in which the Scriptures were familiar as household words. He was only eight years old, when the maid having annoyed him by disturbing some oyster shells which set off his childish garden, he marched into the drawing-room and proclaimed to his astonished parents and their guests, 'Cursed be Sally, for it is written, Cursed is he that removeth his neighbor's landmark.' Something of this temper remained with him to the end of his life. A devoted son and a still more devoted brother, he was a pattern of those domestic virtues which constitute the stronghold of the Puritan faith; and though wide reading and a varied experience of many societies modified any inclination to narrowness, he never lost the strong religious bias and conviction implanted in his mind in early childhood. When he was in India, and busy upon a scheme for the education of the natives which has had very different political results from those its promoters intended, he wrote to his father:—

'The effect of this education on the Hindoos is prodigious. No Hindoo who has received an English education ever remains sincerely attached to his religion. Some continue to profess it as a matter of policy; but many profess themselves pure Deists, and some embrace Christianity. It is my firm belief that, if our plans of education are followed up, there will not be a single idolator among the respectable classes in Bengal thirty years hence.'

This 'cocksureness,' which is perhaps only a changed form of Puritan dogmatism, is characteristic of Macaulay; Lord Melbourne said of him, 'I wish I were as sure of anything as Macaulay is of everything'; but as Macaulay was unusually well-informed, had keen intelligence, and excellent judgment, the drawback is in his case not so serious as it would be in the case of a man less gifted. Associated with it is his tendency to exaggeration and over-emphasis—a fault usually so obvious that it is rarely misleading. He says for instance of some Latin verses of the elder Pitt, written when he was a boy at Eton: 'The matter of the poem is as worthless as that of any college exercise that was ever written before or since.' There was no need of so heavy a sledgehammer to crush so insignificant a fly; but it was a habit that Macaulay could never get rid of. It was partly due to his early initiation to the mysteries of periodical journalism and political debate. Both these were

arenas in which it was the practice to be brisk, emphatic, rhetorical; and the practice fell in only too readily with Macaulay's
natural inclination. But if he has the defects of an artificial style,
in which excessive use is made of balance and antithesis, he has
also its excellences. It is hardly ever possible to hesitate for an
instant as to Macaulay's meaning; it jumps out of the page and
smites you in the face. He is always clear; he is generally forcible;
and though one may become weary of his repeated use of the same
rhetorical devices, he is seldom dull. He selects the facts he wishes
to present with care, and arranges them so as to secure the utmost
lucidity. If he can make his argument more emphatic by a striking
contrast or a telling illustration, he seldom misses the opportunity,
for he had a well-stored mind and an extraordinarily quick wit.
He is unsurpassed as a contriver of historical narrative, to which
he often gives the thrill of fiction. He lacks the cold judicial temper
of the ideal historian, he has the limitations and some of the
prejudices of his time; but when due allowance is made for these
and for his obvious personal idiosyncracies, he remains a sound
guide for the ordinary reader, who is not looking for meticulous
exactitude in historical detail, but for a fair and accurate reproduction of the men and events of a past age. Take for instance his
famous 'third chapter' on the 'state of England in 1685.' He begins
with the population and the distribution of the inhabitants as
compared with the present and with previous times; he discusses
the amount of the national revenue, the way the money was raised
and the way it was spent, the means of national defense, the cost
of civil government; the state of agriculture, the manners and
morals of the country gentry and clergy, the growing wealth and
importance of the provincial towns, the beginnings of the industrial revolution; the port of London, the City, the West End, the
slums, the police, lighting, coffee houses, the roads out of London,
stage coaches, innkeepers, post-horses, newspapers, newsletters,
scarcity of books, female education, immorality of polite literature,
the playhouses, literary patronage, the state of science, of the fine
arts, of the common people, agricultural wages, workmen's wages,
child labor in factories, number of paupers, the progress of civilization. All of these topics are presented with a wealth of illustrative
detail which not only holds the reader's attention but gives him a
lively picture of the life of England at that period.

Macaulay has been reproached by some critics for the smug
satisfaction with which he seems to pat his own generation on
the back for the progress it has made as compared with past times.

There is indeed about him an exuberant optimism which is sometimes disconcerting in view of the more recent history which Macaulay was not to see. Thus, eight years before his death, the close of the Great Exhibition of 1851 moved him almost to tears. He joined heartily in the final thanksgiving service and noted:—'This will long be remembered as a singularly happy year, of peace, plenty, good feeling, innocent pleasure, national glory of the best and purest sort.'

As a matter of fact Macaulay was fully abreast of the moderate liberal opinion of the time. He was not a radical, and when the Chartist Petitioners of 1842 claimed Universal Suffrage, he denied the claim on account of the unequal distribution of property in the United Kingdom and the ignorance of the masses through lack of education, though he admitted that Universal Suffrage had been adopted in the United States 'without producing any very frightful consequences.' His personal position he defined in the following sentences:—'Though I am a faithful and loyal subject of Her Majesty, and though I sincerely wish to see the House of Lords powerful and respected, I cannot consider either monarchy or aristocracy as the ends of government. They are only means. Nations have flourished without hereditary sovereigns or assemblies of nobles; and, though I should be very sorry to see England a republic, I do not doubt that she might, as a republic, enjoy prosperity, tranquillity, and high consideration. The dread and aversion with which I regard universal suffrage would be greatly diminished, if I could believe that the worst effect which it would produce would be to give us an elective first magistrate and a senate instead of a Queen and a House of Peers. My firm conviction is that, in our country, universal suffrage is incompatible, not with this or that form of government, but with all forms of government, and with everything for the sake of which forms of government exist; that it is incompatible with property, and that it is consequently incompatible with civilization.'

Interested as Macaulay was in the machinery of government, he saw that the prosperity of the nation depended more upon the progress of knowledge and individual effort than upon political changes and that the main thing was to preserve internal peace and order. It is for this reason that the third chapter gives so much more space to popular occupations and amusements than to political developments. The great question, as he saw it, was how much wages did the common people receive and what were they able to get with those wages. He cites facts to prove that there had been a notable increase in the prosperity and comfort of all classes, and that the more intense and extensive discontent of his time was due not to greater poverty but to the prevalence of a higher standard of living. In a flight of fancy unusual with him he casts his mind forward to the state of England in the twentieth century, and his prophetic guess is not a bad one. The whole passage is worth quoting:—'It is now the fashion to place the golden age of England in times when noblemen were destitute of comforts the want of which would be intolerable to a modern footman, when farmers and shopkeepers breakfasted on loaves the very sight of which would raise a riot in a modern workhouse, when to have a clean shirt once a week was a privilege reserved for the higher class of gentry, when men died faster in the purest country air than they now die in the most pestilential lanes of our towns, and when men died faster in the lanes of our towns than they now die on the coast of Guiana. We too shall, in our turn, be outstripped, and in our turn be envied. It may well be, in the twentieth century, that the peasant of Dorsetshire may think himself miserably paid with twenty shillings a week; that the carpenter at Greenwich may receive ten shillings a day; that laboring men may be as little used to dine without meat as they now are to eat rye bread; that sanitary police and medical discoveries may have added several more years to the average length of human life; that numerous comforts and luxuries which are now unknown, or confined to a few, may be within the reach of every diligent and thrifty working man.'

The Dorsetshire peasant has received twenty shillings a week and the Greenwich carpenter ten shillings a day; the laboring man is used to have meat once a day; the average length of human life has been prolonged; numerous comforts and luxuries, unknown to Macaulay's generation, are now within the reach of every diligent and thrifty workingman. And even now the Millennium has not yet been reached; it may seem even further off than in Macaulay's day. Macaulay was quite aware that the England of his day was not perfect: he knew that in English towns in the middle of the nineteenth century pestilential lanes existed with a scandalously high death rate. He states that in a good year in his time one out of every ten inhabitants was in receipt of poor law relief, and in a bad year one out of every seven; but he points out that in 1685 the proportion of pauperism was reported as incredibly higher. Nor is he really blind (though he is sometimes accused of being blind) to other than superficial indications of

material prosperity; he could hardly have been his father's son if he had left the imponderable spiritual factors out of his reckoning. He does not, as the following passage sufficiently testifies:—
'It is pleasing to reflect that the public mind of England has softened while it has ripened, and that we have, in the course of ages, become not only a wiser but also a kinder people. There is scarcely a page of the history or lighter literature of the seventeenth century which does not contain some proof that our ancestors were less humane than their posterity. The discipline of workshops, of schools, of private families, though not more efficient than at present, was infinitely harsher. Masters, well born and bred, were in the habit of beating their servants. Pedagogues knew no way of imparting knowledge but by beating their pupils. Husbands, of decent station, were not ashamed to beat their wives. The implacability of hostile factions was such as we can scarcely conceive. . . . Every class doubtless has gained largely by this great moral change: but the class which has gained most is the poorest, the most dependent, and the most defenseless.'

Macaulay was an optimist but not an unreasoning one; he was rather a meliorist, having faith in a better future and doing his share to bring it about. He supported the Bill for the reduction of the hours of employment for women and children in factories from twelve to ten, and used arguments which did equal credit to his head and his heart: 'Rely on it that intense labor, beginning too early in life, continued too long every day, stunting the growth of the body, stunting the growth of the mind, leaving no time for healthful exercise, leaving no time for intellectual culture, must impair all those high qualities which have made our country great. . . . Is it anything in the earth or in the air that makes Scotland more prosperous than Egypt, that makes Holland more prosperous than Sicily? No; it was the Scotchman that made Scotland; it was the Dutchman that made Holland. Look at North America. Two centuries ago the sites on which now arise mills, and hotels, and banks, and colleges, and churches, and the Senate Houses of flourishing commonwealths, were deserts abandoned to the panther and the bear. What has made the change? Was it the rich mold, or the redundant rivers? No: the prairies were as fertile, the Ohio and the Hudson were as broad and as full then as now. Was the improvement the effect of some great transfer of capital from the old world to the new? No; the emigrants generally carried out with them no more than a pittance; but they carried out the English heart, and head, and arm; and the English heart and head and arm turned the wilderness into cornfield and orchard, and the huge trees of the primeval forest into cities and fleets. Man, man is the great instrument that produces wealth.'

He supported a government grant for the elementary education of the poor; and to the education of all classes he contributed more than any other writer of his time. He was perhaps the greatest of periodical journalists; his nephew and biographer Sir G. Otto Trevelyan says of the circulation of the *Essays:*—'The world was not slow to welcome, and having welcomed, was not in a hurry to shelve, a book so unwillingly and unostentatiously presented to its notice. Upward of a hundred and twenty thousand copies have been sold in the United Kingdom alone by a single publisher. Considerably over a hundred and thirty thousand copies of separate essays have been printed in the series known by the name of The Traveler's Library. And it is no passing, or even waning, popularity which these figures represent. Between the years 1843 and 1853 the yearly sales by Messrs. Longman of the collected editions averaged 1,230 copies; between 1853 and 1864 they rose to an average of 4,700; and since 1864 more than six thousand copies have, one year with another, been disposed of annually. The publishers of the United States are still pouring forth reprints by many thousands at a time; and in British India, and on the Continent of Europe, these productions which their author classed as ephemeral, are so greedily read and so constantly reproduced, that, taking the world as a whole, there is probably never a moment when they are out of the hands of the compositor.'

When the first issue of the History came out, a gentleman in Lancashire invited his poorer neighbors to meet regularly in the evening at his house to read it; when it was finished, they passed a vote of thanks to the author for the service he had rendered to popular education or as the resolution put it 'for having written a history which working men can understand.' It was as great a testimony to Macaulay's usefulness as the check for £20,000 which his publishers sent to him on the successful publication of the later volumes and his elevation to the peerage which speedily followed. Macaulay deserved well of his countrymen. He early grasped that principle of an expanding and developing liberty which is the secret of the success of English institutions. In a speech on parliamentary reform in 1832 he said:—'God has decreed that old age shall succeed to manhood, and manhood to infancy. Even so have societies their law of growth. As their strength becomes greater, as their experience becomes more extensive, you can no longer confine them within the swaddling bands, or lull them in the cradles, or amuse them with the rattles, or terrify them with the bugbears of their infancy. I do not say that they are better or happier than they were; but this I say, that they are different from what they were, that you cannot again make them what they were, and that you cannot safely treat them as if they continued to be what they were. . . . You may make the change tedious; you may make it violent; you may—God in his mercy forbid!—you may make it bloody; but avert it you cannot. Agitations of the public mind, so deep and so long continued as those which we have witnessed, do not end in nothing. In peace or in convulsion, by the law or in spite of the law, through the Parliament or over the Parliament, Reform must be carried. Therefore be content to guide that movement which you cannot stop. Fling wide the gates to that force which else will enter through the breach. Then will it still be, as it has hitherto been, the peculiar glory of our Constitution that, though not exempt from the decay which is wrought by the vicissitudes of fortune and the lapse of time in all the proudest works of human power and wisdom, it yet contains within it the means of self-reparation. Then will England add to her manifold titles of glory this, the noblest and the purest of all; that every blessing which other nations have been forced to seek, and have too often sought in vain, by means of violent and bloody revolutions, she will have attained by a peaceful and a lawful Reform.'

Beneath the rhetoric of the parliamentary orator there is the genuine emotion of the patriot who has faith in his country and in those principles of liberty which are indissolubly bound up with his country's greatness. It was the importance of these principles that Macaulay brought home to his countrymen by voice and pen, in his speeches, his essays, his articles, and the long labor of his History. Those who would understand how modern England came to be what she is cannot neglect his writings, for he was not only a writer but a maker of history.

THOMAS CARLYLE
(*1795–1881*)

Thomas Carlyle, born at Ecclefechan, the son of a Scottish stonemason, first attracted the attention of the British public by his articles on German literature in Fraser's (London) Magazine, in which he also published, to the confusion of most of its readers, *Sartor Resartus* (1833–34). The title, 'The Tailor Patched,' heads a burlesque metaphysical treatise on clothes, attributed to a German philosopher; but this is only a cover to enable Carlyle to present a chapter out of his own spiritual autobiography, which again serves but to introduce his judgment on various issues then occupying general attention. The imaginary German philosopher merely acts as a mouthpiece for Carlyle to reveal himself, first in his personal struggles to overcome poverty, sickness, scepticism, and despair, and then as a seer self-appointed to proclaim to his own generation its shortcomings and the remedies for them. Although he defines his attitude as 'speculative Radicalism,' his views do not jibe with those of any of the parties of the time. He 'makes little' of the Elective Franchise about which the political battle was then raging, and scoffs at the idea that freedom can be 'mechanically hatched and brought to light' in the Ballot Box or any other 'discoverable or devisable Box, edifice or steam mechanism,' though he admits it would be 'a mighty convenience; and beyond all feats of manufacture witnessed hitherto.' Carlyle had no faith in democracy; he saw that the supreme problem of his time was 'the cause of the poor,' but he did not see that the possession of the vote would enable the poor man to secure for his condition a degree of national attention that he could not command in any other way. Carlyle could not see that the unenfranchised man was in a condition of servility. 'Fools! Were your Superiors worthy to govern, and you worthy to obey, reverence for them were even your only possible freedom.' The real grievance of the poor, in his view, was their lack of educational opportunity:—'It is not because of his toils that I lament for the poor; we must all toil, or steal (howsoever we name our stealing), which is worse; no faithful workman finds his task a pastime. The poor is hungry and athirst; but for him also there is food and drink: he is heavy-laden and weary; but for him also the Heavens send Sleep, and of the deepest; in his smoky cribs, a clear dewy heaven of Rest envelopes him, and fitful glitterings of cloud-skirted Dreams. But what I mourn over is, that the lamp of his soul should go out; that no ray of heavenly, or even of earthly knowledge, should visit him; but only, in the haggard darkness, like two specters, Fear and Indignation bear him company. Alas, while the body stands so broad and brawny, must the Soul lie blinded, dwarfed, stupified, almost annihilated! Alas, was this too a Breath of God; bestowed in Heaven, but on earth never to be unfolded!—That there should one Man die ignorant who had capacity for Knowledge, this I call a tragedy, were it to happen more than twenty times in the minute, as by some computations it does. The miserable fraction of Science which our united Mankind, in a wide University of Nescience, has acquired, why is not this, with all diligence, imparted to all?'

Carlyle has no patience with the theory of Malthus that the population of Great Britain is outgrowing its food-supply. Is not a full-formed man, he asks indignantly, worth more to the world than a full-formed horse? And if there is not room for him in England, is there not room elsewhere? Why do not the leaders of modern England, like Hengst and Alaric of old, guide these superfluous masses to America and the Colonies? What are the leaders of the nation doing? And he answers sarcastically, 'Preserving their Game.'

To his observant eye England presents the saddest spectacle:— 'The Poor perishing, like neglected, foundered Draught-Cattle, of Hunger and Overwork; the Rich, still more wretchedly, of Idleness, Satiety, and Over-Growth. The Highest in rank, at length, without honor from the lowest; scarcely, with a little mouth-honor, as from tavern-waiters who expect to put it in the bill. Once-sacred Symbols fluttering as empty Pageants, whereof men grudge even the expense; a World becoming dismantled; in one word, the Church fallen speechless, from obesity and apoplexy; the State shrunken into a Police-Office, straitened to get its pay!'

What is Carlyle's remedy? It may be summed up in the one word 'Hero-worship,' by which he means that the national leaders should lead and the followers should follow. How the leaders and followers are to be sorted out he does not explain. The leaders are 'Heaven-chosen,' but how is the choice of heaven indicated? The followers 'cannot but obey,' he asserts; but have they, and will they? When Carlyle proceeded, in a series of lectures delivered in London in 1840, to expound his doctrine of hero-worship with illustrations drawn from history and literature, his choice fell upon Odin, Mahomet, Dante, Shakespeare, Luther, Johnson, Rousseau, Burns, Cromwell, Napoleon. How far, we may ask, did these secure the obedience, or even the respect, of their contemporaries? The most successful were the military leaders, Cromwell and Napoleon, and the political systems they constructed tumbled into dust. In his later choice of Frederick the Great, Carlyle was hardly more fortunate. Moreover, if Carlyle's theory is true, that the heaven-sent leader is sure of recognition, why not let the people at large choose him?

What was it then in Carlyle that won for him the enthusiastic respect of many of his contemporaries and the rather puzzled admiration of posterity? Assuredly not his reactionary political creed, which ran counter to one of the strongest currents of popular feeling in his time. Not even his belief in education and emigration as remedies for over-population, which the experience of another century indicates as probably the best that can be devised. Not the shyness,—the self-conscious timidity—which veiled itself in such intentionally obvious hoaxes as the German clothes-philosopher and in the mannerisms of Carlyle's over-emphatic rhetorical style. It was not so much what Carlyle believed or the eccentric garb in which he expressed his opinions as the intense conviction of his belief and the sincerity of his utterance that won public confidence. The oddity of the theme of *Sartor Resartus* and the perverseness of its mode of presentation kept it from publication in book form in England for seven years, and might have kept it longer unpublished but for the friendly offices of Emerson in securing the issue of American editions in the interim. What interested Emerson was no doubt the sincerity of the book and its religious spirit.

Carlyle took himself quite seriously as a prophet—a Professor of the Science of Things in General—and he uses the grotesque disguise of an obscure German scholar mainly to cloak and excuse this presumption; his ironies of expression, humorous and bitter alike, and his eccentricities of style are rhetorical devices applied to the same end. But he was entirely in earnest about the spiritual state of his countrymen, whom he saw deluded by various false panaceas: the materialism of the current utilitarian philosophy; the inadequacy of merely mechanical improvements of parliamentary government; the impotence of the Manchester School of Political Economy, content with buying in the cheapest market and selling in the dearest; the blind confidence of physical science in its power to weigh and measure all it can see, with supreme disregard of what it cannot see or weigh or measure. All these delusions spring from an incapacity to realize the spiritual values of life, and it was from a desire to rouse his generation to a sense of the transcendental—the sphere beyond the immediate range of the senses—that Carlyle took his place in the pulpit to preach against materialism.

Religions were regarded by Carlyle as vestures, symbols in

which men at this or that stage of culture 'could worse or better bodyforth the Godlike.' The organized religious faiths of his time seemed to him outworn—Hebrew old clothes or other— 'under which no living Figure or Spirit any longer dwells.' The current religious controversies about miracles and the inspiration of the Bible seemed to him meaningless; the birth of a calf was a miracle to him, and inspiration a perennial spring, breaking out in many times and in unexpected places. The official clergy in his own day might be blind leaders of the blind, but religion was still to be found in literature—even in journalism. 'A preaching Friar settles himself in every village; and builds a pulpit, which he calls a Newspaper.'

It was with such unrecognized prophets that Carlyle ranged himself, and he proved a source of inspiration to many whom the organized churches had turned away or failed to interest. Huxley counted the influence of Carlyle among the most potent factors in forming his character and guiding his career; he wrote: '*Sartor Resartus* led me to know that a deep sense of religion was compatible with an entire absence of theology.' Tyndall was equally outspoken in his admiration; John Stuart Mill became a close personal friend. Nor was it only among the leading intellectuals that Carlyle's influence prevailed. As early as 1846 the North British Review testified: 'While other authors may be, in a looser sense, more popular, and more rapidly and eagerly read, we doubt if there is any one whose works have gone more deeply to the springs of character and action, especially throughout the middle classes.'

When Carlyle's authority as a prophet came to be recognized, he was unable to divest himself altogether of the grotesque robes in which he first mounted the pulpit; he continued to take himself more and more seriously, and as he grew older, the voice of the prophet sometimes became a little shrill, and his utterances seemed to some listeners to arise from ill-temper or indigestion rather than from divine inspiration. We have lived to see that his vaticinations as to the evil consequences of the Second Reform Act remained unfulfilled and that still further extensions of the suffrage have as yet brought no catastrophe in their train. The Millennium, it is true, has not yet arrived, but on the other hand things as we see them are decidedly better than they were in Carlyle's day, if we are to accept his testimony, supported by many other witnesses.

It must be admitted that Carlyle's prophecies of impending ruin have been contradicted by the course of events, and the remedies he recommended, so far as they have been applied, have been rather disappointing in their results; but there is still virtue in the sincerity of his utterance, power in his call to duty, life in his devotion to reality, to fact. His doctrine of hero-worship falls ·more and more into disrepute. In the Great War, when the position of England—sometimes even her national existence—seemed at stake, she was saved not by heaven-sent leaders, but by just that 'great heart of the crew' which Carlyle so often derided. Yet his pictures of the great heroes of the past, especially those whom he really loved and admired—Knox, Cromwell, and Burns—still have the glow of inspiration. So too has his sympathetic sketch in *Past and Present* of the work of Abbot Samson of St. Edmundsbury and the life of a medieval abbey, recalled for us with deft touches from a twelfth century chronicle; in these the modern reader may find more pleasure and more profit than in Carlyle's denunciations of the idle aristocracy and short-sighted employing classes of his own day, though his practical suggestions for the relief of the laborers are still worthy of attention. Even his account of the French Revolution, the spirit of which Carlyle hated and despised, has more life in it than his *Latter Day Pamphlets* and other prophetic outbursts as to the political changes of his maturer years. His *Frederick the Great* remains only as a monument of patient research, the value of which is still recognized in Germany, and by professional historians in England, though the ordinary reader finds its bulk too terrifying to be lightly undertaken.

Carlyle finished his *Frederick* in 1865, when he was nearly seventy, and though he lived for sixteen years longer, he did little more literary work that was of any consequence. He continued, however, to exercise his prophetic vocation by word of mouth at his own fireside; after his wife's death in 1866, he fell into a degree of depression almost amounting to despair, and became more than ever 'a veritable Prophet, mourning in sackcloth and ashes the sins of the world.' He and his friend John Stuart Mill had long ago drifted apart; though he still regarded Emerson as 'a spiritual son of mine,' he added a note of interrogation and the remark, 'Yes, in a good degree, but gone into philanthropy and other moonshine'; of another American, Margaret Fuller, to whom Emerson had given a letter of introduction, Carlyle wrote that 'he believed no syllable of that Gospel of Fraternity, Benevolence, and New Heaven-on-Earth preached forth by all manner of "advanced" creatures'; he 'not only disbelieved all that, but treated

it as poisonous cant,—sweetness of sugar-of-lead—a detestable
phosphorescense from the dead body of a Christianity that would
not admit itself to be dead, and lie buried in all its unspeakable
putrescences, as a venerable dead one ought!' Tennyson had once
been regarded by him as 'a most useful, brotherly, solid-hearted
man,' but when the *Idylls of the King* appeared, Carlyle greeted
them 'with profound recognition of the finely elaborated execution, and also of the inward perfection of *vacancy*, and to say
truth, with considerable impatience at being treated so very like
infants, though the lollipops were so superlative.'

Upon the solitary, disillusioned, embittered old man the world
heaped honors and rewards which he received somewhat ironically,
conscious of how much a tithe of such recognition would have
meant to him in the struggles of youth and even of maturity.
Sartor Resartus, which had encountered difficulty in finding a
publisher for years after it was written, was issued in a cheap
popular edition and commanded a large sale; the People's Edition
of his Collected Works was even more successful. He was honored
with a personal interview by Queen Victoria; and her eldest daughter, the German Empress, came to see him in his modest home at
Chelsea. The Conservative Prime Minister, Disraeli, offered him a
baronetcy, a pension, and the Grand Cross of the Bath, all of which
he declined, as 'they would be an encumbrance, not a furtherance
to me.' On his eightieth birthday he received an honorary degree
from Harvard, a gold medal from the University of Edinburgh
(of which he had previously been elected Rector), and a congratulatory address signed by over a hundred of the most distinguished
English men and women of the day. George Meredith greeted
him as 'the greatest of the Britons of his time,' adding, however,
ruefully, that he was a 'heaver of rocks, not a shaper.'

The decline of Carlyle from this pinnacle of fame may be dated
from the publication of his *Reminiscences* as edited by James
Anthony Froude, which were already in the press at the time of
Carlyle's death and appeared immediately after. Carlyle's acid
recollections of such heroes of the national literature as Coleridge,
Lamb, and Wordsworth, made a disagreeable impression, and this
painful impression was deepened when Froude proceeded in the
three years following to publish an official biography, appalling in
its frankness, and the *Letters and Memorials of Jane Welsh Carlyle*.
There could be no question as to Froude's sincerity of purpose, his
substantial competence as a biographer (in spite of occasional
inaccuracy in minor detail), and his genuine and whole-hearted

admiration for Carlyle. But he felt it his duty to tell the whole truth about his idol. The 'feet of clay' in Carlyle's case were a naturally acrimonious and overbearing disposition—his mother foresaw that he would be 'gey ill to live with'—and fits of bad temper induced by the chronic indigestion which resulted from the privations of his childhood and early youth, improper diet, and the sedentary habits of a secluded student. His wife was superior to him in fortune and social position, and not without literary gifts. She wrote excellent letters and had a shrewd wit of her own. When congratulated on the success of the lectures on 'Heroes and Hero-worship,' she retorted that the British public had evidently made up its mind that Carlyle was worth keeping alive at a moderate rate. There can be no doubt that she had a great admiration and affection for Carlyle, and that he had similar feelings for her; not unnaturally, after her death—which occurred very suddenly during his absence from home—he was inclined to exaggerate the ill-temper and unkindness of which he had been guilty toward her and to express his 'remorse' in over-emphatic terms. Thus the discussion which arose tended to center itself, not on Carlyle's character and achievements, but on how he got on with his wife. Their most intimate conjugal relations were debated, often without sympathy or even respect, and the prophet's robe, which Carlyle had worn with some dignity, was torn to shreds. There was truth in what Mrs. Carlyle said: 'I am too like himself in some things— especially as to the state of our livers, and so we aggravate one another's tendencies to despair.' But we need not take literally her remark that Carlyle 'should have had a "strong minded woman" for wife, with a perfectly sound liver, plenty of *solid fat*, and mirth and good humor without end.' No doubt they were both difficult, and there was something in the current comment that if they had married elsewhere 'four people would have been made unhappy instead of two.'

In order to understand Carlyle and his immense influence upon his own time, one must remember that he had a deep realization of himself as a prophet with a message to deliver. He wrote to Lock-hart, then editor of the Quarterly Review: 'I have, and have had for many years, a word to speak *on the condition of the lower classes* in this country.' He despised the journalists who gave the public what it wanted, and he regarded the writer's craft as a sacred calling. He sought the dreary seclusion of Craigenputtock in order, as he told Goethe, 'that I might not have to write for bread, might not be tempted to tell lies for money.' 'The true Church of

England, at this moment,' he wrote, 'lies in the editors of its news-papers. These preach to the people daily, weekly; admonish kings themselves; advising peace or war, with an authority which only the first Reformers, and a long past class of Popes, were possessed of; inflicting moral encouragement, consolation, edification, in all ways diligently "administering the Discipline of the Church."'

Close acquaintance with poverty in his youth and early manhood had fitted Carlyle to insist on its evils, and he did not speak of the abuses of either agriculture or industrialism without acquiring knowledge of the facts. Twice, in 1846 and again in 1849, he made tours in Ireland, under competent guidance, to see for himself the sufferings of the Irish peasant during the famine years. 'Ireland is a perpetual misery to me; lies like a nightmare on my thoughts.' Industrialism he saw face to face—at Birmingham, 'a mean con-geries of bricks, including one large capitalist, some hundreds of minor ones, and perhaps 120,000 sooty artisans in metals and chemical produce. The streets are ill-built, ill-paved; always flimsy in their aspect—often poor, sometimes miserable.' It was a visit to the Lancashire manufacturing district that evoked the lament, 'The mills, oh the fetid, fuzzy, ill-ventilated mills!' And the sight of Merthyr Tydvil, the center of the Welsh coal and iron industry, provoked the outburst (in a letter to his wife), 'About 50,000 grimy mortals, black and clammy with soot and sweat, screwing out a livelihood for themselves in that spot of the Taff valley. Such a set of unguided, hard-worked, fierce, and miserable-looking sons of Adam I never saw before. Ah me! It is like a vision of Hell, and will never leave me, that of these poor creatures broiling, all in sweat and dirt, amid their furnaces, pits, and rolling mills.'

If these things have been, in large part, changed for the better, it is due, to a considerable extent, to Carlyle's influence, exerted not only directly, but indirectly through such writers as Ruskin, Dickens, Canon Kingsley, and William Morris. It was Carlyle's indignation about industrial conditions that met with sympathetic response in the young hearts of Huxley, working in a London slum, and Tyndall, engaged in an ordnance survey near a Lan-cashire factory town.

'Literary fame,' wrote Carlyle in the years of his youthful ambitions, 'is a thing which I covet little'; he desired to do honest and conscientious work as a journalist; and in the bettering of conditions for the laboring poor he achieved the success he was aiming at. Modern criticism is inclined to find his best historical work in *Life and Letters of Oliver Cromwell* (1845), and his best literary work in *The Life of Sterling* (1851), and both judgments are perhaps right; Carlyle's *Cromwell* reversed the established verdict on the character and purposes of the great Puritan statesman, and the biography is free from the rhetorical extravagances of Carlyle's habitual style, which many modern readers find offensive. But both books contain comparatively little of what was most characteristic of Carlyle, either as a thinker or as a writer.

Professor Emery Neff (to whose recent study of Carlyle the present writer is greatly indebted) points out that Carlyle's style is that of a Hebrew prophet, re-inforced by the rhetoric of the contemporary pulpit, the editorial writer, and the political orator; it is still more heavily weighted by much reading of the German romanticists. Though Carlyle could lay it aside for a particular occasion, as in the *Life of Sterling*, it was habitual to him, and it was not an affectation; he used it in his letters and in his conversation. It is an obstacle to the reader of the present day, when rhetoric is out of fashion.

Carlyle as a man, in spite of obvious shortcomings, remains worthy of our admiration. He told the truth with unrestrained bitterness and often with unpardonable exaggeration; but he told the truth as he saw it, and thereby won, not only the respect but also the affection of the greatest among his contemporaries, although they often not only disapproved of the violence with which he expressed his opinions but disagreed with the opinions he expressed. As we have seen, Carlyle despised Tennyson's poetry, but he remained Tennyson's friend. He poured contempt on the scientists, but retained the affection of Huxley and Tyndall. He rejected Christianity, but found a disciple in Canon Kingsley. The Liberalism of John Stuart Mill was as abhorrent to him as his own aristocratic authoritarianism was abhorrent to Mill, but they continued to respect each other, though the close friendship of their earlier acquaintance could not be maintained after the divergence in fundamental principles was made clear. It was Mill who suggested the subject of the *French Revolution*, which was regarded in Carlyle's own time as his most successful piece of historical writing. When the first book was finished, Carlyle lent the only copy of the manuscript to Mill, who, a few days later, came back with the terrible avowal that it had been destroyed. Mill took full responsibility for the catastrophe, but the gossip of the time ran that he had lent the manuscript to his friend, Mrs. Taylor, to read. Mrs. Taylor, enthralled by the narrative, went to bed late leaving the manuscript on the sitting-room table, and the housemaid, who got up early next morning, lit the fire with it. Both men behaved with generosity and self-restraint in this difficult situation, and it caused no break in their affection for each other, though Carlyle had to undergo a long period of light reading before he could face the task of studying his authorities all over again.

JOHN STUART MILL
(1806–1873)

The career of John Stuart Mill marks both the rise and the decline of that 'utilitarian' school of politics and philosophy to which he gave a name and which was a predominating influence in the life and thought of his time. The real founder of the school was Jeremy Bentham (1748–1832), who in turn inherited from the English eighteenth century scientist and radical, Priestley, the phrase 'the greatest happiness of the greatest number,' which was to make Bentham's name famous. Bentham was a disinterested and industrious writer and thinker who exerted a widespread influence not only in the British Isles but in America and on the European Continent. His leading disciple in England was the father of John Stuart Mill, James Mill (1773–1836), the son of a Scottish shoemaker, and the author of a *History of India* which obtained for him an important and lucrative position in the service of the East India Company. Although James Mill had abandoned the Presbyterian faith of his youth and adopted a hedonist philosophy which made happiness the end and rule of life, no one could have practised for himself, and imposed on his son, a more severe regimen of intellectual discipline. Mere sensuous pleasure James Mill despised, and he followed the life of reason with sublime faith and trust. John Stuart Mill wrote in his *Autobiography:* 'So complete was my father's reliance on the influence of reason over the minds of mankind, whenever it is allowed to reach them, that he felt as if all would be gained if the whole population were to be taught to read, if all sorts of opinions were allowed to be addressed to them by word and in writing, and if by means of the suffrage they could nominate a legislature to give effect to the opinions they adopted. Accordingly a democratic suffrage was the principal article of his political creed, not on the grounds of liberty, rights of man, or any of the phrases, more or less significant, by which, up to that time, democracy had usually been defended, but as the most essential of securities for good government.'

John Stuart Mill was educated in accordance with the severe principles and practice of his father. He began to learn Greek at three years of age, undertook the study of universal history at seven, and at sixteen knew as much as the whole teaching staff of an average Cambridge or Oxford College. He then traveled abroad to acquire foreign languages; on his return to England, he went into the Indian Office to work under his father's direction, and began to write for the reviews, especially for the Radical Westminster, which was later united with the London Magazine under his editorship.

The immediate result of this premature intellectual development was depression almost to the point of despair. At the age of twenty young Mill passed through a spiritual crisis of which he tells the story in his *Autobiography*. He asked himself, 'Suppose that all your objects in life were realized; that all the changes in institutions and opinions that you are looking forward to could be completely effected at this very instant, would this be a great joy and happiness to you?' 'And an irrepressible self-consciousness distinctly answered, "No!" At this my heart sank within me: the whole foundation on which my life was constructed fell down. All my happiness was to have been found in a continual pursuit of this end. The end had ceased to charm, and how could there ever again be any interest in the means? I seemed to have nothing to live for.'

From this mood of discouragement Mill gradually escaped by a study of poetry, especially that of Wordsworth, and by a friendship with a Mrs. Taylor, whom he married in 1851. He had already completed his education by writing works on *Logic* (1843) and *Political Economy* (1848), which became standard text books at the universities and did much to mold the liberal thought of the next generation or two. The successive editions of the *Political Economy* mark the steps by which Mill passed from the strict laissez-faire principles to something very like Socialism.

In 1858 the functions of the East India Company were taken over by the Government, and Mill retired from the service with a handsome pension. He published, in the next year or two, essays on *Liberty*, on *Representative Government*, and on *Utilitarianism*, which became classics in virtue of their clear thinking and lucidity of expression. In 1869 he published an eloquent protest against the *Subjection of Women;* he had previously helped to found the first Woman's Suffrage Society, presented a petition to Parliament, and as member for Westminster moved to insert 'persons' instead of 'men' in the Reform Bill of 1867. Defeated in 1868 and still lamenting the loss of his wife some years before, he withdrew to the seclusion of a small estate near Avignon in the south of France, where she was buried. His last years were solaced by the companionship of his step-daughter, Helen Taylor. There he composed *Three Essays on Religion*, which indicate a considerable departure from the rationalistic principles of his early training; he left also to be published after his death the *Autobiography*, which is one of the best examples of that kind of composition.

The elevation of Mill's character and the keenness of his mind made him greatly respected by his contemporaries, and he exercised a widespread and enduring influence. Although his name is usually associated with the doctrine of laissez-faire, in his own thought he interpreted that phrase to mean the removal of those restrictions on trade and industry which were hampering commercial development in the France of the eighteenth century and the England of the first half of the nineteenth. Even upon the doctrine thus interpreted he put severe and increasing limitations in his more mature years, and it was these limitations, rather than the original thesis, that affected his younger readers and followers. He wrote in his *Political Economy*: 'Socialism has now become irrevocably one of the leading elements in European politics. The questions raised by it will not be set at rest by merely refusing to listen to it; but only by a more and more complete realization of the ends which Socialism aims at, not neglecting its means so far as they can be employed with advantage.' He advocated restriction of the right of bequest, or at least the limitation of what anyone should be permitted to acquire by bequest or inheritance, so as to counteract the tendency of inherited property to collect in large masses. He thought the taxes on inheritances and legacies above a certain amount should be as heavy as they could be made without giving rise to evasions—a suggestion adopted by a Liberal Government many years after Mill's death. He drew attention to what has since been recognized as the 'unearned increment' of landed property. 'The ordinary progress of a society which increases in wealth is at all times tending to augment the incomes of landlords; to give them both a greater amount and a greater proportion of the wealth of the community, independently of any trouble or outlay incurred by themselves. They grow richer, as it were in their sleep, without working, risking, or economizing. What claim have they, according to the general principles of social justice, to this accession of riches? In what would they have been wronged if society had, from the beginning, reserved a right of taxing the spontaneous increase of rent, to the highest amount required by financial exigencies?' In order to remedy this injustice he recommended a valuation of all the land in the country—a suggestion which was adopted, first by a Liberal Chancellor of the Exchequer (Lloyd George) and later, in the twentieth century, by a Labor Minister (Snowden). His idea that what the incometax-payer spent on life insurance should be exempt from taxation has long been the English practice, and his contention that elementary education was a responsibility of the state rather than of the parents was fully acknowledged by the Act of 1870.

He was strongly opposed to the view of Carlyle that the humbler workers should be subjected to the control of their natural leaders. 'All privileged and powerful classes,' he wrote, 'have used their power in the interest of their own selfishness.' He was certain that the working-classes of Western Europe would never again submit to the patriarchal or paternal system of Government. 'That question has been several times decided. It was decided when they were taught to read, and allowed access to newspapers and political tracts. It was decided when dissenting preachers were suffered to go among them, and appeal to their faculties and feelings in opposition to the creeds professed and countenanced by their superiors. It was decided when they were brought together in numbers, to work socially under the same roof. It was decided when railways enabled them to shift from place to place, and change their patrons and employers as easily as their coats. The working-classes have taken their interests into their own hands, and are perpetually showing that they think the interests of their employers not identical with their own but opposite to them. Some among the higher classes flatter themselves that these tendencies may be counteracted by moral and religious education; but they have let time go by for giving an education which can serve their purpose. The principles of the Reformation have reached as low down in society as reading and writing, and the poor will no longer accept morals and religion of other people's prescribing. I speak more particularly of our own country, especially the town population, and the districts of the most scientific agriculture and highest wages, Scotland and the North of England.'

He looked forward to a time when the working people would not be contented with the condition of working for wages, but would demand not merely a share in the profits, but a share in the direction and control of the whole undertaking. 'To work at the bidding and for the profit of another, without any interest in the work—the price of their labor being adjusted by hostile competition, one side demanding as much and the other paying as little as possible—is not, even when wages are high, a satisfactory state to human beings of educated intelligence, who have ceased to think themselves naturally inferior to those whom they serve. They may be willing to pass through the class of servants in their way to that of employers; but not to remain in it all their lives. To begin as hired laborers, then after a few years to work on their own account, and finally employ others, is the normal condition of laborers in a new country, rapidly increasing in wealth and population, like America or Australia. But something else is required when wealth increases slowly, or has reached the stationary state, when positions, instead of being more mobile, would tend to be much more permanent than at present, and the condition of any portion of mankind could only be desirable, if made desirable from the first.'

'It appears to me impossible but that the increase of intelligence, of education, and of the love of independence among the working classes, must be attended with a corresponding growth of the good sense which manifests itself in provident habits of conduct, and that population, therefore, will bear a gradually diminishing ratio to capital and employment. This most desirable result would be much accelerated by another change, which lies in the direct line of the best tendencies of the time: the opening of industrial occupations freely to both sexes. The same reasons which make it no longer necessary that the poor should depend on the rich, make it equally unnecessary that women should depend on men, and the least which justice requires is that law and custom should not enforce dependence (when the correlative protection has become superfluous) by ordaining that a woman, who does not happen to have a provision by inheritance, shall have scarcely any means open to her of gaining a livelihood, except as a wife and mother. Let women who prefer that occupation adopt it; but that there should be no option, no other career possible for the great majority of women, except in the humbler departments of life, is one of those social injustices which call loudest for remedy.'

The man who held these views of the position of women and the relations between capital and labor and had the courage to proclaim them when Victorianism was at its height was no ordinary man; he was the prophet of a new age.

JOHN HENRY NEWMAN
(*1801–1890*)

Neither the spiritual influence nor the intellectual activities of John Henry Newman can be understood without some consideration of the position of the Church of England during the formative years of his early manhood. Re-organized by Queen Elizabeth's Protestant advisers after the disastrous religious quarrels of preceding reigns, its articles and services were designed to be inclusive of the more moderate factions of the time, including on the one hand the devout adherents of the older ecclesiastical tradition and on the other the Puritan reformers who desired to go further in the direction of democracy and simplicity than suited the autocratic disposition of either Elizabeth or James. The compromise thus devised was far from satisfactory either to the Catholics or to the Dissenters, but it served to hold the Church together during the turbulent seventeenth century and the sceptical eighteenth century. Men who desired a more conservative liturgy or a simpler form of worship without liturgy were in process of time allowed to go their own way without persecution by the State. Catholic disabilities, except for the sovereign and a few leading officers of state, were removed in 1829, but long before this Nonconformists were 'tolerated,' i.e. they were allowed to worship and educate their children without molestation and they were no longer required to attend Church of England services in order to hold municipal or state offices. The Established Church retained the legal, educational, and social advantages it had acquired by inheritance and tradition; in secure possession of incomes sometimes more than comfortable, sometimes quite inadequate, the clergy sank by the end of the eighteenth century into easy-going ways and in most cases contented themselves with a somewhat perfunctory performance of their sacred duties. George Crabbe (1754–1822) thus describes the typical activities of the average Anglican clergyman of his time—and he himself was a clergyman as well as a poet:

> Fiddling and fishing were his arts; at times
> He altered sermons and he aimed at rhymes;
> And his fair friends, not yet intent on cards,
> Oft he amused with riddles and charades.

The Bishop of Llandaff, who died in 1816, lived in seclusion on Lake Windermere in the North of England, and visited his Welsh diocese only once in thirty-four years; in addition to his bishopric he held sixteen 'livings,' i.e. pastorates of parishes, often widely separated, of which the holder drew the income while the duties were discharged by an ill-paid substitute. The Bishop of London, about the end of the eighteenth century, very gently upbraided his clergy for their constant absence from the parishes to which they were supposed to minister. 'There are, indeed,' he said to them, 'two impediments to constant residence which cannot easily be surmounted; the first is (what unfortunately prevails in some parts of this diocese) unwholesomeness of situation; the other is the possession of a second benefice. Yet even these will not justify a *total* and *perpetual* absence from your cures. The unhealthiness of many places is of late years by various improvements greatly abated, and there are now few so circumstanced as not to admit of residence there in *some* part of the year without any danger to the constitution.'

D. C. Somervell, from whose *English Thought in the Nineteenth Century* the above evidence is mainly quoted, says of the Evangelical movement of the end of the eighteenth and beginning of the nineteenth century, that its most important achievement was to outweigh the influence and authority, within the Church, 'of the old High-and-Dry school, with its complacent tolerance of worldliness and ignorance. The Evangelicals never, perhaps, secured a majority on the episcopal bench, but they provided something more important than bishops; they provided religion.' Elie Halévy, the great French authority on the history of England in the nineteenth century, says of the year 1832, with which the Victorian Era opened: 'It was during this critical year, a few months after the passage of the Reform Bill, that English Evangelicalism may be said to have reached its apogee. It constituted the essence of the Methodist preaching, and in their hatred of Catholics and Latitudinarians the Wesleyans were drawing closer to the Church from which they were sprung. And within the Church the influence of the Evangelicals grew stronger every day. The number of clergymen who had given their formal adherence to the party was estimated at between two and three thousand. The parochial clergy were no longer the keen hunters and hard drinkers they had been a few years earlier. By their preaching and example the Evangelicals had enforced a stricter observance of decorum, and a more obvious regard for the dignity of their vocation. And in the last resort it is to the influence of the Evangelicals that we must attribute the moral reform which Thomas Arnold and several others were effecting at this time with enormous success in the Anglican public schools. Among the aristocracy who governed the country the Evangelicals were bringing the duel into discredit. Among the lower classes they were attacking the use of intoxicating liquors: the first Temperance Societies had just been founded in imitation of an American model, and the House of Commons was shortly to appoint a Committee to consider the advisability of passing legislation with the object of diminishing drunkenness. The credit of the two great humanitarian measures passed by the new parliament, the emancipation of the slaves, and the protection of child labor in factories, belongs to the Evangelicals even more than to the Radicals. Sir Andrew Agnew introduced annually a Bill to prohibit Sunday work in any form whatsoever. He was always defeated, but the number of votes recorded in favor of his Sabbatarian Bill increased every year, and every year the habits of the people, steeped in Evangelical piety, rendered more superfluous the legal enactment of a rule which everybody freely obeyed.

'Men of letters disliked the Evangelicals for their narrow Puritanism, men of science for their intellectual feebleness. Nevertheless, during the nineteenth century Evangelical religion was the moral cement of English society. It was the influence of the Evangelicals which invested the British aristocracy with an almost Stoic dignity, restrained the plutocrats newly risen from the masses from vulgar ostentation and debauchery, and placed over the proletariat a select body of workmen enamored of virtue and capable of self-restraint.'

It was into a London middle-class family of this serious and God-fearing type that John Henry Newman was born at the beginning of the nineteenth century. His father was a London banker, and his mother came of a Huguenot family; he himself described the religious faith in which he was brought up as 'modified Calvinism.' Educated privately until he went to Oxford, he won a scholarship at Trinity College and a fellowship at Oriel. The latter college was the center of what came to be known as the Oxford Movement, of which the main inspiration was an older fellow of the College, the saintly and revered John Keble, who had written some admirable hymns and religious poems, and had served the University as Professor of Poetry. Alarmed at the prospect of attacks upon the Church through the increasing power of the Nonconformist middle class, the advance of science, and the growth of industrialism, this little group of Oxford clerics strove to strengthen the Anglican position by a return to Catholic tradition. Their view was that the Established Church was not a body created by the State but the 'local presence and organ' of 'the Church Catholic and Apostolic, set up from the beginning,' in which every member of the Church of England declared his faith when he recited in the Apostles' Creed the words 'I believe in the Holy Catholic Church.'

As a safeguard against infidelity they strove to emphasize the spiritual mission of the Church of England, to insist upon its divine authority, and to inspire its priesthood with a due sense of the importance of their sacred functions; the priestly power to give absolution from sin and to administer the sacrament of Holy Communion rested, in their view, not upon the interpretation of a solitary text of Scripture, but upon the fact of a divine power communicated by Jesus to the Apostles and by them transmitted from bishop to bishop through the generations from the organization of the primitive Church down to the present time. Young Newman's subtle and versatile but essentially sceptical intellect was attracted by the idea of ecclesiastical authority; he was as certain of the existence of God as of his own existence, but he found himself unable to put the grounds of that certainty into logical shape. In this living, busy world, he could see no reflection of its Creator. 'Were it not for this voice, speaking so clearly in my conscience and my heart, I should be an atheist, or a pantheist, or a polytheist when I looked into the world. . . . Either there is no Creator, or this living Society of men is in a true sense discarded from His presence.' In his view the tendency of reason is toward a simple unbelief in matters of religion. 'No truth, however sacred, can stand against it, in the long run; and hence it is that in a pagan world, when our Lord came, the last traces of the religious knowledge of former times were all but disappearing from those portions of the world in which the intellect had been active and had had a career. And in these latter days, in like manner, outside the Catholic Church things are tending—with far greater rapidity than in that old time, from the circumstances of the age— to atheism in one shape or another.'

When Newman became a fellow of Oriel, he had no doubt that the Church of England was part of the Catholic Church, and that it was invested with divine authority to guide its members in matters of conduct and belief. When he was appointed a fellow, soon after attaining his majority, he declared formally his acceptance of the Thirty-nine Articles, as required of all fellows of Oxford Colleges at that time; for the University was still a close preserve of the Church of England, and was regarded as part of the ecclesiastical organization. Two years later he took Holy Orders and became curate of the Oxford parish of St. Clement's. He soon became distinguished for learning, piety, and fervent eloquence in the pulpit; in 1826 he became tutor of Oriel, and two years later he received the important appointment of Vicar of the University Church of St. Mary's, with a chapelry at Littlemore in the country near by.

If Keble, as has been said, was the inspiration of the Oxford Movement, its intellectual leaders were R. Hurrell Froude and Dr. Pusey. To the latter was due the contemporary name of 'Puseyism,' by which the opponents of the Movement often described its earlier developments; the former (who must not be confused with his brother, J. A. Froude, the biographer of Carlyle), was a specialist in ecclesiastical history. It was a weakness in the Anglo-Catholic position that while the clergy of the Church of England acknowledged the validity of Holy Orders in the Roman Church—through which indeed the English Church drew its line of Apostolic Succession—the Church of Rome refused to acknowledge the validity of Anglican Orders. This led to a controversy in the merits of which Hurrell Froude was an expert, and his discussions with Newman contributed much to unsettle the latter's mind as to the soundness of the Anglican position, both historically and rationally. They went on a Mediterranean tour together in 1832—the first year of the Victorian Era, as we have defined it— visited Rome and many ancient shrines of the Christian faith. At Palermo, where Newman was apparently more attracted by the magnificent churches than repelled by the superstitions of the Sicilian peasantry, he wrote, 'O, that thy creed were sound, thou Church of Rome,' which suggests that only the remnants of the Protestant faith which he had absorbed in his childhood withheld him from accepting Roman Catholicism. He was still obsessed by 'the encircling gloom' of doubts and fears, when on the return voyage he wrote his best known hymn, 'Abide with me, fast falls the eventide.' Arriving in England, he found ecclesiastical Oxford in a state of ferment owing to the introduction of a Bill into Parliament to suppress ten of the twenty-two bishoprics of the Irish Protestant Church, which was ministering to a small fraction of a population mainly Roman Catholic. He reached Oxford in July, 1833, just in time to hear Keble preach a sermon on 'national apostasy,' in which he denounced the Irish Bill as a 'direct disavowal of the sovereignty of God.' Within half a century the Irish Protestant Church was disestablished by the devout Anglican

Premier, W. E. Gladstone, but in 1833 any measure of reform directed at the Protestant Church of Ireland was regarded by conservative churchmen as a blow at the prestige of the Church of England.

Later in 1833 Keble and Newman began the publication of *Tracts for the Times*, intended to strengthen the defense of the Anglo-Catholic position, which at that time embodied the resolve of a recent meeting of the clergy to fight for 'the Apostolic Succession and the integrity of the Prayer Book,' including those vestiges of the Roman ritual remaining in it which had been discontinued and disregarded in course of time by the Protestant clergy of the Church of England. The appointment in 1836 of a liberal churchman, R. D. Hampden, as Professor of Divinity in the University provoked a violent protest from the Anglo-Catholic group and contributed further to upset Newman's mind. He read extensively in the Church Fathers with a view to clear his views as to the contending claims of the Roman and Anglican positions, and was much impressed by St. Augustine's argument against the Donatists, *securus judicat orbis terrarum*—what the whole church accepts must be true. The series of *Tracts for the Times* reached No. 90, which was written by Newman to indicate the position at which he had then arrived. It was an attempt to vindicate his desire to stay in the Church of England by the plea that the Thirty-nine Articles were not directed against the Roman Catholic creed but against popular errors and exaggerations of it, and that the Anglo-Catholic clergy were therefore justified in interpreting the Anglican Articles and Liturgy in a Catholic rather than a Protestant sense whenever the wording would bear a Catholic interpretation.

This appeared to ordinary Englishmen, who regarded the Church of England as Protestant, as an attempt to enjoy the benefits and emoluments of the Established Church while refusing to accept the official statements of its doctrines, as approved by Parliament, in their obvious meaning. There was a great outcry, and at the request of the Bishop of Oxford the series of *Tracts for the Times* was discontinued. Newman was, to use his own phrase, 'on his deathbed as regards membership with the Anglican Church'; he came to the conclusion that the position of the Anglican Church as to Apostolic Succession was untenable and in 1842 withdrew to Littlemore to give full consideration to the seriousness of the conflict in his own mind. In 1843 he retracted all the hard things he had said against the Church of Rome, resigned his

Vicarage of St. Mary's, and preached his last sermon at Little-more. In 1845 he was formally received into the Roman Catholic Church, and a year later went to Rome, where he was ordained priest and accepted the degree of Doctor of Divinity from the Pope.

It is impossible for the present generation to realize the con-sternation, dismay, and resentment caused, not only in clerical circles but among the laity, by Newman's secession. The leading defender of the Anglo-Catholic position and the most eloquent preacher of the Church of England had 'gone over to Rome'; it seemed a fatal blow to the Anglo-Catholic clergy, some of whom followed Newman into the Roman fold while others stayed in the Church of England and justified themselves as best as they could. After a while, the Anglo-Catholic clergy recovered from the blow and became an important group in the Church of England, though the laity, for the most part, remained steadfastly Protestant. An attempt to 'put down ritualism' by Act of Parliament in 1875 failed of its purpose; and an attempt to revise the Prayer Book about half a century later, in spite of the strongest clerical sup-port, could not be put through the House of Commons because the members believed it condoned tendencies toward Roman practice of which the majority of the nation disapproved.

Newman, for the time being, disappeared into the seclusion of the Roman Church, and for many years little or nothing was heard of him by the great world. He emerged to denounce a renegade Roman priest, who brought a prosecution for libel against him; Newman was condemned to a fine of £100, and costs amounting to £14,000. The verdict was generally believed to be unjust, and Newman's expenses were paid by public sub-scription.

He remained, however, subject to much misunderstanding and misrepresentation, for which there seemed no hope of redress until in January, 1864, a leading Anglican divine of strong Protestant sympathies, Canon Charles Kingsley, in a magazine review of Froude's *History*, made the gratuitous *obiter dictum* that 'Father Newman informs us that truth for its own sake need not be, and on the whole ought not to be, a virtue of the Roman clergy.' Newman challenged Kingsley to cite chapter and verse in support of this assertion; Kingsley was unable to do this, but was ill-advised enough to embark upon a controversy with Newman as to the respect of certain Roman Catholic organizations for the truth. Newman, much Kingsley's superior in subtlety of thought and power of argument, had also the facts on his side, and was able to crush his opponent completely. When the dust of battle had settled down, Newman removed the controversial elements from what he had written and left a clear and convincing statement of the successive steps which had led him from the Anglican to the Roman Church. There remained no possible doubt of his sincerity, and his defense, under the title *Apologia pro Vita Sua*, is still one of the best examples of autobiographical writing in the English language.

For a long time Newman was not particularly happy, nor particularly successful, in the Church of his adoption. He went dutifully to Ireland in the hopeless quest of a solution of the problem of higher education for Catholics, of which the main outcome was a masterly series of papers on *The Idea of a University* (1852). He was overshadowed by the superior administrative and political ability of Cardinal Manning, like himself a convert from Anglicanism, but able to accommodate himself more easily to the demands of time and circumstance. Newman took the losing side in the debate about papal infallibility in 1869–70, not that he disbelieved in the doctrine, but he doubted the expediency of an authoritative definition at that particular time. In 1878, having been elected honorary fellow of Trinity College, Oxford, he came back to the scene of his former scholastic and dialectical triumphs to be greeted with affectionate admiration by everybody, for he was now seventy-seven and the bitterness had gone out of the ancient controversies. Next year he received still higher honors, for Leo XIII succeeded to the papal throne and promptly made him a Cardinal. For the rest of his life he lived in seclusion at the Edgbaston Oratory near Birmingham.

To most Americans and most Englishmen, Newman's attitude seems a futile attempt to hark back to the Middle Ages. But one is bound to pay tribute to his sincerity, his intellectual subtlety, and his mastery of a lucid and persuasive style. Once his position is accepted, that, 'apart from an interior and unreasoned conviction, there is no cogent proof of the existence of God,' one arrives easily enough at the conclusion that 'the difficulties of creed and Scripture Canon are unsurmountable unless overridden by the authority of an infallible Church.' To many this seems the negation of reason; to many others it appears the triumph of reason, once reason has been put in its proper place by the acceptance of a premise which is not contrary to reason but superior to it.

JOHN RUSKIN

(*1819–1900*)

John Ruskin was the only child of Scottish parents of the strictest evangelical piety, and his delicate health in childhood made
him their peculiar care. His father was a wine merchant with
his home and headquarters in.London, but in pursuit of business
he traveled in his own carriage all over England and the Scottish
Lowlands, with an occasional tour on the Continent. On these
journeys he frequently took his wife and little boy with him, so
that as a child Ruskin became familiar with most of the high
roads in Great Britain, and nearly all the noblemen's houses in
England. His reading was confined to the daily and diligent study
of the Bible, Pope's *Homer*, Sir Walter Scott, and the great English
poets. Before he was ten he was writing poems on the mountains
of the Lake District in imitation of Wordsworth—and not bad
imitations, either in the quality of the blank verse or in the close
observation of nature. He early learnt the lesson he was to preach
so insistently to the painters, poets, and critics of his time, to
'go to Nature in all singleness of heart, and walk with her laboriously and trustingly, having no other thoughts but how best to
penetrate her meaning and remember her instruction, rejecting
nothing, selecting nothing, and scorning nothing, and rejoicing
always in the truth.' At thirteen he came into contact with the
work of Turner, who had vivified English landscape painting with
the magic and mystery of his romantic imagination. Ruskin was
sixteen when an attack on Turner's work as 'out of Nature,' published in Blackwood's Magazine, roused him to fury, and the boy
wrote and sent to the great artist an impassioned defense, which
Turner made no attempt to publish but sent to the purchaser
of the picture which had provoked the attack. Next year, however, Ruskin's series of articles on 'The Poetry of Architecture or
the Architecture of the Nations of Europe considered in its Association with Natural Scenery and Natural Character' appeared
in the Architectural Magazine; the papers were signed 'Kata
Phusin,' 'according to Nature,' and were commonly believed to
be the work of an Oxford don. The opinion of the anonymous
author was solemnly asked and solemnly given as to the site of a
monument to Sir Walter Scott about to be erected at Edinburgh;
the Committee, however, did not follow the young critic's advice.

All this very naturally convinced Ruskin's parents that they
had produced a genius. His father bought Turner's pictures and

decided to send the boy to the most fashionable of Oxford Colleges, Christ Church. On account of his delicate health, Ruskin had received private tuition at home and had undergone no regular educational discipline, so that it was doubtful whether he could pass the entrance examinations; his father accordingly paid the extra fees necessary for his admission as a 'gentleman commoner.' His mother came to live at Oxford while her son was in residence, and he had tea with her every day; his health was still precarious, but he won the Newdigate prize for English verse composition and took a creditable degree.

The defense of Turner was still dear to the heart of the young devotee, and he settled down at home to the composition of his first book, to be called 'Turner and the Ancients'; it appeared in May, 1843, under the title of 'Modern Painters: their Superiority in the Art of Landscape Painting to all the Ancient Masters proved by examples of the True, the Beautiful, and the Intellectual, from the Works of Modern Artists, especially from those of J. M. W. Turner.' This was the first volume of *Modern Painters*, which rolled on like a snowball, gathering weight and force as it ran, until the fifth volume appeared in 1860. Meanwhile Ruskin had further established his reputation as a writer and critic by the publication of the *Seven Lamps of Architecture* (1849) and *The Stones of Venice* (1851–53); the seven principles of architecture he set out to establish were Truth, Beauty, Power, Sacrifice, Obedience, Labor, Memory; but just as the work of Turner was the starting point of *Modern Painters*, so these two architectural books were to show the supreme excellence of Gothic as compared with Renaissance building, the former depending on 'certain right states of temper and moral feeling,' and arising out of 'a state of pure national faith and of domestic virtue,' and the latter having arisen out of 'a state of concealed national infidelity and of domestic corruption.' All good architecture, he contended, is essentially religious— the production not of an infidel and corrupted people, but of a faithful and a virtuous people, 'inspired by resolute and common purpose and rendering resolute and common fidelity to the legible laws of an undoubted God.' He contrasted this by-gone age of faith and creative power with the slavery of contemporary English industrialism, under which 'the animation of her multitudes is sent like fuel to feed the factory smoke, and the strength of them is given daily to be wasted into the fineness of a web, or racked into the exactness of a line.'

Soon after his graduation, Ruskin's portrait was painted by

a leading artist as 'a young poet seated at a desk with pencil in hand, Mont Blanc in the background.' Frederic Harrison recalls him as he first knew him, nearly twenty years later, as 'a man of slight figure, rather tall (he was five feet ten inches), except that he had a stoop from the shoulders, with a countenance of singular mobility and expressiveness. His eyes were blue and very keen, full of fire and meaning; the hair was brown, luxuriant and curly; the brows rather marked, and with somewhat shaggy eyebrows. The lips were full of movement and character.' His countenance was 'winning, magnetic, and radiant,' full of sparkle and nervous restlessness. It might be supposed that a man with his ardent temperament and good looks would be attractive to women, but his early love-affairs, first with a young French girl and then with Scott's granddaughter, were unfortunate; the young ladies would not listen to him and married elsewhere. He fell into deep despondency, and his parents prescribed marriage as the cure: his mother found a suitable wife for him, as she thought, in a high-spirited beauty whom they knew well, Euphemia Gray. The marriage was not a success, and after five years' trial came to an end by nullification in the courts. Euphemia Gray, who was as fond of fashionable society as Ruskin was devoted to a life of study and quiet, married a successful painter and became Lady Millais. Ruskin returned to his parents' home, his pictures, and his books.

In the next few years Ruskin gave much of his time to lecturing and teaching. He espoused the cause of the young painters known as the 'P. R. B.' (Pre-Raphaelite Brotherhood), and interested himself also in the Christian Socialist Movement, which two Anglican clergymen, Frederick Denison Maurice and Charles Kingsley, had started in London. Kingsley wrote Socialistic novels, and Maurice conducted a college for workingmen in which Ruskin taught. Beyond suffusing a mild Socialistic atmosphere among its devotees and securing a large amount of publicity for social evils, the movement did not travel very far in the direction of Socialism, but it did a good deal in the way of education; Toynbee Hall, University settlements, colleges for workingmen and women, university extension, and various schemes of adult education all received an impulse from this beginning.

Perhaps, however, the most significant achievement of Christian Socialism was to enlist the active interest of Ruskin, who very soon convinced himself that the kind of painting they wanted in London was painting cheeks red with health. His criticisms of art and architecture had always sought a moral basis; he now strove to apply the same tests and standards to political economy, which, in his view, ought not to be regarded as an abstract science, but 'a system of conduct founded on the sciences, and impossible except under certain conditions of moral culture.'

Ruskin was forty years of age, at the height of his power as a writer and of his reputation as an art critic, when the change in his mental attitude was clearly developed. The attack upon the political economy of the Manchester school was not original with him; it had originated with Carlyle, whose disciple he acknowledged himself; it had been enforced by Dickens and Kingsley in popular novels; and John Stuart Mill had suggested practical departures from the theory of laissez-faire which almost amounted to a denial of the doctrine. Ruskin was not an economist and he was not inclined to take the trouble to make himself acquainted with the literature of the subject. The orthodox political economy was to him anathema, and he denounced it with prophetic conviction and emphasis, often without asking himself whether the economists really held the opinions he attributed to them. Nor did he make it clear what general scheme he proposed to substitute for the mercantile and industrial system he assailed with such vigorous and resounding rhetoric. What he did was to awake the public mind to the shortcomings and evils of the existing régime, and the insufficiency of the ideals and standards by which people lived. 'Your ideal of human life,' he told the manufacturers of Bradford in their own town hall, where he had been invited to lecture, 'is that it should be passed in a pleasant undulating world, with iron and coal everywhere underneath it. On each pleasant bank of this world is to be a beautiful mansion, with two wings; and stables and coach-houses, a moderately sized park; a large garden and hot-houses; and pleasant carriage drives through the shrubberies. In this mansion are to live the favored votaries of the Goddess; the English gentleman, with his precious wife, and his beautiful family; always able to have the boudoir and the jewels for the wife, and the beautiful ball dresses for the daughters, and hunters for the sons, and a shooting in the Highlands for himself. At the bottom of the bank is to be the mill; not less than a quarter of a mile long, with a steam engine at each end, and two in the middle, and a chimney three hundred feet high. In this mill are to be in constant employment from eight hundred to a thousand workers, who never drink, never strike, always go to church on Sunday, and always express themselves in respectful language.'

Ruskin also brought back to the consciousness of the English people an ideal for which they might strive, even if he did not indicate the means by which that ideal could be attained—the ideal of a good life. '*There is no wealth but Life*—Life, including all its powers of love, of joy, and of admiration. That country is the richest which nourishes the greatest number of noble and happy human beings.' And again: 'In a community regulated only by laws of demand and supply, but protected from open violence, the persons who become rich are, generally speaking, industrious, sensible, unimaginative, insensitive, and ignorant. The persons who remain poor are the entirely foolish, the entirely wise, the idle, the luckless, the humble, the thoughtful, the dull, the imaginative, the sensitive, the well-informed, the improvident, the irregularly and impulsively wicked, the clumsy knave, the open thief, and the entirely merciful, just, and godly person.'

Naturally such outpourings were not popular in a community which was absorbing by the hundred thousand the gospel of *Self-Help* by Samuel Smiles, who, in this and other volumes, preached the supreme virtues of success and respectability. Ruskin's first full and frank statement of his new convictions was contained in a series of papers in the Cornhill Magazine, afterwards published in book form under the title of *Unto This Last*, taken from a Parable in the New Testament; the outcry aroused was so great that Thackeray, who was then editor, was obliged to discontinue the series. J. A. Froude, the follower and biographer of Carlyle, offered an opening in Fraser's Magazine, of which he was then editor, with the same outcry from subscribers and with the same result. Still, Ruskin was tolerated as a sort of inspired prophet, unquestionably sincere, but probably a bit crazy. He was invited to lecture around London, in Dublin, in Manchester, and in 1870 was appointed Slade Professor of Art at the University of Oxford. He accepted the appointment and held it, with intervals caused by serious breakdowns in his health, until 1884.

The lectures were often not upon art, nor even upon the announced subject of his discourse; but they were very largely attended and must have been a stimulating moral and intellectual force, not only in the life of the university, but in the national life of the next generation. 'I tell you,' he said to his students, 'that neither sound art, policy, nor religion, can exist in England, until, neglecting, if it must be, your own pleasure gardens and pleasure chambers, you resolve that the streets which are the habitation of the poor, and the fields which are the playgrounds of their children, shall be restored to the rule of the spirits, whosoever they are, in earth and heaven, that ordain and reward, with constant and conscious felicity, all that is decent and orderly, beautiful and pure.'

E. T. Cook, one of Ruskin's students and afterwards his biographer, gives us a picture of 'the bent figure with the ample gown,' and the velvet college cap, one of the few remaining memorials of the 'gentleman commoner.' 'The quaintness of his costume —the light home-spun tweed, the double-breasted waistcoat, the ill-fitting and old-fashioned frock coat, the amplitude of inevitable blue tie—accurately reflected something of the quaintness of his mind and talk. If it were not for the peculiarly delicate hands and tapering fingers, denoting the artistic temperament, the Oxford professor might have been taken for an old-fashioned country gentleman.' In repose Ruskin's face had been furrowed into sadness; but the blue eyes, piercing from beneath thick, bushy eyebrows, 'never ceased to shine with the fire of genius; whilst the smile that was never long absent when he lectured, lit up his face with the radiance of a singularly gracious and gentle spirit.'

Ruskin himself had little faith in the efficacy of lectures. He knew that many of his hearers came merely to be amused or in the vain hope 'to get the knowledge it has cost a man half his life to gather, first sweetened up to make it palatable, and then kneaded into the smallest possible pills—and to swallow it homeopathically, and be wise.' But he was not content that they should be listeners only; they must be doers. He organized a school for drawing, and led the enthusiasts for social reform out to mend a neglected bit of road at Hinksey, two or three miles out of Oxford—the Hinksey diggings, as the scoffers called them. They exercised their muscles with the picks and spades Ruskin provided, and did some digging under the direction of Ruskin's gardener; but neither Ruskin nor the gardener knew anything about roadmaking; and the road was, in the end, rather worse than it had been before. The farmers whom it was intended to benefit sat on the fences and jeered.

Before his appointment to the professorship, Ruskin had inherited his father's fortune, amounting to about a million dollars, and during the years of his tenure succeeded in dissipating it in gifts to the university, endeavors to reclaim London slums, to keep the streets clean, to sell good tea at a fair price to the poor, to provide well-made books at a low figure, and to organize the Guild of St. George, 'to slay the dragon of Industrialism.' The Companions of the Order undertook to work with their hands and to use no steam power or machinery for purposes for which their own arms would serve; only three material things were essential— Pure Air, Earth, and Water; and three immaterial things, Aspiration, Hope, and Love. The plan was to buy land which could be cultivated by hand labor and employ 'a happy peasantry, with education, amusements, and art, suitable to their intelligence.' They were to be paid wages at fixed rates until they owned their own land. A Communist farm was actually started but did not last long; spinning and weaving industries by hand were established in the Isle of Man and Lake District—until Ruskin's brain gave way under the strain of anxiety and worry. The letters to workingmen he wrote at this time exhibit already marks not only of extravagance but of incoherence.

In 1871 Ruskin had bought the house called Brantwood standing in its own grounds on a secluded hill above Lake Coniston,— 'five acres of rock and moor and streamlet; and I think the finest view I know in Cumberland or Lancashire.' Here, after his mental collapse in 1884, his last years were spent in quiet. He gave himself up to writing the recollections of his early life, *Præterita*, 'things gone by,' and continued to write till he was over seventy. During the last ten years of the century he was sinking quietly to his end. On his eightieth birthday he received an address signed by the leading men in Great Britain, headed by the Prince of Wales, assuring him of their 'deepest respect, and sincerest affection.' He died just before his eighty-first birthday. A grave in Westminster Abbey was offered, but in accordance with his own request he was buried quietly in Coniston Churchyard.

CHAPTER IV

EARLY VICTORIAN NOVELISTS

CHARLES DICKENS

(1812–1870)

THE death of Jane Austen in 1817 marked the end of the eight-eenth century tradition in the novel, and the death of Scott in 1832 seemed also the end of the romantic novel, so that the writers of fiction left alive at the beginning of the Victorian Era bore names which are now unknown except to students of literary history. It was an open field for newcomers, and one may imagine the glad surprise with which the early works of Dickens were welcomed by an astonished and delighted public. Though Dickens had been in his childhood an ardent reader of *Roderick Random*, *Peregrine Pickle*, *Humphrey Clinker*, *Tom Jones*, *The Vicar of Wakefield*, *Don Quixote*, *Gil Blas*, and *Robinson Crusoe*—the list is his own—he was very little indebted to any of them, except per-haps the first three—all written by Smollett. He created his own manner and his own style; he accumulated his own material, not from books but from life. No great artist seems more independent of his predecessors, and if we wish to penetrate to the secret of his art, we shall learn most about it by listening to what he has to say about it himself. Fortunately, while he was still in his middle years he wrote an autobiographical sketch of his youthful experi-ences, much of which was almost immediately incorporated in *David Copperfield*; the sketch itself he afterwards placed in the hands of his friend, John Forster, for use in his biography. It is mainly from Dickens himself, as quoted by Forster, that the fol-lowing quotations are made.

Dickens's father was a clerk in the navy pay office at Ports-mouth Dockyard. When the novelist was four years old the family removed to Chatham. Not far away, between Rochester and Gravesend on the Canterbury Road, there was a fine large house called Gadshill Place, which the small boy very much admired; and his father said to him, 'If you were to be very persevering, and to work very hard, you might some day come to live in it.' Charles Dickens was very persevering, and worked uncommonly hard;

thirty-five years later he bought Gadshill Place, lived in it the last few years of his life, and died there. He put up an inscription: 'This house, Gadshill Place, stands on the summit of Shakespeare's Gadshill, ever memorable for its association with Sir John Falstaff.' Dickens spent on the house most of the money he made in his last American tour, and entertained there Longfellow, Professor Charles Eliot Norton of Harvard, and many other of his American friends. The best of his childish memories were associated with the neighborhood.

When he was nine, his father removed to London and took a mean house in the poorest part of a poor London suburb. The elder Dickens was already in difficulty with his creditors, and very shortly found himself in the debtors' prison at the Marshalsea. Dickens gave Forster the following account of his first visit:— 'My father was waiting for me in the lodge, and we went up to his room (on the top story but one), and cried very much. And he told me, I remember, to take warning by the Marshalsea, and to observe that if a man had twenty pounds a year, and spent nineteen pounds, nineteen shillings and sixpence, he would be happy; but that a shilling spent the other way would make him wretched. I see the fire we sat before now; with two bricks inside the rusty grate, one on each side, to prevent its burning too many coals. Some other debtor shared the room with him, who came in by and by; and as the dinner was a joint-stock repast, I was sent up to "Captain Porter" in the room overhead, with Mr. Dickens's compliments, and I was his son, and could he, Captain P., lend me a knife and fork? "Captain Porter" lent the knife and fork, with his compliments in return. There was a very dirty lady in his little room; and two wan girls, his daughters, with shock heads of hair. I thought I should not have liked to borrow Captain Porter's comb. The Captain himself was in the last extremity of shabbiness; and if I could draw at all, I would draw an accurate portrait of the old, old brown great-coat he wore, with no other coat below it. His whiskers were large. I saw his bed rolled up in a corner; and what plates and dishes and pots he had, on a shelf; and I knew (God knows how) that the two girls with the shock heads were Captain Porter's natural children, and that the dirty lady was not married to Captain P. My timid, wondering station on his threshold was not occupied more than a couple of minutes, I dare say; but I came down again to the room below with all this as surely in my knowledge as the knife and fork were in my hand.'

The novelist was at the time about ten years old, and the

accuracy of his observation at that age is as remarkable as his power of recollection in after-life. He was to make effective use of these circumstances—both humorous and pathetic—in his great novels, but at the time they were a bitter grief to him. He was a sensitive, precocious boy, deeply imbued with middle-class sentiment and with a strong sense of his own capacity and personal dignity. He felt keenly the humiliation of his father's failure to maintain the social status of the family and the necessity imposed upon his mother of keeping an 'establishment' for the education of young ladies in North Gower Street—which, moreover, never had any pupils. The family was indeed in dire straits, and there was no money to send Charles to school. A relative who had invested his capital in a blacking factory had the happy thought of putting the child of ten to work in it for six or seven shillings a week (equal to about twenty-five cents a day), to keep him out of mischief and eke out the family income. His parents willingly accepted the offer, and thus Charles Dickens began, at that early age, to earn his own living. Again we must quote his own account of it, later utilized, with some modifications, for the unhappy childish experiences of *David Copperfield:*—'It is wonderful to me that, even after my descent into the poor little drudge I had been since we came to London, no one had compassion enough on me— a child of singular abilities—quick, eager, delicate, and soon hurt, bodily or mentally—to suggest that something might have been spared, as certainly it might have been, to place me at any common school. Our friends, I take it, were tired out. No one made any sign. My father and mother were quite satisfied. They could hardly have been more so, if I had been twenty years of age, distinguished at a grammar school, and going to Cambridge.

'The blacking warehouse was the last house on the left-hand side of the way, at old Hungerford stairs. It was a crazy tumble-down old house, abutting of course on the river, and literally overrun with rats. Its wainscotted rooms and its rotten floors and staircase, and the old gray rats swarming down in the cellars, and the sound of their squeaking and scuffling coming up the stairs at all times, and the dirt and decay of the place, rise up visibly before me, as if I were there again. The counting-house was on the first floor, looking over the coal barges and the river. There was a recess in it, in which I was to sit and work. My work was to cover the pots of paste-blacking; first with a piece of oil-paper, and then with a piece of blue paper; to tie them round with a string; and then to clip the paper close and neat all round; until it looked as smart 'as a pot of ointment in an apothecary's shop. When a certain number of grosses of pots had attained this pitch of perfection, I was to paste on each a painted label; and then go on again with more pots. Two or three boys were kept at similar duties downstairs on similar wages. One of them came up, in a ragged apron and a paper cap on the first Monday morning, to show me the trick of using the string and tying the knot. His name was Bob Fagin; and I took the liberty of using his name, long afterwards, in *Oliver Twist*.

'Our relative had kindly arranged to teach me something in the dinner-hour; from twelve to one, I think it was, every day. But an arrangement so incompatible with counting-house business soon died away, from no fault of his or mine; and for the same reason, my small work-table, and my grosses of pots, my papers, string, scissors, paste-pot and labels, by little and little, vanished out of the recess in the counting-house, and kept company with the other small work-tables, grosses of pots, papers, string, scissors and paste-pots downstairs. It was not long before Bob Fagin and I and another boy whose name was Paul Green, but who was currently believed to have been christened Poll (a belief which I transferred, long afterwards, again, to Mr. Sweedlepipe, in *Martin Chuzzlewit*), worked generally side by side. Bob Fagin was an orphan, and lived with his brother-in-law, a waterman. Poll Green's father had the additional distinction of being a fireman, and was employed at Drury Lane theater; where another relation of Poll's, I think his little sister, did imps in the pantomimes.

'No words can express the secret agony of my soul as I sank into this companionship; compared these everyday associates with those of my happier childhood; and felt my early hopes of growing up to be a learned and distinguished man crushed in my breast. The deep remembrance of the sense I had of being utterly neglected and hopeless; of the shame I felt in my position; of the misery it was to my young heart to believe that, day by day, what I had learned, and thought, and delighted in, and raised my fancy and my emulation up by, was passing away from me, never to be brought back any more, cannot be written. My whole nature was so penetrated with the grief and humiliation of such considerations that even now, famous and caressed and happy, I often forget in my dreams that I have a dear wife and children, even that I am a man; and wander desolately back to that time of my life.

'My mother and my brothers and sisters (excepting Fanny in the Royal Academy of Music) were still encamped, with a young servant-girl from Chatham Workhouse, in the two parlors in the emptied house in Gower Street North. It was a long way to go and return within the dinner hour, and usually I either carried my dinner with me, or went and bought it at some neighboring shop. In the latter case, it was commonly a saveloy and a penny loaf; sometimes, a fourpenny plate of beef from a cook's shop; sometimes, a plate of bread and cheese and a glass of beer, from a miserable old public-house over the way; the Swan if I remember right, or the Swan and something else that I have forgotten. Once, I remember tucking my own bread (which I had brought from home in the morning) under my arm, wrapped up in a piece of paper like a book, and going into the best dining-room in Johnson's alamode beef-house in Clare Court, Drury Lane, and magnificently ordering a small plate of alamode to eat with it. What the waiter thought of such a strange apparition, coming in all alone, I don't know; but I can see him now, staring at me as I ate my dinner, and bringing up the other waiter to look. I gave him a halfpenny, and I wish, now, that he hadn't taken it.

'I was such a little fellow, with my poor white hat, little jacket, and corduroy trousers, that frequently, when I went into the bar of a strange public-house for a glass of ale or porter to wash down the saveloy and the loaf I had eaten in the street, they didn't like to give it to me. I remember, one evening, (I had been somewhere for my father, and was going back to the Borough over Westminster Bridge), that I went into a public-house in Parliament Street, which is still there though altered, at the corner of the short street leading into Cannon Row, and said to the landlord behind the bar, "What is your very best—the VERY *best*—ale, a glass!" For the occasion was a festive one, for some reason; I forget why. It may have been my birthday, or somebody else's. "Twopence," says he. "Then," says I, "just draw me a glass of that, if you please, with a good head to it." The landlord looked at me, in return, over the bar, from head to foot, with a strange smile on his face; and instead of drawing the beer, looked round the screen and said something to his wife, who came out from behind it, with her work in hand, and joined him in surveying me. Here we stand, all three, before me now, in my study in Devonshire Terrace. The landlord, in his shirtsleeves, leaning against the bar-window-frame; his wife, looking over the little half-door; and I, in some confusion, looking up at them from outside the partition. They asked me a good many questions, as to what my name was, how old I was, where I lived, how I was employed, etc. To all of which, that I might not commit anybody, I invented appropriate answers. They served me with the ale, though I suspect it was not the strongest on the premises; and the landlord's wife, opening the little half-door and bending down, gave me a kiss that was half-admiring and half-compassionate, but all womanly and good, I am sure.'

A timely legacy released John Dickens from the Marshalsea, and as, though shiftless, he was, according to his son's testimony, the kindest-hearted of men, he was not long in releasing his son from bondage, and sending him to school. But it was long years before the novelist could reconcile himself, even in his own heart, to the recollection of this period of personal degradation. He never spoke of it to anyone until he confided his bitterness of spirit to Forster: 'From that hour until this at which I write, no word of that part of my childhood which I have now gladly brought to a close, has passed my lips to any human being. I have no idea how long it lasted; whether for a year, or much more, or less. From that hour until this, my father and my mother have been stricken dumb upon it. I have never heard the least allusion to it, however far off and remote, from either of them. I have never, until I now impart it to this paper, in any burst of confidence with anyone, my own wife not excepted, raised the curtain I then dropped, thank God.

'Until old Hungerford Market was pulled down, until old Hungerford stairs were destroyed and the very nature of the ground changed, I never had the courage to go back to the place where my servitude began. I never saw it. I could not endure to go near it. For many years, when I came near to Robert Warrens' in the Strand, I crossed over to the opposite side of the way, to avoid a certain smell of the cement they put upon the blacking corks, which reminded me of what I was once. It was a very long time before I liked to go up Chandos Street. My old way home by the Borough made me cry, after my eldest child could speak.'

Better times came to the Dickens family, for the father obtained employment as parliamentary reporter for the Morning Herald, and Charles, now fifteen and employed as an office boy at about fifty cents a day, decided to follow his father's example. To do so he had to become a qualified stenographer, and he has told us, in David Copperfield, with what pains he acquired the art of shorthand according to the Gurney system then in vogue:—'The changes that were rung upon dots, which in such a position meant such a thing and in such another position something else entirely different; the wonderful vagaries that were played by circles; the unaccountable consequences that resulted from marks like flies' legs; the tremendous effects of a curve in a wrong place, not only troubled my waking hours, but reappeared before me in my sleep. When I had groped my way, blindly, through these difficulties, and had mastered the alphabet, there then appeared a procession of new horrors, called arbitrary characters; the most despotic characters I had ever known; who insisted, for instance, that a thing like the beginning of a cobweb meant "expectation," and that a pen-and-ink sky-rocket stood for "disadvantageous." When I had fixed these wretches in my mind, I found that they had driven everything else out of it; then beginning again, I forgot them; while I was picking them up, I dropped the other fragments of the system; in short, it was almost heart-breaking.'

For Dickens, as for David Copperfield, it would have been heart-breaking but for a youthful infatuation for 'Dora,' who, however, did not marry Charles Dickens, and did not die in her youth, but turned up again, fair, fat and forty-four, very much alive, and asked, to his great embarrassment, to be allowed to renew the acquaintance. He called on her with his wife, and they noted in the hall the stuffed effigy of her pet dog Jip.

Dickens was nineteen years old when, after two years' practice as a law court reporter at Doctors' Commons, he obtained permanent employment in the parliamentary gallery. He was still uncertain whether his real powers were as an actor or a writer, but early distinction as a journalist soon put the stage out of his head as a means of livelihood. Speaking to the New York editors during his last American visit, he ascribed his literary success 'to the wholesome training of severe newspaper work.' Presiding in 1865 at the London dinner of the Newspaper Press Fund, he gave an interesting account of his experiences as reporter for the Morning Chronicle and other metropolitan papers: 'I went into the gallery of the House of Commons as parliamentary reporter when I was a boy, and I left it—I can hardly believe the inexorable truth—nigh thirty years ago. I have pursued the calling of a reporter under circumstances of which many of my brethren here can form no adequate conception. I have transcribed for the printer, from my shorthand notes, important public speeches in which the strictest accuracy was required, and a mistake in which would have been to a young man severely compromising, writing on the palm of my hand, by the light of a dark-lantern, in a post-chaise and four, galloping through a wild country, and through the dead of night, at the then surprising rate of fifteen miles an hour. The very last

time I was at Exeter, I strolled into the castle-yard there to identify, for the amusement of a friend, the spot on which I once "took,"
as we used to call it, an election speech of Lord John Russell at
the Devon contest, in the midst of a lively fight maintained by all
the vagabonds in that division of the county, and under such a
pelting rain that I remember two good-natured colleagues, who
chanced to be at leisure, held a pocket-handkerchief over my notebook, after the manner of a state canopy in an ecclesiastical
procession. I have worn my knees by writing on them on the old
back-row of the old gallery of the old House of Commons; and in
the old House of Lords, where we used to be huddled together like
so many sheep—kept in waiting, say until the Woolsack might
want re-stuffing. Returning home from exciting political meetings
in the country to the waiting press in London, I do verily believe
I have been upset in almost every description of vehicle known
in this country. I have been, in my time, belated on miry by-
roads, towards the small hours, forty or fifty miles from London,
in a wheelless carriage, with exhausted horses and drunken post-
boys, and have got back in time for publication, to be received
with never-forgotten compliments by the late Mr. Black, coming
in the broadest of Scotch from the broadest of hearts I ever knew.
These trivial things I mention as an assurance to you that I have
never forgotten the fascination of that old pursuit. The pleasure
that I used to feel in the rapidity and dexterity of its exercise has
never faded out of my breast. Whatever little cunning of hand
or head I took to it or acquired in it, I have so retained that I fully
believe I could resume it tomorrow, very little the worse for long
disuse. To this present year of my life, when I sit in this hall, or
where not, hearing a dull speech (the phenomenon does occur), I
sometimes beguile the tedium of the moment by mentally following the speaker in the old, old way; and sometimes, if you can
believe me, I even find my hand going on the tablecloth, taking an
imaginary note of it all.'

It was in the December number (1833) of the Monthly Magazine
that Dickens saw his first original composition in print. Nine other
sketches appeared in the same magazine up to February, 1835,
and he had already adopted the signature of 'Boz' (the pet name
of his youngest brother), when he had the opportunity of transfer-
ring these contributions to the more lucrative medium of the
newly-founded Evening Chronicle, the monthly having paid
him nothing. This was arranged through George Hogarth, a
fellowworker on the Chronicle, whose daughter Dickens married

early in 1836. About the same time came the announcement of the publication in shilling numbers of the *Posthumous Papers of the Pickwick Club, edited by Boz*. The proposal to Dickens was thus described by him at a later date: 'The idea propounded to me was that the monthly something should be a vehicle for certain plates to be executed by Mr. Seymour; and there was a notion, either on the part of that admirable humorous artist, or of my visitor, that a NIMROD CLUB, the members of which were to go out shooting, fishing, and so forth, and getting themselves into difficulties through their want of dexterity, would be the best means of introducing these. I objected, on consideration, that although born and partly bred in the country, I was no great sportsman, except in regard to all kinds of locomotion; that the idea was not novel, and had already been much used; that it would be infinitely better for the plates to rise naturally out of the text; and that I would like to take my own way, with a freer range of English scenes and people, and was afraid I should ultimately do so in any case, whatever course I might prescribe to myself at starting. My views being deferred to, I thought of Mr. Pickwick, and wrote the first number; from the proof-sheets of which Mr. Seymour made his drawing of the Club and his happy portrait of its founder. I connected Mr. Pickwick with a club, because of the original suggestion; and I put in Mr. Winkle expressly for the use of Mr. Seymour.'

The *Sketches by Boz* in book form and the first numbers of *Pickwick* appeared almost together, and the former was, for a while, much more popular. It was not until the fifth number of *Pickwick*, in which Sam Weller appeared, that the series took the town by storm and people talked of nothing else; of the first number 400 copies were printed, of the fifteenth, 40,000. After the parliamentary session of 1836, the reporters' gallery saw Dickens no more; when *Pickwick* was finished in September, 1837, he had signed contracts for three more novels, and *Oliver Twist* had already begun to appear.

Forster draws a striking picture of Dickens as he first knew him in the early days of his success: 'The features were very good. He had a capital forehead, a firm nose with full wide nostrils, eyes wonderfully beaming with intellect and running over with humor and cheerfulness, and a rather prominent mouth strongly marked with sensibility. The head was altogether well-formed and symmetrical, and the air and carriage of it were extremely spirited. The hair so scant and grizzly in later days was then of a rich brown and most luxurious abundance, and the bearded face of his last two decades had hardly a vestige of hair or whisker; but there was that in the face, as I first recollect it, which no time could change, and which remained implanted on it unalterably to the last. This was the quickness, keenness, and practical power, the eager, restless, energetic outlook on each several feature, that seemed to tell so little of a student or writer of books, and so much of a man of action and business in the world. Light and motion flashed from every part of it.'

It was at this time that Dickens made the acquaintance of his great contemporary and rival, Thackeray. The death of Seymour after the first two numbers of *Pickwick* had been published created a vacancy for an illustrator (soon filled by the choice of Hablot Browne), and Thackeray was still uncertain whether his career was to be that of a painter or a writer. He related the incident himself long after at a Royal Academy dinner at which Dickens was present: 'I can remember, when Mr. Dickens was a very young man, and had commenced delighting the world with some charming humorous works in covers which were colored light green and came out once a month, that this young man wanted an artist to illustrate his writings; and I recollect walking up to his chambers in Furnival's Inn, with two or three drawings in my hand, which strange to say, he did not find suitable.'

Another incident which had a great effect upon Dickens also belongs to this period of his first success. He admired very much all three Hogarth daughters, the eldest of whom he had married; and he was especially devoted to the youngest, Mary, a girl of seventeen of unusual charm. Her sudden death threw him into an agony of grief which he could not control; he was unable to write, and the publication of the *Pickwick* numbers was suspended for two months. His life was permanently saddened by the blow: eleven years later, writing to Forster, he says: 'This day eleven years, poor dear Mary died.' Gradually her place in his affection was taken by her sister Georgina Hogarth, to whom in his will he left his private papers and 'my grateful blessing as the best and truest friend a man ever had.'

As before the completion of *Pickwick* the publication of *Oliver Twist* was begun, so before *Oliver Twist* was finished *The Life and Adventures of Nicholas Nickleby* was already appearing in monthly numbers. *Pickwick, Oliver Twist,* and *Nicholas Nickleby* were all done in the years 1836–39, month by month, with the author seldom more than a week in advance of the printer. Such was the abounding vitality of the young author—Dickens was still in his middle twenties—that none of these earlier works can be said to show any evidence of strain, though there are marks of haste in detail; the novelist's exuberant humor, invention, and creative power of character carry the reader with a rush over any small unevenness of construction.

But Dickens felt the strain himself; and he was also conscious that in the hasty publishing contracts he had made in the first flush of success, he had not done himself justice. Accordingly, he projected in the fall of 1839, a new plan, which would make less demand upon his creative powers and give him a fairer share of the profits which his labors produced. Thus originated the scheme of a weekly periodical which he himself set forth in the following terms: 'I should propose to start as the Spectator does, with some pleasant fiction relative to the origin of the publication; to illustrate a little club or knot of characters, and to carry their personal histories and proceedings through the work; to introduce fresh characters constantly; to reintroduce Mr. Pickwick and Sam Weller, the latter of whom might furnish an occasional communication with great effect; to write amusing essays on the various foibles of the day as they arise; to take advantage of all passing events; and to vary the form of the papers by throwing them into sketches, essays, tales, adventures, letters from imaginary correspondents, and so forth, so as to diversify the contents as much as possible.' The title chosen for the new venture was *Master Humphrey's Clock*, and it made a good start, the forty or fifty thousand circulation of the earlier novels rising to sixty and seventy thousand; but when the readers of the new weekly found that they were not to be entertained by any continuous story, the circulation fell off sharply and Dickens was driven to developing *The Old Curiosity Shop*, which he had begun as a short sketch, into a full-length novel, which, with astounding versatility, he kept going until the death of Little Nell (in spite of numerous requests for her survival) in the seventy-second chapter published early in 1841.

Barnaby Rudge, a historical novel of the eighteenth century, he had had long in mind and completed without difficulty in that year. But he began to feel the need for a long change and rest, and in connection with the project of *Master Humphrey's Clock* he had suggested a visit either to Ireland or to the United States, 'to write from thence a series of papers descriptive of the places and people I see, introducing local tales, traditions, and legends, something after the plan of Washington Irving's *Alhambra.*' This vague design took shape in the voyage to America, begun early in January, 1842. The first welcome to Dickens overwhelmed him with its generosity. He writes to Forster of a public dinner at Boston, a ball and dinner at New York, 'to which I have had an invitation with every known name in America appended to it. But what can I tell you about any of these things which will give you the slightest notion of the enthusiastic greeting they give me, or the cry that runs through the whole country! I have had deputations from the Far West, who have come from more than two thousand miles distance; from the lakes, the rivers, the backwoods, the log-houses, the cities, factories, villages, and towns. Authorities from nearly all the States have written to me. I have heard from the Universities, Congress, Senate, and bodies, public and private, of every sort and kind.'

The rift in the lute was revealed when Dickens in a speech at Boston said that the lack of international copyright was not only unjust to British authors but was, by unfair competition, preventing the development of native American literature. Some newspapers criticized the utterance severely as not merely a lack of tact and a breach of hospitality but a gratuitous interference with a question of domestic politics. Dickens held that he was within his rights, as he was of all men living the greatest loser by the piracy that prevailed. He made another speech on the subject at Hartford and there was a great outcry—as he put it, 'assertions that I was no gentleman but a mere mercenary scoundrel, coupled with the most monstrous misrepresentations relative to my design and purpose in visiting the United States, came pouring in upon me every day.' The New York Reception Committee besought him not to pursue the subject; he refused to listen to them and resented bitterly the attempt to restrict his freedom of speech. The disappointments and dissatisfactions that followed on both sides had their beginnings in the copyright differences, though the causes of them lay deeper. The satires in the early Dickens novels on British institutions led many of his American readers to expect from him a very favorable judgment of their own more democratic society; and when Dickens on his return to England, let loose not only his satiric humor but his righteous indignation on certain features of American life, as he saw it, in *American Notes* and *Martin Chuzzlewit*, the feeling produced in the United States was one of astonished injury. Years healed the breach, and Dickens on his next visit gave ample reparation for the distress he had caused; but for the time being there was a serious estrangement between him and the American public, though he retained the personal sympathy of many American friends.

The sale of *Martin Chuzzlewit* was disappointing, and was not altogether made up for by the enormous popularity of the *Christmas Carol* (1843). Distracted by financial anxieties and difficulties with his publishers, Dickens sought change and rest in a year on the Continent, during which he wrote *The Chimes*, like the *Christmas Carol*, an earnest plea for sympathy with the English poor, whose sufferings were at this time attracting a good deal of attention through the writings of Carlyle and others, though they had no more ardent and convinced spokesman than Dickens himself. It was in the period of distress that produced the repeal of the Corn Laws that Dickens, with the same end in view, wrote, in the spirit of Christian charity, the subsequent Christmas stories, *The Chimes* (1844) and *The Cricket on the Hearth* (1845). A plunge into journalism in 1846 as editor of the newly-founded liberal organ, the London Daily News, tired him out, and led to a second long sojourn on the Continent, where he began *Dombey and Son* (1846–48), still under the strain of shilling numbers, which necessitated his dashing over from Paris to London to supply two pages for an issue which he had underestimated in the writing to that extent—a slip unusual with him. It was as a relief from this pressure that the old idea of a weekly periodical recurred to him, and in 1850 he started Household Words. In the previous year he had begun the publication of what was to prove his life's masterpiece, *David Copperfield*, which was completed in October of 1850. *Bleak House* (1852–53) and *Hard Times* (1854) were less successful; the latter was the first novel he wrote for Household Words; the weekly instalments were easier for Dickens to keep up with, because they were shorter than monthly numbers, but the difficulty of getting sufficient interest into the small space, he acknowledged to Forster, 'was crushing.' He was also exhausting his physical resources in these years by taking an active part in amateur theatricals, for which he not only worked hard as actor and manager but wrote farcical sketches. Overwork resulted in another retirement to the Continent, where he mainly wrote *Little Dorrit* (1855–57). His restless energy was already flagging, and he found himself unable to 'grind sparks out of this dull blade.' He was also worried by domestic difficulties, which culminated in his separating from his wife, and setting up a separate establishment at Gadshill Place in 1858. His younger children and his sister-in-law, Georgina Hogarth, went with him;

the eldest son stayed with his mother. Beyond absolute incompatibility, there was no reason for the separation, and it was no business of anyone's except the few people immediately concerned; but Dickens unwisely published a statement in his own defense in Household Words, and a private letter written to justify himself found its way into the columns of a New York paper without his permission. So, in his excessive desire to avoid scandal, he provoked gossip.

The condition of the poor was the subject that above all others constantly occupied the mind of Dickens, and he was greatly interested in the London Child's Hospital, for which he gave a public reading of the *Christmas Carol* and raised a large amount of money. In 1858–59 he gave paid readings for twenty-four nights in London and made a provincial tour of over a hundred readings, including Ireland and Scotland as well as the principal English cities. In Liverpool he had an audience of over two thousand people, and at many places people were turned away from the doors; he cleared from three hundred to five hundred pounds a week.

Owing to legal difficulties as to the ownership of Household Words, it gave place in 1859 to another weekly, All the Year Round, of which Dickens had complete control and in which he published the best novels of his closing years—*A Tale of Two Cities* (1859) and *Great Expectations* (1860–61). Wilkie Collins contributed to the magazine *The Woman in White*, *No Name*, and *The Moonstone*; he collaborated with Dickens in his less serious work and became his close friend and constant companion; Collins's brother married the elder novelist's daughter. It was a curious feature of the association that the younger novelist influenced the elder more than the elder affected the younger. Not that Dickens gave up the features of his early work which constituted their power—humor and pathos, a lively realization of oddities of character and an intense vitality which gave the little world of each novel a life and movement of its own. But to these he added in his latest novels an element which was obviously due to the type of novel which Wilkie Collins made popular. Collins created or brought to perfection the modern mystery story, especially of crime and the detection of crime—he was the father of the detective novel. For this it was necessary to have a carefully constructed plot, such as we do not find in the early work or even the middle period of Dickens; in his latest work it is a characteristic element and highly elaborated. *Pickwick* has hardly enough plot to hold it together; even the characteristic work of Dickens in his prime, *David Copperfield*, depends for its interest on plot only to a small extent, and that little is not very well worked out. In *The Mystery of Edwin Drood*, which Dickens left unfinished at his death, the plot is so elaborate and was kept such a close secret by the author that it has been found impossible to bring the novel to a satisfactory conclusion, though the attempt has often been made.

Great Expectations presents in this respect a striking contrast with *David Copperfield*, with which it has much in common. Both are novels in the manner of autobiography, the hero telling his own story. *David Copperfield* is very largely the author's own story of the rise to fame and fortune by his own exertions of a gifted child fallen by accident into poverty and degradation, the evil influences of which he escapes by the innate purity and gentleness of his character; with infinite tact Dickens makes his hero tell the story of his success without alienating the sympathy of the reader, for he recounts David's youthful follies and mistakes as well as his achievements. *Great Expectations* offered a more subtle and far more difficult problem; its idea is a more original one, the story of a boy of no great ability but of an engaging simplicity and straightforwardness, who by a lucky accident is taken from the humble surroundings of his childhood to a higher social status, which makes his contacts with the lowly friends of his childhood embarrassing. He is mortified and humiliated to find that his release from poverty is due to the help he has unconsciously given to a convict to escape from the hulks, and though he remains faithful to his strange benefactor after the latter has revealed himself he does so with a constant sense of shame and loss of personal dignity. The element of mystery as to the source of Pip's good fortune is carefully preserved till the story is nearing its end, and *Great Expectations* is by far the best of the later novels, but for human interest and charm it is not equal to the simple tale of the author's childish misfortunes and mature success.

The last years of Dickens had an almost tragic aspect. The straightened circumstances of his youth had not produced in him any inclination towards penuriousness or even carefulness; he was generous and open-handed, and he liked to spend money not only freely but lavishly. His lack of educational and social opportunity as a boy made him anxious to do his very best for his children. Thus, although he earned large sums, he never seemed to have enough. In spite of serious symptoms of failing health, he was induced to undertake more readings year by year from 1861 to

1867, and, when the Civil War was over, to re-visit the United States. It was an even greater success than his first visit. In New York City he read to 40,000 people, and became as well known in its streets as he was in London. On both sides old grievances were entirely forgotten. At a farewell dinner he assured his New York admirers that no future edition of *American Notes* or *Martin Chuzzlewit* should appear without acknowledgment of the politeness, delicacy, sweet temper, hospitality, and consideration for which he had to thank them, and of his gratitude for the respect shown, during all his visit, to the privacy enforced upon him by the nature of his work and the condition of his health.

His physical condition was already serious. Often he had to lie down after a recital, extremely faint, and only stimulants before and during the recitals kept him going. But he cleared twenty thousand pounds from the trip, and on his return to England in May, 1868, he could not resist an offer of eight thousand pounds for a tour in England. He had cut down *David Copperfield* so as to make a continuous narrative and had made of the murder scene in *Oliver Twist* a miniature melodrama; the latter was especially trying to him, and on his arrival at Preston in Lancashire in April, 1869, his physician forbade him to appear and sent him back to London. But after a rest of some months had restored his health to some extent, he was again on the platform, reciting the *Christmas Carol*, followed by the *Pickwick* trial; and his hearers thought he had never read so well. As he closed the volume of *Pickwick*, he thanked the public for their sympathetic attention and announced his retirement. 'In but two short weeks from this time I hope you may enter, in your own homes, on a new series of readings at which my assistance will be indispensable; but from these garish lights I vanish now for evermore, with a heartfelt, grateful, respectful, affectionate farewell.'

The last words refer to *The Mystery of Edwin Drood*, on which he had for some time been at work, and he was still at work on it two months later when he was stricken with an effusion of blood on the brain. Twenty-four hours after, he was dead.

It is not too much to say that his death plunged the whole world into sorrow. The Queen telegraphed 'her deepest regret at the sad news,' and a grave was offered in Westminster Abbey, by the side of the greatest masters of imaginative literature in English; no other monument bore, for so many years, the simple flowers from simple people who loved and admired Dickens. Even that cynical observer of men and things, Thomas Carlyle, now in the most crabbed years of his old age, laid aside for once his habit-ual acerbity and said: 'It is an event world-wide; a *unique* of talents suddenly extinct; and has "eclipsed," we too may say, "the harm-less gaiety of nations." No death since 1866 has fallen on me with such a stroke. No literary man's hitherto ever did. The good, the gentle, high-gifted, ever-friendly, noble Dickens—every inch of him an Honest Man.'

The literary reputation of Dickens, unlike that of most writers extremely popular in their own lifetime, has increased rather than diminished with the lapse of time. Intelligent contemporaneous critics were inclined to depreciate Dickens as a popular favorite and express a preference for Thackeray—a verdict which has been entirely reversed by modern critical opinion. The faults stressed at the time—extreme sentimentalism, exaggerated grotesque humor, conventional morality—are now freely acknowledged, but anyone who because of these drawbacks cannot read Dickens, is now held lacking in artistic sensibility. His place is in the foremost rank of creative artists in English literature, and he seems very likely to keep it. His genuine sympathy with the poor and op-pressed, his insistence on the virtues of common humanity—the kindliness and mutual understanding which now seem more needed than at any previous period of the world's history—his appreciation of the everyday joys of simple life, and his feeling for our most familiar and inevitable sorrows—all this still endears him to the great mass of readers, while the highest intelligences still stand amazed at the intense vitality and energy with which he inspires the numerous and varied creatures of his imagination.

WILLIAM MAKEPEACE THACKERAY
(*1811–1863*)

Thackeray enjoyed all the social and educational advantages of birth and breeding which Dickens lacked and so much regretted. His father and grandfather were in the Indian Civil Service, and having been born at Calcutta he was sent to England as a child to be educated. At Charterhouse, one of the oldest and most famous of English schools, he was remembered as 'a pretty, gentle, and rather timid boy,' who was no good at games and not much better at his studies. He distinguished himself, however, by mak-ing verses, chiefly parodies of the sentimental poems then in vogue; L.E.L.'s touching lyric 'Violets, dark blue violets' turned in young Thackeray's hands into 'Cabbages, bright green cabbages,' and was thought by his schoolfellows to be very clever and original.

At seventeen he was sent to Trinity College, Cambridge, and at eighteen he was taken away again, so that he was evidently no more studious there than he was in London; but he idealized both school and college later, especially Charterhouse, which appears in *The Newcomes* as Grey Friars in allusion to its origin from a monastic foundation. From Cambridge he went to Weimar, and from Weimar to Paris, professing to study art but not doing much beyond amusing and enjoying himself. According to Anthony Trollope, his first biographer, Thackeray never learnt to draw, but was clever as a caricaturist and illustrator. In this capacity he made an unsuccessful application to Dickens to be allowed to illustrate *Pickwick*, as already narrated above; this was in 1836, when both men were in their twenty-fifth year; but Dickens had already his foot on the first rung of the ladder of fame, while Thackeray, though the elder by a few months, was still uncertain which way to take. He felt and expressed a generous admiration for his younger and more precocious rival, and Dickens was quick to respond; when Thackeray went on his American lecture tour of 1855, it was Dickens who presided at the 'send-off' dinner in London, and when Thackeray died, one of the promptest and most sympathetic tributes to his memory came from the pen of Dickens.

The two men differed profoundly, not only in birth and education, but in natural disposition and view of life. Dickens with his exuberant energy and natural self-confidence, early conscious of the power within him and eager for contacts with (and conquests over) his fellows, taking joy in his work and treating his characters as real people with whom he wept in their sorrows and laughed at the drolleries he himself created, was a complete contrast to Thackeray, who was early convinced that all the world was vanity and that all mankind (including himself) suffered from snobbery and other meannesses. He was constitutionally shy and reserved, and showed none of the pleasure Dickens took in the applause and appreciation of others. When Anthony Trollope, to whom, as to Dickens, life seemed a much simpler and more straightforward affair than it did to Thackeray, congratulated him on *Esmond* as his best work, Thackeray replied: 'That is what I intended, but I have failed. Nobody reads it. After all, what does it matter?' When Trollope insisted on the general appreciation of *Esmond*'s character, Thackeray rejoined: 'If they like anything, one ought to be satisfied. After all, Esmond was a prig.' This mood of self-distrust and self-depreciation was habitual with Thackeray, who regarded his characters as mere puppets and himself as a mere showman, who should be content if he contrived to pull the strings successfully and gratify the public.

His personal history was in part accountable for this depressed and sceptical view of life. The easy circumstances of his youth, which Dickens would have regarded as most enviable, were almost his ruin. Inheriting, when he came of age, a fortune which brought in an income of five hundred pounds a year, he dissipated it in foolish extravagances and equally foolish speculations, so that a year or two later he found himself penniless. Grim necessity drove him to journalism, and he became a regular contributor to Fraser's Magazine, to the New Monthly Magazine, and to Punch after its foundation in 1840. He had already developed, at school and college, a gift for satire, and his favorite theme was the snobbery of his fellowcreatures. This was the constant subject of his earlier work: the *Yellowplush Papers*—life seen from the footman's point of view, which is copied from that of his masters; his various 'Sketch Books,' illustrating and ridiculing the weaknesses of his neighbors across the Channel and the Irish Sea; *The History of Samuel Titmarsh and the Great Haggarty Diamond*, a satire of city life; burlesques of various popular authors, parodying their peculiarities of style and manner. The work of this period which seems most deserving of permanent regard is a picaresque romance in autobiographical form entitled *The Memoirs of Barry Lyndon* (1844). The hero tells his own adventures, as a card-sharper, bully, and liar; as a heartless wretch, who had neither love nor gratitude in his composition, who had no sense even of loyalty; who regarded gambling as the highest occupation to which a man could devote himself, and fraud as always justified by success; a man possessed by all meannesses except cowardice. And the reader is so carried away by his frankness and energy as almost to rejoice when he succeeds, and to grieve with him when he is brought to the ground. So says Trollope, and he is a competent judge of his own craft. Thackeray gives his hero the solitary virtue of courage, and he uses him as an example of the fact that even the meanest of God's creatures has his own form of self-esteem. He uses him also as a kind of devil's advocate who attempts to justify himself by claiming that he is really just as good as anyone else. 'They cry fie now upon men engaged in play; but I should like to know how much more honorable *their* modes of livelihood are than ours. The broker of the Exchange who bulls and bears, and buys and sells, and dabbles with lying loans, and trades upon state secrets,—what is he but a gamester? The merchant who deals in teas and tallow, is he any better? His bales of dirty indigo are his dice, his cards come up every year instead of every ten minutes, and the sea is his green-table. You call the profession of the law an honest one, where a man will lie for any bidder;—lie down poverty for the sake of a fee from wealth; lie down right because wrong is in his brief. You call a doctor an honorable man,—a swindling quack who does not believe in the nostrums which he prescribes, and takes your guinea for whispering in your ear that it is a fine morning. And yet, forsooth, a gallant man, who sits him down before the baize and challenges all comers, his money against theirs, his fortune against theirs, is proscribed by your modern moral world! It is a conspiracy of the middle-class against gentlemen.' But, even if *Barry Lyndon* is an exceedingly clever *tour de force* as a picture of a great scoundrel, it is mainly of interest as a preliminary study for the portraits of the more human figures of Mr. and Mrs. Rawdon Crawley in *Vanity Fair*.

Thackeray had just begun his journalistic career in 1837 when he married. His wife had three daughters and then fell ill of a nervous disease which developed into mental derangement. Fortunately the two daughters who survived grew up into unusually bright, intelligent girls, and he found consolation in their society. One became well known as a writer under the name of Mrs. Richmond Ritchie; the younger married Leslie Stephen, editor of the Dictionary of National Biography and a leading man of letters. As little girls they were Thackeray's constant care. He writes in one of his ballads:—

> I thought as day was breaking,
> My little girls were waking,
> And smiling, and making
> A prayer at home for me.

It was for their sake that when he felt his financial position still insecure, even after the success of *Vanity Fair*, he applied (unsuccessfully) for a permanent position in the Civil Service, and later—with the same result—for the secretaryship of the British Legation at Washington. It was for their sake that he undertook the distasteful task of preparing and delivering in London courses of lectures which were afterwards repeated in the United States. The first course was *The English Humourists of the Eighteenth*

Century, and as published in book form offered a substantial contribution to literary criticism, for which he was well qualified by
his studies for *Esmond*, published in 1852. His second course of
lectures, *The Four Georges*, was of a more popular character and
dealt in a freely satirical and anecdotal fashion with British
sovereigns who were, in some people's opinion, too recent in date
for him to take such liberties with them. As a lecturer Thackeray
won esteem by the clearness of his utterance and the excellence of
his matter, which he read from a manuscript; but he took no such
delight in these public appearances as did Dickens, who prepared
for a lecture as if it were a dramatic performance and recited it
from memory with the same energy and skill in presentation as
if he had been actually on the stage. The public readings of the
later life of Dickens were dramatic performances, of which Thackeray would have been quite incapable.

Thackeray was obliged to 'pen many a line for bread' before he
established his reputation in the world of letters by the publication
of *Vanity Fair*. This great novel appeared in 1847-48 in twenty-
four monthly numbers (instead of the twenty affected by Dickens)
and was issued by Bradbury and Evans whom a year or two before
Dickens had made his publishers instead of Chapman and Hall.
Hereafter Thackeray was a prominent figure in the London clubs
and the literary world. 'His face and figure, his six feet four in
height, with his flowing hair, already nearly gray, and his broken
nose, his broad forehead and ample chest, encountered everywhere either love or respect.' Thackeray, in spite of his shyness,
was a sociable person and full of fun and jollity in superficial contacts, but in the depths of his nature he was saddened by his wife's
illness and his own indifferent health. A severe illness interrupted
the writing of *Pendennis*, which appeared in numbers in 1848-50;
Esmond, which came next, was published in book form in 1852;
but he reverted to the plan of monthly numbers for *The Newcomes* (1854-55).

In 1857 Thackeray contested the parliamentary seat of Oxford
in the Liberal interest, and polled 1,017 votes against 1,070 for his
successful opponent. In the same year appeared the first number
of *The Virginians*, the twenty-fourth in 1859. In the latter year
he undertook the editorship of Cornhill, one of the first of the
shilling magazines; it sprang at once into a circulation of a hundred
thousand, at that time an unprecedented figure. Thackeray was
not a good editor; he was neither methodical, nor industrious, nor
able to hurt people's feelings; and after two years he was glad to

hand over to his successor a large number of unpublished manuscripts which he had been unwilling to refuse because the contributors needed the money. He continued, however, to write for
the magazine, and after completing in its columns the *Adventures
of Philip* he began for it a new novel, *Denis Duval*, of which three
numbers were published after his death. He still had the future
of his children in mind and it was for their sakes that he built in
1862 a new house, into which he moved, only to die in it on Christmas Eve, 1863. The house sold for £2,000 more than what it had
cost, and Thackeray was able to leave for his children a provision
of half as much again as the fortune he had squandered in his youth.

Thackeray's satirical genius was much more hampered than that
of Dickens by the conventions of the Victorian Era. Dickens
adapted himself to the limitations set on the discussion of sex
with astonishing ease; the seduction of Little Emily by Steerforth
in *David Copperfield* is narrated with a conventional propriety
which could give no offense. Thackeray's more critical spirit felt
itself cramped in telling the truth as he saw it. In the Preface to
Pendennis he complains that 'since the author of *Tom Jones* was
buried, no writer of fiction among us has been permitted to depict
to his utmost power a MAN. We must shape him, and give him a
conventional simper. Society will not tolerate the Natural in our
Art. . . . Even the gentlemen of our age we cannot show as they
are, with the notorious foibles and selfishness of their lives and
their education. You will not hear—it is best to know it—what
moves in the real world, what passes in society, in the clubs,
colleges, mess-rooms,—what is the life and talk of your sons.' So
the amours of the young Pendennis had to be draped and sentimentalized, represented not as they actually would have been but
as the Victorian parent liked to suppose that they were. Even so,
the author complained that many ladies remonstrated and subscribers left him because of his realistic tendencies. It is Thackeray's misfortune that his yieldings to the sentimental objections
of lady subscribers have made his picture of life in *Pendennis* and
The Newcomes so untrue that the modern reader finds it insipid.
In *Vanity Fair* he recounted the escapades of Becky Sharp with
skilful reticence, but left the reader to form his own conclusions as
to what really happened. He says, after the great scene in which
her husband returns home unexpectedly and finds her alone with
the amorous Lord Steyne, 'Was she guilty or not? She said not;
but who could tell what was truth which came from those lips; or
if that corrupt heart was in this case pure.' Similarly, when Becky

is banished from polite society and re-appears in a very different world at the end of the book, the author takes the discerning reader into his confidence: 'We must pass over a part of Mrs. Rebecca Crawley's biography with that lightness and delicacy which the world demands—the moral world, that has perhaps no particular objection to vice, but an insuperable repugnance to hearing vice called by its proper name. There are things we do and know perfectly well in Vanity Fair, though we never speak of them: as the Ahrimanians worship the devil, but don't mention him: and a polite public will no more bear to read an authentic description of vice than a truly-refined English or American female will permit the word breeches to be pronounced in her chaste hearing. And yet, Madame, both are walking the world before our faces every day, without much shocking us. If you were to blush every time they went by, what complexions you would have! It is only when their naughty names are called out that your modesty has any occasion to show alarm or sense of outrage, and it has been the wish of the present writer, all through this story, deferentially to submit to the fashion at present prevailing, and only to hint at the existence of wickedness in a light, easy, and agreeable manner, so that nobody's fine feelings may be offended. I defy anyone to say that our Becky, who has certainly some vices, has not been presented to the public in a perfectly genteel and inoffensive manner. In describing this siren, singing and smiling, coaxing and cajoling, the author, with modest pride, asks his readers all round, has he once forgotten the laws of politeness, and showed the monster's hideous tail above water? No! Those who like may peep down under waves that are pretty transparent, and see it writhing and twirling, diabolically hideous and slimy, flapping against bones, or curling round corpses; but above the water-line, I ask, has not everything been proper, agreeable, and decorous, and has any the most squeamish immoralist in Vanity Fair a right to cry fie? When, however, the siren disappears and dives below, down among the dead men, the water of course grows turbid over her, and it is labor lost to look into it ever so curiously. They look pretty enough when they sit upon a rock, twanging their harps and combing their hair, and sing, and beckon to you to come and hold the looking-glass; but when they sink into their native element depend upon it those mermaids are about no good, and we had best not examine the fiendish marine cannibals, reveling and feasting on their wretched pickled victims. And so, when Becky is out of the way, be sure that she is not particularly well employed, and that the less that is said about her doings is, in fact, the better.'

It is upon the creation of the character of Becky Sharp and her various contacts with the world of fashion that Thackeray's permanent reputation rests. It was a world which he had known intimately but which in his heart he more than half despised. Though he has not a little liking for the entertainment provided in Vanity Fair, the general impression he receives from it and conveys to the reader is more melancholy than mirthful; he is not really taken in either by his own or other people's hilarity. Even his own characters give him no joy of creation; he introduces them to the reader in the preface as Puppets—skilfully managed and successfully displayed—but still Puppets, which at the end of the story are hustled back into the box by the showman, 'for our play is played out.' It is curious that Dickens, the professed moralist, was essentially a public entertainer, most anxious to please his readers; while Thackeray, the professed entertainer of the public, was at heart a moralist who could not help coming forward to preach a sermon in his own person from time to time. When he can let his characters play their own parts, tell their own story, and convey indirectly the moral lesson involved in their experience of life, Thackeray is magnificent, but when he pushes himself forward as the author-moralist, most modern readers find him tiresome.

It is probably for this reason that modern critics have chosen *Esmond* as his most perfect work. The full title is *The History of Henry Esmond Esq., a Colonel in the Service of Her Majesty Queen Anne, written by Himself.* The device of autobiographical authorship is admirably maintained, not only in the style but in Esmond's attitude towards the persons and the events which he is supposed to relate. Thackeray said Esmond was a prig, and his hero certainly took as serious and depressed a view of life as Thackeray himself. But he is, like his creator, a thorough gentleman, for all his preaching, and this is the reason why the portrait commands the sympathies of the reader. It is also the reason why Thackeray's personality, which comes so vividly and directly through all his work, wins the admiration of the discerning public. Professor George Saintsbury says in his *Consideration of Thackeray:* 'I remember having, some thirty years ago, delight of battle for at least an hour by, and not far from, Kensington clock, on the subject of Thackeray, with the late Mr. Henley. At last, apropos of exactly what I have forgotten, I happened to say, "And this, you see, is because he was such a gentleman." "No," said Henley, "it is because he was such a genius." "Well," I said, "my dear Henley, suppose we put it, that it is because he was such a genius who was also a gentleman." So we laughed and shook hands and parted. And really I am inclined to think that these words were, and are, "the conclusion of the whole matter" about Thackeray.'

ANTHONY TROLLOPE
(*1815–1882*)

Dickens and Thackeray together created the vogue of the Victorian novel and their supremacy in that important field of popular literature was clearly and fully recognized by their contemporaries; but it was not undisputed. The various activity of Edward G. E. L. Bulwer (1803–73), who became Lord Lytton in 1866, won for him a vast popularity but no permanent reputation; the tawdry melodrama of *The Last Days of Pompeii* (1834) cannot be regarded as a serious contribution to historical fiction, any more than Disraeli's early stories can be said to have given any significance to that dubious product, the political novel; this early Victorian fiction gives the modern reader, as Hugh Walpole puts it, 'the shudder of electric light upon plush.' Charles Kingsley's historical novels *Hypatia* (1851) and *Westward Ho!* (1855) have stood the test of time better than his political novels *Yeast* and *Alton Locke*, already referred to above as documents of the Christian Socialism movement of the mid-nineteenth century. Thomas Hughes, another leader of that movement, is still remembered as the author of *Tom Brown's School Days* (1857). A third university don, Charles Reade, holds a place in our memory as the author of *The Cloister and the Hearth* (1861), an admirable historical novel of the period preceding the Renaissance. Wilkie Collins (1824–89), the friend and collaborator of Dickens, was, as Professor Elton puts it, 'master of the regular gambit of the detective story; first the "exposition," then the crime, then a succession of traps into which the reader falls. One false plausible clue no sooner leads him to grief than he is up again snatching at another; till at last the true one is put into his hand. It has been hidden all along in a host of small conditions and incidents. A better eye than our own, or than any of the characters possessed would have seized it. . . . Collins is so consistent and clever that he gives a kind of pleasurable false satisfaction to the reasoning faculty.' But this kind of fictional invention is of its nature short-lived and gives place to later contrivances with the promise of novelty.

The work of Anthony Trollope has a more enduring fame, and as a personality his vigorous and imposing figure commands our interest. He disliked the 'over-emphasis' of Dickens, and was a devoted friend and admirer of Thackeray, whose life he wrote (not very successfully) for the English Men of Letters Series. In his youth he combined the educational opportunities of Thackeray with the miseries of the childhood of Dickens. His Micawber-like father had a sufficient social position to send him to first-rate schools but not enough money to keep him there in comfort or even to pay his fees regularly. When he was still a small boy at Harrow, the headmaster stopped him in the street and asked him 'with all the clouds of Jove upon his brow and all the thunder in his voice, whether it was possible that Harrow School was disgraced by so disreputably dirty a little boy as I.' When he was in his teens, it seemed to him that all hands were against him, masters as well as boys; he felt convinced in his own mind, that he had been flogged 'oftener than any human being alive.' He went to Harrow at seven and left it at nearly nineteen. 'During the whole of those twelve years no attempt had been made to teach me anything but Latin and Greek, and very little attempt to teach me those languages. I do not remember any lessons either in writing or arithmetic. French and German I certainly was not taught.' He obtained, not through any deserts or abilities, but by personal influence, a small post in the Civil Service, a postal clerkship which after seven years' drudgery brought him a yearly income of less than seven hundred dollars; during all that time he was hopelessly in debt.

The circumstances of Trollope's youth must be realized if we are to understand the point of view with which he faced life. As he trudged through the muddy lanes which led from the dilapidated farmhouse where his father lived to Harrow School, he records in his *Autobiography*, 'I was always telling myself that the misery of the hour was not the worst of it, but that the mud and solitude and poverty of the time would insure me mud and poverty and solitude through my life. Those lads about me would go into Parliament, or become rectors and deans, or squires of parishes, or advocates thundering at the Bar. They would not live with me now—but neither should I be able to live with them in after-life.' Trollope was born into the English upper middle class, and, like Dickens, he was acutely sensitive of the peril of losing his social position and the opportunities of social contact which a secure position implied. His humble position in the Postal Service gave him a bare living—hardly that; it gave him no chance of the social and intellectual pleasures afforded by a recognized status in the upper middle class. The way he saw to make sure of that status and of the opportunities it ensured was through literature.

Trollope belonged to a literary household. His father had ruined the financial prospects of the family by excessive interest in an ecclesiastical encyclopedia; his mother had to some extent revived the family fortunes, after a vain attempt to sell fancy goods in Cincinnati, Ohio, by an amusing satire on the *Domestic Manners of the Americans*. His brother and his sister had each written novels; literary ambition was regarded in the family as almost a disease, and when he announced that he also was embarking on a literary career, the news was received with consternation. His mother, however, was sympathetic and secured him a publisher who promised half profits. There were no profits, so that young Trollope got nothing beyond the satisfaction of seeing his first novel in print.

The Macdermots of Ballycloran (1847) was a story of Irish life, but not after the manner of the Irish novel which Charles Lever and Samuel Lover had already popularized in *Harry Lorrequer* (1839) and *Handy Andy* (1842); in these the shiftless poverty of the Irish peasant and the shiftless extravagance of the Irish landlord had been made the subject for drollery. The line taken by Trollope was not the humorous grotesque, but the conscientious realism he was afterwards to apply to the English scene, or the Australian, or wherever his steps happened to turn. The heroine of his first novel is introduced with her hair in papers—'and the very papers themselves looked soiled and often used. Her black hair had been hastily fastened up with a bit of old black ribbon and a comb boasting only two teeth, and the short hairs round the bottom of her well-turned head were jagged and uneven, as though bristling with anger at the want of that attention which they required. She had no collar on, but a tippet of different material and color from her frock was thrown over her shoulders. Her dress itself was the very picture of untidiness; it looked as though it had never seen a mangle; her sleeves drooped down, hanging despondently below her elbows; and the tuck of her frock was all ripped and torn.'

Trollope had gone to Ireland in the postal service in 1841, when he was twenty-six. The salary was only a hundred pounds a year, but he had a generous traveling allowance, and his real income was four times that amount. Living in Ireland was cheap so that he was able to marry, to keep within his means, and to get his first novel published. Another Irish novel followed, *The Kellys and the O'Kellys* (1848); it had no better success than the first—the publisher lost money by it and the author received nothing—but Trollope was not easily discouraged. He cherished the saying of an old family servant, 'It's dogged that does it.'

His opportunity came after ten years of persistent literary labor, his promotion in the postal service, and his return to England, where he rode about the country inspecting rural postal delivery districts and making himself thoroughly acquainted with the English countryside and the county families, whom he met also on the hunting field. He writes in his *Autobiography:*—'In the course of my Post Office job I visited Salisbury, and while wandering there one midsummer evening round the purlieus of the cathedral I conceived the story of *The Warden*—from whence came that series of novels of which Barchester, with its bishops, deans and archdeacons, was the central site.' It was his pride that he added a new county to the English Shires, that of Barsetshire, which is the scene of half a dozen of his best novels:—*The Warden* (1855), *Barchester Towers* (1857), *Doctor Thorne* (1858), *Framley Parsonage* (1861), *The Small House at Allington* (1864), and *The Last Chronicle of Barset* (1867). *The Warden* was the first of Trollope's novels to bring in any financial return, and he always regarded the book with affection, 'as I made £9.2.6 by the first year's sale'—rather less than fifty dollars. His first real success was *Barchester Towers; Framley Parsonage* made its appearance at the beginning of 1860 in the opening issues of the new Cornhill Magazine, edited by Thackeray. On October 23, 1859, Trollope wrote to Thackeray offering his services; Thackeray's reply was to ask for a three volume novel to be published serially, beginning in January. This left an interval of six weeks after arrangements were made. Trollope had nothing on hand, but he was not going to let such an opportunity slip; he accepted the commission, had the instalments ready as planned, and the story was one of his best. His own summary of it might be taken as a prescription for a Trollope novel:—a little fox-hunting and a little tuft-hunting, some Christian virtue and some Christian cant, no heroism and no villainy, much church but more love-making.

A source of great satisfaction to Trollope a little later was his election to the Garrick Club early in 1861. There he met the celebrities of the literary and dramatic world, played whist nearly every afternoon between tea and dinner, and said to himself that he had satisfied his heart's desire:—'I now felt that I had gained my object. In 1862 I had achieved that which I contemplated when I went to London in 1834, and towards which I made my first attempt when I began the *Macdermots* in 1843. I had created for myself a position among literary men, and had secured to myself an income on which I might live in ease and comfort—which ease and comfort have been made to include many luxuries. From this time for a period of twelve years my income averaged £4,500 a year.'

Serial publication proved in fact an excellent thing for Trollope's pocket, but a bad thing for the quality of his work and his permanent reputation. He wrote too much: it was his boast at the end of his life that he had produced more than Voltaire and 'more than twice as much as Carlyle.' In 1868 his fee for a novel was a little over fifteen thousand dollars—a large sum at that date. But in 1870 there began the first stage of a decline, clearly traced by Michael Sadleir in *Trollope, A Commentary*. 'The second stage began in 1876, after which date the market sagged dangerously. From then to the end of his life there was rapid decadence.'

The final blow to Trollope's reputation was struck by himself in his *Autobiography*, published after his death. There he told how regularly and even mechanically his work as a writer had been done. Rising at five o'clock, he exacted from himself a minimum of 2,500 words before breakfast; then he went off to the drudgery of the Post Office, which he never allowed himself to neglect; twice or thrice a week he went hunting, during the season; he was full of social engagements and a constant presence at his club in the afternoon. But he never omitted his daily toll of composition; he wrote in railway trains, on shipboard when sea-sick during a gale, when visiting friends or abroad on official business. Beside some fifty novels he wrote 'political articles, critical, social, and sporting articles for periodicals without number.' Most of his miscellaneous volumes of travel, biography, and commentary are 'now quite dead and no resurrection for them is to be expected.' So says his most recent biographer, Hugh Walpole, who is certainly not lacking in appreciation for his subject. Of the novels, too, the greater number are dead beyond recall.

Trollope contended that just as he never allowed his literary work to interfere with his official duties at the Post Office, so he never wrote at a speed that prevented him from doing his best.

But his biographers have disallowed the claim. Hugh Walpole is clear on this point: 'It is not possible for us to be shocked as his contemporaries were by the assertion that authors write for money, but it is at the same time a quite legitimate inquiry whether, in any individual artist's case, writing for money has damaged the art. In Trollope's case it quite certainly has done so. To write by the clock is not at all inartistic unless the clock becomes of more importance than the art, as unquestionably in Trollope's case it did at times become—as for instance when we hear of him finishing a novel ten minutes before the allotted hour and beginning at once another in order that the time should be properly filled.'

But when all necessary deductions are made on account of Trollope's mercenary motives and mechanical methods, he remains a conscientious and competent craftsman, whose best work has stood the test of time and in recent years has come back into favor with the critics and with the public. Hawthorne long ago praised it as essentially English—'solid, substantial, written in the strength of beef and through the inspiration of ale.' Hugh Walpole praises Barsetshire as a place of escape from the restlessness of modern life: 'An English sun shines down upon it, English hedges bound it in, the little streets of little English towns have their place in it. It is a country where it is always afternoon; the sturdiness and courage of his own honest spirit pervade its atmosphere.' To Trollope's contemporaries the Barsetshire world appeared a true and lifelike picture of a society they knew and loved. Frederick Harrison testifies to Trollope's 'inimitable truthfulness and curious delicacy of observation. The dignitaries of the cathedral close, the sporting squires, the county magnates, the country doctors, and the rectory home, are drawn with a precision, a refinement, an absolute fidelity that only Jane Austen could surpass. There is no caricature, no burlesque, nothing improbable or overwrought. The bishop, the dean, the warden, the curate, the apothecary, the duke, the master of foxhounds, the bishop's wife, the archdeacon's lady, the vicar's daughter, the governess, the undergraduate,—all are perfectly true to nature. So, too, are the men in the clubs in London, the chiefs, subordinates, and clerks in the public offices, the ministers and members of Parliament, the leaders, and rank and file of London "society." They never utter a sentence which is not exactly what such men and women do utter; they do and they think nothing but what such men and women think and do in real life. Their habits, conversation, dress, and interests are photographically accurate, to the point of illusion. It is not high art, but it is art. The field is a narrow one, the actors are ordinary. But the skill, grace, and humor with which the scenes are caught, and the absolute illusion of truthfulness, redeem it from the commonplace.'

It has been objected that Trollope's clergy, like Trollope himself, have no spiritual vision. His clerical heroes are always gentlemen, and sometimes scholars, but we seldom see them as priests, exercising religious functions. Trollope expressly excluded from his picture of them their spiritual interests and activities: 'describing, as I have endeavored to do, such clergymen as I see around me, I could not venture to be transcendental.' Nor, in a larger sense, does he deal in his novels with spiritual issues. 'There were no poets in Barsetshire. About these solid stone-walled country houses, these firm and guarded rectories, these sun-lit country roads, there hang no sunset skies of mysterious colors, the moons when they rise are available for croquet-parties but cast no shadows, the cathedral windows fling no varied lights, there are no bats in Trollope's belfries.' So writes Hugh Walpole, making the best defense he can for Trollope on this issue. We must take Trollope for what he can give, and what he can give is very good as far as it goes. The Victorian public had no desire to see the mysteries of religion dragged into a novel of everyday life.

CHARLOTTE AND EMILY BRONTË
(1816–1855, 1818–1848)

With his somewhat limited outlook and genuine desire to please and profit his readers Trollope generally accommodated himself readily enough to the Victorian conventions. He had one story rejected by Thackeray for Cornhill because it dealt with an irregular love affair and another refused by Dr. Norman MacLeod, a popular Presbyterian divine who was also editor of Good Words, because it described dancing with too much enthusiasm. But Trollope moderated the passions of his heroes and heroines to suit popular prejudices, and editors and publishers were satisfied that he was not dangerous. Oddly enough, it was left for two unsophisticated girls in a provincial parsonage to break the bonds that kept the Victorian novel in swaddling clothes. It was the Brontë sisters who brought into English fiction, as J. B. Priestley puts it, 'the thrilling if sometimes strident voice of passionate and romantic womanhood.'

Beside Charlotte and Emily there was a younger sister, Anne, who also wrote poetry and fiction, but her more timid literary efforts have gradually faded out of the picture. Altogether, the three sisters produced seven novels, and to these there must be added an eighth—the story of their own frustrate passions and literary ambitions achieved too late.

They were daughters of an Irish evangelical clergyman named Prunty, who, having changed his name to the more fashionable form of Brontë, the title of Lord Nelson's Italian dukedom, emigrated to the North of England, and married there a Cornish woman who brought him an annuity of fifty pounds, bore him six children in six years, broke down in health after the birth of the sixth, and shortly afterwards died. The year before (1820), the Rev. Patrick Brontë had been appointed to the perpetual curacy of Haworth with a salary of a thousand dollars a year and a house; according to Mrs. Gaskell, the first and best-informed of the many biographers of Charlotte Brontë, he was an eccentric man who wakened the household for its daily tasks by firing a pistol early in the morning out of his bedroom window; even during his wife's lifetime he took his meals alone. His eccentricities were doubtless increased by living in a small and remote manufacturing village, on the edge of a bleak Yorkshire moor; he was a man of intelligence and a poet, though not a very good one; to the day of her death Charlotte deferred at times to his literary judgment, not always to the advantage of her work.

Left with six little motherless children, Brontë called his sister-in-law from Cornwall to his aid; accustomed to a softer climate, she found the stone floors of the parsonage, the prevailing damp and cold, little to her liking, and took refuge in her bedroom. For a while Brontë taught the children himself; but it soon became evident that the elder ones should be sent away to school. It happened that about that time a cheap boarding school for clergymen's children was founded at Cowan Bridge, not many miles away. In 1824, first the two elder girls, and then Charlotte and Emily, were admitted as pupils. The discipline was severe, the situation unhealthy, the diet insufficient and ill-cooked: in the spring of 1825, the two elder children were sent home to die; it was evident that the two younger ones could not get through another winter there, and they too were withdrawn. Charlotte thus at the age of nine took on the responsibilities of the eldest daughter of the house. She was of small size, but well proportioned, with thick, soft brown hair and reddish brown eyes, which glowed with interest or indignation when she was excited—the rest of her features plain, large, and ill-set—a crooked mouth and a large nose; the whole impression was that of a tiny girl, plain-looking but attractive, and unusually sensitive and intelligent. The parsonage at Haworth and the village itself were unhealthy, and Charlotte suffered from constant weakness; 'all her life was but labor and pain.'

These details are necessary, not only for the appreciation of her character, but for the understanding of her work. If she had any gift of invention she exhausted it in the romantic tales she wrote as a child; her mature novels are mainly founded on things she had heard with her own ears or had seen with her own eyes; the places and the people are imaginatively realized from actual life; when a critic of *Jane Eyre* objected to one of its romantic incidents as incredible, she exclaimed, 'But it is a true thing: it really happened.'

This is the explanation of the 'coarseness' with which the Victorian critics often reproached her, to her very great pain. The Northern farmers, manufacturers, and workmen among whom she lived were independent and angular characters, blunt in speech and downright in action. For the first half of her life Charlotte Brontë was hardly out of the bounds, not only of Yorkshire, but of the wildest and most desolate region in it; what wonder that she was always shy in society and unusually direct and abrupt, in speech and correspondence. When George Henry Lewes, who had been most generous in his praise of *Jane Eyre*, wrote a review of *Shirley* in which he made some reserves, she sent him a tart note of fifteen words: 'I can be on my guard against my enemies, but God deliver me from my friends.' Her lack of contact with polite society led her into errors of taste and limited her range, but saved her from some of the pitfalls which beset the more sophisticated writers of her time. Even Mrs. Gaskell, with her genuine admiration and affection for Charlotte Brontë, gave in to the 'critical, unsympathetic public' so far as to admit 'the existence of coarseness here and there in her works' and pleaded, 'It was but skin-deep. Every change in her life was purifying her.' Charlotte Brontë herself was as much puzzled by the charge during her lifetime as she would have been mortified by the apology if she had been alive to know of it; and the modern reader is equally at a loss. Where was the 'coarseness' in *Jane Eyre*, the author frankly asked Mrs. Gaskell, of which the critics complained. Mrs. Gaskell's answer was that 'love was treated with unusual breadth, and that the kind of intercourse was uncommon and uncommonly described.' So too Harriet Martineau, another personal friend, about Charlotte Brontë's last novel, *Villette*: 'All the female characters, in all their thoughts and lives, are full of one thing, or are regarded by the reader in the light of that one thought—love. It begins with a child of six years old, at the opening—a charming picture—and it closes with it at the last page; and so dominant is this idea—so incessant is the writer's tendency to describe the need of being loved—that the heroine, who tells her own story, leaves the reader at last under the uncomfortable impression of her having either entertained a double love, or allowed one to supersede another without notification of the transition. It is not thus in real life. There are substantial, heartfelt interests for women of all ages, and under ordinary circumstances, quite apart from love: there is an absence of introspection, an unconsciousness, a repose in women's lives—unless under peculiarly unfortunate circumstances—of which we find no admission in this book; and to the absence of it may be attributed some of the criticism which the book will meet with from readers who are no prudes, but whose reason and taste will reject the assumption that events and characters are to be regarded through the medium of one passion only.'

Thus, in sheer innocence of heart, Charlotte Brontë opened for the modern novel a gate which her more intelligent and sophisticated contemporaries would have kept closed or feared to touch. Though she recognized the passion in her own and every healthy woman's heart, she is not open to Harriet Martineau's accusation of regarding it as the only or even the main interest in woman's life. At the age of thirty, when she had gone through at least one passionate experience and had refused more than one suitor whom she did not love, she wrote to an older, unmarried friend congratulating her on the enjoyment of an intelligent and useful maturity: 'It seems that even "a lone woman" can be happy, as well as cherished wives and proud mothers. I am glad of that. I speculate much on the existence of unmarried and never-to-be-married women now-a-days; and I have already got to the point of considering that there is no more respectable character on this earth than an unmarried woman, who makes her own way through life, quietly, perseveringly, without support of husband or brother; and who, having attained the age of forty-five or upwards, retains in her possession a well-regulated mind, a disposition to enjoy simple pleasures, and fortitude to support inevitable pains, sympathy with the sufferings of others, and willingness to relieve want as far as her means extend.'

The fact is that in *Jane Eyre* she portrayed a woman of natural but controlled passion because she looked into her own heart; and her appreciation of the necessity of an independent intellectual and economic life for women came from her own hard experience. When she was twenty, she wrote to Southey asking him for advice about her literary ambitions and sending him samples of her poetical work. After a lapse of two months, he wrote telling her that 'Literature cannot be the business of a woman's life, and it ought not to be.' She accepted the reproof with patient humility— but she went on writing. A little while before, she had accepted a position as teacher in a ladies' school so that her only brother Branwell could go to London to study art; unfortunately he turned out to be not only irresponsible but dissipated, and of his un- doubted artistic ability nothing now remains as evidence except the portrait of his three sisters now in the National Gallery— showing Charlotte as 'a little, rather prim-looking girl of eighteen, and the two other sisters (girls of sixteen and fourteen) with cropped hair and sad, dreamy-looking eyes.' When Anne was nineteen she went out as a governess, and only the lack of oppor- tunity prevented the oldest sister from following her example. She writes to a friend: 'I am as yet "wanting a situation," like a housemaid out of place. By the way, I have lately discovered that I have quite a talent for cleaning, sweeping-up hearths, dust- ing rooms, making beds etc.; so, if everything else fails, I can turn my hand to that, if anybody will give me good wages for little labor. I won't be a cook; I hate cooking. I won't be a nursery- maid, nor a lady's-maid, far less a lady's companion, or a mantua- maker, or a straw-bonnet maker, or a taker-in of plain work. I won't be anything but a housemaid.' When she did get a place as governess to the children of a wealthy Yorkshire manufacturer, she was not happy in it; she had no gift for teaching and she did not understand children, for she had never really been a child herself—only a precocious girl lost in the manufacture of ro- mances, dramas, poems, and short stories. She was soon home again, busy with writing when she had done house-cleaning and ironing the linen while Emily did the cooking, there being at the time no maid. She comments: 'I am much happier blackleading the stoves, making the beds, and sweeping the floors at home, than I should be living like a fine lady anywhere else.' A second place as governess was more congenial, for the family was more considerate of her personal dignity, though she had to do plain sewing in addition to teaching two children to earn a meager salary of less than a hundred dollars a year, from which deductions were made for her laundry.

It was evident that literary ability, intelligence, and high character were not enough; the Brontë sisters must have more accomplishments if they were to make their way in the world. So in February, 1842—when Charlotte was twenty-five and Emily twenty-three—the two sisters left their native county for the first time to become pupils in a school at Brussels conducted by M. and Madame Héger. Stern Protestant provincials, they found the Catholic atmosphere bitterly uncongenial, but they had set their hearts on learning, and M. Héger was an intelligent, well-informed man, and a capable teacher. They were recalled home in the fall by the death of the aunt who had taken their mother's place in the Brontë household. Emily, who always sickened and pined when she was away from the Yorkshire moors, was glad to stay at Haworth, and when Charlotte returned to Brussels at the beginning of 1843, she returned alone. She was now a teacher in the school and as such came into closer contact with M. Héger, who gave her private instruction, and was somewhat embarrassed when he found that his brilliant pupil had conceived an ardent affection for him, especially as his wife was evidently aware of the situation. But he took things quietly, acted with exemplary prudence and self-restraint, and filed away the passionate letters that Charlotte sent to him after her final return home. Mrs. Gaskell saw them after Charlotte's death when she was gathering material for her *Life of Charlotte Brontë*, but with Victorian reserve suppressed all reference to this episode in the Brussels chapter of the official biography. It was not until 1913—some seventy years after the letters were written and the people concerned in them were all dead—that M. Héger's heirs allowed Charlotte Brontë's letters to be published in the London Times. Modern biographers have been inclined to treat this as the central incident in Charlotte Brontë's life, and it was certainly of importance, both for her spiritual and literary development. The Times remarked editorially in publishing the letters: 'All her life she was in love with an ideal; and so far as Héger was her ideal, she was in love with him and knew it.' Professor Elton, however, cannot see that the words 'in love' are applicable even in this sense. 'The letters breathe the far-off devotion of a pupil; a hectic desire, which does not lessen our respect, for encouragement and recognition; an immense solitariness of spirit; and nothing more.'

The purpose of the sojourn in Brussels had been the establishment of a school at Haworth to be conducted by the three sisters, for Emily was still at home and Anne still working as a governess. The scheme came to naught, partly for lack of pupils, partly on account of the behavior of Branwell, who was also at home, refusing to work, and indulging in debauches of drink and opium when he found the opportunity. In these circumstances literature was the only possible resource, and it happened that one day in the autumn of 1845, Charlotte accidentally lighted on a collection of verse in Emily's handwriting. She found some of them of unusual merit, possessing 'a peculiar music, wild, melancholy, and elevating.' She was convinced that they were worth publication, and as Anne revealed the fact that she also had a hidden store of verses, the three sisters agreed to arrange for the publication of a small selection of their poems under the pen-names of Currer, Ellis, and Acton Bell, which preserved the identity of the separate authors under initials, but hid even their sex from a too inquisitive public. The poems appeared accordingly from a London publishing house (at the authors' expense) in May, 1846, but the public showed no curiosity about either the authors or the poems, only two copies being sold. Undaunted, the three sisters asked the publishers' advice as to the joint issue of three novels—one by each of the three authors. The proposition was courteously declined, and the applicants were advised to try each story by itself. Accordingly *The Professor* by Currer Bell, *Wuthering Heights* by Ellis Bell, and *Agnes Grey* by Acton Bell made the round of the London publishing offices. The two latter were accepted, but *The Professor* (founded on Charlotte's experiences in Brussels) found a welcome nowhere. Smith Elder & Co., however, though not disposed to publish the MS., offered to consider another novel from the same hand, containing more exciting narrative and more varied interest. This encouraging offer came into Charlotte's hands early in August, 1847, and she at once replied that she had already in hand and almost completed a second narrative in three volumes which she hoped would meet the publishers' requirements. Before the end of the month it was finished and forwarded to London. *Jane Eyre* was immediately accepted and sent to press; it was published by the middle of October, and by December was exciting universal attention—some of it hostile, but most of it favorable and even enthusiastic.

Wuthering Heights by Ellis Bell and *Agnes Grey* by Acton Bell appeared before the end of the year, and there arose a belief that the three Bells were all the same person (the identity and even the sex of the authors being still kept a profound secret). This soon caused complications in the arrangements made by Smith Elder & Co. with their American representatives, and they wrote to Charlotte Brontë accordingly; Charlotte and Anne started the same day for London to prove their separate identity, and the leading member of the publishing firm (who did not yet know whether the Bells were men or women) was very much astonished when Currer and Acton Bell revealed themselves in his office as 'two young ladies dressed in black, of slight figure and diminutive stature, looking pleased yet agitated.' They were still more agitated when, later in the day, the publisher's wife called to take them to the opera; and, somewhat self-conscious in their country traveling clothes, they sat in a box, Charlotte 'pleasureably excited,' and Anne 'calm and gentle.'

This was on a Saturday in July, 1848, and on Tuesday morning, after three days of hectic entertainment, they were on their way home again. It was a sad situation that faced them on their return. Their brother Branwell, beloved in spite of his weaknesses and even his vices, was seriously ill, and died two months later. Before the year was out, Emily was dead; and the death of Anne followed in May, 1849.

Jane Eyre sprang from a discussion among the sisters as to whether the heroine of a novel needed to be beautiful as well as good. Charlotte denied the necessity, and when the other two persisted, she retorted, 'I will prove to you that you are wrong; I will show you a heroine as plain and as small as myself, who shall be as interesting as any of yours.' But she added, in telling the story, '*Jane Eyre* is not myself, any further than that.' One wonders whether the latter avowal, though no doubt sincere, is altogether correct. Jane's early hardships at Lowood School are certainly taken from the misfortunes of the Brontë sisters at Cowan Bridge, especially those of the eldest sister, Maria; and Jane's governessing doubtless owes something to Charlotte's experiences in that capacity; the story of a mad wife kept in seclusion on a great estate is said to be founded on a local legend, though the melodrama in which this situation is invested may be due to the publishers' demand for thrilling incident. *Shirley* also owes a good deal to stories of the countryside about the Luddite riots of 1812–14, though the novelist refreshed these local recollections by consulting a file of the Leeds Mercury for that period. The heroine is modeled upon her sister Emily, and the 'three curates,' as well as other characters, were recognizable portraits of people still living in the neighborhood. Indeed, the identity of the scenery and the personages with actualities speedily led to the identification of the novelist with Charlotte Brontë; and her authorship was publicly acknowledged. On later visits to London she met Thackeray and other literary celebrities, but she shrank from notoriety, feeling that her solitary life had disqualified her for society. Her fame attracted the attention of the local land-owners, and at the house of one of them in the Lake District she met her fellowworker in the art of fiction, Mrs. Gaskell, who soon became a fast friend, and was to be her biographer when her short life came to an end. Mrs. Gaskell, in a letter written at the time of this first meeting, described Charlotte Brontë as 'a little lady in a black gown . . . more than half a head shorter than I am; soft brown hair, not very dark; eyes (very good and expressive, looking straight and open at you) of the same color as her hair; a large mouth; the forehead square, broad, and rather overhanging.'

Villette, her last novel, was the recast of the unsuccessful *Professor* which procured her the opportunity of publishing *Jane Eyre*. The hero, Paul Emanuel, is the M. Héger of her Brussels days, as he appeared to her imaginative recollection in later years, when all pain had gone out of her old attachment. About the time of its publication she received a proposal of marriage from the Rev. Arthur Bell Nicholls, her father's curate, and after some delay, due to her father's opposition, she accepted it. It seemed as if at last, after the hardships and bereavements that had beset her path in life since her mother's death when she was a little child, she was to have a season of calm enjoyment, for Mr. Nicholls was willing to come to live at the parsonage so that Charlotte could give her aged father the care he needed to the end of his days. They were married in June, 1854, and after a visit to Ireland to see Mr. Nicholls's family, settled down at Haworth. In November they went for a walk on the moors and were overtaken by heavy rain. Charlotte caught cold and was unable to regain her strength. She sank lower and lower, and one day in March, wakening for a moment from stupor, she overheard her husband praying that God would spare her. 'Oh!' she whispered, 'I am not going to die, am I? He will not separate us, we have been so happy.' Before the end of the month she was dead.

About Charlotte Brontë and her work there has been as much discussion among both English and French critics as about any novelist of the last hundred years. In recent criticism there has been an inclination to esteem Emily as the more original genius, and, as Charlotte herself was the first to point out, the greater poet. Certainly nothing in the work of the two other sisters has the power of thought and the terseness of expression of Emily's *Last Lines:*—

> No coward soul is mine,
>   No trembler in the world's storm-troubled sphere:
> I see Heaven's glories shine,
>   And faith shines equal, arming me from fear.
>
> O God within my breast,
>   Almighty, ever-present Deity!
> Life—that in me has rest,
>   As I—undying Life—have power in Thee!
>
> Vain are the thousand creeds,
>   That move men's hearts: unutterably vain;
> Worthless as withered weeds
>   Or idlest froth amid the boundless main,
>
> To waken doubt in one
>   Holding so fast by thine infinity;
> So surely anchored on
>   The steadfast rock of immortality.
>
> With wide-embracing love
>   Thy spirit animates eternal years,
> Pervades and broods above,
>   Charges, sustains, dissolves, creates, and rears.
>
> Though earth and man were gone,
>   And stars and universes cease to be,
> And Thou wert left alone,
>   Every existence would exist in Thee.
>
> There is not room for Death
>   Nor atom that his might could render void:
> Thou—THOU art Being and Breath,
>   And what THOU art may never be destroyed.

Wuthering Heights conveys with more intensity than any other novel the grim independent spirit of the lonely dwellers on the wild Yorkshire moors, which Emily never left without reluctance and always returned to with rejoicing. 'Wuthering' is a word of the local dialect meaning storm-swept, full of the noise of tempest in the air, 'atmospheric tumult.' 'The action is laid in hell,' said Dante Gabriel Rossetti, 'only it seems places and people have English names there.' The story makes a disagreeable impression, even on those who are the readiest to acknowledge its power. E. F. Benson, the last Brontë biographer, thinks Branwell Brontë 'wrote the first two chapters, and was to some extent a collaborator in the rest'; but the evidence produced is insufficient to outweigh Charlotte's explicit declaration that Emily was far too proud to accept any outside help, and that Branwell never knew what his sisters had done in literature. He died within a year of the publication of *Wuthering Heights*, when the secret of its authorship was still most closely kept; during the last year or two of his life his health was already broken down by drink and drugs.

It is odd that Mr. Benson, while robbing Emily of the credit of independent authorship on the one hand, on the other exalts her above Charlotte, both as a woman and as a writer. On the evidence available, it seems best to attribute *Wuthering Heights* entirely to Emily's somber imagination; except Branwell's own word—and that at second-hand—there is nothing to show that he had anything to do with it. Matthew Arnold, on the internal evidence of the poems and the novel, wrote that Emily Brontë's soul

> Knew no fellow for might,
> Passion, vehemence, grief,
> Daring, since Byron died.

It is not necessary to depreciate Charlotte in order to extol Emily. Charlotte may have been, as Mr. Benson says, 'prejudiced, obstinate, censorious, difficult'; but she was also, as another recent critic (Naomi Royde-Smith) points out, 'brave, patient, wise, unselfish, ardent, witty; unworldly and yet prudent; scrupulous, yet able to circumvent her intolerable tyrant of a father; austere, yet at moments soft and feminine; virginal, yet passionate; a better novelist than Emily, and undoubtedly a greater woman.'

From the point of view of literary achievement, there can be no doubt of Charlotte's superiority. She stands midway between the impetuous and extravagant Emily and the gentle and patient Anne, who faded out of literature as she faded out of life. *Wuthering Heights*, as Professor Elton points out, is 'superficially awkward and inexperienced work, with its Chinese-box narratives, its intricate intermarriages, and its vagueness as to imaginary dates.' Charlotte's novels are well-constructed as well as well-written, professional—not amateur work. After *Jane Eyre*, the 'novel of passion' could never be the same again. 'The two sisters,' again to quote Professor Elton 'did more to assert the spiritual rights and equalities of their sex than all the pamphleteers from Mary Woolstonecraft to John Stuart Mill. . . . They have left the soundest and most imaginative statement of claim from the feminine standpoint.' This claim was the ground of Charlotte Brontë's quarrel with George Henry Lewes, whom she never entirely forgave; in the offending article in the Edinburgh Review, he began his examination of her novels with a discussion headed 'mental equality of the sexes?' and 'female literature'; throughout, the fact of the author's sex is never forgotten. Charlotte Brontë (and this is the reason why to the end she preferred to appear as 'Currer Bell') asserted her right to be judged not as a woman, or as a woman-novelist, but simply as a novelist; she not only asserted this right; she proved it.

MRS. GASKELL
(1810–1865)

Mrs. Gaskell's biography of her friend Charlotte Brontë has perhaps withdrawn attention from her own novels, for it immediately excited controversies of which the echoes have not even yet died away. The intimate friend of Charlotte Brontë during the last years of her life, she devoted more than a year to the consideration of the material put at her disposal by the family, visited all the scenes,—not very numerous,—connected with the subject, and took every possible pains to secure accuracy; but some of the statements made to her by Charlotte Brontë were questioned by people still living and had to be withdrawn. It is still true, however, that, as Sir A. W. Ward said half a century ago, 'the substantial accuracy of the picture has not been successfully impugned.'

Elizabeth Cleghorn acquired the name under which she is familiar to students by her marriage to the minister of the leading Unitarian church in Manchester. She had been brought up at Knutsford in Cheshire, only fifteen miles away, but sufficiently far removed in those days to offer a complete contrast to the bustle, grime, poverty and riches of the metropolis of the Lancashire cotton trade. To quote Professor Hugh Walker: 'It lies in the midst of characteristically English scenery. Great parks with stately trees and still meres, and old Halls which carry the imagination back for hundreds of years, surround it, and oak-timbered houses are still to be seen in the streets. The little town was then a veritable Sleepy Hollow.' Mrs. Gaskell gave a faithful and loving picture of this quaintly charming rural community in *Cranford*. A local Victorian Guidebook says: 'Cranford is all about Knutsford; my old mistress, Miss ——, is mentioned in it, and our poor cow—she did go to the field in a large flannel waistcoat, because she had burned herself in a limepit.'

Removal to the busy streets of Manchester by her marriage in 1832 and contact with the lives of poor working folk could not but impress her mind with the contrast between the Arcadia she had left and the industrial Inferno into which she was then plunged. She was a girl of unusual beauty, refinement, and intelligence, and early showed capacity for literary composition, but it was not until the death of her only boy in 1844 that she sought consolation, on her husband's advice, in the creation of a long work of fiction. The result was her first novel *Mary Barton*, which found a publisher after the usual difficulties encountered by a beginner, and appeared in 1848—the year after *Jane Eyre*. As a sympathetic study of the sufferings and wrongs of the Lancashire cotton operatives, it at once attracted the favorable attention of Carlyle and Dickens, as well as of a large reading public. The manufacturers, first by correspondence in the Manchester Guardian and then through their spokesman W. R. Greg, complained that they had been maligned; and Professor Oliver Elton, who as professor first at Manchester and then at Liverpool, should speak from knowledge, remarks: 'certainly she chooses some stony examples of the tribe.' Mrs. Gaskell was much surprised and distressed by the charge of unfairness, and after some years of diligent inquiry she made amends to the Lancashire manufacturers in another novel, *North and South*, which gives evidence of 'greater impartiality and riper reflection,' in the opinion of Sir A. W. Ward, for many years Principal of what is now the University of Manchester.

Cranford and *North and South* appeared in Household Words under the editorship of Dickens, who had a very high opinion of Mrs. Gaskell's genius. She contributed also to Cornhill, and was in the midst of writing for it what some thought would have been her best novel, *Wives and Daughters*, when she died, very suddenly, from heart disease.

In spite of an occasional inclination for melodrama, Mrs. Gaskell's romance moves in a gentler sphere than that of the two Brontë sisters; she has genuine sympathy for the oppressed, but none of their fierce indignation and fiery passion. She was truly fond of Charlotte Brontë and very sorry for her; but she did not share her view of life. 'I thought,' she says, 'that human lots were more equal than she imagined; that to some, happiness and sorrow came in strong patches of light and shadow (so to speak), while in the lives of others they were pretty equally blended throughout.' This difference in point of view rested partly, no doubt, upon a difference in temperament; but mainly, one would think, upon a difference in experience. Mrs. Gaskell had a happy youth, and in spite of the anxieties and bereavements common to the human lot in every station, a happy and successful maturity. She knew nothing of the cramping of soul which results from the humiliations of poverty and the denial of opportunity to a restless and passionate spirit.

GEORGE BORROW

(1803–1881)

It may seem to be begging the main question about Borrow's work to include him in a chapter about novelists; but it is hard to say under what other heading it should be classified. It had much in common with the picaresque novel of vagabond adventure, but is really a new genre—a story which professes to be and mainly is autobiographical, but deals freely with persons, events, and dates for purposes of romantic effect. About one half of *The Bible in Spain* (1843), which was the first of his publications to win general attention, was made up of the regular reports he had sent to the Committee of the British and Foreign Bible Society about the work he was doing as their representative and agent. But it is hardly likely that he sent in as a report the elaborate sophistications by which he justified himself when he wanted to go to Cape Finisterre, and found sufficient reason for the trip in meditation upon the vast amount of good (from the point of view of eternity) that might be done by the distribution of one copy of the New Testament, which was all that remained in his colporteur's knapsack. He was a vagabond from his youth up, with a strong liking for gypsies, wandering tinkers, and other Bohemians of the less respectable sort. He had a wide but not accurate knowledge of languages, was a fierce Protestant, a lover of good ale, and a practitioner, as well as an admirer, of the noble art of self-defense. His account in *Lavengro* (1851) of his battle with the Flaming Tinman is one of the classics of pugilism, and the subsequent episode of his sojourn in the dell with Isopel Berners (who had acted as his second) is one of the oddest experiences recounted in

fiction. According to his story he lived with her as a brother for
weeks, teaching her Armenian verbs when the relations between
them threatened to become too difficult for his comfort. She was
born in the poorhouse (as she calls it the 'great house') at Long
Melford but had learnt to 'fear God and take her own part,' so
that she was quite able to protect herself and keep at a distance
any man whose intentions seemed to be too on-coming. She is
one of the most independent and engaging young women in literature, and a great testimony to Borrow's power of character creation, but as an episode of actual experience, this part of the tale
seems 'too good to be true.' The reader is, however, very sorry
when Borrow sends her off to America; and no less sorry when, at
the end of the autobiographical sequel, *Romany Rye* (The Gypsy
Gentleman), he brings the narrative to a close. The two books
together bring the story of Borrow's life down from his infancy
to 1825, when he was twenty-two years of age. He seems to have
been about thirty-eight when the plan of writing his life was conceived and nearly fifty-four when he completed it, so far as it went.
Lavengro: the Scholar, the Gypsy, the Priest appeared in 1851 and
The Romany Rye in 1857. The dates forbid the possibility of a
contemporary record; and the latter book ends with the author's
declaration of his intention of going to India. He never went to
India, though he said he learnt the gypsy language in Moultan.
After the romantic incidents recounted in the two autobiographical
books, we know little of Borrow until 1832, when he traveled in
Russia as an agent of the British and Foreign Bible Society,
learnt Turkish (according to his own account, 'there was a time
when I wrote it better than any other language,') helped to trans-
late the New Testament into Manchu, and eventually settled down
in East Anglia, where he had been born. His philological books,
even of the gypsy tongue with which he was best acquainted, were
never held of much account by the professional philologists, but as
a writer of romantic travel and adventure he is unsurpassed. In
1854 he made a long walking tour in Wales, with his wife and step-
daughter, and jotted down his adventures by the way in four
notebooks, which he afterwards expanded into *Wild Wales, Its
Peoples, Language, and Scenery*. No one else who ever traveled
over the same ground had anything like so many strange encoun-
ters, but enthusiastic Borrovians contend that nothing is truer
than Borrow's travel books, though they admit that he paid little
regard to such trifles as time and place. Adventures are to the
adventurous, and Borrow's tall and vigorous figure, his white

hair, black clothes, wideawake hat, were distinctly out of the ordinary. One wonders, however, whether a band of Irish reapers on the Welsh coast really mistook Borrow for a popular Irish priest of the time, Father Toban, and insisted on receiving a blessing from him in 'Holy Latin,' under threat of a beating if he refused. But the incident, if not exact fact, is well invented, and falls in well with Borrow's romantic character. It was what he would have done, if the opportunity had offered itself.

CHAPTER V

EARLY VICTORIAN POETS

ELIZABETH BARRETT	ROBERT BROWNING
(1806–1861)	*(1812–1889)*

NEARLY a century after the beginning of the Victorian Era, a successful dramatist enabled the British and the American public to realize that 50 Wimpole Street had been the scene of one of the most romantic episodes of the romantic nineteenth century. It was at this house that the two poets, Elizabeth Barrett and Robert Browning, fell in love with each other, from this house that she escaped secretly to be married to him in a neighboring church, and from this house that a few days later she ran away to Italy. Their life together in Florence was 'a true poem' and produced some of the finest poetry of the Victorian Era.

There was nothing scandalous about the elopement. Miss Barrett was forty years old and Browning was thirty-four; they belonged to highly respectable well-to-do families of the Non-conformist middle class, and each had an established position in the intellectual and literary world of London, where they both lived; not the slightest breath of malicious gossip could mar either's reputation. The most severe comment made upon the event was that of William Wordsworth, then poet laureate and ordinarily the mildest of men: 'So Robert Browning and Elizabeth Barrett have gone off together. Well, I hope they may understand each other—nobody else could.'

As a perverse view of the situation this could only be matched by the remark of Miss Barrett's father: 'I have no objection to the young man, but my daughter should have been thinking of another world.' Barrett was a religious fanatic, and his objection to the marriage of his daughters was carried almost to the point of monomania. 'If a prince of Eldorado,' said Elizabeth Barrett to her sister Arabel, 'should come with a pedigree of lineal descent from some signory in the moon in one hand, and a ticket of good behavior from the nearest Independent chapel in the other——' 'Why, even then,' interrupted Arabel, 'it would not *do*.' Barrett's 'other-worldliness' in the case of his eldest daughter found some excuse in the precarious state of her health. A delicate and precocious child, crippled by a spinal injury through a riding accident in her girlhood, she had never recovered from the shock of her brother's death by drowning, which happened in her thirty-fourth year; she lived in almost complete seclusion, 'occupied, upon her sofa, with her books and papers—her Greek dramatists and her Elizabethan poets.' 'A bird in a cage,' she said, 'would have as good a story'; and 'I lived with visions for my company, instead of men and women . . . nor thought to know a sweeter music than they played to me.' Her timidity and nervousness were probably due in part to her father's habit of praying, aloud and at length, by her bedside whenever her conduct did not meet with his entire approval. Yet he was a man 'of integrity in business, of fortitude in adversity, of a certain stern piety,' and, in his own peculiar way, an affectionate father.

Fortunately Elizabeth Barrett was able to console her solitude by her devotion to literature. As a child she had written an epic poem, *The Battle of Marathon*, which was printed for private circulation before she left school, and her first publication, at the age of twenty, was a versified *Essay on Mind*, after the manner of Pope's *Essay on Criticism*. She read Homer in the original at the age of eight, and later extended her Greek studies to all the Greek poets, beside reading the whole of the Old Testament in Hebrew. She produced a youthful translation of the *Prometheus Vinctus* of Æschylus, and published also an Essay on *The Greek Christian Poets*, with many translations. Yet there was nothing of the blue-stocking in her disposition. *The Cry of the Children*, from which a stanza was quoted in our second chapter, shows her interest in contemporary social problems, and in literary London she had a few friends who were allowed to see her when she felt strong enough to receive visits. Miss Mitford, who knew her well, describes her at this time as a 'slight, delicate figure, with a shower of dark curls falling on each side of a most expressive face, large tender eyes, richly fringed by dark eyelashes, and a smile like a sunbeam.' Nathaniel Hawthorne, who knew her later, speaks of her as 'a pale, small person, scarcely embodied at all. . . . It is wonderful to see how small she is, how pale her cheek, how bright and dark her eyes. There is not such another figure in the world, and her black ringlets cluster down into her neck and make her face look whiter.'

Robert Browning's early life presents as complete a contrast to that of Elizabeth Barrett as could well be expected between people of identical literary and intellectual interests. His father and mother belonged to the same class of intelligent Nonconformists ('My father was a scholar and knew Greek'), and though, as the son of a Nonconformist, admission to public schools and the older universities was denied to him, he had a good private education and attended classes in the newly founded University College in London. At the age of twelve he was writing verses in the manner of Byron, and at fourteen his mother bought him the poems of Shelley and Keats—apparently his own choice for a birthday present. His youthful admiration for Shelley led him to profess atheism and practise vegetarianism, but these youthful vagaries passed in a year or two, leaving behind them a genuine devotion to Shelley's genius as a poet and philosopher. His own predilection for poetry was encouraged by his father, who bore all the expenses of the publication of his early poems *Paracelsus* (1835), *Sordello* (1840), and the *Bells and Pomegranates* series (1841–46). His first published poem *Pauline* (1833) was paid for by a devoted aunt. Browning took full advantage of this early appreciation and encouragement, and wrote of it in later years as follows: 'It would have been quite unpardonable in my case not to have done my best. My dear father put me in a condition most favorable for the best work I was capable of. When I think of the many authors who have had to fight their way through all sorts of difficulties, I have no reason to be proud of my achievements. My good father sacrificed a fortune to his convictions. He could not bear with slavery, and left India [the West Indies], and accepted a humble banking-office in London. He secured for me all the ease and comfort that a literary man needs to do good work. It would have been shameful if I had not done my best to realize his expectations of me.'

The Browning of these earlier days is described by a fellow-student of Greek at University College as 'a bright, handsome youth, with long black hair falling over his shoulders.' He was fond in these earlier as in later days of vigorous physical and social activities. He 'sang, danced, rode, boxed and fenced'! his voice is described as 'flute-like, clear, sweet, and resonant.' He was short and slight, but his movements were graceful, and he held his head high. His face was one of rare intelligence and full of changing expression. Macready, the leading actor of the day, was greatly impressed by Browning's 'simple and enthusiastic manner' and noted in his diary 'that he looks and speaks more like a youthful poet than any man I ever saw.' Another observer describes his hair as dark brown and hanging in wavy masses upon his neck. To another he appeared 'slim, dark and very handsome. And—may I hint it?—just a trifle of a dandy, addicted to lemon-colored kid gloves and such things, quite "the glass of fashion and the mold of form." But full of ambition, eager for success, eager for fame, and, what is more, determined to conquer fame and to achieve success.' One of his friends wrote to another in 1844: 'Browning's conversation is as remarkably good as his books, though so different: in conversation anecdotical, vigorous, showing great thought and reading, but in his language most simple, energetic, and accurate. From the habit of good and extensive society he has improved in this respect wonderfully. We remember him as hardly doing justice to himself in society; now he is quite the reverse—no one could converse with him without being struck by his great conversational power—he relates admirably; in fact, altogether I look upon him as *to be* our foremost literary man.'

With these qualifications it was no wonder that Browning was a favorite in the London literary world. He soon counted among his friends Carlyle, Dickens, Wordsworth, and Landor, and at a dinner at which it was expected one of the two last-mentioned would respond to the toast of 'The Poets of England' the slight and graceful figure of Browning rose at the call of the chair. After the dinner Macready said to the young poet, 'Write me a play, and keep me from going to America.' So *Strafford* was written and produced at Covent Garden theater in 1837, just before Queen Victoria came to the throne; but it failed to save Macready from the fate he dreaded and the theater from closing. The play, however, was issued by the publishers at their own expense and the loss fell upon them and not, as in the case of Browning's previous publications, upon his relatives.

Browning was from the beginning an unpopular poet. A reviewer of *Pauline* described it as 'a piece of pure bewilderment,' and *Paracelsus* was condemned as diffuse. In deference to the latter criticism Browning attempted to be extremely concise in his next long poem, *Sordello*, and the result was that there was general agreement that it was incomprehensible. Mrs. Carlyle, who was certainly one of the most intelligent women then alive, said she could not make out whether the hero was a man, a city, or a book. Tennyson said he understood only two lines of it—the first, 'Who will may hear Sordello's story told,' and the last line—'Who would has heard Sordello's story told'; and both were lies. But the most amusing story of the Victorian public's inability to understand *Sordello* is told of Douglas Jerrold, the famous contributor to Punch. He was recruiting at Brighton after a long illness, and in the course of his convalescence a parcel arrived from London which contained, among other things, this new volume of *Sordello*. The doctor had forbidden Jerrold the luxury of reading, but in the absence of his wife and her sister, who were nursing him, he indulged in the illicit enjoyment. A few lines put Jerrold in a state of alarm. Sentence after sentence brought no consecutive thought to his brain. At last the idea crossed his mind that in his illness his mental faculties had been wrecked. The perspiration rolled from his forehead, and smiting his head, he sat down on the sofa, crying 'O God I am an idiot!' When his wife and her sister came back, he pushed the volume into their hands and demanded what they thought of it. He watched them intently while they read; at last his wife said, 'I don't understand what the man means; it is gibberish.' The delighted humorist sank back into his seat with a sigh of relief: 'Thank God I am not an idiot!'

The charge of obscurity, so often made against Browning during his lifetime and after, calls perhaps for no defense in an age when the younger poets no longer regard lucidity as a virtue; but there are one or two things that should be said. We must accept Browning's disclaimer of any intentional obscurity. He wrote to an admirer who drew attention to this accusation:—'I can have little doubt that my writing has been in the main too hard for many I should have been pleased to communicate with; but I never designedly tried to puzzle people, as some of my critics have supposed. On the other hand, I never pretended to offer such literature as should be a substitute for a cigar or a game of dominoes to an idle man. So, perhaps, on the whole I get my deserts, and something over—not a crowd, but a few I value more.' But there can be no doubt that Browning often made more demands upon the reader's intelligence than the ordinary man is able or willing to meet. Some of the poems are extremely difficult, for one or more of three reasons: (1) allusions to little-known facts or incidents; (2) an abbreviated sentence-construction, difficult to follow on account of the omission of pronouns or particles; (3) lightning-like transitions of thought which leave the ordinary reader puzzled or gasping. The difficulty last-mentioned is the most serious, and it is admitted by Browning in answer to an inquiry from Ruskin, who found himself unable to understand the sequence of thought in one of the poems of *Men and Women* (1855): 'For your bewilderment more especially noted—how shall I help *that?* We don't read poetry the same way, by the same law; it is too clear. I cannot begin writing poetry till my imaginary reader has conceded licenses to me which you demur at altogether. I know that I don't make out my conception by my language; all poetry being a putting the infinite within the finite. You would have me paint it all plain out, which can't be; but by various artifices I try to make shift with touches and bits of outlines which *succeed* if they bear the conception from me to you. You ought, I think, to keep pace with the thought tripping from ledge to ledge of my "glaciers," as you call them; not stand poking your alpenstock into the holes, and demonstrating that no foot could have stood there;—suppose it sprang over there? In *prose* you may criticize so—because that is the absolute representation of portions of truth, what chronicling is to history—but in asking for more *ultimates* you must accept less *mediates*, nor expect that a Druid stone-circle will be traced for you with as few breaks to the eye as the North Crescent and South Crescent that go together so cleverly in many a suburb.' Certainly there was no suburban regularity of plan in *Sordello*. The first prerequisite for understanding Sordello's story is some knowledge of medieval Italy, of the political and literary conditions in a place and time remote from the interests, even of the vast mass of intelligent readers; then there is a certain tortuousness in the construction of the plot as well as in the composition of particular lines or passages of the poem; finally, there is the difficulty of the theme itself, the central thought to be elucidated. Browning wrote of *Sordello* many years later: 'The historical decoration was purposly of no more importance than a background requires; and my stress lay on the incidents in the development of a soul: little else is worth study.'

The immediate result of the chill reception of *Sordello* was that Browning found himself obliged to publish his poems at his own risk. This was the origin of the *Bells and Pomegranates* series, cheap issues in yellow paper wrappers, sold at that time for a few cents and now hardly obtainable for many more dollars. For the name of the series the poet offered by way of explanation a reference to *Exodus* XXVIII. 34, which speaks of the bells and pomegranates adorning the hem of the high priest's robe, interpreted to suggest 'a mixture of music with discoursing, sound with sense, poetry with thought.'

Elizabeth Barrett, already well established in popular favor, had recognized in *Paracelsus* 'the expression of a new mind,' and she gave a welcome to the *Bells and Pomegranates* series by an appreciative couplet in her versified romance *Lady Geraldine's Courtship* (1844), expressing a pleasurable expectation of further issues:

Or from Browning some 'Pomegranate' which, if cut deep down the middle,
Shows a heart within, blood-tinctured, of a veined humanity.

Browning, encouraged by a friend of his family, who was Elizabeth Barrett's cousin (John Kenyon), wrote in January, 1845, to Miss Barrett to express his gratitude for the compliment and something more than admiration for his fellow poet and her work. 'I love your verses with all my heart, dear Miss Barrett,' he began, and later in the letter he added 'I love you too.' So began a correspondence which afterwards made perhaps the most remarkable of all collections of love letters: it was all preserved with the exception of one letter—a proposal of marriage sent to Miss Barrett after their meeting face to face. When they had exchanged a number of letters he asked to be allowed to visit her; she protested that there was nothing to see in her; she was not a flower, but 'a weed, fit for the ground and darkness.' When the proposal came, she insisted that he must not only withdraw it, but forget that he had ever made it. Browning asked for the return of his letter, and destroyed it. But when a lover is bidden to disappear, and invited to re-appear in the character of a friend, 'wise guardian-angels smile at each other, gently and graciously.' It was not long before Miss Barrett asked to have the offending letter back again, and after a short secret engagement the poet-lovers were quietly married at a church near her home. A few days later, with equal secrecy, they left for the Continent.

This was in September, 1846. A friend who met Mrs. Browning in Paris described the change in her health as not so much an improvement as a transformation. After traveling about for a while, the Brownings settled down at Casa Guidi, Florence, where a son was born to them in 1849. There they received many visitors of distinction in the literary and artistic world, who have left abundant testimony to the harmony and beauty of their married life. Among these that of Thackeray's daughter, Mrs. Richmond Ritchie, may be quoted because of the picture drawn with a few strokes of the pen:—'Those among us who only knew Mrs. Browning as a wife and as a mother have found it difficult to realize her life under any other conditions, so vivid and complete is the image of her peaceful home, of its fireside where the logs are burning, and the mistress established on her sofa, with her little boy curled up by her side, the door opening and shutting meanwhile to the quick step of the master of the house, and to the life of the world without, coming to find her in her quiet corner. We can recall the slight figure in its black silk dress, the writing apparatus by the sofa, the tiny ink-stand, the quill-nibbed penholder, the unpretentious implements of her work.'

The two poets worked independently, and did not show each other their poems till they were finished. It was at Pisa, on their way to Florence, that Mrs. Browning slipped into her husband's hands the poems she had written during his courtship of her, for her more facile and emotional genius was the first to respond to the stimulus of their happiness. The sonnet series was first printed privately, but was published in 1850 under the title *Sonnets from the Portuguese*. In their combination of elevation of thought, simplicity and directness of feeling, and musical tenderness they are unsurpassed. One may be quoted from among many others of nearly equal beauty:—

> How do I love thee? Let me count the ways,
> I love thee to the depth and breadth and height
> My soul can reach, when feeling out of sight
> For the ends of Being and ideal Grace.
>
> I love thee to the level of everyday's
> Most quiet need, by sun and candle-light.
> I love thee freely, as men strive for Right;
> I love thee purely, as they turn from Praise.
>
> I love thee with the passion put to use
> In my old griefs, and with my childhood's faith.
> I love thee with a love I seemed to lose
> With my lost saints,—I love thee with the breath,
> Smiles, tears, of all my life!—and, if God choose,
> I shall but love thee better after death.

Mrs. Browning was intellectually stirred as well as emotionally excited by coming out of her dark chamber into the light of day. She took a deep interest in the resurgence of Italian nationalism and the desire for union and independence. *Casa Guidi Windows* (1851) and *Poems before Congress* (1860) express her lively sympathy with the policy of Cavour, whose death in 1861 seems to have been a contributing cause to her own. Already ill, she seemed unable to survive the shock and died not long after. The city of

Florence was grateful to her for her interest in their national aspirations and at once placed on the walls of Casa Guidi a memorial tablet bearing the following inscription, composed by the poet Tommaseo: 'Here wrote and died Elizabeth Barrett Browning, who in her woman's heart reconciled a scholar's learning with a poet's soul and made of her verse a golden ring between Italy and England.'

It is to this inscription that Browning refers in the dedication of his great poem *The Ring and the Book* to his dead wife, with its allusion to 'that rare gold ring of verse the poet praised, Linking our England to his Italy.' The whole passage is an example of the feeling which in Browning at his best merges with his intellectual discernment and his religious faith:—

> O Lyric Love, half angel and half bird
> And all a wonder and a wild desire,—
> Boldest of hearts that ever braved the sun,
> Took sanctuary within the holier blue,
> And sang a kindred soul out to his face,—
> Yet human at the red-ripe of the heart—
> When the first summons from the darkening earth
> Reached thee amid thy chambers, blanched their blue,
> And bared them of the glory—to drop down,
> To toil for man, to suffer or to die,—
> This is the same voice: can thy soul know change?
> Hail then, and hearken from the realms of help!
> Never may I commence my song, my due
> To God who best taught song by gift of thee,
> Except with bent head and beseeching hand—
> That still, despite the distance and the dark,
> What was, again may be; some interchange
> Of grace, some splendor once thy very thought,
> Some benediction anciently thy smile:
> —Never conclude, but raising hand and head
> Thither where eyes, that cannot reach, yet yearn
> For all hope, all sustainment, all reward,
> Their utmost up and on,—so blessing back
> In those thy realms of help, that heaven thy home,
> Some whiteness which, I judge, thy face makes proud,
> Some wanness where, I think, thy foot may fall!

Only once during her lifetime did Browning address a poem directly to his wife—the *One Word More. To E. B. B.*, which completes the two volumes of *Men and Women*, dramatic monologues done by Browning during his residence at Florence and constituting the finest collection of his shorter poems. But there are several indirect allusions to her, not only in this Florentine series, but in others. *By the Fireside*, one of the most charming poems of *Men and Women*, drew its setting from the woods about Bagni di Lucca, a summer resort between Florence and Pisa, which the Brownings visited in 1853; its spiritual atmosphere, however, comes from their own fireside at Casa Guidi, and it is not going too far to identify the hero of the poem with Browning himself, sitting there and indulging in fancies about his old age:—

> How well I know what I mean to do
>   When the long dark autumn-evenings come:
> And where, my soul, is thy pleasant hue?
>   With the music of all thy voices, dumb
> In life's November too!
>
> I shall be found by the fire, suppose,
>   O'er a great wise book as beseemeth age,
> While the shutters flap as the cross-wind blows
>   And I turn the page, and I turn the page,
> Not verse now, only prose!
>
> My perfect wife, my Leonor,
>   Oh heart, my own, oh eyes, mine too,
> Whom else could I dare look backward for,
>   With whom beside should I dare pursue
> The path gray heads abhor?
>
> With me, youth led . . . I will speak now,
>   No longer watch you as you sit
> Reading by fire-light, that great brow
>   And the spirit-small hand propping it,
> Mutely, my heart knows how—
>
> When, if I think but deep enough
>   You are wont to answer, prompt as rhyme;
> And you, too, to find without rebuff
>   Response your soul seeks many a time
> Piercing its fine flesh-stuff.

In 1851 the Brownings took their boy to London in the hope of effecting a reconciliation with Mrs. Browning's father, but Barrett was irreconcilable, left town, and refused to answer letters. The Brownings, however, met Carlyle, who took a fancy to them and insisted on going with them as far as Paris on the return journey.

They were in London again in 1855 to see *Men and Women* through the press, and met Tennyson and the Rossettis. Dante Gabriel Rossetti, in a letter written at the time, described an evening spent at the Brownings' as 'truly a night of the gods, not to be remembered without pride and pang.' Tennyson read *Maud*, which had just been published, and Browning followed with a sprightly rendering of *Fra Lippo Lippi* from *Men and Women*.

It was during the first return visit that Bayard Taylor had the good fortune to catch the Brownings on his way through London and left on record his impression of Browning at thirty-nine, with his lively, cheerful manner, quick voice, and perfect self-possession —more like an American than an Englishman. 'His dark hair was already streaked with gray about the temples. His complexion was fair, with perhaps the faintest olive tinge, eyes large, clear, and gray, nose strong and well cut, mouth full and rather broad, and chin pointed, though not prominent. His forehead broadened rapidly upwards from the outer angle of the eyes, slightly retreating. The strong individuality which marks his poetry was expressed not only in his face and head, but in his whole demeanor. He was about the medium height, strong in the shoulders, but slender at the waist, and his movements expressed a combination of vigor and elasticity.'

There is no question but that at this time Browning had reached his full maturity and was at the height of his poetic productivity. In *Men and Women* he maintains a high standard of excellence, and is less subject than he was, both before and after, to the overbalancing of emotion by intellectual, psychological, argumentative considerations. Italy not only enriched his imagination but provided him with subjects of high romantic interest. It supplied the background and sometimes more than the background of some of the best poems he ever wrote, *Love Among the Ruins*, *Fra Lippo Lippi*, *A Toccata of Galuppi's*, *By the Fireside*, *The Statue and the Bust*, *The Patriot*, *Andrea del Sarto*, *Old Pictures in Florence*, '*De Gustibus*,' *The Guardian Angel*, *Two in Campagna*, and *A Grammarian's Funeral*, all of which first appeared in *Men and Women* and must therefore have been composed in the Florentine period.

Italy supplied also the subject for his most massive achievement, *The Ring and the Book*, a poem of over twenty thousand lines which nineteenth century readers labored over with enthusiasm, but which now ranks with Spenser's *Faery Queen* among the works of genius which few people have read to the end. Oddly enough, the story itself formed the basis of a romantic drama which a popular

American actor found the medium for his ability; but there was not much of Browning left in *Caponsacchi* beyond romantic atmosphere. The old Roman murder story Browning discovered in a 'old yellow book' he picked up for a lira at a secondhand bookstall in Florence as he was crossing the square of San Lorenzo. This famous case of the seventeenth century resulted in the conviction and execution of a brokendown Count, Guido Franceschini, who married a young girl (Pompilia) of humble birth for her money and then subjected her to a series of humiliations and petty persecutions which drove her to run away from her husband's roof under the protection of a young priest who took pity on her (Caponsacchi). Guido, with four assassins, pursued and murdered her, along with her parents. The chief interest of the poem lies in the character of the child-wife Pompilia (evidently modeled on Mrs. Browning) and her relation to Caponsacchi, whom Guido accused of committing adultery with her, not only falsely but insincerely, as Browning holds and as was held at the time by the Pope of that period, to whom the case was referred for ultimate decision. There are long, dreary, and difficult stretches in the poem, but it contains many beautiful and touching passages, if one has time and patience to seek them out. It was published in 1868–69 and made a great impression upon the public of that day.

After burying his wife in the Protestant cemetery at Florence, Browning left the city for ever. He settled in London and for some years devoted his main attention to his son's education. Later he went out a great deal into society and became one of the social as well as the literary personages of the English metropolis. Every few years, up to the date of his death, he published a volume of poems, some of them long and philosophical, either by way of psychological analysis or by way of metaphysical argument, some of them in the form of the dramatic monologue, in which he excelled. Of the latter the most notable collection was *Dramatis Personæ* (1864), which included some of his best religious poems— *Abt Vogler, Rabbi Ben Ezra, A Death in the Desert, Caliban upon Setebos,* and *Prospice.* To the end of his life Browning retained a firm faith in the liberal evangelicalism which he had adopted in his youth.

In the last years of his life he spent much of his time in Venice, with his son, who had married an American lady, and bought a house on the Grand Canal, the Palazzo Rezzonico. Here he was taken ill in December, 1889, and died on the same day that his last volume of poems was published—*Asolando,* so named from a hill city near Florence to which Browning was much attached. In the Epilogue he gave final testimony to his belief in a future life of beneficent activity, speaking of himself as:—

One who never turned his back but marched breast forward,
  Never doubted clouds would break,
Never dreamed, though right were worsted, wrong would triumph,
  Held we fall to rise, are baffled to fight better,
      Sleep to wake.

ALFRED TENNYSON
(*1809–1892*)

Tennyson's reputation as a poet and thinker was much more violently attacked than Browning's in the twentieth century, doubtless because he was much more popular and reflected more completely Victorian prejudices and limitations. Tennyson, moreover, adopted and developed the traditional style in poetry, from which Browning tried to escape; the latter was, also, greatly influenced by John Donne, whose poetry is just now (1934) very much in fashion. The attack upon Tennyson was twofold, first upon the poverty and conventionality of his ideas; and, in the second place, upon the conventional form in which his ideas were expressed. Protests on both counts were made by his contemporaries. Carlyle, in spite of his deep admiration for Tennyson as a man, saw in the *Idylls of the King* only 'the inward perfection of *vacancy*'; and Meredith wrote in a letter to a friend: '*The Holy Grail* is wonderful, isn't it? The lines are satin lengths, the figures Sèvres china. I have not the courage to offer to review it; I should say such things. To think! it's in these days that the foremost poet of the country goes on fluting of creatures that have not a breath of vital humanity in them, and doles us out his regular five-feet with the old trick of the vowel endings. The Euphuist's tongue, the Exquisite's leg, the Curate's moral sentiments, the British matron and her daughter's purity of tone:—so he talks, so he walks, so he snuffles, so he appears divine.—I repeat with my Grannam—to think!—and to hear the chorus of praise too! Why, this stuff is not the Muse, it's Musery. The man has got hold of the Muses' clothes-line and hung it with jewelry.' This was in 1869, and at that date Meredith was lamenting (privately) that the public had corrupted so fine a natural singer. 'In his degraded state I really believe he is useful, for he reflects as much as our Society chooses to show of itself. The English notion of

passion, virtue, valor, is in his pages.' Half a century later Harold
Nicolson won critical fame by pointing out that Tennyson, by
nature a purely lyrical poet, the lineal successor of Keats and
Coleridge, was perverted by the Philistine spirit of the Victorian
Era into a sort of 'Secretary for Poetry in the Government of
Queen Victoria and Prince Albert.' F. L. Lucas, the latest of
Tennysonian critics, sums up the views of the younger generation
in the charges that as a thinker Tennyson was not only incom-
petent, but insincere:—'Tennyson's metaphysics, they feel may
have been poor but honest, though even there he cheated a good
deal in letting the wish be father to the thought; but his moralizing
they find past all endurance. The *Idylls of the King* are the apotheo-
sis of a prig; his discussion of feminism begins in a picnic and is
drowned by a wedding-bell; his politics consisted at home in hedg-
ing, abroad in that type of cackling bluster which was to end in
hatching, to its own ridiculous consternation, the dragon's egg of
the war.' The best defense Mr. Lucas can find is that (1) it is
unreasonable to expect poets to be profound thinkers; and (2) with
Tennyson, as with other writers, the only sane course is to enjoy
the good and forget the rest. The 'rest' is indeed apparently well
on its way to be forgotten; the danger is that some things that
are really good will not be remembered; and that Tennyson will
be dismissed with contempt by young people who do not know
his work and have not enough wit to judge whether it is good or
bad.

Tennyson's sympathy with what might be called the forward
view in political and social matters has been already noted in
Chapter II; and it is also noteworthy that on the day the Reform
Bill was passed, he and his brothers, sons of a Lincolnshire rector,
astonished the villagers of Somersby by ringing the church bells.
At Trinity College, Cambridge, he was a member of a small society
called The Apostles, young men who took themselves very seriously
and in some cases attained important positions in after-life. Of
these the most promising was thought to be the famous historian's
son, Arthur Hallam, who became Tennyson's most intimate
friend and was engaged to be married to his sister, Emily. All
accounts of Tennyson in his college days represent him as a person
of extraordinary attractiveness—an Apollo for beauty and a
Hercules for strength:—'A figure rising to six feet was crowned by
a head which already suggested the large kingliness notable in
later years. Above the broad brow the hair lay dark and thick,
falling in waves over the ears, with a hint of gold in it for the light

to find. The face made a general impression of haughty fastidious-ness, of an intense sensibility balanced by a high preoccupation, the eyes being large, luminous, and heavy-lidded, the nose strong, even dictatorial, but slender also and rarely chiseled, the lips full, but so shapely in their curves as to suggest a scorn of license, which was re-inforced by the pointed chin. Foreign and romantic in its swarthiness, the face was yet commandingly aristocratic; it was even more cultivated than sublime. The aquiline nose, steady eyes, and somewhat deprecating mouth contended with the large-ness of head and brow and the luxuriant hair to leave upon the onlooker a conflicting impression both of power and of preciosity.' (Hugh I'Anson Fausset).

Even before he went to college Tennyson's poetic vocation was manifest: in 1827 he and his elder brother, Charles, issued a volume of poems, and a kindly bookseller paid them ten pounds for the copyright. In 1829 he won the Chancellor's Medal for English verse with *Timbuctoo;* in 1830 he published *Poems chiefly Lyrical* and was fairly launched on a poetical career. A perfervid eulogy by Arthur Hallam in the Englishman's Magazine provoked a smart retort from 'Christopher North,' the pen-name of a well-known Scotch critic, in Blackwood's Magazine; and Tennyson's next volume, *Poems 1833,* brought a stinging article from the Quarterly. Tennyson, who was sensitive to criticism, was much discouraged, and did not publish again for nearly ten years, saying he had had 'abuse enough.'

Owing to his father's death, Tennyson left Cambridge in 1831, without a degree but without regret. The tutors had taught him nothing, 'feeding not the heart'; but in after-years he looked back to the discussions with his fellow-students in their rooms:—

> Where once we held debate, a band
>   Of youthful friends, on mind and art,
>   And labor, and the changing mart,
> And all the framework of the land.

His father's successor at Somersby was kind enough to leave the family in possession of the rectory for some years, and Tenny-son settled down there, contentedly enough, to perfect his poetic gift and give long hours to study. He had a regular programme, beginning the week with history and German, and ending it with Italian and Greek, with chemistry, botany, electricity, animal physiology, and mechanics to fill the interim. 'He observed the facts of Nature with marvellous patience and recorded them with

lavish exactitude.' He was fully conscious of the mystery lying
behind little things:—

> Flower in the crannied wall,
> I pluck you out of the crannies,
> I hold you here, root and all, in my hand,
> Little flower—but *if* I could understand
> What you are, root and all, and all in all,
> I should know what God and man is.

He read Lyell's *Geology* and *Vestiges of the Natural History of
Creation*, a popular precursor of evolutionary doctrine by an
anonymous writer (long after revealed as an enterprising Scottish
publisher, Robert Chambers), who argued that the earth was 'the
result not of any immediate or personal exertion on the part of the
Deity, but of natural laws which are expressions of His will.' It
was this interest in early Victorian science, which for Tennyson
included physics, geology, astronomy, and anthropology, that
enabled him, at any rate in appearance, to anticipate Darwin and
to win from Huxley the tribute that he was the only modern poet,
perhaps the only poet since Lucretius, who had taken the trouble
to understand the work and method of men of science. The unexpected death of Arthur Hallam in 1833 drove Tennyson to
attempt to reconcile traditional religion with scientific discovery:

> Are God and Nature then at strife
>   That Nature lends such evil dreams?
> So careful of the type she seems,
>   So careless of the single life . . .
>
> 'So careful of the type?' but no,
>   From scarped cliff and quarried stone
> She cries, 'A thousand types are gone:
>   I care for nothing, all shall go.
>
> 'Thou makest thine appeal to me:
>   I bring to life, I bring to death:
> The spirit does but mean the breath:
>   I know no more.' And he, shall he,
>
> Man, her last work, who seemed so fair,
>   Such splendid purpose in his eyes,
> Who rolled the psalm to wintry skies,
>   Who built him fanes of fruitless prayer,

> Who trusted God was love indeed
>   And love Creation's final law—
> Though Nature, red in tooth and claw
>   With ravine, shrieked against his creed—
>
> Who loved, who suffered countless ills,
>   Who battled for the True, the Just,
> Be blown about the desert dust,
>   Or sealed within the iron hills?

Such were the meditations that filled Tennyson's inner life between Hallam's death and the publication of *In Memoriam* (1850). His external life was comparatively uneventful. After his mother left Somersby, the family experimented without much success in search of a suitable home, and Tennyson, who had long been engaged, was unable to marry for lack of means. He began to be well known in London and made friends. 'One of the finest-looking men in the world,' wrote Carlyle, 'I do not meet in these late decades such company over a pipe.' Mrs. Carlyle was equally enthusiastic: 'He is a very handsome man and a noble-hearted one, with something of the gypsy in his appearance, which for me is perfectly charming.'

The *Poems* of 1842, issued after much hesitation and with some trepidation, included some of the finest work Tennyson ever did— *Morte d'Arthur*, the first treatment by him of the Arthurian legend and the best; *Locksley Hall*, so much better in its youthful aspiration than the pessimistic and embittered *Locksley Hall Sixty Years After*, which he wrote in his disillusioned old age. Best of all was *Ulysses*, which breathed a more manly air than Tennyson had hitherto exhibited and used a more masculine utterance:—

> Though much is taken, much abides; and though
> We were not now that strength which in old days
> Moved earth and heaven; that which we are, we are;
> One equal temper of heroic hearts,
> Made weak by time and fate, but strong in will
> To strive, to seek, to find, and not to yield.

The 1842 volume was a great success, both with the critics and the public. But, even so, Tennyson did not have enough to marry on. In an evil hour he put his money into 'The Patent Decorative Carving and Sculpture Co.,' an attempt to combine art, machinery, and philanthropy, which was a ghastly failure, and might have been a still more ghastly failure if it had been a success. Fortunately, something was saved from the wreck by the prevision of Tennyson's rich relatives, who insured the promoter's life and were able to collect on his opportune death. A year later Carlyle's influence secured Tennyson a government pension of a thousand dollars a year, and *The Princess* (1847) was a popular success; it had just enough of a forward view as to the education of women, and just enough of a compromise with conventional opinion, to be liked by everybody; the charming connective lyrics by which the poem is now chiefly remembered were inserted in the later edition of 1850. After the publication of *In Memoriam* in the latter year Tennyson was able to marry ('The peace of God came into my life before the altar when I wedded her,' he said of his wife long after). In the same year he became poet laureate in succession to Wordsworth, and he was soon making five hundred pounds a year; with money borrowed from his publisher, he was able to acquire, at Farringford in the Isle of Wight, an estate upon which he lived happily for the rest of his life. 'Here was to be found all that was pure, cultured, and gracious, in that upper middle-class home life of which the Victorian age can rightly boast the achievement. It was perhaps the one ideal realized by that age, and, at its best, the one entirely satisfactory contribution to the art of life.' (Fausset).

It has been suggested that by this time Tennyson had expressed all the ideas he had in him and that afterwards all he did was to exercise and develop his art of expression. *Maud* (1855) was certainly not calculated to increase respect for Tennyson as a thinker; it is described as 'a monodrama,' and the one speaker, beginning as a neurotic, and passing through a phase of mania, has hardly recovered complete nervous equilibrium at the end of the poem. The dramatic cloak might shield the poet from criticism of some of the extravagances of expression; but the opinions seem to be really Tennyson's own; and if we are to give him credit for the onslaught on the vices of industrialism, it is difficult to forgive him for his laudation of the virtues of militarism. It was the time of the Crimean War, in which nobody concerned came out with credit except the common soldier and Florence Nightingale. By sheer stupidity a brigade of light cavalry received orders to charge the Russian guns and obeyed. Tennyson's imagination was fired by a phrase in the Times, 'some one had blundered,' and in a few minutes he struck off his *Charge of the Light Brigade;* the martial accents of this patriotic poem were soon echoing from one end of the country to the other; and from that moment Tennyson was the people's darling. They had certainly little to be proud of either in the conduct of the campaign or in the results of the shocking waste of men and money on the field and in the hospitals; as a Conservative Foreign Minister, Lord Salisbury, cynically remarked, long after, the English people of that time 'put their money on the wrong horse'; they ought to have backed the other side.

Maud springs from a short lyric first printed in 1837:—

> O that 'twere possible
> After long grief and pain
> To find the arms of my true love
> Round me once again!

Someone asked Tennyson what it meant; and he revolved the answer in his own mind till the little lyric expanded itself into a drama, in which 'different phases of passion in one person take the place of different characters.' The plot, such as it is, is that of Scott's *Bride of Lammermoor*, brought up to date by topical allusions to speculators, promoters, pickpockets, burglars, babykillers, adulterators, dishonest tradesmen, cotton spinners, and other supposed representatives of modern industrialism. There is even a dash of modern science:—

> A monstrous eft was of old the Lord and Master of Earth,
> For him did his high sun flame, and his river billowing ran,
> And he felt himself in his force to be Nature's crowning race.
> As nine months go to the shaping an infant ripe for its birth,
> So many a million of ages have gone to the making of man:
> He now is first, but is he the last? Is he not too base?

Tennyson varies his meters with remarkable versatility to the varying mood of his monologuizing hero, and there are some good resounding lines about the hypocrisies of modern society; but, like *The Princess*, *Maud* will be chiefly remembered for its lyrics, beginning with:

> A voice by the cedar tree
> In the meadow under the Hall!
> She is singing an air that is known to me,
> A passionate ballad gallant and gay,
> A martial song like a trumpet's call!
> Singing alone in the morning of life,
> In the happy morning of life and of May,
> Singing of men that in battle array,
> Ready in heart and ready in hand,
> March with banner and bugle and fife
> To the death, for their native land.

So, on to

> O let the solid ground
> Not fail beneath my feet

and

> Birds in the high Hall-garden
> When twilight was falling,
> Maud, Maud, Maud, Maud,
> They were crying and calling.

Then

> Go not, happy day,
> From the shining fields,
> Go not, happy day,
> Till the maiden yields.

and

> I have led her home, my love, my only friend,
> There is none like her, none.

Even 'Come into the garden, Maud,' which became fearfully hackneyed as a popular song, has that musical power which Tennyson at his best possesses in such an extraordinary degree. He has not, and knew he had not, the simple direct singing quality of Burns, who was much more in touch with reality and human emotion; but in the lyric of the literary type Tennyson is unexcelled.

Of his attempts at epic, in *The Idylls of the King*, and at drama in *Queen Mary*, *Harold*, and *Becket* there is not much that need be said. The plays afforded a suitable medium for Sir Henry Irving, Ellen Terry, and the Lyceum Company (including the scene-painter) to exercise their remarkable talents, but they are neither good acting drama—the characters never come alive—nor even good closet drama—they cannot be read without boredom. The *Idylls* were an attempt to Victorianize Malory and the Mabinogion and to make over King Arthur in the likeness of Prince Albert; the attempt failed, because the medieval material would not lend itself to such treatment. The Victorian spirit and the Victorian conventions were too alien from the original, and the medieval trappings made the modern ideas sound hollow and even absurd.

In Tennyson's later period the modern reader will probably find most satisfaction in the stirring ballad of the Last Fight of the Revenge, founded upon the contemporary accounts of Sir Walter Raleigh and Linschoten; and in the dialectical poems, if he does not find the dialect too difficult. In these Tennyson at last came

into touch with reality and with a kind of humanity he knew and
appreciated. The *Northern Farmer* (Old Style) was inspired by
the dying words of a farm-bailiff, 'God A'mighty little knows what
He's about, a-taking me. An' Squire will be so mad an' all'; and
the New Style farmer with his

> Coom up, proputty, proputty—that's what I 'ears 'im saäy—
> Proputty, proputty, proputty—canter an' canter awaäy,

was also taken directly from life. Both these poems, as well as
The Spinster's Sweet–Arts, show Tennyson to have been by no
means deficient in a quality some of his critics have denied him—
the gift of humor. The old maiden lady, identifying her cats with
her former suitors, whose names she gives them, is a charmingly
comic figure.

In his last years Tennyson became more and more a national
possession. To the ageing Queen he was no longer a court official
but a personal friend, who talked to her about Albert, shared her
profound conservatism, and expressed her own conception of her
character and purposes better than she could herself:

> Her court was pure; her life serene;
>   God gave her peace; her land reposed,
>   A thousand claims to reverence closed
> In her as mother, wife, and Queen.
>
> And statesmen at her council met
>   Who knew the seasons when to take
>   Occasion by the hand, and make
> The bounds of freedom wider yet
>
> By shaping some august decree,
>   Which kept her throne unshaken still,
>   Broad based upon her people's will
> And compassed by the inviolate sea.

His increasing popularity resulted in an increased income, and
he was able to acquire a second country place, beautifully situated,
Aldworth in Surrey. After twice refusing a baronetcy, he accepted
a peerage. The great ones of the nation came to him as honored
guests, the small ones crowded railway stations to see him pass by.
He played his part well, and usually maintained a stately dignity,
getting more and more handsome in his old age; but occasionally
he could be humorously gruff. To the end of his life he enjoyed

reading *Maud* aloud to his guests, and once, after reading the stanza about 'birds in the high Hall-garden, calling Maud, Maud,' he turned to a fair young thing by his side and asked 'What birds'? Taken by surprise, she blushingly stammered 'Nightingales, I suppose.' 'No,' he retorted sententiously, 'Crows.' When Longfellow and his daughters came to visit him, one of the young ladies was sitting at the foot of a staircase and heard her host (of whom she was in mortal terror) coming downstairs behind her. To hide her embarrassment she hastily snatched up and opened the nearest volume, which happened to be a copy of Longfellow's poems—probably a presentation copy, placed there for the occasion. Tennyson glanced over her shoulder and remarked, 'I should have thought you had enough of that at home.' To an older lady, who commented upon Dr. Johnson's table manners and said 'he stirred his tea with his finger—and a dirty one at that,' he made the retort, 'The dirt was in your own mind, Madam.' She had spirit enough to come back with the reply, 'I came to see a lion—not a bear.'

Tennyson's ideal knight

> Who reverenced his conscience as his king;
> Whose glory was, redressing human wrong;
> Who spoke no slander, no, nor listened to it;
> Who loved one only and who clave to her—

contrasted ludicrously with the actual knights of Queen Victoria, who gained their spurs in trade, or politics, or the law, and were merely respectable representatives of a commercial civilization. But in itself the ideal was not an unworthy one, and the people of Dante's or Shakespeare's or Milton's time fell just as short of Christian standards of perfection. This 'hard-boiled' age may see in the difference between the actual and the imagined merely hypocrisy, but there was at any rate an element of beauty in the ideal which Tennyson expressed almost with his dying breath:—

> Sunset and evening star,
>   And one clear call for me!
> And may there be no moaning of the bar,
>   When I put out to sea,
>
> But such a tide as moving seems asleep,
>   Too full for sound and foam,
> When that which drew from out the boundless deep
>   Turns again home.

Twilight and evening bell
  And after that the dark!
And may there be no sadness of farewell,
  When I embark;

For though from out our bourne of Time and Place
  The flood may bear me far,
I hope to see my Pilot face to face
  When I have crossed the bar.

PART II
MID-VICTORIANS
(*1860–1880*)

CHAPTER VI

MID–VICTORIANS

(*1860–1880*)

THE Middle Period is naturally the most characteristically Victorian of the three divisions we have, for the purposes of convenience, adopted. It has lost the aristocratic elegance of the eighteenth century; and has not yet acquired the democratic and socialistic tendencies which mark the last years of the nineteenth. It is the *bourgeois* period *par excellence*—the reign of the middle class, triumphant and confident; their ideas, their standards, their prejudices prevail. Only during the middle years of the century, says a recent writer in the London Times Literary Supplement, were 'values secure, individualism clearly triumphant, all for the best in the best of all possible worlds—for, though poets and prophets might attack this or that abominable excrescence, they were chary indeed of attacking the foundations, and the scientists and agnostics, though they rejected God, were in no doubt about the imperative claims of morality.' The most important book published in 1859 was undoubtedly Darwin's *Origin of Species;* but perhaps the most characteristic was Smiles' *Self-Help*, which sold twenty thousand copies the first year and a hundred and fifty thousand within thirty years, in addition to many other books by the same author on the same theme; the successive volumes might be called *Thrift, Character, Duty*, or what not, but they all preached the same smug doctrine that to be industrious was to be successful, to be successful was to be happy, and the boy who followed in the footsteps of the Edisons, Eastmans, and Fords of Mid-Victorian England was fulfilling all possible requirements, both for this world and for the next. Matthew Arnold, the great contemporary critic of Mid-Victorianism, crystallized the gospel according to Smiles in 'the beautiful sentence Sir Daniel Gooch quoted to the Swindon workmen, which I treasure as Mrs. Gooch's Golden Rule, or the Divine Injunction "Be ye perfect" done into British—the sentence Sir Daniel Gooch's mother repeated to him every morning when he was going to work: "Ever remember, my dear Dan, that you should look forward to being some day manager of that concern."'

THE EVOLUTION THEORY

The popular catchword of the evolution theory, 'the survival of the fittest,' fell in well enough with the middle-class conception of life, though the successful business men who used the phrase probably imported into it a providential sense not intended by the scientist: to the successful business man the fact that he had vanquished his competitors was an indication of the divine approval; his survival was to the scientist merely an indication that he had succeeded in adapting himself to his environment. The rapid acceptance of the theory, not only by the scientists but by the general public, was no doubt due in part to the common conviction that this was the best of all possible worlds, England the best of all existing nations, the middle class 'the backbone of England,' and the manufacturing districts the stronghold of the middle class, 'what Lancashire said to-day England would say to-morrow,'— and the rest of the world, no doubt, the day after. Nevertheless, the triumph of the idea of evolution was one of the most remarkable changes of opinion in the history of mankind, not only for the swiftness with which it was accomplished but for its far-reaching implications. The Copernican theory, which revolutionized the traditional conception of the place of the earth in the universe, had not been accepted by so intelligent and highly educated a man as John Milton more than a century later, and its implications are even yet very insufficiently absorbed by the average man. The evolution theory, which revolutionized the traditional conception of man's relation to the other animals, was accepted by almost every intelligent man within a generation, although its implications with reference to orthodox religious beliefs were very hotly discussed from the first.

The idea of evolution, somewhat vaguely conceived, was not new. As R. S. Lull pointed out in *The Ways of Life* (1925), Aristotle 'had substantially the modern conception of the evolution of life from a primordial soft mass of living matter.' When the medieval Church undertook the reconciliation of the teaching of Aristotle with the text of Holy Scripture, its leaders had the good sense to avoid a clash between the account of Creation given in the first chapter of *Genesis* and the discoveries or theories of science. St. Augustine offered an easy way of escape by accepting the opening verse of the Bible story—'In the beginning God created the heaven and the earth'—as fundamental truth and treating the rest as allegory. St. Thomas Aquinas, more metaphysically, said God made all created things *causaliter*—that is, God was the original Cause of all Being. It was later theologians who insisted on a literal interpretation of the Scriptural story and involved the Church in a difficult position from which it has not, even yet, altogether succeeded in disentangling itself.

It was a Protestant divine, Archbishop Ussher (1581–1656), who made matters worse by putting into the margin of the English Bible definite dates as to the occurrence of the events narrated in the Scriptural record, founded, it is true, upon that record as he understood it, but bound to cause embarrassment when his hard and fast interpretation of the ancient documents became stereotyped in popular tradition. There was not only the definite date of 4004 B.C. as the year of Creation, which brought the Scriptural record into conflict with modern geology, but as the discovery of fossils proceeded, it became more and more difficult to reconcile the existence of all these huge animals with the dimensions of Noah's Ark; there was not room for them. To account for the omission of any reference to these prehistoric animals in the Deluge of Genesis, the ecclesiastical geologists had invented the theory of previous catastrophes to provide for their disappearance, and the necessary catastrophes had reached the number of twenty-seven by the beginning of the Victorian Era. Then the English geologist, Sir Charles Lyell, overturned the elaborate catastrophic theory by the simple suggestion that it was reasonable to suppose that the behavior of the earth in prehistoric time was similar to its behavior in historic time. Lyell also demanded geologic ages far exceeding in extent the time allowed by Archbishop Ussher's chronology; but as Lyell himself was an orthodox believer and a man of great tact and suavity, the clergy were not alarmed by his 'uniformitarian' theory, which made little impression upon the popular imagination, though it had in it the germs of a revolution in the popular conception of the order of nature.

Lyell was not an evolutionist at the time of the publication of his *Principles of Geology* (1830–33), and he succeeded in maintaining a judicious reserve on that burning issue up to the time of his death (1875), although he was repeatedly pressed by Darwin to give public expression to his acceptance of the theory. The controversy as to the origin of species had been going on since the beginning of the century, and the French naturalists had given a certain vogue to their theory of 'transformisme,' which was really evolution under another name. There were a million known species to account for, and the traditional explanation of a supernatural creation of each of them became increasingly difficult to accept; the rival theory, that of 'spontaneous generation,' was evidently no explanation at all; and the general similarity in structure between fish and reptile, bird and beast, naturally suggested a connection by way of descent or development. The great French naturalist Buffon laid stress upon the importance of environment, and his successor Lamarck, in his *Philosophie Zoologique* (1809) suggested that species were evolved by the transmission of acquired characteristics; that the giraffe, for instance, got his long neck by striving to reach the higher leaves on the tall palm trees. Lamarckism is still a recognized school of evolutionary thought, though the transmission of acquired characteristics is not a theory generally accepted by modern zoölogists. Darwin's suggestion, that the antelopes with the long necks survived in conditions under which the short-necked ones disappeared, still meets with more general approval. But it should be clearly understood that Darwin's contribution was the theory of the process of natural selection, and that he did not originate the name or the idea of evolution. His contemporary, Herbert Spencer, published in 1852 an essay entitled *The Development Hypothesis*, in which the theory of evolution is fully and clearly set forth; and in 1858 Spencer issued a programme for a series of works dealing with astronomic evolution, geologic evolution, the evolution of life in general, and evolution in individual organisms. Darwin's *Origin of Species* was not published until 1859.

Darwin contributed not only a reasonable explanation of the process by which the development of species might be supposed to have taken place, but also a mass of evidence, carefully collected and systematically arranged, in support of the probability of the idea of evolution. Born in 1809, he was at the time of the publication of the *Origin of Species* fifty years of age, and had spent more than half his life up to that time in the accumulation of his material. In the years 1831–36 he was serving as a naturalist on H.M.S. Beagle during a long voyage of exploration and scientific investigation, and was especially impressed by the fauna and flora of the secluded Galapagos Islands. Lyell's *Principles of Geology* altered his entire view of the species problem, but it was reading the Essay of Malthus on *Population* that gave him the suggestion of the struggle for life and the survival of the individuals and species best fitted to adapt themselves to their environment. This was in 1838, when he had already begun to make notes for the purpose of his investigation, and in 1842 he was able to draw up a first sketch of his theory of natural selection. But he continued to work quietly and steadily at Downe, for he was by disposition a modest and retiring naturalist, disinclined to invite public attention and shrinking somewhat fearfully from premature publication. He liked to work deliberately and to think things over; an investigation of the habits of the earthworms on his own lawn, begun in 1836, was not brought to a conclusion till 1881, and he would not have published the *Origin of Species* in 1859, if his hand had not been forced by circumstances. Fortunately, the wealth of the Wedgwood Potteries, which came to him, partly by inheritance, partly by marriage with his cousin, provided him with an income which placed him beyond the need of earning money. Thus, though he communicated with various other scientists in Europe and America as to what he was doing, it was only in 1856 that he began to set in order and transcribe the evidence he had gathered together during the previous twenty years.

He was still engaged in this laborious process of literary composition in 1858 when he received a communication from A. R. Wallace, a younger scientist working in the same field, which completely upset the philosophic calm of the retiring naturalist in his contemplative seclusion. Wallace, studying the prolific vegetation and animal life he had come into contact with during a voyage on the River Amazon, had leapt at one bound to the same conclusion as Darwin had arrived at by years of patient research and cogitation—that natural selection was the process by which the evolution of species was effected. Wallace wrote out an account of his discovery and sent it to Darwin, as the older and more influential scientist, asking him for help in getting it published. Darwin's first impulse was to publish Wallace's paper and say nothing about his own work. But ultimately, through the interposition of Sir Charles Lyell and of Sir Joseph Hooker, the leading botanist of the time, Wallace's paper and a summary of his own work which Darwin had drawn up some years before were issued contemporaneously in the Proceedings of the Linnæan Society in 1858.

As Sir Arthur Keith observed lately, these innocent-looking scientific papers contained intellectual dynamite, but either people were not aware of it, or being aware of it, they made up their minds to handle the package gingerly, for very little fuss was made about it. Sir Richard Owen, the leader of the conservative school of scientists and the President of the British Association for that year, in his annual address made a passing reference to the two papers and remarked that he had been struck himself by the possible importance of natural selection as a conception to be taken into consideration in connection with the theory of the development of species. He was convinced, however, that this had nothing to do with the origin of man: the structure of man's brain was in itself enough to set him quite apart from the rest of the animal creation.

THE CHURCH INTERVENES

So matters rested until the publication of *The Origin of Species by means of Natural Selection* by Charles Darwin in 1859. Darwin, though he was naturally taken aback at the prospect of being forestalled by Wallace, was careless about popular esteem; he said he would be satisfied if the book convinced three men—the leading geologist, Lyell; the leading botanist, Hooker; and Thomas Henry Huxley, who was already acquiring a reputation as a teacher of zoölogy at a London college. Huxley had seen the proofs, and by a stroke of extraordinary luck the review copy sent to the London Times was forwarded to him, with the request that he would write an article upon it. No one then living was so well qualified by knowledge and literary ability for the task, and Huxley performed it with enthusiasm. The widespread attention commanded by the Times review made it clear that a clash between the scientists and the theologians could no longer be avoided, and both sides girded themselves for the fray; there was even a tacit agreement upon a pitched battle at the annual meeting of the British Association for the Advancement of Science in 1860, which happened to be at Oxford. The Bishop of Oxford, a versatile and popular prelate named Samuel Wilberforce, duly coached by Sir Richard Owen, the leader of the older scientific school, was chosen to open the debate on behalf of the Church, and as Darwin refused to be coaxed away from his garden and study at Downe, the lot of leading the defense fell upon Huxley. The Bishop, who was unable from lack of scientific knowledge, to discuss Darwin's theory on its merits, attempted to win a rhetorical victory by ridicule and a personal challenge to Professor Huxley to say whether he traced his monkey ancestry through his grandfather or his grandmother. Huxley skilfully turned the tables upon his antagonist, and won a striking personal triumph in debate as well as a victory for evolution in the first skirmish. But this part of the story will find a more appropriate place in our account of Huxley's career. The clergy had chosen as their fighting ground the question of man's relation to the other animals, and the evolutionists accepted this issue; Huxley and Darwin presented their views in separate books, Huxley in *Man's Place in Nature* (1863) and Darwin, who had rather avoided this issue in the *Origin of Species*, in *The Descent of Man* (1871). These were the outstanding literary and scientific contributions to the evolution controversy, which raged furiously for about twenty years, conducted vigorously—and sometimes bitterly—with tongue and pen by both sides. The result was an indisputable victory for the evolutionists. Huxley lived to attend another meeting of the British Association at Oxford in 1894, at which Lord Salisbury, the leader of the Conservative party and Lord Chancellor of the University, declared as President of the Association that the theory of evolution had been accepted, with substantial unanimity, by the scientific world. Huxley wrote to his friend Hooker: 'It was queer to sit there and hear the doctrines you and I were damned for, thirty-four years ago, enunciated as matters of course, disputed by no reasonable man.'

BIBLICAL CRITICISM

Not all the clergy, it is fair to say, treated Darwin's presentation of the theory of evolution with contempt and derision. Frederick Temple, afterwards Headmaster of Rugby, Bishop of Exeter, and Archbishop of Canterbury, the Sunday after the debate between the Bishop of Oxford and Professor Huxley, in the University Church of St. Mary's, preached a sermon to the Members of the British Association in which he gave 'a learned and friendly exposition of the Darwinian theory.' Temple and Jowett, who later became famous as Master of Balliol College, Oxford, were both contributors to *Essays and Reviews* (1860), a volume encouraging a more liberal view of church doctrine and practice. Temple wrote: 'He is guilty of high treason against the faith who fears the result of any investigation, whether philosophical, or scientific, or historical.' The book was formally condemned by the assembled bishops, at the instigation of the Bishop of Oxford, but the condemnation did not prevent the future promotion of the authors.

A more serious mistake on the part of the ecclesiastical authorities was their treatment of J. W. Colenso (1814–83), Bishop of Natal. Sent out to South Africa as a missionary bishop, Colenso took in hand the conversion of a Zulu chief, and they had many conversations together about the wanderings of the Israelites in the desert, a subject which interested the chief, as he had a first-hand knowledge of pastoral, nomadic life. The upshot was that the bishop did not convert the chief, but the chief brought the bishop to the conviction that the Bible account of the journey of the Israelites to the promised land contained serious inaccuracies. He embodied the results of further reflection on these matters in a commentary entitled *The Pentateuch and the Book of Joshua Critically Examined* (1862–79). His conclusions shocked the local clergy so much that they met in solemn conclave, and in 1863 Colenso was deposed and excommunicated by the Bishop of Cape Town. He appealed to the English law courts and was re-instated (1866); but the prolonged litigation and the accompanying controversy had a considerable share in undermining the authority of the Church. D. C. Somervell remarks: 'Most of what Colenso said is now accepted as obviously true, and the educated clergy of to-day, far from deploring the spread of such knowledge, are more inclined to deplore the fact that large sections of the nominally religious laity take so little intelligent interest in their Bibles that they are apt to be shocked when they happen to come across facts which are the commonplaces of Biblical scholarship.'

An even more flagrant instance of clerical short-sightedness was the reception given to Professor J. R. Seeley's *Ecce Homo* (1865). Without questioning Christ's divinity, he stressed the human side of Jesus of Nazareth in his book, which was entirely sympathetic and reverent in tone. But it was 'furiously abused' by Dr. Pusey, the Anglo-Catholic divine, and Lord Shaftesbury, the Evangelical leader, described it as 'the most pestilential volume ever vomited forth from the jaws of Hell.'

Matthew Arnold, the leading critic of this middle period, saw that the blind ecclesiastical hostility to modern investigation of the Christian monuments and refusal to accept the results of scholarship would work harm to religion, and he attempted to act as a mediator between the contending parties. He counted himself a faithful member of the Church of England, and he defended its interests against the attacks of the militant Nonconformists, whose life he imaged as 'a life of jealousy of the Establishment, disputes, tea meetings, openings of chapels, sermons,' contrasting this with 'an ideal of a human life completing itself on all sides, and aspiring with all its organs after sweetness, light, and perfection.' The Puritan middle class, in his view, was too much obsessed by two prevailing fears—the fear of bankruptcy and the fear of eternal damnation; put positively, their absorbing interests were, he thought, making money and saving their own souls. To his mind there was too much Hebraism—the Old Testament religion of material prosperity—and too little Hellenism—Arnold's own Gospel of 'Sweetness and light'—in the way of life of the Non-conformist middle class, whom he described as 'Philistine' in their crass material interests, as against the aristocratic 'Barbarians' and the ignorant 'Populace' of Victorian England. Yet from his father, Dr. Thomas Arnold, the famous Headmaster of Rugby, Matthew Arnold had inherited a deep conviction of the importance of morals—he defined religion as 'morality touched by emotion,' and said conduct was three-fourths of life; he had a high admiration for the Hebrew conception of God: 'the Eternal Power, not our-selves, which makes for righteousness.' But he found in the middle class, together with energy, enterprise, self-reliance, seriousness, 'a narrow range of intellect and knowledge, a stunted sense of beauty, a low standard of manners, and a defective type of religion.' His remedy for this state of things was culture. 'Culture,' he wrote, 'has two characters. On one side it is knowledge, and is prompted by the impulse to know things, on the other side it is reform, and it is prompted by the desire to make truth prevail.' Arnold devoted most of his mature life, apart from his official duties as a school inspector, to 'a disinterested endeavor to learn and propa-gate the best that is known and thought in the world,' and to make wisdom and the will of God prevail. But as he regarded the Bible mainly as literature, subject to the canons of literary interpreta-tion and investigation, his airy dismissal of the ideas of miraculous intervention and divine inspiration offended the orthodox; it was only the already heterodox who found in his pages consolation and encouragement.

SOCIAL AND POLITICAL DISCUSSION

Arnold's view of life was essentially literary and academic, and it was therefore not likely to appeal to the submerged class, not as yet blessed with the opportunities of universal elementary education. In *Culture and Anarchy* (1869), he defined this class, with manifest lack of sympathy, in the following terms: 'But that vast portion, lastly, of the working class which, raw and half-developed, has long lain half-hidden amidst its poverty and squalor, and is now issuing from its hiding-place to assert an Englishman's heaven-born privilege of doing as he likes, and is beginning to perplex us by marching where it likes, meeting where it likes, bawling what it likes, breaking what it likes,—to this vast residuum we may with great propriety give the name of *Populace*.' When he delivered an address to the Workingmen's College at Ipswich in

1879, he gave to it the condescending Latin title: 'Ecce convertimur ad Gentes' (Lo! we turn to the people). As a matter of theory, he could adopt the Greek maxim, 'Follow after equality,' but he never ventured to recommend the adoption of the maxim in practice.

While Arnold was discussing subjects of eternal significance with an airy lightness, the politicians were giving intense seriousness to matters of little permanent interest. The characteristic representative of this school was William Ewart Gladstone (1809–98), once the rising hope of the Tory party, but driven by political vicissitude into the Liberal ranks, where he soon made a name for himself by his conscientious high-mindedness, financial ability, and oratorical powers. The son of a Liverpool merchant but educated at Eton and Oxford, he was a conservative by instinct and a High Churchman by conviction; but he became the idol of the Nonconformist middle class and came to rely on them for support in his policies of moderate reform. Along with Lord John Russell he submitted to Parliament in 1866 a project for the further extension of the franchise, but was defeated in the House of Commons, and his great rival Disraeli came into power.

Benjamin Disraeli (1804–81) was in almost every respect Gladstone's antithesis. He was a Jew by race, and a Christian only by the accident of baptism at the intervention of a friend of the family, who thought that for English life christening would give him a better start than circumcision; his father, Isaac Disraeli, who had won fame as the author of *Curiosities of Literature*, acquiesced, being absolutely indifferent to the value of either rite for any purpose whatever. Nominal Christianity did not save young Disraeli from persecution at Christian schools, but he took gaily and courageously to the life of a penniless literary and political adventurer who had his way to make by his own ability in spite of all drawbacks. Although he had aired some youthful radical opinions and expressed sympathy with the Chartists, he found his political opportunity in the disorganization of the Tory party after the repeal of the Corn Laws by Sir Robert Peel, and by sheer audacity and political astuteness forced his leadership upon the reluctant country gentlemen who remained Conservatives during the long years of opposition to successive Whig governments. Having succeeded in throwing the Whigs out of office on their franchise bill, as Chancellor of the Exchequer in a Conservative government which represented only a minority of the House of Commons, he introduced a Reform Bill of his own, extending the suffrage to all ratepayers, and carried it with the help of his political opponents, who strengthened its provisions very considerably in the course of its passage. In the two political novels *Sybil* (1845) and *Tancred* (1847), in which he set forth the programme of the Young England party Disraeli had suggested that the Conservatives might play the upper and lower classes against the middle class, which he disliked and upon which the Whigs depended for support. In a still earlier political novel, *Coningsby*, Disraeli makes the political hack, Mr. Tadpole, exclaim: 'The time has gone by for Tory Governments; what the country requires is a sound Conservative Government.' 'A sound Conservative Government,' said Taper musingly. 'I understand: Tory men and Whig measures.' It was this policy, rather than that of social and economic reform, that Disraeli adopted in passing the Second Reform Bill (1867). His avowed motive was to 'dish the Whigs'; 'he had caught the Whigs bathing and stolen their clothes.' The appeal to the new electorate brought the Liberals back into power, and Gladstone, on the retirement of Lord John Russell, succeeded inevitably to the leadership of the party and the premiership. He passed some useful and necessary reforms—disestablished the Irish Church, carried the first Irish Land Bill, abolished the purchase of officers' commissions in the army and the exaction of religious tests at the universities, introduced vote by ballot instead of the open voting which put farmers and workmen at the mercy of their landlords and employers, and established a system of compulsory elementary education to be administered by local school boards with the aid of grants from the central government. 'We must educate our masters,' said Robert Lowe, one of Gladstone's ministers, and the education of the proletariate, following inevitably upon the extension of the suffrage, was the most important step towards enabling the masses to liberate themselves from the various tyrannies, social and economic, which oppressed them.

These seem rather scanty instalments of social reform, even if we include progressive factory legislation and statutes to secure the legal position of trades unions, under pressure from the Trade Union Congress, which was organized in 1868. But the time for genuinely socialistic legislation was not yet. The middle class, in spite of being swamped by the working-class vote after 1867, still exercised a predominant influence. An attempt to make the nation healthy by state interference about the middle of the century was abandoned as premature, provoking the remark from the Times: 'We prefer to take our chance of cholera and the rest, rather than be bullied into health.' The Christian Socialist movement of which Canon Kingsley was the leading exponent in his pamphlet *Cheap Clothes and Nasty*, and his novels *Alton Locke*, *Yeast*, and *Two Years Ago*, died away for lack of sufficient response from public opinion. Even Gladstone's moderate reforms excited violent antagonism and his party was defeated at the polls in 1874.

Disraeli became Prime Minister, and found himself for the first time supported by a solid Conservative majority in the House of Commons. But he made no attempt to carry out the social and economic reforms suggested in *Sybil* and *Tancred*. He had, as a matter of fact, little interest in domestic questions and treated them in a somewhat cavalier fashion. When the evolution debate was going on, he addressed a meeting of clergy on the subject in the following strain: 'Gentlemen, the question is whether man is descended from the apes or the angels; I am on the side of the angels.' Similarly, when liberalism in church doctrine was a burning question, Disraeli consented to the appointment of a leading Liberal, Arthur Stanley, as Dean of Westminster, because Stanley was a favorite with Queen Victoria, but he added the cynical admonition: 'Remember, Mr. Dean; no dogma, no dean!'

Disraeli had chosen as his fighting ground for the election the neglect by the Liberal Government of imperial issues. It is true that, twenty years before, Disraeli had spoken slightingly of 'these wretched colonies which will all be independent in a few years and are a millstone round our necks,' but in 1872 it was the Liberals that he was reproaching for alienating the colonies and bringing about the disintegration of the Empire. Not that he did anything for the colonies when he got into office. He bought the Suez Canal shares and secured the passage to India, but at the same time involved the British Government in serious responsibilities later, first in Egypt and afterwards in Palestine; he made the Queen Empress of India, and she made him Earl of Beaconsfield. He defeated the designs of Russia on the North West frontier of India and at the Hellespont; but six years of this kind of imperialism was all the British public could stand, and in 1880 they recalled Gladstone to power.

POETRY AND FICTION

In poetry and fiction the achievements of the Middle Period were far less brilliant than in science and the application of science to industry. Browning and Tennyson both did their best work before 1860, and the newcomers were not only men of inferior power but of a different spirit. Matthew Arnold felt himself the victim of an age of doubt and transition between two worlds, one dead, the other powerless to be born. Hearing the receding wave on Dover Beach, he is reminded of the ebb of faith; and even the returning surge brings only 'the eternal note of sadness in.'

> Ah, love, let us be true
> To one another! for the world, which seems
> To lie before us like a land of dreams,
> So various, so beautiful, so new,
> Hath really neither joy, nor love, nor light,
> Nor certitude, nor peace, nor help for pain;
> And we are here as on a darkling plain
> Swept with confused alarms of struggle and flight,
> Where ignorant armies clash by night

Arnold's friend, Arthur Hugh Clough, is overwhelmed by the same doubts and fears: for him the voyage of life is a mystery of which the beginning and the end are alike dark:

> Where lies the land to which the ship would go?
> Far, far ahead, is all her seamen know.
> And where the land she travels from? Away,
> Far, far behind, is all that they can say.

Swinburne is more certain, but certain only of extinction:

> From too much love of living,
>   From hope and fear set free,
> We thank with brief thanksgiving
>   Whatever gods may be
> That no life lives for ever;
> That dead men rise up never;
> That even the weariest river
>   Winds somewhere safe to sea.

In fiction also the mighty masters of the earlier period have finished their work before 1860. Thackeray died in 1863 and Dickens in 1870; the last great novel to be accredited to the latter is *Great Expectations*, which began to appear in 1860 and completed publication in 1861. The new novelists, Samuel Butler, George Eliot, Meredith, and Hardy, are, with the possible exception of Hardy, not equal in creative power to their predecessors, and they are all perplexed by doubt and questionings as to the purpose of life, both here and hereafter.

Of the English drama between 1860 and 1880 there is no need to say anything here, for there is hardly any drama worth saying anything about; and what little is to be said is better reserved to a later chapter.

CHAPTER VII

MID-VICTORIAN SCIENTISTS, PUBLICISTS, HISTORIANS, AND ESSAYISTS

CHARLES DARWIN
(*1809–1882*)

DARWIN was the son of a Shrewsbury doctor, and, since Shrewsbury has a famous school, he went there as a matter of course. His mother was the daughter of the great potter, Wedgwood, and Darwin later married his cousin, a granddaughter of the same, so that he came in for a double portion of the income inherited from the Etruria Pottery Works. It was this that made possible Darwin's life as an independent research worker, unburdened by teaching or administrative duties, so that it may be said that evolution was subsidized out of the profits of the Wedgwood pottery. But when Darwin was a boy, the knowledge that he would not have to work for a living appeared to have disadvantages. He did no good at school, and was no more industrious at either Edinburgh or Cambridge University. Neither the medical profession nor the Church aroused in him any enthusiasm, though he had no strong objection to either. He was fond of sport and became an excellent shot, so that his father said to him in despair, 'You care for nothing but shooting, dogs, and rat-catchers, and you will be a disgrace to yourself and all your family.'

Darwin left Cambridge with a pass degree and no particular object in life. But he had shown enough interest in natural science to be recommended by the university authorities to Captain Fitzroy, of H.M.S. Beagle, who was starting on a voyage round the world, and was willing to give up a part of his cabin to any young man who would volunteer to go with him without pay as naturalist. Darwin offered himself and was accepted. He had been rather extravagant at Cambridge and said to his father apologetically that he would be 'deuced clever to spend more than his allowance whilst on board the Beagle.' His father answered him, with a smile, 'But they tell me you are very clever.'

It was on the Beagle, in Darwin's opinion, that his education began; up to that point he had been wasting his time. He now developed his powers of observation: studied attentively Lyell's *Principles of Geology*, which was of the highest service to him; investigated the geology of all the places visited; collected animals of all classes, briefly describing and roughly dissecting many of the rare ones; and kept a journal, in which he set down with much pains all he had seen. These special studies were, however, of no importance compared with the habit of energetic industry and concentrated attention then acquired. In the autobiographical *Recollections of the Development of my Mind and Character* which Darwin put together in 1876 for his wife and children, he wrote: 'Everything about which I thought or read was made to bear directly on what I had seen or was likely to see; and this habit of mind was continued during the five years of the voyage. I feel sure that it was this training which has enabled me to do whatever I have done in science.' It was at this time too that he discovered, though unconsciously and insensibly, that the pleasure of observing and reasoning was a much higher one than that of sport, and in Good Success Bay, Tierra del Fuego, he made up his mind that he could not employ his life better than in adding a little to Natural Science.

The voyage lasted from December 27, 1831, to October 2, 1836. On his return to England Darwin settled down in lodgings, first in Cambridge and then in London, to prepare the scientific results for publication. The first to be completed was the *Journal of Researches*, published in 1839 as part of Captain Fitzroy's book on the voyage of the Beagle, and six years later issued independently in a second edition, which had a good sale for many years. Darwin had none of Huxley's brilliance in exposition and liveliness of style, but he had a supreme regard for the truth and an intense desire to arrange and state his facts as logically and effectively as he could. 'No nigger with lash over him could have worked harder at clearness than I have done.'

In 1837 he obtained a grant of a thousand pounds from the Government for the publication of the *Zoology of the Voyage of the Beagle*, and early in the following year was elected Secretary of the Geological Society, which after three years he gave up on account of the state of his health. The greater part of his time in London was devoted to a book on *The Structure and Distribution of Coral Reefs* (1842), which completely upset previous theories on the subject. He had married early in 1839 and the first three years of his married life were spent in Upper Gower Street, London; but his health continued to be very unsatisfactory. He suffered from palpitation of the heart and violent sickness of the stomach if he were excited by a lively conversational evening or overtired by excessive work. Indeed, it was only by the constant care of a devoted wife that Darwin was able to accomplish what he did and to live to an active old age. London with its bustle and hurry was seen to be impossible for him, and in the fall of 1842 they bought a house a quarter of a mile from the village of Downe (or Down as Darwin preferred to spell it), to which the ordinary means of access at that time involved a coach-drive of twenty miles. Even now, when the house has become national property and is a shrine for Darwin worshippers, it is still remote from railways, and only a dull haze of smoke that sometimes clouds the sky suggests the neighborhood of London.

It was in his London lodgings in July, 1837, that Darwin opened his first notebook for facts in relation to the *Origin of Species*, about which he had long reflected, and on which he never ceased working for the next twenty years. 'During the voyage of the Beagle' (he writes in the Autobiography) 'I had been deeply impressed by discovering in the Pampean formation great fossil animals covered with armor, like that on the existing armadillos; secondly, by the manner in which closely allied animals replace one another in proceeding southwards over the Continent; and thirdly, by the South American character of most of the productions of the Galapagos archipelago, and more especially by the manner in which they differ slightly on each island of the group, none of the islands appearing to be very ancient in a geological sense.

'It was evident that such facts as these, as well as many others, could only be explained on the supposition that species gradually become modified; and the subject haunted me. But it was equally evident that neither the action of the surrounding conditions, nor the will of the organisms (especially in the case of plants) could account for the innumerable cases in which organisms of every kind are beautifully adapted to their habits of life—for instance, a woodpecker or a treefrog to climb trees, or a seed for dispersal by hooks or plumes. I had always been much struck by such adaptations, and until these could be explained it seemed to me almost useless to endeavor to prove by indirect evidence that species have been modified.

'After my return to England it appeared to me that by following the example of Lyell in Geology, and by collecting all facts which bore in any way on the variation of animals and plants under domestication and nature, some light might perhaps be thrown on the whole subject.'

Darwin began by collecting facts on a wholesale scale, more especially with respect to breeding under domestication, both of plants and animals, and by abstracting whole series of scientific journals and transactions of learned societies, so that in later life he was astonished at his youthful industry. He soon perceived that selection was the keystone of man's success in making useful races of animals and plants; but how selection could be applied to organisms living in a state of nature remained for some time a mystery.

'In October, 1838,' (again to quote his autobiographical record) 'I happened to read for amusement Malthus on *Population*, and being well prepared to appreciate the struggle for existence, which everywhere goes on, from long-continued observation of the habits of animals and plants, it at once struck me that under these conditions favorable variations would tend to be preserved and unfavorable ones to be destroyed. The result of this would be the formation of new species. Here, then, I had at last got a theory by which to work; but I was so anxious to avoid prejudice that I determined not for some time to write even the briefest sketch of it. In June, 1842, I first allowed myself the satisfaction of writing a very brief abstract of my theory in pencil in thirty-five pages; and this was enlarged during the summer of 1844 into one of two hundred and thirty pages, which I had fairly copied out and still possess.

'But at that time I overlooked one problem of great importance; and it is astonishing to me, except on the principle of Columbus and his egg, how I could have overlooked it and its solution. This problem is the tendency in organic beings descended from the same stock to diverge in character as they become modified. That they have diverged greatly is obvious from the manner in which species of all kinds can be classed under genera, genera under families, families under sub-orders, and so forth; and I can remember the very spot in the road, whilst in my carriage, when to my joy the solution occurred to me; and this was long after I had come to Downe. The solution, as I believe, is that the modified offspring of all dominant and increasing forms tend to become adapted to many and highly diversified places in the economy of nature.

'Early in 1856 Lyell advised me to write out my views pretty fully, and I began at once to do so on a scale three or four times as extensive as that which was afterwards followed in my *Origin of Species;* yet it was only an abstract of the materials which I had collected, and I got through about half the work on this scale. But my plans were overthrown, for early in the summer of 1858 Mr. Wallace, who was then in the Malay Archipelago, sent me an essay *On the Tendency of Varieties to depart indefinitely from the Original Type;* and this essay contained exactly the same theory as mine. Mr. Wallace expressed the wish that if I thought well of his essay, I should send it to Lyell for perusal.'

The circumstances which led to the joint publication with Wallace in the *Journal of Proceedings of the Linnæan Society* (1858) have been narrated in Chapter VI. The joint production attracted very little attention, the only public notice of them Darwin could remember being a comment by a Dublin professor that all that was new in them was false, and what was true was old. The reception of the *Origin of Species* on its publication in November, 1859, was very different. It was an abstract of an abstract of voluminous notes, and therefore, as Darwin put it, 'a stiff book' to read; Huxley found it 'one of the hardest books to understand thoroughly,' and described Darwin's style as that of 'a sort of miraculous dog,' who strays this way and that when he is going home but always gets there sooner or later. In spite of these difficulties the first edition sold out on the day of publication and a second edition of three thousand copies soon afterwards; sixteen thousand copies were sold within the next twenty years. For a book of its kind and the reading public of the day, its sale was remarkable.

Darwin took little part in the heated debates that followed. On Lyell's advice he avoided controversy, 'as it rarely did any good and caused a miserable loss of time and temper.' Although from the beginning he was convinced that man must come under the same law as the other animals, in the *Origin of Species* he never discussed the derivation of any particular species, contenting himself with the remark that his work would 'throw light on the origin of man and his history.' For a long time he had collected notes on the subject for his own satisfaction without any intention of publishing; but when the discussion aroused, at the meeting of the British Association and elsewhere, by the publication of the *Origin of Species* showed that the issue could not be avoided, he set to work to collect more material; then he had to spend three years in arranging it and writing it out. So it was 1871 when the *Descent of Man* appeared, and even so Darwin felt that a second and largely corrected edition was called for in 1874. A by-product of the investigation was the *Expression of the Emotions in Men and Animals* (1872).

Darwin's later work was of a more specialized character—*Insectivorous Plants* (1875) was the result of sixteen years' observations, and was followed by *The Effects of Cross- and Self-Fertilization* (1876) and *Power of Movement in Plants* (1880). In 1881 he sent to the printers the manuscript of *The Formation of Vegetable Mold through the Action of Worms*, the outcome of investigations continued, mainly on his own lawn at Downe, for over forty years.

Before the publication of the *Origin of Species*, Darwin said he would be satisfied if he succeeded in convincing three men—Lyell, Huxley, and Hooker. He lived long enough to see his main conclusions accepted by the scientific world. He died full of years and honors, and was buried in Westminster Abbey, near the tomb of Sir Isaac Newton. His verdict on his own life was: 'I believe that I have acted rightly in steadily following and devoting my life to Science. I feel no remorse from having committed any great sin, but have often and often regretted that I have not done more direct good to my fellow-creatures.' This was an addendum to the autobiography, in which he noted with regret his loss of interest in poetry and pictures, music and works of imagination generally except novels, which he liked to have read to him aloud, if they were moderately good and ended happily. He goes on to say: 'This curious and lamentable loss of the higher æsthetic tastes is all the odder, as books on history, biographies, and travels (independently of any scientific facts which they may contain), and essays on all sorts of subjects interest me as much as ever they did. My mind seems to have become a kind of machine for grinding general laws out of large collections of facts, but why this should have caused the atrophy of that part of the brain alone, on which the higher tastes depend, I cannot conceive. A man with a mind more highly organized or better constituted than mine, would not, I suppose, have thus suffered; and if I had to live my life again, I would have made a rule to read some poetry and listen to some music at least once every week; for perhaps the parts of my brain now atrophied would thus have been kept active through use. The loss of these tastes is a loss of happiness, and may possibly be injurious to the intellect, and more probably to the moral character, by enfeebling the emotional part of our nature.'

Darwin was often questioned by correspondents as to his religious faith and the compatibility of any religious faith with belief in evolution. He left a long statement on the subject in his Auto-biography, from which the following extracts are made:—'Whilst on board the Beagle I was quite orthodox, and I remember being heartily laughed at by several of the officers (though themselves orthodox) for quoting the Bible as an unanswerable authority on some point of morality. I suppose it was the novelty of the argument that amused them. But I had gradually come by this time, i.e. 1836 to 1839, to see that the Old Testament was no more to be trusted than the sacred books of the Hindoos.

'With respect to immortality, nothing shows me [so clearly] how strong and almost instinctive a belief it is, as the consideration of the view now held by most physicists, namely, that the sun with all the planets will in time grow too cold for life, unless, indeed, some great body dashes into the sun and thus gives it fresh life. Believing, as I do, that man in the distant future will be a far more perfect creature than he now is, it is an intolerable thought that he and all other sentient beings are doomed to complete annihilation after such long-continued slow progress. To those who fully admit the immortality of the human soul, the destruction of our world will not appear so dreadful.

'Another source of conviction in the existence of God, connected with the reason and not with the feelings, impresses me as having much more weight. This follows from the extreme difficulty or rather impossibility of conceiving this immense and wonderful universe, including man with his capacity of looking far backwards and far into futurity, as the result of blind chance or necessity. When thus reflecting, I feel compelled to look to a First Cause having an intelligent mind in some degree analogous to that of man; and I deserve to be called a Theist. This conclusion was strong in my mind about the time, as far as I can remember, when I wrote the *Origin of Species*, and it is since that time that it has very gradually, with many fluctuations, become weaker. But then arises the doubt—can the mind of man, which has, as I fully believe, been developed from a mind as low as that possessed by the lowest animals, be trusted when it draws such grand conclusions?

'I cannot pretend to throw the least light on such abstruse problems. The mystery of the beginnings of things is insoluble by us, and I for one must be content to remain an Agnostic.'

Darwin's influence on scientific thought was twofold: (1) He established the theory of evolution as the process by which species have been developed; no one now expects science to return to the belief in special creation previously held. (2) He put forward natural selection as the means by which the process has been and is carried on; on this point there still prevails considerable difference of opinion. A. R. Wallace in 1889 suggested a 'spiritual influx' to explain man's higher qualities. Upon this suggestion Professor Lloyd Morgan founded his doctrine of 'emergent evolution' involving the appearance in the world of new kinds of being, which were not contained in the precedent conditions; he distinguishes three stages in evolution, which he calls 'life, mind, spirit,' declaring that 'spiritual value stands at a higher emergent level than economic, moral, esthetic, or intellectual values.' In the first decade of the present century Driesch offered an 'entelechy or directive soul' as the motive force of development, and Bergson was responsible for the term 'évolution créatrice,' interpreted by Bernard Shaw as the Life Force. More recently, Professor William MacDougall assumed conscious purpose or direction in evolution, and Professor E. W. MacBride asserted that the driving force in evolution is the struggle of the individual organism itself, which modifies its character. But all these scientists and philosophers are at one in accepting the evolutionary process as the basis of their theories, and it remains true that Darwin transformed the world of modern thought. Sir Arthur Keith, in his presidential address to the British Association in 1927, said: 'By a logical analysis of his facts Darwin reconstructed and wrote a history of man. Fifty-six years have come and gone since that history was written; an enormous body of new evidence has poured in upon us. We are now able to fill in many pages which Darwin had perforce to leave blank and we have found it necessary to alter details in his narrative, but the fundamentals of Darwin's outline of man's history remain unshaken. Nay, so strong has his position become that I am convinced that it never can be shaken.'

THOMAS HENRY HUXLEY
(1825–1895)

Huxley was a great scientist but something more; he was interested not merely in zoölogy, but in the influence of science on education, religion, and the general thought of his time. He was a man of letters and a great personality. Only a man of great intellectual resources and moral courage could have triumphed over the disappointments of his early career. 'Kicked into the world without guide or training,' to use his own words, he found in Carlyle the inspiration to high aims and noble endeavor. He thus sums up the agents of his redemption from the follies of youth: '*Sartor Resartus* led me to know that a deep sense of religion was compatible with the entire absence of theology. Secondly, science and her methods gave me a resting place, independent of authority and tradition. Thirdly, love opened up to me a view of the sanctity of human nature and impressed me with a deep sense of responsibility.' Born at Ealing, a London suburb, he won honors as a struggling medical student and at twenty-one obtained the post of assistant surgeon for research purposes on H.M.S. Rattlesnake. When he returned four years later he had become (to quote from Prof. Virchow) 'a perfect zoölogist and a keen-sighted ethnologist. How this was possible anyone will readily understand who knows from his own experience how great the value of personal observation is for the development of independent and unprejudiced thought. For a young man who, besides collecting a rich treasure of positive knowledge, has practised dissection and the exercise of critical judgment, a long sea voyage and a peaceful sojourn among entirely new surroundings afford an invaluable opportunity for original work and deep reflection. Freed from the formalism of the schools, thrown upon the use of his own intellect, he soon forgets the dogmas of the prevailing system, and becomes first a sceptic and then an investigator.' It was through this change that there arose the Huxley who was to make so deep a mark upon the thought of his own time.

Important as were the results of the four years' cruise for Huxley's mental development and the researches which he conducted, he had bitter disappointments before he could establish for himself the position of usefulness and influence upon which he had set his heart. The Admiralty refused to help him to publish the results of his investigations and after repeated postponements summarily ordered him in 1854 to join his ship as an acting surgeon. He refused and was struck off the navy list. In the meantime he had received the highest scientific honors but no position which promised him a permanent income for the work he wished to do. He became a fellow of the Royal Society in 1851, won the Royal Medal in 1852; but he applied in vain for vacant chairs of Zoölogy at Toronto, Canada, at Aberdeen in Scotland, at Cork in Ireland, and at King's College, London. His health broke down and he was greatly discouraged; he even thought of giving up Zoölogy altogether and turning to commercial chemistry or squatting or store-keeping in Australia, for he was engaged to an Australian girl he had met on the voyage, Miss Heathorn of Sydney, N.S.W. It was her encouragement that saved him from losing heart altogether. In answer to a letter in which she urged him to pursue the things for which he was most suited, he wrote on July 6, 1853: 'My course in life is taken. I will *not* leave London. I *will* make myself a name and a position as well as an income by some kind of pursuit connected with science, which is the one thing for which nature has fitted me if she has ever fitted anyone for anything.'

His devotion to science was at last rewarded. His income from books and reviewing made him independent of his half-pay as a naval surgeon. In 1854 he was appointed to a lecturership at the Government School of Mines and a little later became Naturalist to the Geological Survey. Other appointments followed and when Miss Heathorn returned to England in 1855 he was able to marry and settle down to regular work as a teacher and investigator. He helped to revolutionize the teaching of Zoölogy and was not content to restrict his energies to his own students. He took a leading share in the foundation of a scientific review (now known as 'Nature'), and he addressed himself to the task of bringing science home to the people. 'I am sick of the dilettante middle class,' he says, 'and mean to try what I can do with these hard-handed fellows who live among facts. . . . I want the working classes to understand that science and her ways are great facts for them, that physical virtue is the basis of all other, and that they are to be clean and temperate and all the rest—not because fellows in black with white ties tell them so, but because these are plain and patent laws of nature which they must obey "under penalties."'

Huxley became one of the most successful of popular lecturers, because he always gave the working people of his best. He took pains to be absolutely clear and took nothing for granted, but he gave them the results of his own most recent work and at the same time continued ardently to prosecute research. He writes under date of New Year's Eve, 1856, his good resolutions: 'That the three years to come must still be "lehrjahre" [years of apprenticeship] to complete training in principles of histology, morphology, physiology, zoölogy, and geology by monographic work in each department; 1860 will then see me well grounded and ready for any special pursuits in either of these branches. . . . In 1860 I may further look forward to 15 or 20 years meisterjahre [mastership], and with the comprehensive views my training will have given me, I think it will be possible in that time to give a new and healthier direction to all biological science. To smite all humbugs, however big; to give a nobler tone to science; to set an example of abstinence from petty personal controversies and of toleration for everything but lying; to be indifferent as to whether the work is recognized as mine or not.'—These were the aims he set before himself on entering the year 1857.

In 1859 a new direction was given to Huxley's energies by the publication of Darwin's *Origin of Species*. Huxley was for so long the most prominent champion of the theory of evolution that his name was for a time more closely connected with it in the popular mind than that of either Darwin or Spencer, who embraced it long before they succeeded in making him a convert. It was not until the *Origin of Species* was in his hands that Huxley owned himself convinced. Huxley, who was already regarded as a leading authority in biology, was one of the three scientists Darwin especially wished to convert, and the prompt adhesion of Huxley proved of paramount importance. Darwin disliked controversy, and he had not Huxley's gift of making things clear to the uninitiated. As late as 1888 Huxley writes, 'I have been trying to set out the argument of the *Origin of Species*, and reading the book for the nth time for that purpose. It is one of the hardest books to understand thoroughly that I know of.' This being the case in 1888, the difficulty of understanding Darwin's argument when it was new and had to overcome a dead wall of prejudice may be imagined. Huxley had the book before publication and was able to some extent to prepare the way for it. An accident enabled him to render conspicuous service from the start. The Times reviewer, who knew nothing whatever of the subject, appealed to Huxley for help and the article which first drew the attention of the British public to Darwin's work was, with the exception of a few introductory sentences, from Huxley's pen.

Another accident gave Huxley a recognized place in the forefront of the battle which soon raged between the opponents of the theory of evolution and its supporters. We have already seen how the Bishop of Oxford, Dr. Samuel Wilberforce, was put up at the Oxford meeting of the British Association in 1860 'to smash Darwin.' The Bishop, with the skill of a practised rhetorician, selected the theory of the descent of man and the apes from a common ancestor as his main ground of attack, and turning to Prof. Huxley asked him whether it was through his grandfather or through his grandmother that he traced his monkey ancestry. Huxley, grasping the mistake in tactics which his adversary had made by giving this personal tone to the discussion, smote his knee, and turning to Sir Benjamin Brodie who sat next to him on the platform said 'the Lord hath delivered him into my hands.' After the Bishop had finished his speech, Huxley was called for by the audience and said with some scorn, 'I am here only in the interests of science, and I have not heard anything which can prejudice the case of my august client.' In answer to the Bishop's joke about the monkey, he explained that the suggestion was of descent through thousands of generations from a common ancestor, and went on: 'But if this question is treated, not as a matter for the calm investigation of science, but as a matter of sentiment, and if I am asked whether I would choose to be descended from the poor animal of low intelligence and stooping gait, who grins and chatters as we pass, or from a man endowed with great ability and a splendid position, who should use these gifts to discredit and crush humble seekers after truth, I hesitate what answer to make.' This is the version of A. G. Vernon Harcourt, but there is no exact report of what Huxley actually said. The historian J. R. Green, then an undergraduate, perhaps comes nearer to the words used: 'I asserted—and I repeat—that a man has no reason to be ashamed of having an ape for his grandfather. If there were an ancestor whom I should feel shame in recalling, it would rather be a man—a man of restless and versatile intellect—who, not content with an equivocal success in his own sphere of activity, plunges into scientific questions with which he has no real acquaintance, only to obscure them by an aimless rhetoric, and distract the attention of his hearers from the real point at issue by elegant digressions and skilled appeals to religious prejudice.' Whatever question there may be as to the exact words Huxley used—and he himself never admitted that he applied to the Bishop's success the term 'equivocal'—there can be no doubt that the effect of the retort was tremendous. The end of the sentence was lost in a tumult of applause. Some people jumped out of their seats in the excitement of the moment, one lady fainted and had to be carried out. Instead of the evolutionists being crushed, they came out of the debate triumphant, and from that day forth the Bishops recognized that in Huxley they had to meet a scientist who could wield the weapons of debate with no less skill than the most practised speaker or writer among them.

Huxley followed up his success at Oxford by lectures on the subject in London and Edinburgh, and soon became known to the public as the most active champion of the new theory. But his services to the doctrine of evolution went beyond popular exposition and defense. As has been already noted, the utmost ridicule and obloquy were directed against the suggestion that man and the apes were descended from a common ancestor, and it was to this point that Huxley directed his researches. At the Oxford meeting Professor Owen, who had primed the Bishop for his famous speech, stated that the brain of the gorilla presented more differences, as compared with the brain of man, than it did when compared with the brains of the very lowest monkeys. Huxley gave the statement a flat contradiction and pledged himself to justify that unusual procedure elsewhere. He redeemed this promise in numerous papers published in the scientific periodicals and in his first book, *Evidence as to Man's Place in Nature* (1863). He was warned that the publication of this book would involve him in endless misrepresentation and abuse, but he persisted and the consequence was that, as his son, Leonard Huxley, says in the biography from which much of this is quoted, 'for the next ten years he was commonly identified with the championship of the most unpopular view of the time; a fighter, an assailant of long-established fallacies, he was too often considered a mere iconoclast, a subverter of every other well-rooted institution, theological, educational, or moral.' As to the importance of Huxley's contribution to the discussion of evolution, Sir Arthur Keith says: 'It settled for all time that man's rightful position is among the primates, and that, as we anatomists weigh evidence, his nearest living kin are the anthropoid apes.'

What his aims actually were may be gathered from a letter to his wife written in 1873: 'The part I have to play is not to found a new school of thought or to reconcile the antagonisms of the old schools. We are in the midst of a gigantic movement greater than that which preceded and produced the Reformation and really only the continuation of that movement. But there is nothing new in the ideas which lie at the bottom of the movement, nor is any reconcilement possible between free thought and traditional authority. One or the other will have to succumb after a struggle of unknown duration, which will have as side issues vast political and social troubles. I have no more doubt that free thought will win in the long run than that I sit here writing to you, or that this free thought will organize itself into a coherent system, embracing human life and the world as one harmonious whole. But this organization will be the work of generations of men, and those who further it most will be those who teach men to rest in no lie, and to rest in no verbal delusions.'

From this time until his retirement from the Government Service in 1885 Huxley was very much occupied as the head of the Department of Biology in the College of Science, Inspector of Fisheries, and member of numerous Royal Commissions. He was Secretary and afterwards President of the Royal Society. He still lectured and wrote a great deal, was Lord Rector of Aberdeen University, one of the original members of the London School Board, and keenly interested in all educational subjects.

In the fall of 1876 Huxley went to the United States, mainly to visit his favorite sister, who was living at Nashville, Tennessee, and whom he had not seen for thirty years. He was invited by he citizens to address them and spoke with his usual frankness as to the difference between the evolutionists' view of the history of the earth and that commonly received. He said: 'It is so widely different that it is impossible to effect any kind of community, any kind of parallel, far less any kind of reconciliation between these two. One of these must be true. The other is not.' The speech was received not only with courtesy but with enthusiasm—in odd contrast with subsequent legislation in Tennessee as to the teaching of evolution in schools and the Scopes trial which took place half a century later than Huxley's visit.

Strangely enough, the one outbreak of intolerance during Huxley's visit to America was in connection with his inaugural address at the foundation of Johns Hopkins University at Baltimore. What was more important was that he left behind him his former colleague in London, Henry Newell Martin, who as professor of biology introduced Huxley's methods of teaching and research to the New World. A year or two later Dr. Henry Fairfield Osborn brought the Huxley method to Princeton and afterwards to Columbia University and New York City.

In 1885 Huxley resigned his professorship of biology at the School of Science and his inspectorship of fisheries, and delivered his farewell address as President of the Royal Society. During the last ten years of his life he was actively engaged in numerous controversies with various Bishops, Mr. Gladstone, Herbert Spencer, Frederick Harrison (the leader of the English Positivists), the Duke of Argyll, and the chief officials of the Salvation Army. He was always ready to run a tilt against loose thinking or obedience to authority unsupported by reason, and few controversialists have spoken their minds with more vigor and effectiveness. He lived to receive numerous honors from the Government and the universities, was invited to lecture on evolution at Oxford, and heard Lord Salisbury as Chancellor acknowledge that the theory of evolution had received the unanimous assent of the scientific world.

His achievement in science was undoubtedly less than that of Darwin, in philosophy less than that of Spencer, for he was distracted from scientific research by the various other subjects which engaged his attention. But in active public service and in influence upon his own generation, he was not excelled by either. He was greater than either as a man of letters, his style being one of the most effective instruments for its purpose in the whole range of English literature. He writes: 'the fact is that I have a great love and respect for my native tongue and take great pains to use it properly. Sometimes I write essays half-a-dozen times before I can get them into the proper shape.'

Although Huxley's education was early turned in the direction of science, he did not cease to take an interest in literature. The study of Carlyle led him as a youth to learn German that he might read Goethe; on the Rattlesnake he taught himself Italian in order to become acquainted with Dante; he afterwards learnt Greek that he might read Homer and Aristotle; but he always attached the utmost importance to the great models in English prose. It was to him an astonishing scandal that graduates should be turned out of the English universities 'ignorant of the noble literature which has grown up in these islands during the last three centuries,' and he had no patience with the 'current superstition that whoso wishes to write and speak English well should mold his style after the models furnished by classical antiquity.' 'For my part' (he continues) 'I venture to doubt the wisdom of attempting to mold one's style by any other process than that of striving after the clear and forcible expression of definite conceptions; in which process the Glassian precept, "first catch your definite conceptions," is probably the most difficult to obey. But still I mark among distinguished contemporary speakers and writers of English, saturated with antiquity, not a few to whom it seems to me, the study of Hobbes might have taught dignity; of Swift, concision and clearness; of Goldsmith and Defoe, simplicity.'

Whether he gained the qualities of his own style by diligent study, or by a natural lucidity of mind, or by both, his own writing remains a model for those engaged in exposition or in controversy. He would not have spent his strength in controversy so willingly if he had not had a natural inclination for it. When his old friend, Dean Shaler, Professor of Geology of Harvard University, advised him to leave the Bishops alone, Huxley replied, 'No, I like it and it does me good. When my digestion is out of order, nothing helps me so much as a course in episcopophagy.' Bishop-eating was, in fact, his favorite sport. Once a student appeared before him as examiner with a dismal paper; he had the place of the heart's mitral valve wrong. Huxley, however, passed him. 'Poor little beggar! I never got them correctly myself until I reflected that a Bishop is never in the right,' he said. The mitral valve is on the left, and 'mitral' suggested Bishop.

When in 1869 he became a member of the Metaphysical Society, composed of leading representatives of various religious beliefs, Huxley invented the word Agnostic to set forth his own point of view. But he was really further removed than Darwin from the sceptical detachment the word would seem to imply. Huxley had a consuming zeal for what he believed to be the truth, worthy of the founder of a new religion. In a correspondence with Canon Kingsley on the occasion of the death of his first-born, he wrote: 'One thing people shall not call me with justice, and that is—a liar.' And in *Science and Education* he set forth his view that the ideal university 'should be charged with that enthusiasm for truth, that fanaticism of veracity, which is a greater possession than much learning; a nobler gift than the power of increasing knowledge.' Perhaps Huxley's zeal for truth was not always according to knowledge, and he may be fairly charged with some responsibility for the passionate dogmatism that afflicted the champions of science at the turn of the century; but he also taught them that unflinching respect for the truth which was and is their greatest glory.

JOHN TYNDALL
(1820–1893)

Tyndall was not quite equal to his friend and fellowworker Huxley, either as a thinker or as a writer, so that the impression he made upon his contemporaries was smaller, and has undergone to a greater extent the inevitable effacement of time. Born in Ireland of English stock, he obtained at an early age a post in the Irish ordnance survey and did his work well enough to be transferred to England. While working at Preston in Lancashire, he came into contact with the poverty and degradation of the cotton operatives and miners in the neighborhood, and found an echo to his own heartfelt indignation in the early fulminations of Carlyle, whose influence was strong upon him for the rest of his life.

Feeling that his educational opportunities had been insufficient, he gave up his position for further study in Germany at the Universities of Marburg and Berlin. Returning to England, he became a friend of Huxley, and together they applied for professorial vacancies at Toronto, Canada, and Sydney, New South Wales, but without success. In 1853, however, Tyndall was appointed Professor of Natural Philosophy at the Royal Institution, London, and worked there with Faraday, whom he succeeded as Superintendent; on his retirement in 1887 he was appointed honorary 'professor. In the course of his investigations into the flow of glaciers, he became an ardent and an accomplished Alpine climber and built a cottage for himself at Bel Alp, above the Rhône valley. He had also a house at Hindhead in Surrey, where he died, after prolonged illness, from an overdose of chloral accidentally administered.

Tyndall did not feel impelled, as Huxley did, to constitute himself 'something between maid-of-all-work and gladiator-general for Science,' and he took a far less prominent part in the controversies of the time. But he could speak boldly and trenchantly when occasion offered itself. His presidential address at the Belfast meeting of the British Association for the Advancement of Science in 1874 created a sensation, not only among men of science but among the general public who read reports of it in the newspapers and more especially among the clergy. Tyndall attempted to reverse the limitations which religion had imposed upon science by imposing, on behalf of science, limitations on the sphere of dogmatic theology. He said: 'All religious theories, schemes, and systems, which embrace notions of cosmogony, or which otherwise reach into the domain of science, must, in so far as they do this, submit to the control of science, and relinquish all thought of controlling it. Acting otherwise proved disastrous in the past, and it is simply fatuous to-day.' He went on to argue that scientific investigation showed that life was 'indissolubly joined' with matter. 'Every meal we eat, and every cup we drink, illustrates the mysterious control of Mind by Matter. Believing as I do in the continuity of Nature, I cannot stop abruptly where our microscopes cease to be of use. Here the vision of the mind authoritatively supplements the vision of the eye. By an intellectual necessity I cross the boundary of the experimental evidence, and discern in the Matter, which we in our ignorance of its latent powers, and notwithstanding our professed reverence for its Creator, have hitherto covered with opprobrium, the promise and potency of all terrestrial life.'

Naturally the clergy resented this attempt to 'put the boot on the other leg.' Belfast is a stronghold of Presbyterianism, and the local Presbytery promptly denounced Professors Huxley and Tyndall as 'ignoring the existence of God and advocating pure and simple materialism.' Tyndall retorted that if the statement were amended to read 'ignoring the existence of our God, and advocating what we consider pure and simple materialism,' he would have accepted it as 'objectively true,' i.e. a true statement of the Presbytery's opinion. Neither he nor Professor Huxley accepted the common description of themselves as materialists without qualification.

HERBERT SPENCER

(1820–1903)

Herbert Spencer came of Huguenot and Quaker stock and might fairly be described as a born dissenter. He was throughout his life a strong individualist, and his whole system of thought was based upon the right of every man to do what he wills so long as he does not trench upon the similar rights of any other man. At the age of thirteen he showed that independence of mind which was to characterize his whole life; his parents had difficulty on account of their poverty in providing for his education, and they gladly accepted the offer of a clerical uncle to take charge of him. Little Herbert was taken to his uncle's parsonage for a visit and was left there, but within two weeks he was at home again; he had not been consulted, and he had walked the whole distance—over a hundred miles—48 the first day, 47 the second, and the rest of the distance on the third. Having thus asserted his independence, he went back contented to his uncle's house and settled down quietly to his studies.

The manufacturing towns of Derby and Nottingham, in which Spencer's childhood was spent, and the grim houses in a monotonous row, in which his parents lived, as well as their stern religious creed, drove him as a mere child to the pleasures of the mind and inculcated an early sense of personal responsibility. His education was mathematical rather than literary, and though he enjoyed such outdoor sports as skating, riding, and fishing, he took no pleasure in games for their own sake; exercise in the open air was to him merely a means for the maintenance of health. When, at fifteen, he published his first article, it was a reply to a criticism of poor law administration, and his main point was that the critic disregarded the fact that the whole system of man's responsibility and of his future reward or punishment depends on his being 'diligent in business, fervent in spirit, serving the Lord.'

What difference mixing with other young men at College and taking part in the ordinary associations of healthy youth might have made to Spencer's health and view of life is an object for speculation. The force of circumstances drove him to earn his living at the age of sixteen as a railway engineer; he became a neat draughtsman and invented two mechanical contrivances—a 'velocimeter' and a 'dynamometer'—for measuring (1) the speed and (2) the tractive power of a locomotive. But his intellectual interests drew him into journalism, and beside magazine articles, he wrote a pamphlet *On the Proper Sphere of Government* and a book on *Social Statics* (1851) which attracted considerable attention. He made the acquaintance of G. H. Lewes, George Eliot, Huxley, and other radical thinkers of the time; for five years he was subeditor of the London Economist, and he wrote articles for other reviews—on 'The Development Hypothesis,' on 'The Theory of Population,' and on 'The Philosophy of Style' (1852). In 1853 a small legacy freed him from the necessity of earning a living by journalism, and he was able to devote all his energies to an important book he had projected for some time, *The Principles of Psychology*. It was completed and published in 1855, but at the cost of a nervous breakdown, which compelled him for the rest of his life to give the first place to the consideration and preservation of his health. He 'disciplined himself to amusements' and said in recommending his example to another philosopher: 'though at first you may, in consequence of having wedded yourself to work, find amusement dreary and uninteresting, you will in course of time habituate yourself to it, and begin to find life more tolerable.' In the country he found tearing trees up by the roots and splitting them up for firewood the most pleasurable form of exercise, but as life in London did not offer much opportunity for it, he took to playing cards (he paid his losses but refused to accept winnings) and billiards, at which he acquired a moderate proficiency, though he was fond of quoting the remark of another member of the Athenæum Club, that excessive skill at the game was a mark of an ill-spent youth.

In spite of his insufficient means and broken health, Spencer set himself resolutely to no less an undertaking than the working out of a whole system of philosophy founded on modern scientific methods and principles. He sought in vain for an appointment—

in the Indian Administration, on the Education Commission, or in the Consular Service—that would give him a moderate income and sufficient leisure to pursue his philosophic enquiries; and he was thus driven to the ancient resource of publication by subscription. At twenty years of age Spencer had studied Lyell's *Principles of Geology*, and, rejecting the adverse arguments, had adopted the development hypothesis, on which, after ten years of reflection, he published an essay which created a sensation. In 1860 he sent out an appeal to his English and American disciples and admirers, requesting subscriptions for his projected philosophical series. There was a generous response to the appeal, and another opportune legacy secured him a small income if the subscriptions kept up; if they did not, there would not be enough to pay the printer's bill, to say nothing of providing the author with a living. By June, 1862, the first instalment of the 'system of synthetic philosophy,' entitled *First Principles*, was published; Part I dealt with the Unknowable under the headings (1) Religion and Science; (2) Ultimate Religious Ideas; (3) Ultimate Scientific Ideas; and (4) The Relativity of All Knowledge; Part II dealt in the main with the Law of Evolution.

With this first important step accomplished, Spencer took a short holiday and then set to work on the *Principles of Biology*, which began publication in January, 1863. It was a tremendous affair, in two volumes of three parts each, with a dozen appendices, dealing with the evolution of life in all its forms and the laws that govern its development. With the number of the *Biology* published in December, 1865, came a notice from the author that on the completion of the volume the series would cease. The reasons were financial, and Spencer was at once urged by his English and American subscribers to continue; generous financial aid was forthcoming. Henry Ward Beecher wrote from New York: 'The peculiar condition of American society has made your writings far more fruitful and quickening here than in Europe. We are conscious of great obligations to you, and perplexed because we cannot acknowledge them as we could were we your fellow-citizens.' This was accompanied by a testimonial in the form of a money gift of seven thousand dollars, of which the subscribers begged Spencer's acceptance. He was surprised, touched, and pleased, and agreed to go on with the work.

His immediate task was to get out a revised edition of the *First Principles;* then he enlarged the *Principles of Psychology* so as to fit into the more comprehensive scheme of the series. This was accomplished in 1870, when he was encouraged by the widespread recognition of his work and the greater circulation which began to provide him with a sufficient income. He was gratified by his election to the Athenæum for 'distinguished eminence in science,' and he came almost to make this celebrated club his home. He was invited to stand for Parliament and for the Rectorship of three of the Scottish Universities, and was offered numerous honorary degrees and membership of various scientific societies, which he invariably declined. His next great undertaking was the *Principles of Sociology*, which began to appear in 1876 and was brought to a conclusion twenty years later. Meanwhile the *Principles of Ethics*, which began publication in 1879, was completed in 1893. Later editions of some other parts of the series were prepared, and *First Principles* appeared in a sixth and finally revised edition in 1900, when its author was eighty years of age—forty years after the issue of the circular which outlined the scope and general plan of the series. It was an astounding achievement, almost without parallel in literary history.

Spencer felt that he had fulfilled his obligations to the subscribers with the completion of the series as planned in 1896. When he dictated the last words in August of that year, he rose slowly and shook hands with his secretary. 'I have finished the task I have lived for' he said, and sat down, regaining immediately his usual composure. The leading members of the political and scientific world, in a congratulatory address on the completion of his great work, expressed their appreciation 'of the great intellectual powers it exhibits and of the immense effect it has produced in the history of thought; nor are we less impressed by the high moral qualities which have enabled you to concentrate those powers for so many years upon a purpose worthy of them, and, in spite of all obstacles, to carry out so vast a design.'

On his death in 1903 the chorus of praise was renewed. 'In the whole story of the searchers for truth,' said the London Times, 'there is no instance of devotion to noble aims surpassing his— courage, baffling ill-health and proof against years of discouragement, unwearied patience, wise economy of powers and confidence in the future recognition of the value of his work.'

Spencer's long life of celibate devotion to study produced in him certain oddities which became inseparable from the popular conception of his personality; he was extremely methodical, keeping his keys in one pocket, his knife in another, and every one of his papers in its assigned place. He was fussy and dictatorial about small details—'such as how to light a fire or revive it when it was low, the hanging of pictures, the colors in a carpet, or of the flowers on a dinner table, the proper shape of an inkstand, and a thousand other matters; and he allowed what he thought an unreasonable way of doing these things, even when they had nothing to do with himself, to unduly disturb his peace.' In spite of his absorption in his allotted task, he could not help making an effort to rectify whatever seemed to him an evil. Thus, although he had no experience of the care of children, he wrote to a young married woman of his acquaintance an interminable letter—or rather lecture—on the clothing of her little girls: 'There is an enormous amount of mischief consequent upon the uneven circulation which is caused by uneven covering. The rationale of the matter is a very simple one. The vascular system constituted by the heart and by the ramifying system of blood vessels is a closed cavity having elastic walls. Of necessity, if you constrict the walls of any part of this cavity, the blood has to go somewhere, and it is thrust into some other parts of the cavity. If the constriction is great and extends over a considerable area, the pressure of blood throughout the unconstricted vessels becomes great, and if any of them are feeble they dilate, producing local congestion.' And so on, for pages after pages. To an old friend, when they had both arrived at an age when most men are toothless—Spencer was then nearly eighty—he wrote a similar dissertation on the importance of mastication. 'That you a scientific man should not recognize the importance of mastication is to me astonishing.' Always the fervid apostle of personal liberty for himself, he sometimes failed to recognize, in practice, its appreciation by others, and he allowed trifling *contretemps* to upset his equilibrium. Thus he wrote to Andrew Lang: 'I continually meet with paragraphs about myself, many absurd and many utterly baseless. An American interviewer described me as always wearing white gaiters. I never wore any in my life. It was said that I invariably carry an umbrella, and a bulky one. For many years past I have not walked at all, and when I did walk I never carried an umbrella unless it was raining or obviously certain to rain. It is said that I take my meals alone and dislike dining with others. Absolutely the reverse is the fact. I dislike to take a meal alone. I was asked by a lady whether it was true that I lived chiefly on bread and coffee; a statement absolutely baseless. I was asked whether I changed my occupation every ten minutes—a statement which had a certain slight basis, but an extremely small one. I saw a paragraph stating that on one occasion I could not manage my sister's children. The only sister I ever had died when two years old.'

These little weaknesses had their favorable side. If he was meticulous about reference to himself and his writings—and his sensitiveness in this respect involved him in endless controversies and bitter quarrels—he was equally scrupulous in giving credit to others. Till he was over eighty, he replied unfailingly to a continuous stream of begging letters and applications for interviews, 'requests for photographs, autographs, mottoes, sentiments, for advice in the bringing up of children, on the organization of schools, on the management of debating societies, for expressions of his matured opinions on all manner of topics, ranging from the industrial situation in New Zealand to divorce in Italy.'

His somewhat irritable self-consciousness communicated itself to his methods of work. He could not continue to read an author he did not agree with, and a slight difference of opinion made him throw down the book, never to take it up again. Thus, being asked his opinion of Robert Louis Stevenson he replied: 'I began to read many years ago *Travels with a Donkey in the Cevennes*, but was so disgusted with his treatment of the donkey that I gave it up quickly and never looked into another of his books for many years.' He was frequently reproached for dealing with the authorities he consulted in the same way, i.e. selecting facts favorable to his theories and disregarding the rest. His scientific friends deplored his failure to acquaint himself with the whole of the facts on which judgment should be formed. Darwin said of Spencer's *Biology:* 'It is wonderfully clever, and I dare say mostly true. . . . If he had trained himself to observe more, even at the expense, by the law of balancement, of some loss of thinking power, he would have been a wonderful man.' Huxley said Spencer's idea of a tragedy was the slaying of a beautiful theory by an ugly fact. Galton gives a curious example of Spencer's weakness in this respect. They were talking, in Galton's anthropometric laboratory, of the difficulty of accounting for peculiarities in the patterns of finger tips. Spencer interrupted Galton's account of his investigations with an elaborate theory based on the supposition that the sudorific glands were protected by the ridges. Galton let him go on, and then remarked that there was only one difficulty—the supposition was contrary to the fact.

Spencer had a much greater reputation abroad than in his own country. While German idealism was the prevailing cult in English academic circles, the German universities were discussing Spencer with profound seriousness. The English scientists, who were nearly all specialists in some branch of knowledge, regarded his wide range of learning with some distrust. His intense individualism ran counter to the socialistic tendencies of his time, and since his death his reputation has rather lost than gained. His early recognition of the importance of the theory of evolution and his extraordinary industry and energy in applying it to various branches of knowledge made him an important influence in his own lifetime, and he may be said to have created a new science—that of sociology. But the immense volumes of his Synthetic Philosophy are now little read. He is better known by the shorter essays he did by the way—his little books on Education and the Philosophy of Style. In spite of his lack of religious belief, Spencer was a characteristic Victorian in his stern individualism, his profound seriousness, his entire devotion to his self-appointed task, and the monumental industry with which he accomplished it.

SIR HENRY MAINE
(*1822–1888*)

The evolutionary theory affected other fields of thought beside the geological and biological sciences most immediately concerned; phrases like 'the struggle for life' and 'the survival of the fittest' passed quickly into common talk, without being always perfectly understood; the importance of heredity and environment was much discussed, by men of letters as well as scientists; 'origins' and 'influences' became the main principles of investigation in various departments of intellectual activity. The study of law as a social institution, begun by Jeremy Bentham, was continued by Sir Henry Maine, who had a distinguished career as a student and teacher at Cambridge before going out to India to complete the codification of Indian law begun by Macaulay. His Indian experience confirmed him in his view of law as a function of human living in community rather than a collection of statutes or a set of abstract principles. His *Ancient Law* (1861), *Village Communities* (1871), *The Early History of Institutions* (1875), and *Dissertations on Early Law and Custom* (1883) not only added a great deal to knowledge, but suggested a new and fruitful point of view. His *Popular Government* (1885) presented anti-democratic arguments at a time when Gladstone's and Bright's advocacy of a further extension of the franchise under the plea of 'trusting the people' made democracy popular.

WALTER BAGEHOT
(*1826–1877*)

Bagehot in his *Physics and Politics* (1872) attempted to apply evolutionary principles to forms of government and to elucidate the laws of their development; but his more successful efforts were his studies of the *English Constitution* (1865–67) and *Lombard Street* (1873), in both of which he showed a most unusual gift of seeing things as they are and showing how they work instead of contenting himself with the theory of what they should be and how they are supposed to work. This is still the most difficult problem of professors both of political economy and of political science; it is so much easier to construct theories than to make out how things actually happen in human experience and what are the real forces underlying the façade protecting most institutions from all but the most piercing scrutiny. Bagehot was fitted, by nature and by familiarity with affairs, to get behind appearances, and he had an extraordinary gift for stating in plain and familiar language what he saw.

He was the son of a West of England banker, and it was perhaps his good luck rather than his misfortune, that, his father being a Unitarian, he was barred from the Universities of Oxford and Cambridge; he was sent to London to the recently founded University College, and after taking his degree read for the Bar, though he never practised law. After completing his legal qualifications, he returned to work in the head office of his father's bank at Langport, in Somerset, where he was born. Not very far from his home was the great house of Claverton Manor, formerly owned by Ralph Allen, the 'Squire Allworthy' of *Tom Jones*, and at this time in possession of James Wilson, then Financial Secretary to the Treasury, the owner and director of the Economist, and a leading authority on matters of finance and of national policy connected with finance. It must have been with feelings of some trepidation as well as excitement that in January, 1857, the young banker visited Claverton Manor on the invitation of its owner to discuss certain topics of banking and public finance; he found Mr. Wilson in bed, owing to a riding accident, but the absence of the host from the family table was more than made up for by the presence of his six daughters. Bagehot was sisterless, and had led a somewhat secluded life owing to the need of his mother (who was subject to occasional fits of insanity) for the constant attention of his father and their only son. The six sisters had no brother, and what could be more delightful for both sides? Bagehot was full of humor and high spirits, tall and thin, with rather narrow, square shoulders, 'a mass of black wavy hair; a dark eye, with depths full of slumberous playful fire; a ruddy skin that bespoke active blood, quick in its rounds; the lithe figure of an excellent horseman; a nostril full, delicate, quivering, like that of a blooded racer.' All the girls adored him, and he was exceedingly happy in their companionship. He chose the eldest and was married to her the following year. The young couple settled down at a house above Clevedon, about midway between the two family seats, and by means of frequent visits to London, made the acquaintance of the leading people of the time. Mr. Wilson was delighted to be useful to his brilliant son-in-law, and when he was sent out to India as Chancellor of the Indian Exchequer in 1859, he left the direction of the Economist in Bagehot's hands. On Wilson's unexpected death in 1860, Bagehot took charge of his affairs and became the head of his father-in-law's family, to their great relief and satisfaction. He accordingly moved to London and took up quarters in the family house. He became editor of the Economist as well as director of its policy, and wrote a great deal for it as well as for the Spectator, the National Review, and the Fortnightly. It was in the review just mentioned that the *English Constitution* first appeared as a series of nine articles spread over eighteen months; in the year in which the *English Constitution* was concluded, *Physics and Politics* began.

Lombard Street was issued in 1873 in book form without previous serial publication. President Woodrow Wilson, who was a great admirer of Bagehot, described *Lombard Street* as 'the most outwardly serious of his writings. It is his picture of the money market, whose public operations and hidden influences he exhibits with his accustomed, apparently inevitable, lucidity. He explains, as perhaps only he could explain, the parts played in the market by the Chancellor of the Exchequer, whose counsellor he often was, by the Bank of England, and by the joint-stock banks, such as his own in Somersetshire; the influences, open and covert, that make for crisis or for stability—the whole machinery and the whole psychology of the subtle game and business of finance. There is everywhere the same close intimacy between the fact and the thought. What he writes seems always a light playing through affairs, illuminating their substance, revealing their fiber.' A living financial authority, Hartley Withers, remarks that after the lapse of so many years 'it is a wonderful achievement that a book dealing with the shifting quicksands of the money market should still be a classic of which no one who wishes to understand the subject can afford to be ignorant.'

Bagehot stood three times for Parliament, always unsuccessfully, the last time in 1865; in the last dozen years of his life he was often invited to stand again, but persistently refused. He probably exerted more influence as the confidential adviser of the Chancellor of the Exchequer of both parties than he would have done as a member of the House of Commons, a position for which his peculiar abilities did not fit him; he saw too much of both sides of a question or a situation to be a strong partisan, though his opinions, once formed, were clear cut and pronounced with vigor and emphasis. His written work, admirable as it is, seems to fall short of the extraordinary impression he made upon his contemporaries. He was a professional journalist and had to meet, first of all, the needs of the hour. In so doing he succeeded in giving permanent value to work which was originally intended to satisfy the immediate occasion. There was a good deal of good work of this kind done by Victorian prose-writers that has been inevitably, if not deservedly, forgotten. It is Bagehot's distinction that his journalism has kept alive so much longer than that of his fellows.

THE HISTORIANS

Two contending impulses appear in the endeavors of Victorian historians: (1) to be lively and picturesque, giving to history the movement and interest of a Scott novel, after the manner of Macaulay and Carlyle; (2) to be scientifically detached and accurate, supporting every statement by exact evidence, after the manner of Stubbs, Creighton, and Gardiner. The former school has the disadvantage of appearing to write from a point of view previously established, rather than working toward a conclusion from the facts as they are disclosed; the latter school is frequently subject to the charge of being, except to the professional student, unreadable. The Victorians had excellent practitioners in both kinds. In the picturesque style J. A. Froude, the disciple and biographer of Carlyle, was as good as his master; 'he never fails to be interesting, and his admirable English gives a charm to everything he wrote.' J. R. Green, another writer of a vivid, romantic style, has been often decried by professional historians as a 'popularizer,' but his *Short History of the English People* (1874) brought to great masses a knowledge, accurate in the main, of the struggles of the nation towards self-government and self-expression in various commercial industrial, intellectual, and spiritual activities which previous historians had too often neglected.

William Edward Hartpole Lecky (1838–1903) won his spurs in a different field. A graduate of Trinity College, Dublin, he was only twenty-seven when he astonished the reading public by the ripeness and fulness of his knowledge as shown in the *History of the Rise and Influence of the Spirit of Rationalism in Europe*. In four years he consolidated his reputation with the *History of European Morals from Augustus to Charlemagne*. He conceived of history not as 'a series of biographies, or accidents, or pictures, but a great organic whole,' and he offered these early works as essays in that conception of history as a science. Nearly nine years elapsed before he published the first two volumes of *A History of England in the Eighteenth Century*, and it was more than twenty years before the set of eight volumes was completed. As an Irishman he was naturally interested in the relations between Ireland and England, and the discussion of this subject came to bulk larger than he had originally intended, so that he found it advisable to deal with this theme in a separate work entitled *History of Ireland in the Eighteenth Century*. With an eminently judicious mind, Lecky was well qualified to apply his own idea of a philosophic conception of history and 'to disengage from the great mass of facts, those which relate to the permanent forces of the nation, or which indicate some of the more enduring features of national life.' In questions of such immediate interest as the relations between Ireland and England, it was impossible for Lecky to please all parties, but there can be no question of his desire to be just. His last word, or at any rate the message of his maturity, was, like Sir Henry Maine's, a rather gloomy view of the future of democratic government. *Democracy and Liberty* (1894) foresaw with apprehension the coming of the Socialistic tendencies which were to prevail before and after the end of Victoria's reign.

Another Irishman who early in life won repute as a historian was James (later Viscount) Bryce, who was born at Belfast in 1838. After taking his degree at Trinity College, Oxford, he became a fellow of Oriel, and almost immediately attracted attention by a brilliant prize essay on the *Holy Roman Empire* (1864). He was appointed Regius Professor of Civil Law at the University in 1870 and held the chair for nearly a quarter of a century. Elected to the House of Commons in 1880, he became a member of the Cabinet in 1892, holding various offices while the Liberal Government was in power until 1907, when he became British Ambassador to the United States. His great work on the *American Common-wealth* was first published in 1888, and at once established itself as an authority on American institutions on account of the fulness of its information, its judicial fairness of spirit, and the business-like lucidity of its style; a new and revised edition was published in 1910. His tenure of the Ambassadorship was remarkable for the sympathy and good judgment which he brought to bear on all subjects affecting the relations between Great Britain and the United States. In the later years of his life he undertook an extensive study of the methods of government of the English-speaking democracies all over the world, which was published in 1921, under the title of *Modern Democracies*. His general conclusion was that while democracy is spreading, as a system of government it shows signs of decay, the reputation and authority of elected legislatures having declined in almost every country: 'In some they are deemed to have shown themselves unequal to their tasks, in others to have yielded to temptations, in others to be too sub-servient to party, while in all they have lost some part of the re-spect and social deference formerly accorded to them.' The extension in many directions of the sphere of government, which began in the United States about half a century ago, and has been carried furthest in New Zealand and Australia, has made demo-cratic government more difficult by the creation of a powerful bureaucracy. The complexity of modern government makes effec-tive popular control almost impossible, and increases the tempta-tions of Ministers by swelling the amount of patronage at their disposal. It was in this somewhat discouraged mood that Lord Bryce came in 1921, not very long before his death, to attend a conference on international relations and to pay his last visit to the United States. Newspaper readers and newspaper editors were rather surprised at the depressed tone of his addresses and were inclined to attribute it to old age; but it need hardly be said that his forebodings have been more than justified by subsequent events.

JOHN MORLEY
(1838–1923)

John Morley, to those who knew him or knew of him in his later life, comes to mind as a leading Liberal Minister, Secretary for Ireland under Gladstone, and Secretary for India under Camp-bell-Bannerman and Asquith, resigning in 1914 at the beginning of the War. In recognition of his political services he was raised to the peerage under the title of Viscount Morley of Blackburn, the Lancashire manufacturing town in which he was born. But probably the most influential period of his life was the fifteen years 1867–82 during which he was editor of the Fortnightly Review. The son of a provincial doctor, he had been educated at Oxford, and had considerable experience as a journalist before he went into politics. For a time he was editor of the Pall Mall Gazette, of Macmillan's Magazine, and also of the important series of critical biographies known as the English Men of Letters. To the populace he was known as the man who spelt Gladstone with a capital and God with a little g, and his conduct of the Fortnightly Review with its gospel of free intellectual and social expansion was regarded as sympathetic with heterodoxy, especially in religion. Morley admitted that in one half-year 'nearly every number contained an attack by some powerful writer, either on theology as a whole, or on some generally accepted article of theological belief.' Huxley invented the term Agnosticism, but it was largely Morley who made that attitude fashionable in intellectual circles. He was the friend of Mill, Huxley, Spencer, Meredith, Leslie Stephen, George Eliot, Matthew Arnold—all the leaders of the attack upon religious orthodoxy. His essay On Compromise (1874) was an uncompromising protest against half-heartedness and timidity in the avowal of heterodox beliefs: truth should always be the foremost consideration. The whole group had in common a denial of special revelation and a stout insistence on morality. Morley was even more unbending than his friend and master Mill, and in spite of his strong affection and admiration he regarded Mill's posthumous essay on Theism as a sort of intellectual scandal, not merely 'as an infelicitous compromise with orthodoxy, but, what was far more formidable, as actually involving a fatal relaxation of his own rules and methods of reasoning.' Oddly enough, Morley regarded Mill's sympathetic view of socialism as part of the same weakness. Morley's own attitude was more uncompromising. In his Life of Cobden (1881) he reviews almost regretfully the factory acts and poor laws passed for the protection of the working-class up to that date, and remarks, somewhat acidly, that in England 'where socialism has been less talked about than any other country in Europe, its principles have been most extensively applied.' He acquiesced reluctantly in the further socialistic legislation that followed, but drew the line at supporting the Eight Hours Bill for Miners, although his election agent warned him, almost with tears, that his opposition would cost

him his seat for Newcastle-upon-Tyne, where the miners' vote
was decisive. The miners respected the consistency of 'honest
John,' as they called him, enough to return him at that election,
but later he was defeated and had to seek a seat in Parliament
elsewhere.

In his later years Morley showed the same courage and con-
scientiousness in dealing with sedition in India, and when he retired from public life in 1914, it was with universal respect. His
greatest literary work is his monumental *Life of Gladstone* (1903),
though he also wrote monographs on *Voltaire* (1871), *Rousseau*
(1873), *Diderot and the Encyclopædists* (1878), *Burke* (1879), *Walpole* (1890), and *Cromwell* (1900), all done with the probity and
distinction characteristic of the writer as it was of the man. The
last years of his active life were given to the publication of his
Recollections (1917), in which he quotes an early criticism of himself as 'a writer who præter-calmly, sub-silently, super-persua-
sively, but subtly and potently, is exercising influence on the most
advanced and most earnest thought of the present generation;
who by a refined, destructive criticism is solving the faith of thousands, but is not contributing an iota to the reconstruction of a
systematic body of thought which can help the educator in floating
the tiniest skiff on the troubled waters of life.' It is characteristic
of Morley's intellectual detachment that he accepted this estimate,
as, on the whole, just. He comments upon it that it was far beyond
either his capacity or his ambition to produce 'a systematic
body of thought.' He aspired to be no more than 'a comrade in
the struggle for thought, and the wrestle for truth.' As such, he
made his mark upon his generation, and was esteemed alike for
the uprightness of his character, and the intellectual insight which
he brought to bear upon problems both of public policy and of
literary criticism.

CHAPTER VIII

MID-VICTORIAN NOVELISTS

SAMUEL BUTLER

(*1835–1902*)

To the disintegration of accepted beliefs, which was character-istic of this Middle Period, no one contributed more than Samuel Butler. He brought to the attack no array of indisputable scientific facts or weighty ethical arguments but the more destruc-tive weapons of ridicule, satire, irony, and paradox. To the 'other-worldliness' of such a simple maxim as 'Ye cannot serve God and Mammon,' he opposed his favorite doctrine of compromise: 'Granted that it is not easy, but nothing that is worth doing is ever easy. Easy or difficult, possible or impossible, not only has the thing got to be done, but it is exactly in doing it that the whole duty of man consists. And when the righteous man turneth away from his righteousness that he hath committed and doeth that which is neither quite lawful nor quite right, he will generally be found to have gained in amiability what he has lost in holiness. If there are two worlds (and that there are I have no doubt) it stands to reason that we ought to make the best of both of them, and more particularly of the one with which we are most immediately concerned.'

For more than a generation Butler was treated in the same way as his greater disciple, Bernard Shaw. The element of surprise in his sayings caused them to be treated as merely amusing. It was in 1907 that Shaw wrote in his Preface to *Major Barbara:*—'The late Samuel Butler, in his own department the greatest English writer of the latter half of the nineteenth century, steadily in-culcated the necessity and morality of a conscientious Laodicean-ism in religion and of an earnest and constant sense of the im-portance of money. It drives one almost to despair of English literature when one sees so extraordinary a study of English life as Butler's posthumous *Way of all Flesh* making so little impression that when, some years later, I produce plays in which Butler's extraordinary fresh, free and future-piercing suggestions have an obvious share, I am met with nothing but vague cacklings about

Ibsen and Nietzsche, and am only too thankful that they are not about Alfred de Musset and George Sand. Really, the English do not deserve to have great men.'

Not only in matter but in method and manner Shaw was much indebted to Butler. Both provoke the interest of the reader by asserting the opposite of some universally accepted commonplace so that the reader has to ask himself how much of the traditional doctrine and how much of the contradiction is true. In this way the reader's attention is gained and he is forced to think for himself—which is no doubt the first object of the writer. But the reader's attention, once gained, has to be kept; and a series of paradoxes, following each other, however brilliant, produces the fatigue of a succession of fireworks. The device of understatement, of irony, has to be used to keep the reader's attention from flagging; and sometimes the author will be driven to talking plain commonsense, if only for the sake of variety.

Naturally such a writer begins with a profound disbelief in popular morality and orthodox theology; but he must have positive principles of his own to put in their place, and he must illustrate his attack on the old landmarks with a constantly diversified play of wit and humor, or he will not only fail to win the reader's sympathy but he will not hold his attention. No doubt, when Butler appeared on the Mid-Victorian scene, the foundations of orthodoxy were already beginning to crumble—much more so than most people were at the time aware of. But it needed skill and knowledge to bring the tottering bulwarks to the ground and clear the way for something else.

At first sight, no one would have chosen Samuel Butler for this heroic task. Blue-eyed, pale, and slight, with dark hair and a half sardonic, half melancholy expression, his appearance was almost insignificant, his disposition shy to the point of timidity, his upbringing strictly orthodox, his family tradition clerical. His father was a clergyman, his grandfather a bishop, his mother a woman of strict evangelical principles, his sisters models of piety. It must have been the reaction from a religious atmosphere, said sometimes to happen in a clergyman's family, that drove Samuel Butler in the opposite direction.

He was born at Langar Rectory, in Nottinghamshire, and was sent to Shrewsbury School, of which his grandfather had been headmaster. He took a first class in classics at Cambridge when he was twenty-three. Being still rather young for the hereditary clerical profession, he was sent to act as lay reader in a London parish by way of preparation for the priestly office. But doubts had already begun to arise in Butler's mind as to the efficacy of the sacrament of baptism; he observed that the baptized members of his boys' club behaved just as badly as the unbaptized, and came to the conclusion that the ceremony had failed of its promised effect to make them 'members of Christ, children of God, and inheritors of the Kingdom of Heaven.' He communicated his doubts to his father, who was scandalized by this matter-of-fact way of testing a doctrine of the Church, and asked him what he wanted to do. 'To be a painter,' said the young man, but his father would not hear of painting as a profession. So the Prodigal Son went off to New Zealand with the portion of goods that fell to his share, and invested his money in a sheep-run. The sheep-run did well, and in 1864 Butler was able to return to England with eight thousand pounds instead of the four thousand his father had advanced to him.

In five years' solitude on his New Zealand sheep-run, Butler had ample time to think things over and to make up his mind about some of the problems which had perplexed his youth. He examined carefully the evidence for the Resurrection of Christ given in the Four Gospels, and found it insufficient to induce belief, as the accounts were in his opinion not only inconsistent but contradictory; he published his conclusions in a fifty-page tract on his return to England, and some years later used the material for a book called *The Fair Haven*. Although in New Zealand his hut was eighteen miles from the nearest human habitation and three days' journey on horseback from a bookseller, he managed to get hold of Darwin's *Origin of Species* soon after its publication and contributed three articles on it to a New Zealand newspaper. In them we see in embryo the ideas he was afterwards to develop in *Erewhon* as to the future subjection of man to the machine. In one headed 'Darwin among the Machines,' he suggests that the machines have almost achieved an independent existence in everything except the development of reproductive organs. 'It is true that these organs may be ultimately developed, inasmuch as man's interest lies in that direction; there is nothing which our infatuated race would desire more than to see a fertile union between two steam-engines; it is true that machinery is even at this present time employed in begetting machinery, in becoming the parent of machines often after its own kind, but the days of flirtation, courtship, and matrimony appear to be very remote, and indeed can hardly be realized by our feeble and imperfect imagination.' In this letter, published on June 13, 1863, we have already Butler's ideas presented in characteristically quizzical fashion with his own turn of phrase and irresponsible humor.

On his return to London Butler took three rooms and a pantry at 15 Clifford's Inn and lived there (he was a confirmed bachelor) to the day of his death. His first idea was to devote himself to art and he worked hard at painting for some years before he realized that his real strength lay not with the brush but with the pen. It was not until 1872 that he put his ideas into shape in a novel of adventure obviously modeled on *Gulliver's Travels*. In the ease and directness of his style—'just common, simple straightfor-wardness,' as he said himself—he resembles Swift, but he has none of Swift's fierceness of attack, his vehemence of onslaught— arising, no doubt, from the fierce indignation with the human race that corroded his heart. Butler finds the human race amusing, and wishes his readers to share his amusement. If a comical idea occurs to him, he cannot keep it to himself, but must communicate it to his reader, even at the expense of his own argument. He despises the worship of Mrs. Grundy, and yet he makes the evan-gelical hero of *Erewhon* admit that the 'high Ydgrunites' are altogether likeable and admirable, 'being inured from youth to exercises and athletics of all sorts, and living fearlessly under the eye of their peers, among whom there exists a high standard of courage, generosity, honor, and every good and manly quality.'

Erewhon is a Utopia—being indeed the word Nowhere spelled backwards—but it is neither an ideal community nor, like Swift's Lilliput, a bitter satire on contemporary England. It is nearer the latter, but without Swift's bitterness. The story begins with a somewhat romanticized description of the New Zealand moun-tains near his sheep-run, for which he used some of the letters he had written home and two articles he had contributed to his College Magazine. He also worked into the account of *Erewhon* the papers on Darwin mentioned above, an article on 'The World of the Unborn,' which he had already written but had not yet suc-ceeded in getting published, and the substance of two other papers which became the chapters on the Musical Banks and the trial of a man for suffering from consumption. Thus the fragments existed before the story, and the story in its construction retains marks of its fragmentary composition; but it remains one of the most original things Butler ever did. Nearly thirty years later he published a sequel entitled *Erewhon Revisited*, which purports to tell the story of the religion the hero unintentionally founded by his escape from Erewhon in a balloon, leaving behind him an illegitimate son, the son of Yram who had befriended him in prison. The sequel has the virtue which Butler claimed for it of being more of an organic whole, having been written in six months on a plan previously conceived; but it has not the interest or the originality of *Erewhon*, the ideas of which took Butler ten years to work out.

The main ideas set forth in the two books are these: (1) The danger of the mechanical side of modern civilization developing to such an extent that men become merely servants of the machines; in Erewhon this is guarded by forbidding the use of all mechanical contrivances invented after a certain date, fixed by compromise at 271 years before the passage of the statute. (2) The Erewhonian view of crime as disease and of disease as crime, so that a young man convicted of suffering from pulmonary consumption, after previous convictions for minor complaints and 'aggravated bronchitis,' is sentenced to 'imprisonment with hard labor for the rest of your miserable existence . . . and two tablespoonfuls of castor oil daily until the pleasure of the court be further known.' On the other hand, in a case where a young man had been swindled out of his property by his guardian, it was the young man who was punished for allowing himself to be swindled; he was sentenced to apologize to his guardian (presumably for leading him into temptation) and to receive twelve strokes with a cat-of-nine-tails. (3) The satire on the Established Church under the guise of Musical Banks, which everybody honors by marks of outward respect, but nobody takes seriously. 'The Musical Banks paid little or no dividend, but divided their profits by way of bonus on the original shares once in every thirty thousand years.' (4) The real religion, the worship of the goddess Ydgrun (Mrs. Grundy). 'Ydgrun certainly occupied a very anomalous position; she was held to be both omnipresent and omnipotent, and was sometimes both cruel and absurd. . . . Take her all in all, however, she was a beneficent and useful deity, who did not care how much she was denied so long as she was obeyed and feared, and who kept hundreds of thousands in those paths which make life tolerably happy, who would never have been kept there otherwise, and over whom a higher and more spiritual ideal would have had no power.' (5) Satire on the mathematical and classical training in the Universities of Oxford and Cambridge (Colleges of Unreason, where nothing is taught that is of any practical value). It will be seen that Butler managed to put his finger on most of those conventions and hypocrisies which the younger generation in the twentieth century made their chief ground of complaint against the Victorian Era.

In both books Butler ascribes to the Erewhonians his own peculiar notions about immortality. He believed in immortality of a sort, but not of the ordinary sort. His belief was something like George Eliot's idea of the Choir Invisible of those who live in lives made better by their presence; but while the emphasis in George Eliot's view is chiefly on moral influence, Butler's hope of survival rests mainly on intellectual or artistic achievement. It is briefly set forth in the Erewhonian epitaph:—

> I fall asleep in the full and certain hope
>   That my slumber shall not be broken;
>   And that though I be all-forgetting,
>   Yet shall I not be all-forgotten,
> But continue that life in the thoughts and deeds
>   Of those I loved,
> Into which, while the power to strive was yet vouchsafed me,
>   I fondly strove to enter.

His personal conviction is more clearly expressed in the sonnet:

> Not on sad Stygean shore, nor in clear sheen
> Of far Elysian plain, shall we meet those
> Among the dead whose pupils we have been,
> Nor those great shades whom we have held as foes;
> No meadow of asphodel our feet shall tread,
> Nor shall we look each other in the face
> To love or hate each other being dead,
> Hoping some praise, or fearing some disgrace.
> We shall not argue saying, ''Twas thus' or 'Thus,'
> Our argument's whole drift we shall forget;
> Who's right, who's wrong, 'twill be all one to us;
> We shall not even know that we have met.
>   Yet meet we shall, and part, and meet again,
>   Where dead men meet, on lips of living men.

During the thirty years which separated the publication of *Erewhon*, Butler's first book, from that of *Erewhon Revisited*, the last of his books issued in his lifetime, he was busily engaged with various literary, scientific, artistic, and musical projects. *Erewhon* scored an unlooked for success; the first edition was sold out in three weeks and the type had all to be set again for a new edition. If Butler had been willing to exploit this vein, he might easily have made himself a popular writer; but he left the composition of

Erewhon Revisited till most of his first readers had died or forgotten him. In the meantime he went on with literary undertakings which interested him, but which the public did not care about. His immediate concern was with the problem of the Resurrection which he had already discussed in a tract published before he left New Zealand. He now recast his material in a very different form, taking as his model Defoe's ironical pamphlet, *The Shortest Way with the Dissenters*. Butler imagined two evangelical clergymen, brothers, one dead and the other living. The deceased brother, John Pritchard Owen, was supposed to have written a serious evangelical treatise 'in defense of the miraculous element of our Lord's ministry upon earth, both as against rationalistic impugners and certain orthodox defenders.' The living brother, William Bickersteth Owen, was credited with a memoir of the author of the treatise. The brothers existed only in Butler's imagination, and the treatise was a hoax, for the arguments in defense of the Resurrection were presented in such a way as to be ridiculous when closely examined. But Butler (who published *The Fair Haven* anonymously as he had done with *Erewhon*) had copied the style of the evangelical tract so well that the religious papers were taken in by it and reviewed it accordingly. They were naturally very indignant when Butler issued another edition with his own name and acknowledged the deception he had practised.

Having seriously offended the Church, Butler next undertook a quarrel with the scientists. He thought that while Darwin's presentation of the evidence in support of the evolution theory was overwhelming, the process of natural selection was insufficient to explain the phenomena, and that variation was due less to chance and environment and more to cunning and effort, design or memory, conscious or unconscious. Habit and memory were, in Butler's opinion, the means by which variations were developed and transmitted, and in this view he is borne out by some recent investigators in the field. Professor E. W. MacBride, a leading London biologist, said in 1932: 'An acquired character is primarily an acquired habit, and evidence is accumulating on all sides that acquired habits have an influence on the habits of the offspring. This influence is slow, and often takes a long time to manifest itself. There is a long latent period, and only when a new habit has become ingrained for many generations does it affect visible structure. I have found through my acquaintance with experts on the evidence for evolution, both those who study fossils and those who study existing races, that more and more are being driven to the conclusion that the inheritance of acquired habit has been the method by which the evolution of species has proceeded. In my address last year I gave a number of cases in which direct experimental proof of the inheritance of acquired habit had been obtained. It is utterly unscientific to put forward natural selection as an alternative theory to the inheritance of acquired habit, because natural selection simply means that some live and others die. No evolution would be possible unless the some who live differ from those who die, and if we refuse to believe in those differences being brought about by habit the only alternative is to attribute them to chance, and this, in my opinion, is not a scientific method of reasoning at all.'

Butler expounded his theories in a series of books: *Life and Habit* (1877); *Evolution Old and New*, or *A Comparison of the Theories of Buffon, Dr. Erasmus Darwin, and Lamarck with those of Charles Darwin* (1879); *Unconscious Memory* (1880); *Luck or Cunning as the Main Means of Organic Modification? An Attempt to Throw Additional Light upon Charles Darwin's Theory of National Selection* (1886). All these Butler published at his own expense and at a considerable loss; the public did not buy them, and the biologists paid no attention to them. Unfortunately Butler confused the issue with a personal quarrel with Charles Darwin, first as to the credit given by Darwin in the *Origin of Species* to his predecessors; and secondly as to the credit given to Butler himself in some of Darwin's later publications. Darwin appears to have been technically guilty of an oversight, but Butler's accusation of a lack of good faith was absurd and recoiled upon the head of the accuser.

In his own cranky, wrongheaded fashion Butler knew what he was doing, or thought he did. He wrote in 1883: 'If my books succeed after my death . . . let it be understood that they failed during my life for a few very obvious reasons of which I was quite aware, for the effect of which I was prepared before I wrote my books, and which on consideration I found insufficient to deter me. I attacked people who were at once unscrupulous and powerful, and I made no alliances. I did this because I did not want to be bored and have my time wasted and my pleasures curtailed. I had money enough to live on, and preferred addressing myself to posterity rather than to any except a very few of my own contemporaries. Those few I have always kept well in mind. I think of them continually when in doubt about any passage, but beyond these few I will not go. Posterity will give a man a fair hearing; his own times will not do so if he is attacking vested interests, and

I have attacked two powerful sets of vested interests at once. (The Church and Science.) What is the good of addressing people who will not listen? I have addressed the next generation and have therefore said many things which want time before they become palatable. Any man who wishes his work to stand will sacrifice a good deal of his immediate audience for the sake of being attractive to a much larger number of people later on. He cannot gain this later audience unless he has been fearless and thoroughgoing, and if he is this, he is sure to have to tread on the corns of a great many of those who live at the same time with him, however little he may wish to do so. He must not expect these people to help him on, nor wonder if, for a time, they succeed in snuffing him out. It is part of the swim that it should be so. Only, as one who believes himself to have practised what he preaches, let me assure anyone who has money of his own that to write fearlessly for posterity and not get paid for it is much better fun than I can imagine its being to write like, we will say, George Eliot and make a lot of money by it.'

Butler was not content merely to antagonize the Church and Science. An opportunity to score off people or to say something humorous about them in a not unkindly way was more than he could resist. In 1874 his Canadian investments were doing badly and he went out to Montreal to look after them. There he met in a Museum a janitor engaged in skinning an owl and asked him why the statue of the Discobolus was pushed into a corner. 'Because,' answered the janitor (according to Butler's report), 'he is vulgar; he has no pants on.' On this basis (perhaps partly imagined) Butler constructed a satirical *Psalm of Montreal*, with the refrain 'O God! O Montreal!' and reaching its climax in the lines:

'Thou callest trousers "pants" and I call them trousers.
Therefore thou art damned to hellfire for everlasting!'
O God! O Montreal!

Butler thought later that he ought to have presented the MS. of this poem to the City of Montreal, but he had given it to some one else before that happy thought occurred to him. The poem was printed in the Spectator in 1878 and was much sought after as one of Butler's most humorous efforts before it appeared in more permanent form.

When he was not too busy chaffing the colonials and insulting the scientists, Butler painted pictures and composed music. An oratorio he wrote on 'The Return of Ulysses' directed his attention to the *Odyssey*, and after reading it very carefully he arrived at the entirely original conclusion that it was written by a woman, that the authoress was the heroine Nausicaa, and that she lived at Trapani in Sicily. To verify this remarkable hypothesis he visited Sicily and other parts of Italy several times, staying for weeks together at a country inn at Calatafimi near Trapani. The results of this freak of Butler's were twofold: he translated Homer into an easy colloquial prose, erring as far in the direction of undue familiarity as previous versions had done in stiffness and reserve; and a street of Calatafimi was named after him. Otherwise no one paid any attention to his Homeric theory.

Having no luck with the classical professors, Butler next tried the Shakespearean scholars, who were full of theories about the identity of 'Mr. W. H.' described by Shakespeare as 'the only begetter' of his sonnets. Butler's theory was simple: W. H. was an entirely obscure person named William Hughes, who had sold the sonnets to a bookseller because he needed the money. This did not please the professors of English any more than *The Authoress of the Odyssey* had pleased the classicists.

There is no telling what other heresies would have occurred to Butler's ingenious brain if he had not soon after been overtaken by death. But he left behind him two bombs to be exploded for the delight of the irreverent and the scandal of the good. One was a novel *The Way of All Flesh*, on which he was at work from 1872 to 1885 and which was not published till 1903. It is largely autobiographical in character and describes his parents, teachers, pastors, and masters with a satiric irreverence which amounted almost to a scandal. Butler anticipated, if he did not originate, the revolt against the family which was one of the chief characteristics of twentieth century society. He says of 'The Family' in his *Notebooks:* 'I believe that more unhappiness comes from this source than from any other—I mean from the attempt to prolong family connection unduly and to make people hang together who would never naturally do so.'

The *Notebooks* were five or six manuscript volumes which Butler left to his literary executor. He had accumulated the entries in them during his daily attendance for years at the British Museum Library, not by levying on the works of other authors, but by jotting down such wise or witty thoughts as occurred to him from time to time. Many of these he used in his published works as opportunity offered; others were left to be given to the world in the selections from the *Notebooks* published in 1912 and 1934. For the reader who desires a taste of the Butler flavor they afford the readiest access to his wit. Amid much that is erratic and extravagant, they contain many things that are not only well said but acutely observed. For instance, 'A man will feel the loss of money more keenly than loss of his bodily health, so long as he can keep his money. Take his money away and deprive him of the means of earning any more, and his health will soon break up; but leave him his money and, even though his health breaks up and he dies, he does not mind it so much as we think. Money losses are the worst, loss of health is next worse, and loss of reputation comes in a bad third. All other things are amusements provided money, health, and good name are untouched.'

Butler was a curious mixture of a man of sound judgment and an inspired crank, and in his books, as no doubt in real life, his moods vary with extraordinary quickness. In spite of recurring extravagances and paradoxes, he often sets forth the homeliest truth in the simplest fashion, as when he says that the glory of God is best advanced by advancing that of man, and that the glory of man is 'good breeding,' the latter phrase being interpreted to signify both nature and nurture. Most of us would accept his definition of nice people as those who have 'good health, good looks, good sense, experience, a kindly nature, and a fair balance of cash in hand.' They are the people to whom 'all things work together for good.' 'We love God,' Butler adds slyly, 'because He first loved us.'

GEORGE ELIOT
(1819–1880)

George Eliot was a striking example of the combination of Victorian earnestness with an intellectual independence which impelled her to reject the Victorian tradition and to defy the Victorian conventions; she accepted the Victorian morality in its essence and Victorian religion in its spirit, but refused to submit to the forms of either. She paid the penalties for heterodoxy and declined what she regarded as the opiates of the orthodox faith, but continued to accept its obligations as binding upon herself and others.

She was the daughter of Robert Evans, a builder and carpenter of Welsh origin, who had established himself by his diligence and uprightness as the trusted agent of the Arbury estate in Warwickshire; the owner, Sir Roger Newdigate, represented the University of Oxford in Parliament for thirty years in the second half of the eighteenth century and founded the Newdigate prize for English poetry. Mary Ann Evans was born at Arbury Farm, but within a few months of her birth the family moved to Griff, 'a charming red-brick, ivy-covered house on the Arbury estate,' which was the home of Marian (as she later preferred to call herself) for the first twenty-one years of her life. She went to school in the neighboring towns of Nuneaton and Coventry and had (for the time) a good education, interrupted when she was sixteen by the illness and death of her mother, whose place she was called upon to take in her father's household. She became an 'exemplary housewife' and acquired an interest and skill in household arts which she never lost, but she did not neglect her intellectual development, studying French, German, and Italian as well as English literature. Her mind at nineteen (she records at the time) presented 'an assemblage of disjointed specimens of history, ancient and modern; scraps of poetry picked up from Shakespeare, Cowper, Wordsworth, and Milton; newspaper topics; morsels of Addison and Bacon, Latin verbs, geometry, entomology, and chemistry; reviews and metaphysics—all arrested and petrified and smothered by the fast-thickening everyday accession of actual events, relative anxieties, and household cares and vexations.' With a man's force of genius in her, she had to suffer (as she put it many years later) 'the slavery of being a girl.' Her 'slavery' went beyond subjection to the conventional restrictions of her time and the physical limitations of her sex: it extended to her emotional nature. She was always, to the day of her death, in despair about her own powers and ambitions, dependent upon some one else for stimulus and encouragement, passionately devoted in those early years to her father and her brother, and after her father's death, when she was thirty, writing: 'The only ardent hope I have for my future life is to have given to me some woman's duty, some possibility of devoting myself where I may see a daily result of pure calm blessedness in the life of another.'

When she was twenty-one, her brother took over the business at Griff, and father and daughter removed to a semi-detached house in Foleshill Road, Coventry. The removal was the occasion for a change in her intellectual and religious point of view. Hitherto she had moved in a circle of narrow, evangelical opinion: her father was a 'churchman of the old school,' and she had an aunt who was a Methodist preacher, the original of the Dinah Morris of *Adam Bede*. At Coventry the Evanses lived next door to the sister of a sceptical ribbon-manufacturer, Charles Bray, who had just published a book entitled *The Philosophy of Necessity*. Bray had married into a local Unitarian family and his brother-in-law, Charles Hennell, was the author of an *Enquiry into the Origin of Christianity*, which had great influence on the impressionable mind of Marian Evans, already unsettled by previous reading. By the time she was twenty-two, she had become sufficiently clear in her new convictions to refuse to go to church—a decision which greatly upset her orthodox father. The discussion on this point became so acute as to threaten a separation, and Marian gave way to the family tradition. On fuller reflection her impulse 'to withhold the slightest sanction from all that contains even a mixture of supposed error' seemed to her premature. Speculative truth began to appear 'but a shadow of individual minds.' Agreement between intellects seeming unattainable, she turned to the truth of *feeling* as the only universal bond of union. So she continued to go to church with her father, and he on his part tolerated her friendship with the sceptical Brays and Hennells.

The upshot of her break with orthodoxy was not an attitude of antagonism but a feeling of sympathy with all forms of religious belief, which proved of primary importance when she undertook imaginative work. In her intellectual maturity she wrote to a personal friend: 'I have too profound a conviction of the efficacy that lies in all sincere faith, and the spiritual blight that comes with no faith, to have any negative propagandism in me. In fact I have very little sympathy with Freethinkers as a class, and have lost all interest in mere antagonism to religious doctrines.' And again, to the same friend: 'As for the forms and ceremonies, I feel no regret that any should turn to them for comfort if they can find comfort in them; sympathetically I enjoy them myself. But I have faith in the working-out of higher possibilities than the Catholic or any other Church has presented; and those who have strength to wait and endure are bound to accept no formula which their whole souls—their intellect as well as their emotions—do not embrace with entire reverence. The "highest calling and election" is to *do without opium*, and live through all our pain with conscious, clear-eyed endurance.'

Meanwhile, friendship with the liberal group at Coventry led to her further identification with sceptical thought. Charles Hennell was engaged to a young lady who had undertaken the translation of the most important sceptical book of the time, the *Life of Jesus*, by Strauss; and when the young lady married, the work fell by natural reversion into the hands of Marian Evans.

She found the task laborious and often uncongenial, but she went
through with it and it was published anonymously in 1846. Although by this time the breakdown of her father's health and her
devoted care of him made a heavy tax on her energies, she turned to
another difficult piece of translation, Spinoza's *Tractatus Theo-
logico-Politicus*, and laid this aside to make a version of Ludwig
Feuerbach's *Essence of Christianity*, which was published in 1854.
It was her only publication bearing the name of Marian Evans.

Her father's death in 1849 freed her from the necessity of living
at Coventry, and after traveling and resting for a while to recover
her health, in 1851 she settled down in London as assistant editor
of the Radical Westminster Review. Her work brought her into
contact with many of the London intellectuals, and she formed a
close friendship with Herbert Spencer, who at the end of 1851
made her acquainted with George Henry Lewes. Lewes was literary editor of a weekly periodical and known as the author of
popular books on drama, philosophy, and science. He was versatile rather than profound, plain-looking—Douglas Jerrold called
him 'the ugliest man in London'—but attractive by his brilliance
as a talker, his wit and gaiety. Lewes had been deserted by his
wife, who had left him with three children to take care of; he had
poor health and an insufficient income. Circumstances prevented
him from obtaining a divorce, and in 1854 Marian Evans became,
in everything except the legal tie, Mrs. Lewes. She asserted her
right to that name, with a complete conviction that she was entitled to it, and resented being addressed as 'Miss Evans,' having
accepted all the responsibilities of a married woman. She was an
affectionate mother to his three boys and gave new heart and
courage to her husband in his illness and depression. Five years
after their union, he wrote in his diary: 'Since then my life has
been a new birth. To her I owe all my prosperity and my happiness.' No legally-wedded pair could have exceeded their devotion
to each other.

Without the stimulus of her husband's encouragement it seems
likely that George Eliot (as we must now call her) would never
have written fiction, and without his constant support and help it
is certain that she could never have accomplished the succession
of stories and novels that filled the rest of their joint lives. She
had indeed previously had a vague dream that some time or other
she might write a novel, but had never gone further than an introductory chapter describing a Staffordshire village and the life of
the neighboring farmhouses. When Lewes was in Germany with

her in 1854–55 completing his *Life of Goethe*, she read him, one evening in Berlin, this introductory chapter, and he was struck with it as a bit of concrete description. When they came back to England and she was busy writing reviews and articles for the Westminster Review, he began to say very positively, 'You must try and write a story,' and one morning, in a half dream, half daze, there came into her head the title, 'The Sad Fortunes of the Reverend Amos Barton.' This struck Lewes as 'capital' and with his encouragement she began on September 22, 1856, and finished on November 5 a story under that title, planned as the first of a series to be called 'Scenes of Clerical Life.' The pen-name under which this and all her future work appeared was chosen by her because George was Lewes's Christian name and Eliot was a good, mouth-filling, easily pronounced word. It was agreed that Lewes should submit the story to Blackwood's Magazine as the work of an anonymous friend. It was accepted, and published in the magazine in 1857; when the first part appeared, John Blackwood sent Lewes a letter of congratulation and a check for fifty guineas—a very welcome addition to the family exchequer. Two more stories were written during the year, and early in 1858 the three were published together in two volumes. Copies were sent to Dickens, Thackeray, and Mrs. Carlyle; all were appreciative and curious about the new author; Thackeray thought it was a man, Dickens guessed that it was a woman, and Mrs. Carlyle had the ingenious suggestion that it must be a man of middle age, 'with a wife from whom he has got those beautiful feminine touches.' The third story, *Mr. Gilfil's Love-Story*, was especially admired for its idyllic charm.

Before *Scenes of Clerical Life* appeared in book form, George Eliot had begun a full length novel, *Adam Bede*, the germ of which was an anecdote told her nearly twenty years earlier by her Methodist aunt, wife of her father's younger brother. This Mrs. Evans had given spiritual consolation to a country girl convicted of the murder of her illegitimate baby, had induced her to confess, and accompanied her in the cart to the place of execution. When George Eliot was writing *Scenes of Clerical Life*, she related this incident to Lewes, and he remarked that it would make a fine element in a story. She thought of it first as one of the series of *Scenes*, but on consideration reserved it for independent treatment. So were conceived the characters of Hetty Sorrel and her seducer, Arthur Donnithorne; her lover, Adam Bede, was molded on the character of George Eliot's father and one or two incidents in his early life. Adam's fight with Arthur Donnithorne in the wood and his marriage to the Methodist evangelist at the end of the book were due to suggestions from Lewes and have been considered by some critics unfortunate additions to the original story as it first shaped itself in George Eliot's mind. On the whole, however, there can be no doubt that she was greatly indebted to Lewes for advice and encouragement, and when the manuscript was finished, she gave it to him with an inscription setting forth that it would never have been written but for the happiness which his love had conferred on her life.

Blackwood was greatly pleased with *Adam Bede*, and offered eight hundred pounds for four years' copyright, which was promptly accepted. Its success on publication in February, 1859, was immediate and overwhelming; by July it had gone into a fourth edition, all of which was sold in two weeks. Blackwood doubled the payment agreed upon for the copyright, and the author declined an offer of twelve hundred pounds from an American publisher for her next story. With her first novel George Eliot had won a first place among contemporary writers of fiction, with only Dickens and Thackeray ahead of her, and had secured an income which put an end to the financial anxieties of the Lewes family.

In her next novel, *The Mill on the Floss*, George Eliot drew even more deeply on the recollections of her childhood and youth. As *Adam Bede* was woven round the characters of her father and her aunt, so *The Mill on the Floss* was woven round her childish affection for her brother Isaac and her separation from him by her union with Lewes. Maggie Tulliver in her passionate ardor, her demand for affection, and her intellectual and spiritual ambitions is Mary Ann Evans, placed indeed in very different circumstances and confronted by a different problem, which was solved by the author for her heroine in a directly opposite sense from that she had adopted in her own life. Her union with Lewes was in defiance of convention and family tradition; Maggie Tulliver's renunciation of her lover was in submission to family tradition and what society held to be the moral law. Recognizing her own case as exceptional, George Eliot was careful in her novels—perhaps over careful—to stress the duty of fidelity to matrimonial obligations and consideration for the feelings of others even under the sway of an overpowering passion. The pervading moral atmosphere of her novels is stern and even bleak, and her ethical teaching is conveyed both in the treatment of character and plot and in direct precept. This has no doubt contributed to alienate the present generation of readers as much as it won the approval and support of the Puritan middle class of her own time.

The success of *The Mill on the Floss* was immediate and unmistakable. Blackwood agreed to pay two thousand pounds if the subscription edition reached four thousand, and more in proportion; the actual issue went beyond 6,000. After three months in Italy George Eliot and Lewes came back to establish themselves in a new house, and in spite of weariness of body and some depression of spirit, a sudden inspiration came to her at the beginning of 1861 for a new story, *Silas Marner*, which was completed in two months and published in one volume, as it was less than the full novel length. Perhaps on account of its simple structure and lack of elaboration it has held the favor of the public better than her great novels.

During the visit to Italy in 1860, George Eliot was fired with the idea of writing a historical romance of Florentine life at the end of the fifteenth century, with the career and martyrdom of the Catholic evangelist Savanarola as its central theme. When she left England she felt that she had exhausted her store of memories of English provincial society as she had known it in her youth, and that she must absorb some new life and gather fresh ideas. But while the novelist's absorption of the life of her childhood and youth was spontaneous and unconscious, the acquisition of the life of another time and place—especially one so far removed as fifteenth century Florence—was a deliberate process of intensive study. She was at all times a tremendous reader, in several languages, and it seems likely that this continuous intellectual exertion was responsible for the prolonged headaches, physical weakness, and mental depression from which she frequently suffered. She plunged into the study of Florentine history with conscientious ardor, but soon found that the reading of books, however laboriously prolonged and exhaustive, was not sufficient. In the spring of 1861 she spent over a month at Florence, 'looking at streets, buildings, and pictures, hunting up old books at shops or stalls, or reading at the Magliabecchian Library,' always with the help of her devoted husband. In the autumn she was back in England, utterly despondent and dejected, studying Florentine history, topography, and costume in endless books, but incapable of constructing anything. It was only at the beginning of 1862 that she was able to make a real start with *Romola* and the last stroke was not added till June, 1863, when she handed the completed manuscript to Lewes with the inscription: 'To the Husband whose perfect love has been the best source of her insight and strength, this manuscript is given by his devoted wife, the writer.' The work of composition took more out of her than ever before. 'I began it,' she said, 'a young woman—I finished it an old woman.' Lewes thought 'it ploughed into her more than any of her other books.' From a professional point of view it was a success; she received seven thousand pounds for its serial publication in the Cornhill Magazine. Artistically, it was a failure; she not only failed to re-capture the spirit of the time and place, but she did not succeed in giving to her characters the natural life, ready wit, and easy movement which had distinguished her earlier work. Even in the opinion of her friendliest critics, *Romola* marks the decline of her genius.

She returned to the provincial sphere of her early successes, but either the field was worked out or her hand had lost its cunning. Her next novel, *Felix Holt, the Radical* (1866) was based upon a girlish recollection of an election riot about the time of the passage of the first Reform Bill, fortified by a diligent study of the file of the London Times for 1832–33. The novel was enriched by a rather melodramatic family scandal and an elaborate legal complication about a will, but it lacked vitality and it lacked charm. The Cornhill Magazine was unwilling to pay five thousand pounds for it, but it was accepted at that price by Blackwood.

Middlemarch was George Eliot's supreme and most elaborate effort to portray provincial life as she had seen it as a little girl in the years just before the first Reform Act. It was begun in 1869, delayed by ill health, and not finished till 1872. It is a big book, developing at length the love stories of Dorothea Brooke, Rosamond Vincy, and Mary Garth, as they are intermingled with the social and political life of a provincial town. Two of the three resulting marriages are failures, and the prevailing tone of the book is sad—even sadder than that of her previous work. As a study of the total life of a community in its various ramifications, *Middlemarch* has always won critical admiration, but the modern reader seldom cares to have his fiction encumbered with so much psychological analysis and moral earnestness.

During the last years of her life George Eliot occupied a position of undisputed dignity and authority in the intellectual world. Her house in Regent's Park was a sort of temple, of which she was the presiding deity, and Lewes the lively and good-humored attendant priest. She was received with honor at Oxford and Cambridge,

and perhaps the best account of the impression she made upon her
contemporaries in her later years is that given by a Cambridge
don, Frederick Myers, of a meeting with her at her visit to the
latter university in 1873: 'I walked with her once in the Fellows'
Garden of Trinity, on an evening of a rainy May, and she, stirred
somewhat beyond her wont, and taking as her text the three words
which have been used so often as the inspiring trumpet-calls of
men—the words *God*, *Immortality*, *Duty!*—pronounced with terrible earnestness how inconceivable was the *first*, how unbelievable
the *second*, and yet how peremptory and absolute the *third*. Never,
perhaps, had sterner accents affirmed the sovereignty of impersonal
and uncompromising law. I listened and night fell; her grave,
majestic countenance turned towards me like a Sybil's in the gloom;
it was as though she withdrew from my grasp, one by one, the two
scrolls of promise, and left me the third scroll only, awful with inevitable fates.'

The death of Lewes in 1878 left her prostrate with grief, for
she was absolutely dependent upon his constant companionship.
She said of herself: 'It is hard to believe long together that anything is "worth while" unless there is some eye to kindle in common with our own, some brief word uttered now and then to imply
that what is infinitely precious to us is precious alike to another
mind.' In *The Mill on the Floss* she insists again and again on her
heroine's 'need of being loved,' 'the hunger of the heart—as peremptory as that other hunger by which Nature forces us to submit to the yoke.' This dependence upon affection was as true of
Maggie Tulliver's creator as of Maggie herself, and though contemporary opinion was somewhat scandalized by George Eliot's
marriage at sixty to a much younger man, a New York banker
named John Walter Cross, the step was in absolute accord with
the demands of her nature. They traveled together in Italy and
came back to England in the autumn of 1880. They had hardly
settled into their new house in Cheyne Walk, Chelsea, before
George Eliot sickened and died. Her grave is in Highgate Cemetery, next to that of George Henry Lewes.

It seems unlikely that the work of George Eliot will ever regain
the esteem in which it was held by her contemporaries. In spite
of her equivocal position in society on account of her irregular
union with Lewes—perhaps all the more on account of it—she
held the ethical purpose of her novels of no less importance than
their artistic merits, and her didacticism—sometimes rather
heavy-handed, it must be confessed—is now quite out of fashion.

sanity

Her conscious life was conducted under the steady pressure of a sense of duty, and it was never an easy, and seldom a pleasant life. Its spirit is finely expressed by what is generally regarded as the most moving passage in her poetry:

> O may I join the choir invisible
> Of those immortal dead who live again
> In minds made better by their presence: live
> In pulses stirred to generosity,
> In deeds of daring rectitude, in scorn
> For miserable aims that end with self,
> In thoughts sublime that pierce the night like stars,
> And with their mild persistence urge man's search
> To vaster issues.

GEORGE MEREDITH
(1828–1909)

Meredith was the acknowledged leader of the English and American intelligentsia during the latter part of the Victorian Era, and during his long and active career as an author exercised a widespread influence, not only on literature, but on public opinion as to many important questions. His first volume of poems was published in 1851, his first important novel in 1859; the establishment of his reputation may be dated from the publication of *Diana of the Crossways* and the first collected edition of his novels in 1885. A 'limited edition' of his complete works in thirty-two volumes was begun in 1896, and there were numerous other editions thereafter. Though he never became a popular author, his works were carefully—even devoutly—read by the more thoughtful public on both sides of the Atlantic, and his high-minded attitude to life and letters made a deep and abiding impression.

His climb to fame was unusually painful and laborious. The son and grandson of Portsmouth tailors, he was conscious in his youth of the snobbishness of the 'county' society and perhaps of his own reactions to it; he portrayed them, amusingly and satirically, in his early novel *Evan Harrington*, but he seems to have remained somewhat sensitive on the subject long after he had reached maturity. His father's lack of business ability and the death of his mother when he was five years old made his early education erratic and unprofitable; he gained little beyond dislike for the scholastic and especially for the religious ministrations of his childhood. 'I remember,' he records, 'how all love of the

Apostles was belabored out of me by three Sunday services of prodigious length. *Corinthians* will forever be associated in my mind with rows of wax candles and a holy drone overhead, combined with the sensation that those who did not choose the road to Heaven, enjoyed by far the pleasantest way. I cannot hear of *Genesis*, or of the sins of amorous David, or of Hezekiah, without fidgetting in my chair, as if it had turned to the utterly unsympathetic Church-wood of yore. In despair, I used to begin a fresh chapter of the adventures of St. George (a serial story, continued from Sunday to Sunday), and carry it on till the preacher's voice fell. Sometimes he deceived me (I hope, not voluntarily) and his voice bade St. George go back into his box, and then ascended in renewed vigor once more; leaving me vacant of my comforting hero; who was not to be revived, after such treatment. I have known subsequent hours of ennui: but nothing to be compared with those early ones.'

Meredith had pleasanter memories of the Moravian School at Neuwied on the Rhine, to which he was sent at the age of fourteen. His sensitive nature received a strong impression from the religious atmosphere of the place, and though he later rejected the evangelical dogmas he had accepted with the enthusiasm of youth, the moral training he received made a permanent mark on his mind and character. Returning to England, he went to London, where his father had set up in business as a tailor, and became articled clerk in the office of a London lawyer, who was more interested in his own literary ambitions than in the practice of his profession. It was for a manuscript magazine conducted by his employer that Meredith wrote his first published poem, which was printed in 1849 in Chambers's Journal. Through him, too, Meredith made literary acquaintances, among them the son and daughter of the eccentric novelist, Thomas Love Peacock. The daughter was a young widow, of brilliant wit and striking beauty, and Meredith fell an immediate victim to her charms; they were married in 1849, when Meredith was only twenty-one. 'No sun warmed my roof-tree,' Meredith said long after; 'the marriage was a blunder; she was nine years my senior.' As a matter of fact, the young couple seldom had a roof-tree to warm. Having little money, they lived for a time with Peacock in London, and then dispersedly in lodgings and boarding-houses, settling down ultimately in rooms at Seaford in Sussex. Here, in 1858, the final rupture took place; Mrs. Meredith went off to Italy with a lover, who deserted her. She returned to England and sought a reconciliation

with her husband, but he was inexorable. In 1861, on her deathbed, she asked him to come to see her, but he refused; he reluctantly allowed their little boy to see his mother before she died.
   This crisis in Meredith's life found literary expression in a series
of fifty poems published in 1862 under the title *Modern Love*. In
the first poem the wedded pair are already estranged:

> Like sculptured effigies they might be seen
> Upon their marriage-tomb, the sword between;
> Each wishing for the sword that severs all.

The husband's offense was that 'in Love's deep woods, he dreamt
of loyal Life.' He wished to be not merely an ardent lover, but
a man with work to do 'worthy of the world.'

> Oh, had I with my darling helped to mince
> The facts of life, you still had seen me go
> With hindward feather and with forward toe,
> Her much-adored delightful Fairy Prince.

Outwardly they keep up appearances, and present to their friends
the spectacle of a perfectly united pair:

> At dinner, she is hostess, I am host.
> Went the feast ever cheerfuller? She keeps
> The Topic over intellectual deeps
> In buoyancy afloat. They see no ghost.
> With sparkling surface-eyes we ply the ball:
> It is in truth a most contagious game:
> HIDING THE SKELETON, shall be its name.
> Such play as this, the devils might appal!
> But here's the greater wonder; in that we
> Enamored of an acting nought can tire,
> Each other, like true hypocrites, admire;
> Warm-lighted looks, Love's ephemerioe,
> Shoot gaily o'er the dishes and the wine.
> We waken envy of our happy lot.
> Fast, sweet, and golden, shows the marriage-knot.
> Dear guests, you now have seen Love's corpse-light shine.

Each seeks consolation—or at least, distraction—in another
attachment. There is a moment when reconciliation seems possible:

> We saw the swallows gathering in the sky,
> And in the osier-isle we heard them noise.
> We had not to look back on summer joys,
> Or forward to a summer of bright dye:

But in the largeness of the evening earth
Our spirits grew as we went side by side.
The hour became her husband and my bride.
Love that had robbed us so, thus blessed our dearth!
The pilgrims of the year waxed very loud
In multitudinous chatterings, as the flood
Full brown came from the West, and like pale blood
Expanded to the upper crimson cloud.
Love that had robbed us of immortal things,
This little moment mercifully gave,
Where I have seen across the twilight wave
The swan sail with her young beneath her wings.

But she believes he is sacrificing himself for her sake and leaves him so that he may be free to seek the lady of his true desires. When next he sees her, she is at the point of death.

'Now kiss me, dear! it may be now!' she said.
Lethe had passed those lips, and he knew all.

In the final poem Meredith sums up the thoughts on life suggested to him by his own bitter experience of passionate love and its frustration by contact with the facts of a workaday world.

Thus piteously Love closed what he begat:
The union of this ever-diverse pair!
These two were rapid falcons in a snare,
Condemned to do the flitting of the bat.
Lovers beneath the singing sky of May,
They wandered once; clear as the dew on flowers:
But they fed not on the advancing hours:
Their hearts held cravings for the buried day.
Then each applied to each that fatal knife,
Deep questioning, which probes to endless dole.
Ah, what a dusty answer gets the soul
When hot for certainties in this our life!—
In tragic hints here see what evermore
Moves dark as yonder midnight ocean's force,
Thundering like ramping hosts of warrior horse,
To throw that faint thin line upon the shore.

Without the help of any biographical clue, it is not surprising that the critics failed to understand or appreciate *Modern Love*. Meredith was himself conscious that it 'could only be apprehended by the few who would read it many times'; he looked 'to a severe drubbing from the Reviewers'; and he got it. His friend Swinburne protested at the lack of comprehension of 'a work of such subtle strength, such depth of delicate power, such passionate and various beauty'; and he pointed to Meredith as 'one of the three or four poets now alive whose work, perfect or imperfect, is always as noble in design as it is often faultless in result.' But in 1862 Swinburne protested in vain.

Meredith had no better luck with his first great novel, *The Ordeal of Richard Feverel*. Left by the desertion of his wife with the responsibility of bringing up their little son, he turned his thoughts to the subject of education, and found an outlet for them in a novel about a boy, similarly bereft of a mother's care and brought up by an eccentric and misogynist father. The story turns on the seduction of the youth by a London adventuress, and the episode is described in a lively fashion which gave offense to the reviewers and (what was more important) to the chief circulating library (Mudie's) which refused to send the book out to its readers. As at this date the circulating library was the main avenue of access for the reading public to the three volume novel then in vogue, this amounted to a virtual suppression, and Meredith's chances of success as a writer of fiction were seriously affected. A reputation for impropriety might not have hurt him so much if it had not been accompanied by the criticism that his work was extremely hard to understand; the combination not only denied him for many years the general appreciation every writer desires, but it seriously diminished his income. His real ambition was to write poetry, but after the reception of the volume containing *Modern Love*, he said: 'Truly the passion to produce verse in our region is accursed. I ask myself why I should labor, and, for the third time, pay to publish the result, with a certainty of being yelled at, and haply spat upon, for my pains.' Of his novels he wrote to Swinburne in 1867: '*Vittoria* passes to the limbo where the rest of my works repose,' and to his son the following year: 'My novels have been kept back by having had to write on newspapers—the only things that paid.'

To those who associate the name of Meredith with Radical opinions it must seem odd that both the newspapers for which he wrote were Conservative; for eight years he wrote editorials for the Ipswich Journal, and in 1866 he went to the Italian front in the struggle against Austria as war correspondent for the Morning Post, of which his friend Hardman was editor. His main source of income was his salary (£250 a year) for acting as reader to the publishing firm of Chapman & Hall; one of their regular clients was Anthony Trollope, to whom the firm paid an average of £4,500 a year for copyrights, so that it is no wonder that Meredith was discontented. He toiled at the readership for thirty years after the publication of *Richard Feverel*, and was glad to eke out his income during the earlier part of the period by reading aloud to an old lady. It was no exaggeration, but literally the truth that Meredith wrote to a friend: 'I get so small a sum of money for my work that I am always in harness, always jogging for a shilling, and to be let loose in a paddock for an hour is a thing unknown to me.'

The curtailment of Meredith's leisure by lack of means was perhaps less important than the effect of unpopularity upon his attitude to the public and to his work. He remarked with some bitterness: 'Who really cares for what I say? The English people know nothing about me. There has always been something anti-pathetic between them and me. With book after book it was the same outcry of censure and disapproval. The first time or two I minded it; then I determined to disregard what people said alto-gether, and since then I have written only to please myself.' The bitterness remained even after the cause for it had disappeared. In 1881 he described himself, and with reason, as 'an unpopular writer.' But there was no reason why in 1902, after his position as the leading writer of his day had been fully established and acknowledged, he should still describe himself as 'an unpopular novelist and an unaccepted poet.'

The change from neglect to a restricted popularity may be def-initely marked. In 1883 Mark Pattison wrote: 'Mr. Meredith is well known by name, to the widest circle of readers—the novel readers. By name, because his name is a label warning them not to touch.' This evidence of unpopularity is confirmed by the report of a conversation which took place a year or two earlier between George Eliot and John (afterwards Lord) Morley, then editor of the Fortnightly Review, in which one of Meredith's stories was then running as a serial. George Eliot asked Morley if it pleased the readers of the Review, and Morley, who was aware that publishers gave Meredith 'little welcome,' answered as best he could. George Eliot then informed him that she had discovered only one admirer of the Meredith novel, and even him she had convicted of missing two whole numbers without noticing a gap. But in 1884, when the Fortnightly published *Diana of the Cross-ways*, there was a change for the better, which was emphasized, especially in the United States, when the novel appeared in book form in 1885. 'The touch of American money,' Meredith wrote a year or two later, 'has impressed me with concrete ideas of fame,' and in one of the last letters he wrote he cordially acknowledged that the run of his novels 'started from American appreciation.' In a letter to Professor G. P. Baker, written in 1887, Meredith gave thanks for the assurance that 'Harvard has the works, and that Young Harvard reads them,' adding, a little wistfully: 'In England I am encouraged but by a few enthusiasts.'

The 'enthusiasts,' though few, were influential, including Thomas Carlyle, John Morley, Sir Leslie Stephen, Sir Sidney Colvin, R. L. Stevenson, W. E. Henley, Algernon Swinburne, Dante Gabriel Rossetti, J. M. Barrie, and other people of importance or promise in the literary world. *The Ordeal of Richard Feverel* was followed by other studies of adolescence depending in part upon the experiences of the author's own youth, and by a political novel, *Beauchamp's Career*, suggested by the unsuccessful candidacy of his friend Maxse for a seat in the House of Commons. But this earlier reputation was mainly founded upon *The Egoist*, a psychological novel giving proof of Meredith's remarkable insight into character and of his mastery of his own peculiar style. In the same year (1879) he published the *Essay on Comedy*, in which he developed his own ideas of the purpose of the novel as a satire on human egotism in its myriad forms. The Comic Spirit is the spirit of criticism which reveals to men their own weaknesses and shortcomings. 'Whenever men wax out of proportion, overblown, affected, pretentious, bombastical, hypocritical, pedantic, fantastically delicate; whenever it sees them self-deceived or hoodwinked, given to run riot in idolatries, drifting into vanities, congregating in absurdities, planning shortsightedly, plotting dementedly; whenever they are at variance with their professions, and violate the unwritten but perceptible laws binding them in consideration one to another; whenever they offend sound reason, fair justice; are false in humility or mined with conceit, individually, or in the bulk—the Spirit overhead will look humanely malign and cast an oblique light on them, followed by volleys of silvery laughter.'

Meredith looked for the exercise of this wholesome corrective of social faults in the influence of cultivated women, to whom he appealed in the Essay to exercise their natural prerogative. 'They are blind to their interests in swelling the ranks of the sentimentalists. Let them look with their clearest vision abroad and at home. They will see that where they have no social freedom, Comedy is absent: where they are household drudges, the form of Comedy is

214 LEADERS OF THE VICTORIAN REVOLUTION

primitive: where they are tolerably independent, but uncultivated, exciting melodrama takes its place and a sentimental version of them. . . . But where women are on the road to an equal footing with men, in attainments and in liberty—in what they have won for themselves, and what has been granted them by a fair civilization—there, and only waiting to be transplanted from life to the stage, or the novel, or the poem, pure Comedy flourishes, and is, as it would help them to be, the sweetest of diversions, the wisest of delightful companions.'

In *Diana of the Crossways* Meredith strove to give an example of the application of his theories to life. The heroine was, by the author's confession, partly modeled upon a famous beauty of an earlier day, Mrs. Caroline Norton, a granddaughter of Sheridan and a witty and valiant defender of the rights of her sex. She was concerned in two notorious scandals of her time, as the co-defendant with Lord Melbourne in a suit for divorce brought by her first husband, and as the supposed culprit in the betrayal of the secret of the impending repeal of the Corn Laws by the Government in 1845. Mrs. Norton's innocence in the first scandal was established by a law court, in the second by the subsequent revelation that the 'secret' was communicated to Delane, then editor of the Times, by Lord Aberdeen himself. But this was not known at the time Meredith wrote, and his acceptance of the current belief that Mrs. Norton had 'blabbed' to the Times editor involved him in the difficult problem of reconciling this grave indiscretion with the high character and keen intelligence of his heroine. His solution of the difficulty was not a very probable one, and in later editions of the novel Meredith printed a prefatory note to the effect that the charge against Mrs. Norton in connection with the repeal of the Corn Laws was a 'baseless calumny.' The inconsistency in the character of his heroine was left unremedied. His conception of Diana is nevertheless a great achievement; in spite of her failings, she is a magnificent figure, communicating, like other Meredith women, the inspiring impression of 'a height of sky, a belief in nobility,' which becomes a permanent possession of the sympathetic reader.

In the year of the success of *Diana of the Crossways* (1885) Meredith sustained a heavy blow in the death of his second wife, Marie Vulliamy, to whom he was devotedly attached. He gave expression to his thoughts on mortality in *A Faith on Trial*— one of his finest and most philosophical poems. The rest of his life he passed enjoying the sympathy of many friends and the adoration of many admirers, in the charming Flint Cottage he had made his home, beautifully situated on the lower slope of Box Hill in Surrey. His plea, in *Diana*, for the emancipation of women—especially from the bondage of an uncongenial marriage,—was re-inforced in later novels, equally 'fortified by philosophy'—*One of our Conquerors* (1891), *Lord Ormont and his Aminta* (1894), and *The Amazing Marriage* (1895). In the same period he published noteworthy volumes of poems, also mainly philosophical in character—*A Reading of Earth* (1888), *Odes in Contribution to the Song of French History* (1898), and *A Reading of Life* (1901). Both his novels and his poems were too difficult for popular comprehension, partly on account of the subtlety of their thinking, but more because of the tortured style in which the ideas were expressed. Meredith accepted what he regarded as the logical consequences of the evolution theory which was the main feature of scientific discovery in his time, and abandoned the belief in a future life which had been the central doctrine of his ancestral creed; but he retained a firm faith in the spiritual significance of life and in the validity of Christian ethics. He found in the achievements of mankind in the past a strong hope for progress in the future, and took over Wordsworth's transcendental view of Nature, or, as he preferred to put it, Earth. So he exhorted his generation to accept the earthly life, on its spiritual as well as its material side, as 'footway to the God of Gods:'

> Earth your haven, Earth your helm,
> You command a double realm:
> Laboring here to pay your debt,
> Till your little sun shall set;
> Leaving her the future task;
> Loving her too well to ask.

THOMAS HARDY
(1840–1928)

As we pass from Meredith's novels to Hardy's, we notice a complete change of atmosphere. In the former, we live in the refined air of drawing-room or library, among cultivated people, who direct their lives and control their emotions by their own intelligence, their material circumstances going on unchanged, for the most part, from year to year. In Hardy's novels we are in the open air or in humble dwellings where a change of material circumstance falls like a blow of fate, against which the helpless victims contend in vain, or do not make even a show of resistance. The Meredith heroines are women of intellect and character; 'what pitiful antagonists of destiny these rural people of Mr. Hardy make,' exclaimed an American critic; 'the intelligence of mortals is wholly inactive in the combat.' His women are indeed magnificent creatures, so far as their emotions, and especially their passions, are concerned; but for steadfastness of will and sureness of judgment they are often lamentably deficient. Hardy, indeed, in *A Pair of Blue Eyes*, re-inforces the general theme of the novel with outspoken comments on 'those stealthy movements by which women let their hearts juggle with their brains,' and on 'woman's ruling passion—to fascinate and influence those more powerful then she.' 'Decision, however suicidal, has more charm for a woman than the most equivocal Fabian success.' The habit of self-dispraise, he says in the same novel, is 'a peculiarity which, exercised towards sensible men, stirs a kindly chord of attachment that a marked assertiveness would leave untouched, but inevitably leads the most sensible woman in the world to undervalue him who practises it. Directly domineering ceases in the man, snubbing begins in the woman; the trite but no less unfortunate fact being that the gentler creature rarely has the capacity to appreciate fair treatment from her natural complement.' The contrast between Gabriel Oak and Bathsheba in *Far From the Madding Crowd*, between Clym Yeobright and Eustacia in *The Return of the Native*, and between the hero and heroine of *Jude the Obscure* reflects the same conviction in the author's mind that women are generally creatures of temperament, swayed this way and that by passionate emotion, often to their own undoing.

One consequence of this difference of outlook is that the world of Hardy's novels seems less hopeful than the more sheltered arena in which Meredith's men and women struggle against circumstance and learn wisdom by their own misadventures. Again and again, in the conclusions of his novels and in the more outspoken confidences of his poems—especially in his vast poetic drama *The Dynasts*—Hardy expressed his conviction of man's helplessness—and still more of woman's—in the grip of circumstance or overmastering passion.

Yet the conditions of Hardy's life were peculiarly fortunate. Born of parents of a good country stock with moderate means, he received a fair education and a professional training as an architect which enabled him to earn his own living until he had gained an independent position in the literary world. He wedded the love of his youth and lived with her in harmony and comfort for many years. After her death, his old age was protected and cherished by the devoted affection of his second wife, who had been his secretary. His novels brought him in an income sufficient for his modest wants, and as he grew older he received abundant proofs of the veneration with which he was regarded. Although Meredith had been refused burial in Westminster Abbey on account of his unorthodox religious belief, a resting-place for Hardy's ashes was offered by the ecclesiastical authorities both at his village church and at the Abbey, and funeral services were held at both, with every mark of public sorrow and respect. It was probably some deep-seated acceptance in Hardy's mind of a dark Fate and a bitter human lot, inherited from remote ancestors or acquired by contact with the neighboring peasantry, which gave him that gloomy view of life described by his critics as pessimism. It seems a fair description of the philosophic background of his novels and poems, though in personal contacts Hardy was quiet, placid, cheerful, and good-tempered.

Hardy was fortunate also in his first literary advisers. When he was twenty-eight years old and had spent five years in a London architect's office, Hardy submitted to Macmillan & Co. the MS. of a three volume novel entitled *The Poor Man and the Lady*. It purported to be written 'by the Poor Man,' who was in some particulars identical with Hardy himself, being a Dorsetshire youth of humble origin, but of good education. 'The Lady' was of a much superior class, and the story, which had what one would now call a strong Socialistic tendency, found its main interest in the obstacles of rank and fortune interfering with their love for each other. This induced Alexander Macmillan and his reader John (afterwards Lord) Morley, to decline the novel; still, they were impressed by its literary merits, and gave Hardy an introduction to another London publishing firm, Chapman and Hall. This led to interviews, first with Chapman and then with Chapman's reader, George Meredith, who advised Hardy that such a sweeping satire on the upper classes and established institutions would antagonize the conventional reviewers, not only in dealing with this novel, but with any future work by the same author. He recommended Hardy not to publish *The Poor Man and the Lady*, but to write another novel, free from social bias. Moreover, he pointed out that it was necessary, in order to win popular favor, that a novel should have a plot of a complicated and sensational character.

This was an odd prescription to be given by Meredith, who never himself took this way of winning the attention of the public; but it must be considered with due regard to the popular taste of the time and the masterpieces of fiction then in favor. There was Charles Reade's *The Cloister and the Hearth*, and Richard Blackmore's *Lorna Doone*, both of them rattling tales of adventure and conflict. But most popular of all was the type of mystery story introduced by Wilkie Collins with *The Woman in White* in 1860 and brought to perfection by Dickens in the closing years of his career. It was certainly this kind of story that young Hardy proceeded to produce in obedience to Meredith's advice. *Desperate Remedies* is a mystery story of the deepest dye—a mystery of love rather than of crime, although a murder is revealed in the final solution. It is concerned with the fortunes and misfortunes of two heroines (both named Cytherea), and the marriage of the second to the illegitimate and unacknowledged son of the first. It is doubtful at the time of the marriage (1) whether he is married already; (2) whether his first wife is still alive; (3) whether a lady he passes off as his legal wife is really the same woman; and (4) whether the first wife has been criminally put out of the way. There are the most elaborate and exciting entanglements right up to the last chapter, in which all is made clear and the hero is safely married to the younger and poorer Cytherea, who succeeds to the wealth of the older heroine at her opportune death. The plot is an extremely complicated one, full of coincidences and contrivances, to an extent beyond anything in Hardy's later work. All that reminds us of his later style is the humorous conversation of the peasant characters.

Desperate Remedies was offered to Macmillan & Co., and declined; it seems not to have been submitted to Chapman and Hall; it was published by Tinsley at the author's expense; Hardy put up £75 and got £60 back out of the proceeds of the sale, so that he was only £15 out of pocket. For Hardy's next venture, *Under the Greenwood Tree*—a rustic idyll with hardly a vestige of plot—Tinsley offered £30 and actually paid £40. Tinsley gave still better terms for *A Pair of Blue Eyes*, a well-written story with an exciting plot, of which the scene was laid on the romantic coast of Cornwall where Hardy met and courted his young wife. She encouraged him to drop architecture and go on novel writing, and her advice was borne out by a request from Leslie Stephen (who had been impressed by the rural charm of *Under the Greenwood Tree*), for a serial to be published in the Cornhill Magazine. *Far*

From the Madding Crowd began publication there in January, 1874, which may be taken as the date of Hardy's decisive success as a novel writer. It not only established his popularity, but marked his first successful combination of an exciting plot with the charm, romance, and humor of country life and country people. Another exciting serial—lacking the latter elements—*The Hand of Ethelberta*, was published in the Cornhill Magazine of 1876.

In 1878 appeared in book form what is regarded by many as Hardy's masterpiece, *The Return of the Native*. It presents his conception of Nature as a mysterious force, alien and often apparently hostile to man, without sympathy for his desires and ambitions, and without pity for his weaknesses. Eustacia Vye, the heroine, is a victim of her desire to escape from the awful loneliness of Egdon Heath and to satisfy the cravings of her sensuous disposition. When the grim severity of her environment combines with her own inner weakness to drive her to destruction, she exclaims (and Hardy evidently intends to convey a certain amount of sympathy with her exclamation): 'O, the cruelty of putting me into this ill-conceived world! I was capable of much; but I have been injured and blighted and crushed by things beyond my control! O, how hard it is of Heaven to devise such tortures for me, who have done no harm to Heaven at all!'

Hardy's 'austere artistic code' had led him to condemn the minor pair of lovers to similar frustration, the gentle Thomasin to perpetual widowhood and her devoted Diggory Venn to final disappearance from the Heath, 'nobody knowing whither,' but the editor of the Belgravia Magazine, in which the story was first published, protested against the separation of the two innocent lovers in whom the reader had become interested and insisted upon a happy ending. Hardy, with a nonchalance unusual with him, acquiesced in the change, and allowed it to stand when the novel was published in book form, with a warning to the reader that he considered his original conclusion more consistent with the scheme of the novel as he had planned it.

The austerity of the plot is happily mitigated by its picturesque setting, in which the peasant figures fall naturally into place. Their superstitions, their fondness for ancient usages, and their homely and often humorous wisdom give the story a warmth and color which do much to relieve its severity of outline. It is difficult to conceive what the novel would be without the bonfire and the wedding festivities, the play of St. George and the Dragon, the raffle, the village dance, and the burning of the waxen image of

Eustacia by Susan Nonsuch, for all these are part of the action, and cannot be conceived in isolation from it. To a degree perhaps unknown outside of Hardy's work, they give a complete representation of the life of an entire community, and not mere glimpses of the lives of a few individual members.

Hardy's declared purpose was to show that in these sequestered spots 'dramas of a grandeur and unity truly Sophoclean are enacted in the real, by virtue of the concentrated passions and closely-knit interdependence of the lives therein.' His ideal was Greek tragedy, and in *The Return of the Native*, he may justly be said to have attained it. There is the same great sweep of harmonious design, which in view of Hardy's earlier profession one may without pedantry call architectonic. The novel is magnificently constructed; the story moves easily on the heights of human destiny, without haste or wasted effort, and with a perfection of workmanship in detail of which we are only conscious after careful examination. One scene of impassioned or humorous interest succeeds another, and we follow with ever heightened attention to the appointed end; it is only then that we perceive how every smallest part fits into its place to make the perfect whole. This unity of impression comes mainly from unity of conception, but it is assisted by the subordinate unities of time and place which are in their way no less characteristic of *The Return of the Native* than of Greek tragedy as it was interpreted by Aristotle and succeeding analysts. The story opens with the Fifth of November bonfires about which the fates of Thomasin and Eustacia center, and passes to the Christmas Festival which welcomes 'the return of the native' and brings as its ultimate consequence the marriage, first of Thomasin and Wildeve, and then of Eustacia and Clym Yeobright. The last hot day of August conducts Clym's mother to her doom, and the unintentional signal fire of the following Fifth of November leads, on the next day, to the fatal flight of Eustacia and Wildeve. Within a year and a day the principal characters have run their appointed courses, and Hardy is so little concerned with what happens to the other characters that he does not much care whether Thomasin and Diggory are married or not.

Hardy's next novel, *The Trumpet Major* (1880) was a pleasant story, but inferior in artistic power and interest. About the time that it was published it was discovered that he was seriously ill, suffering from an internal hemorrhage, and he was compelled to lie for months on an inclined plane with his head lower than the rest of his body. In this uncomfortable position, enduring considerable pain, he persisted in fulfilling his contract to finish *A Laodicean*, of which publication had already begun in Harper's Magazine. It was one of his poorest novels, as might have been expected from the conditions under which most of the work was done. But enforced solitude and meditation in a recumbent position gave Hardy time to think about the purpose and methods of his art, and he made some jottings which are still of interest. They run: 'The real, if unavowed, purpose of fiction is to give pleasure by gratifying the love of the uncommon in human experience, mental or corporeal. This is done all the more perfectly in proportion as the reader is illuded to believe the personages true and real like himself. Solely to this latter end a work of fiction should be a precise transcript of ordinary life: but the uncommon would be absent and the interest lost. Hence, the writer's problem is how to strike the balance between the uncommon and the ordinary so as on the one hand to give interest, on the other to give reality. In working out this problem, human nature must never be made abnormal, which is introducing incredibility. The uncommonness must be in the events, not in the characters; and the writer's art lies in shaping that uncommonness while disguising its unlikelihood, if it be unlikely.'

It is his belief that 'the uncommonness must be in the events' that sets Hardy apart from the realistic movement of his time. As he puts it in a memorandum made some years later, 'a story *must* be striking enough to be worth telling. Therein lies the problem—to reconcile the average with that uncommonness which alone makes it natural that a tale or experience would dwell in the memory and induce repetition.'

Two on a Tower, published in the Atlantic Monthly in 1882, was certainly uncommon enough in its events, for a bishop, by marriage to a lady of rank, provides for the legal paternity of a child whose real father is a young astronomer. But it can hardly be said that Hardy's art has succeeded in this instance in shaping the uncommonness so as to disguise its unlikelihood. He was more successful with *The Mayor of Casterbridge* (1886), the plot of which unfolds itself from the unusual incident of the sale by a drunken man of his wife and child to a passing sailor, though it could be proved that such an event, though uncommon, was not unknown in England at the time of which Hardy wrote—the first quarter of the nineteenth century. In thus brutally disposing of his wife and child, Michael Henchard acts in accordance with his character, which has a strongly marked vein of perverse obstinacy. His repentant vow of abstinence from liquor and his rise by dogged industry to be a successful business man and Mayor of Caster-bridge, is all in accordance with Hardy's conception of Henchard as a man of great powers and serious weaknesses. His fall is no less consistent with his character than his rise; the young Scotch-man Farfrae, whose subtle power of adapting himself to a situation is strikingly contrasted with Henchard's rugged energy, naturally gets the better of every encounter in which it is possible for intel-ligence to outwit mere brute force. Farfrae defeats Henchard in business, becomes Mayor in his stead, robs him of his Lucetta, and finally wins away from him his last companion and comfort, Elizabeth-Jane. Henchard leaves Casterbridge after a quarter of a century of toil, as poor as he had come to it—a broken, solitary man. 'Externally there was nothing to hinder his making another start on the upward slope, and by his new lights achieving higher things than his soul in its half-formed state had been able to accomplish. But the ingenious machinery contrived by the Gods for reducing human possibilities of amelioration to a minimum—which arranges that wisdom to do shall come *pari passu* with the departure of zest for doing—stood in the way of all that.'

So Henchard, with grim determination, accepts his lot as 'an outcast, an encumberer of the ground, wanted by nobody, and despised by all.' Dying alone he pins to his bed-head his last will and testament:

'That Elizabeth-Jane Farfrae be not told of my death, or made to grieve on account of me.

& that I be not bury'd in consecrated ground.

& that no sexton be asked to toll the bell.

& that nobody is wished to see my dead body.

& that no murners walk behind me at my funeral.

& that no flours be planted on my grave.

& that no man remember me.

To this I put my name.'

Michael Henchard is the most original and remarkable of Hardy's character studies of poor mortals whipped and subjugated by the Fates. Though he is made at times the sport of sheer mis-chance, one feels more in his case than in any other of Hardy's portrayal of an individual destiny, that his misfortunes are in-evitable, being mainly the natural outcome of defects in his own character; it is not so much that he is robbed of wealth and happi-ness; he throws them away. Yet the reader cannot help a feeling of sympathy and admiration for Henchard, even in his worst fits of stubborn unreason. He is a rebel against the established order, in the moral as in the physical world, but there is something magnificent in his defeat.

While writing *The Mayor of Casterbridge* Hardy was building a house for himself about a mile outside Dorchester, the scene of the story; and here he lived quietly to the end of his days, with occasional excursions to other parts of England and abroad. It was at Max Gate (as he called his new house) that in 1887 he wrote *The Woodlanders*, which in after-years he was inclined to regard as in some respects his best novel. The scene is cast in the more remote countryside of 'The Hintocks,' and the woodland atmosphere is admirably preserved. The Fates, though stern, are less harshly severe than in the other great novels. Grace Melbury, with her gentle charm, has to make the best of the faithless and sensual Fitzpiers as a husband; her true lover, Giles Winterborne, ends in frustration and death; the faithful Marty South is condemned to a life of poverty and bereavement; yet her final lament at Winterborne's grave has a resigned and pathetic beauty, which affords some consolation for the sense of disappointment felt by the reader who still has a lingering desire for a happy ending. 'Now, my own own love, you are mine, and on'y mine; for she has forgot 'ee at last, although for her you died! But I—whenever I get up I'll think of 'ee, and whenever I lie down I'll think of 'ee. Whenever I plant the young larches I'll think that none can plant as you planted; and whenever I split a gad, and whenever I turn the cider-wring, I'll say none could do it like you. If ever I forget your name let me forget home and heaven! . . . But no, no, my love, I never can forget 'ee; for you was a good man, and did good things!'

In *The Woodlanders* Hardy was tempted to challenge current conventions as to sex and marriage, and resisted the temptation. In *Tess of the d'Urbervilles; a Pure Woman Faithfully Presented* (1891) he made the challenge, and received a prompt response. The editor of Murray's Magazine had asked to see the manuscript with a view to serial publication; he immediately declined it 'on the score of its improper explicitness.' It was then offered to the editor of Macmillan's Magazine, who had also asked for it, and it was as promptly declined, for the same reason. By this time, Hardy had become more wary; he saw that no magazine editor would accept the story, as it stood, for serial publication, and he could not afford to issue it in volume form only. He accordingly went through his manuscript again and removed or modified the offending passages, which had to be re-written in different colored ink so that the originals could be easily replaced in preparing the manuscript for publication in book form. This shortened and amended version was submitted to the editor of the Graphic, and accepted. But when the instalments came to be printed, the editor refused to publish the chapter containing the account of the baptism of Tess's illegitimate child, and it had to be omitted. He also objected to the description of Angel Clare carrying Tess and the three other dairymaids in his arms across a flooded lane. 'He suggested that it would be more decorous and suitable for the pages of a periodical intended for family reading if the damsels were wheeled across the lane in a wheelbarrow.' This was accordingly done; but Hardy swore that he would free himself from the necessity of supplying serial fiction for family reading as soon as he could.

It was not only on sex questions that Hardy expressed himself more freely in *Tess* than in any previous novel; with a new candor he expressed his passionate indignation at the injustice of the human lot. Take, for instance, his view of the chances in life of Tess and the other children in the Durbeyfield family: 'All these young souls were passengers in the Durbeyfield ship—entirely dependent on the judgment of the two Durbeyfield adults for their pleasures, their necessities, their health, even their existence. If the heads of the Durbeyfield household chose to sail into difficulty, disaster, starvation, disease, degradation, death, thither were these half-dozen little captives under hatches compelled to sail with them—six helpless creatures, who had never been asked if they wished for life on any terms, much less if they wished for it on such hard conditions as were involved in being of the shiftless house of Durbeyfield. Some people would like to know whence the poet whose philosophy is in these days deemed as profound and trustworthy as his song is breezy and pure, gets his authority for speaking of "nature's holy plan."'

Equally bitter in its scornful irony is his reflection on Tess's first betrayal: 'Darkness and silence ruled everywhere around. Above them rose the primeval yews and oaks of The Chase, in which were poised gentle roosting birds in their last nap; and about them stole the hopping rabbits and hares. But, might some say, where was Tess's guardian angel? where was the Providence of her simple faith? Perhaps, like that other god of whom the ironical Tishbite spoke, he was talking, or he was pursuing, or he was in a journey, or peradventure he was sleeping and not to be awaked.'

Finally, when the black flag has been hoisted above Winchester gaol, signifying that Tess has paid the last penalty of the law, his irony is again directed, not at the inadequacy of human institutions, or the wickedness of mankind, but at the folly of supposing that such a fate as that of Tess can be reconciled with the hypothesis of a divine government of the world. '"Justice" was done, and the President of the Immortals (in Æschylean phrase) had ended his sport with Tess.'

It has been suggested, and perhaps with reason, that Hardy loaded the dice against Tess to a point not justified by common human experience. Fortunately, in order to enjoy the novel as a work of art, the reader is not obliged to subscribe to the author's comments upon the mischances of his characters. It is perhaps more melodramatic in its plot, and less even in its construction than *The Woodlanders, The Mayor of Casterbridge*, and *The Return of the Native;* but it is on a greater scale and more affecting as a picture of human destiny than any of them. As in *The Return of the Native*, which perhaps comes nearest to it in the scope and range of its emotional effects, Hardy has shown great dramatic skill in setting the different 'phases' of his narrative (like the acts of a tragedy) to significant scenes. Tess's girlhood is associated with the village of Marlott, her first fall with Tantridge, and the neighboring estate of The Chase. 'The Rally' takes place in the beautiful Froom Valley, and the melodramatic incidents following Tess's marriage in the ancient manor-house of Wellbridge. Retribution comes to Tess in the bare and stony surroundings of Flintcomb-Ash farm, and renewed temptation in Kingsbere, the original home of the D'Urbervilles and their last resting-place. Tess's second lapse from purity and her terrible vengeance are assigned to a lodging house in the fashionable watering place of Sandbourne (Bournemouth), and the story takes on the unsympathetic color of its surroundings. But the interest rises again as Tess makes her way with Angel Clare through the steepled Melchester (Salisbury) to Stonehenge, and the climax of her capture is of Hardy's best.

Tess provoked a violent controversy. A London hostess said all she had to do was to mention the name of the heroine at a dinner table and the excited guests at once divided into two violent factions, like contending parties on a distracted jury. But the heated discussion aroused by *Tess* was nothing in comparison with the hubbub caused by the publication in 1895 of Hardy's next novel, *Jude the Obscure*, which first had to be laboriously altered for Harper's Magazine, and when published in volume form provoked a howl of indignation all round the English-speaking world. Hardy received with reasonable scepticism the statement of an English bishop that he had thrown the book into the fire, as he knew that fires were not frequent in midsummer and the book would not easily burn; but he was rather staggered by the receipt of a packet of ashes from Australia, said to be the result of a holocaust of the 'iniquitous novel'; libellous letters and postcards came in profusion. Hardy held to his own view that *Jude* 'makes for morality more than any other book I have written,' though he admitted that artistically it was not all he would have liked it to be. But he was disgusted at the intolerant attitude of the British and American public, and determined to write no more novels, preferring to express himself henceforth in verse. 'To cry out in a passionate poem,' he wrote in 1896, 'that (for instance) the Supreme Mover or Movers, the Prime Force or Forces, must be either limited in power, unknowing, or cruel—which is obvious enough, and has been for centuries—will cause them merely a shake of the head; but to put it in argumentative prose will make them sneer, or foam, and set all the literary contortionists jumping upon me, a harmless agnostic, as if I were a clamorous atheist, which in their crass illiteracy they seem to think is the same thing. . . . If Galileo had said in verse that the world moved, the Inquisition might have let him alone.'

The upshot was the issue in 1898 of *Wessex Poems*, composed for the most part between 1865 and 1870, but not hitherto published. In these he gave expression without reserve to the dark moods in which he regarded the destiny of mankind as affording much cause for grief, and not much for hope, much less for congratulation. In his diary he wrote that the man of fifty who won't own that his birthday is an April Fool's Day for him, is 'a rogue or a fool, a hypocrite or a simpleton.' But this was when he was still feeling bitter about the reception of *Jude the Obscure*. He did not realize that in the next thirty years he was to publish a dozen volumes of pessimistic poetry which would be received with respectful admiration by an adoring public. Few people read the three parts of *The Dynasts* published in 1904–08, but everybody regarded the author with veneration. It was an unreasoning affection on the part of the great public, and increased as the poet advanced in years and he took his place with simple dignity among the great men who 'burnt brightlier towards their setting-day.' He was even encouraged by the welcome given to *Wessex Poems*

to bid farewell to the nineteenth century in a strain that was almost cheerful. In the last month of the dying century he heard
'an aged thrush, frail, gaunt, and small' amid the bleak twigs
overhead flinging out 'a full-hearted evensong of joy illimited':

> So little cause for carolings
>   Of such ecstatic sound
> Was written on terrestrial things
>   Afar or nigh around,
> That I could think there trembled through
>   His happy good-night air
> Some blessed Hope, whereof he knew
>   And I was unaware.

CHAPTER IX

MID–VICTORIAN POETS

MATTHEW ARNOLD
(*1822–1888*)

MATTHEW ARNOLD wrote to his mother in 1869, when his poetical career was practically over: 'My poems represent, on the whole, the main movement of mind of the last quarter of a century, and thus they will probably have their day as people become conscious to themselves of what that movement of mind is, and interested in the literary productions which reflect it. It might be fairly urged that I have less poetical sentiment than Tennyson, and less intellectual vigor and abundance than Browning; yet, because I have perhaps more of a fusion of the two than either of them, and have more regularly applied that fusion to the main line of modern development, I am likely enough to have my turn, as they have had theirs.' So far, the verdict of posterity has not borne out Arnold's favorable estimate of his future reputation, for the public has continued to regard Tennyson's confident nationalism and melodious verse and Browning's buoyant optimism as more characteristic of Victorian achievement than the less confident and more melancholy strain of Arnold. He is chiefly remembered for his elegiac poems—*The Scholar Gypsy* and *Thyrsis*, in which he laments his friend Clough and the Oxford of the past, for the lines written in Rugby Chapel commemorating his father, and for his well-turned appreciations of Sophocles, Shakespeare, Goethe, Wordsworth, or less illustrious figures in the past. His more imitative Greek poems are neglected, and of his narrative poems the best known is *The Forsaken Merman* with its plaintive refrain of desertion and despair.

In his lyrics generally there is the same note of disillusion. The series of poems apparently suggested by a youthful love affair in Switzerland—perhaps more imagined than experienced—expresses doubt and misgiving rather than rapturous devotion. Even in the most ardent moment of pursuit he hears the voice of the divine mentor, 'Be counselled, and retire.'

Forgive me! forgive me!
Ah, Marguerite, fain
Would these arms reach to clasp thee!
But see! 'tis in vain.

In the void air, towards thee,
My stretched arms are cast;
But a sea rolls between us—
Our different past!

To the lips, ah! of others
Those lips have been prest,
And others, ere I was
Were strained to that breast;

Far, far from each other
Our spirits have grown;
And what heart knows another?
Ah! Who knows his own?

No wonder the maiden wooed in this half-hearted fashion let
her hand lie languid in that of her lover, her cheek grew pale, her
speech grew rare, and the upshot was estrangement:

Yes! in the sea of life enisled,
With echoing straits between us thrown,
Dotting the shoreless watery wild,
We mortal millions live *alone*.

Who ordered, that their longing's fire
Should be, as soon as kindled, cooled?
Who renders vain their deep desire?—
A God, a God their severance ruled!
And bade betwixt their shores to be
The unplumbed, salt, estranging sea.

Ten years later, when the poet revisits Berne, he does not even
seek the scene of his youthful passion, but gives way to the most
depressing (and apparently gratuitous) suppositions:

Ah, shall I see thee, while a flush
Of startled pleasure floods thy brow,
Quick through the oleanders brush,
And clap thy hands, and cry: *'Tis thou!*

Or hast thou long since wandered back,
Daughter of France! to France, thy home;
And flitted down the flowery track
Where feet like thine too lightly come?

> Doth riotous laughter now replace
> Thy smile; and rouge, with stony glare,
> Thy cheek's soft hue; and fluttering lace
> The kerchief that enwound thy hair?

Nor does the young poet find consolation in Nature, to whom he turns for refuge in his distress. In the poem entitled *Resignation*, addressed to his favorite sister, Arnold writes:

> Enough, we live!—and if a life,
> With large results so little rife,
> Though bearable, seem hardly worth
> This pomp of worlds, this pain of birth;
> Yet, Fausta, the mute turf we tread,
> The solemn hills around us spread,
> This stream which falls incessantly,
> The strange-scrawled rocks, the lonely sky,
> If I might lend their life a voice,
> Seem to bear rather than rejoice.

'The something that infects the world' infects also the poet's soul. In the glory of *A Summer Night* he is still conscious of the

> unquiet breast,
> Which neither deadens into rest,
> Nor ever feels the fiery glow
> That whirls the spirit from itself away,
> But fluctuates to and fro,
> Never by passion quite possessed
> And never quite benumbed by the world's sway?—

He is forever

> Wandering between two worlds, one dead,
> The other powerless to be born

Even a bacchanalian view of 'The New Age' gives not a joyful prospect of the future but mainly a regretful glance at the past:

> The epoch ends, the world is still.
> The age has talked and worked its fill—
> The famous orators have shone,
> The famous poets sung and gone,
> The famous men of war have fought,
> The famous speculators thought,
> The famous players, sculptors, wrought,

The famous painters filled their wall,
The famous critics judged it all. . . .
The one or two immortal lights
Rise slowly up into the sky
To shine there everlastingly,
Like stars over the bounding hill.
The epoch ends, the world is still.

Nature not only gives him no joy but suggests sorrowful reflections. On Dover Beach, with a calm sea, a full tide, a fair moon, a sweet night air, the mere recurrence of the waves on the beach brings 'The eternal note of sadness in.'

The Sea of Faith
Was once, too, at the full, and round earth's shore
Lay like the folds of a bright girdle furled.
But now I only hear
Its melancholy, long, withdrawing roar,
Retreating, to the breath
Of the night-wind, down the vast edges drear
And naked shingles of the world.

This pervasive melancholy was perhaps a part of Arnold's natural constitution. In his most charming lyric, *Requiescat*, he cannot keep out the personal note:

Strew on her roses, roses,
And never a spray of yew!
In quiet she reposes;
Ah, would that I did too!

Her mirth the world requirèd
She bathed it in smiles of glee.
But her heart was tirèd, tirèd,
And now they let her be.

Her life was turning, turning,
In mazes of heat and sound.
But for peace her soul was yearning,
And now peace laps her round.

Her cabined, ample spirit,
It fluttered and failed for breath.
Tonight it doth inherit
The vasty hall of death.

Although the young Arnold is aware that men 'have such need of joy,' he 'looks languidly round on a gloom-buried world.'

> Joy comes and goes, hope ebbs and flows
>   Like the wave;
> Change doth unknit the tranquil strength of men.
>   Love lends life a little grace,
>   A few sad smiles; and then,
>   Both are laid in one cold place,
>   In the grave.

This tendency may have been encouraged by the atmosphere of ethical otherworldliness in which Arnold grew up under his father's influence. At Oxford he was greatly affected by Newman, whose essentially sceptical mind shook Arnold's confidence in the liberal and evangelical ideas in which he had been brought up, without giving him a consolatory faith in the authority of the Catholic Church. In his academic career Arnold achieved a modified success. He won the prize for poetry at Rugby and a Balliol scholarship. At Balliol he won the Newdigate prize for English poetry, but got only a second class in the final examination for Classical Honors. He was, however, elected to an Oriel Fellowship, which gave him a sufficient income to look around and make up his mind what he wanted to do. He taught classics for a time at Rugby and apparently did not like it. He tried the law and abandoned it; he refused to accept his father's suggestion that he should study medicine. After some time spent in travel he decided on a political career and became private secretary to Lord Lansdowne, President of the Council in Lord John Russell's Government. But after a year or two he fell in love with the daughter of Sir William Wightman, Judge of the Queen's Bench; as his secretarial salary did not permit him to marry, he accepted a government position as Inspector of Schools, and was married the same month, June, 1851. He discharged the duties of an inspector of elementary schools for thirty-five years with conscientious boredom, mitigated by nomination to government commissions on education which brought him into contact with Continental thinkers, and by his election in 1857 to the Professorship of Poetry at Oxford.

The Oxford Chair gave Arnold an opportunity of which he took full advantage. Up to that time the lectures had been delivered in Latin, and the few hundred dollars' salary had been regarded merely as a plum to be allotted to a Low or High Church clergyman in accordance with the religious sympathies of the majority of the electors. Arnold lectured in English and made his courses the medium for the establishment of something like a canon of English criticism. Selected lectures, with other writings, were published in the two series of *Essays in Criticism*, and exercised a widespread influence. He defined criticism as 'a disinterested endeavor to learn and propagate the best that is known and thought in the world,' and insisted that it should be European rather than national in scope and spirit. Europe should be regarded 'as being, for intellectual and spiritual purposes, one great confederation, bound to a joint action and working to a common result; whose members have, for their proper outfit, a knowledge of Greek, Roman, and Eastern antiquity, and of one another.' The subjects of the essays were selected from this point of view, and, if we include the *American Discourses*, covered also the United States, which Arnold visited for a lecture tour in 1883–84.

Long before this Arnold had changed his center of interest from literary to social and religious subjects. Up to 1861 he still cherished an intention of giving 'the next ten years earnestly to poetry.' The abandonment of this good resolution was probably due to his appointment on the Middle Class Schools Inquiry Commission in 1865; the investigation gave him an appalling impression of the absorption of middle-class intelligence in making money by trade and manufacture. 'Your middle-class man thinks it the highest pitch of development and civilization when his letters are carried twelve times a day from Islington to Camberwell, and from Camberwell to Islington, and if railway trains run to and fro between them every quarter of an hour. He thinks it is nothing that the trains only carry him from an illiberal dismal life at Islington, to an illiberal dismal life at Camberwell, and the letters only tell him that such is the life there.'

Arnold's attitude toward the middle class was too patronizing and supercilious for his counsels to have much effect upon any but the most intelligent members of it, and not always upon them, for a leading Nonconformist editor rejected his advice as 'the monotonous bray of the well-accredited ass.' It is doubtful whether Arnold ever understood the Puritan spirit, and his caricatures of it often infuriated instead of persuading; but his endeavors to effect a combination between Hebraism and Hellenism were not entirely fruitless. He encouraged a more liberal interpretation of the Bible, and a higher appreciation of it as literature apart from dogma. His pleas for the organization of secondary education

helped to bring about the establishment of schools which eventually made the middle class more intelligent, more liberal-
minded, more tolerant, and less absorbed in merely commercial
pursuits.

Arnold's judgment of his own poetic achievement is quoted
above. His earlier estimate of his powers (1853) was more modest
and perhaps hits nearer the mark: '*The Scholar Gypsy* at best
awakens a pleasing melancholy. But this is not what we want.

> The complaining millions of men
> Darken in labor and pain—

what they want is something to animate and ennoble them—not
merely to add zest to their melancholy or grace to their dreams.'
His friend J. A. Froude said, shrewdly enough, about the same
date: 'I admire Matt. to a very great extent. Only I don't see
what business he has to parade his calmness and lecture us on
resignation when he has never known what a storm is, and doesn't
know what he has to resign himself to. I think he only knows the
shady side of nature out of books. Still I think his versifying and
generally his esthetic power is quite wonderful.' Clough also put
his finger on Arnold's characteristic weakness when he declared
the poems to be 'the productions of a scholar and a gentleman; a
man who has received a refined education, seen refined "society,"
and been more in the world, which is called the world. . . . More
refined, therefore, and more highly educated sensibilities—too
delicate, are they, for common service? A calmer judgment also,
a more poised and steady intellect, the *siccum lumen* [dry light]
of the soul; a finer and rarer aim perhaps, and certainly a keener
sense of difficulty, in life.' This also explains the somewhat top-
lofty attitude of Arnold both in his literary criticism and his social
essays. He assumed as an undergraduate at Oxford the pose of a
man of the world and never seemed able to drop it. We find it
running through his correspondence with Clough (from which the
above estimates are taken) as well as through all his public lectures,
his poems, and his prose. It is a form of donnishness which is
particularly exasperating to the ordinary man and greatly hindered
the free communication of the message Arnold wished to convey.
He had valuable ideas which are not yet out of date; he was a
prophet of beauty and wisdom, an apostle of sweetness and light—
if he could only have worn the academic robes with a less self-
conscious air of polite detachment.

A. H. CLOUGH
(*1819-1861*)

Arthur Hugh Clough was a fellow student and friend of Matthew Arnold, and aroused contemporary expectations of achievement which failed of realization. Born at Liverpool, he was taken before his fourth year to Charleston, South Carolina, by his father, who taught him Latin grammar and arithmetic, while his mother cultivated his imagination by reading to him Pope's translation of Homer. When he was ten years old the family returned to England, and he was sent to Rugby to be under the care of Dr. Arnold. He was a model pupil and won every honor the School had to offer, including a Balliol scholarship. At Oxford, like Matthew Arnold, who followed him to Balliol College, he came under the influence of Newman, became unsettled in his religious convictions, gained only second class honors, and was appointed to an Oriel fellowship, later to a tutorship at the same college. Inability to reconcile his religious views with the Thirty-nine Articles of the Church of England led him a few years later to resign his fellowship and tutorship, and for a while he traveled on the Continent with Emerson, whom he charged with a message to Longfellow that a reading of the *Evangeline* hexameters had led him to adopt the same measure for his first long poem, *The Bothie of Tober-na-Vuolich*, the outcome of visits to the Highlands during the Long Vacation with reading parties of Oxford undergraduates. During these years he was much concerned with the Chartist agitation and the Irish famine, and became an ardent advocate of social reform. In 1849 he was appointed to the headship of a residential hall of the University of London, but found the work uncongenial, and sailed to Boston to establish himself as a tutor to Harvard undergraduates at Cambridge, Mass. But a year later he was back in London, having accepted a position in the Education Office, which gave him a moderate but regular salary and enabled him to marry. For seven years he led a happy and secluded life, but the hard work and confinement preyed on his vitality and in 1860 his health broke down altogether. Short holidays proving ineffectual, he went in the following year to Florence, only to die.

Clough's friends were attracted by his high intelligence, the charm of his personality, and his eager devotion to the public welfare; with greater physical vigor he might have made a deeper and wider impression on the life of his time. But he was hampered by ill health and his mind was racked by religious doubt. He was unable to retain his hold on the evangelical dogmas he had accepted under Dr. Arnold's teaching; but he relinquished them with painful regret. Celebrating Easter Day at Naples, he records with profound melancholy his loss of faith in the central doctrines of Christianity:

> Eat, drink, and die, for we are souls bereaved:
> Of all the creatures under heaven's wide cope
> We are most hopeless, who had once most hope,
> And most beliefless, that had most believed.
> Ashes to ashes, dust to dust;
> As of the unjust also of the just—
>   Yea of that Just One, too!
> It is the one sad Gospel that is true—
>   Christ is not risen!

Matthew Arnold pointed out, affectionately but firmly, to Clough that he did not sufficiently desire and earnestly strive towards assured knowledge, activity, happiness. 'You are too content to *fluctuate*, to be ever learning, never coming to the knowledge of the truth.' Clough had not even faith in the triumph of the new truth at which he had arrived after so much suffering. He was haunted by the thought that perhaps it was better to retain the old belief.

> The souls of now two thousand years
> Have laid up here their toils and fears,
> And all the earnings of their pain—
> Ah yet consider it again!

Bitterest of all was the reflection that the world was indifferent alike to the old thought and the new; it did not consider either enough to cleave to one or to reject the other. And Clough's own life seemed wasted. His early triumphs had justified high ambitions and the hope of great achievements. Yet all that was left after twenty years of struggle was a thin volume of poetry and letters and an almost forgotten gravestone in the Protestant Cemetery at Florence.

DANTE GABRIEL ROSSETTI
(1828–1882)

Rossetti was only twenty years of age when he united with two other painters, Millais and Holman Hunt, and the sculptor Woolner, to found the Pre-Raphaelite Brotherhood, which appeared to contemporary opinion a reactionary and negligible movement towards medievalism, but was really, as a modern art critic has pointed out, a revolt—'and a valuable and successful one, against the ugliness of industrialism and the apathy of the Victorians to the hideousness of their homes and their furnishing and decorating of public buildings and churches.' Backed by the authority of Ruskin, who found in the principles of the Brotherhood an application of his own gospel of the worship of nature and truth, the young painters made for themselves a distinct place in the life and art of the time; but Rossetti's literary work, published in the Brotherhood's magazine, The Germ, and other periodicals, attracted little attention. When public interest was excited, it was in a way not altogether favorable to the poet-painter.

Early in his artistic career Rossetti fell in love with a young model, a girl of humble origin but of exceptional beauty, Elizabeth Siddall, and after long waiting on account of insufficient means he was able in 1860 to marry her. Rossetti was of an ardent, dreamy, impracticable disposition, and the marriage was not entirely happy; two years later, in a desperate mood, Elizabeth Rossetti put an end to her life. Rossetti, in an agony of remorse, buried in her coffin the poems he had written to her and for her. Some of them had been circulated in manuscript among his friends, of others no other copy was extant. A friend who had done a great deal for Rossetti in his bereavement persuaded him in 1869 to allow an application to the Home Secretary for authority to exhume the buried poems, and they were published the following year. The book appeared, as Sir Edmund Gosse put it, 'after such expectation and tiptoe curiosity as have preceded no other book in our generation,' and the impression it made upon the public was commensurate with the sensational conditions under which it was produced. But an anonymous critic, angered perhaps at the outburst of popular enthusiasm for a poet hitherto almost unknown, made the poems the center for attack upon what he called 'The Fleshly School of Poetry,' published in a leading review. The article was exceedingly bitter in tone, reeking with what Swinburne called 'rancid morality,' and illustrated its invectives by lines or phrases torn from their context and twisted to give an impression of sensuality quite beyond the author's intention or their real meaning. Already in a very nervous condition, Rossetti became obsessed by the belief that he was the object of a campaign of 'widespread calumny and obloquy, not less malignant and insidious than unprovoked and undeserved.' He had a serious breakdown from which he emerged a physical wreck; he suffered severely from sleeplessness, and the chloral he took as a remedy made matters worse, bringing on in 1881 a paralytic stroke, which resulted in his seclusion and death.

Rossetti's poetry has a distinctive place in English literature. A master of felicitous phrase and melodious meter, he was unsurpassed as a translator. His versions of Dante's predecessors and contemporaries, of Dante himself, and of Villon are poems of exquisite and abiding beauty. His ballads also are exceedingly effective, combining the medieval spirit with the perfection of modern versification. His latest critic, Lord David Cecil (*The Great Victorians*, 1932) sees in him the greatest exponent in English of a devotion to beauty in art, in nature, and especially in woman, which embodies an elevated though impractical philosophy, 'a strenuous, athletic, chaste self-dedication to what it conceived to be the highest; utterly different from the sensual self-indulgence that its enemies represented it.'

This pursuit of beauty is 'a passion that is conscious of its own mortality, that feels the decay implicit in its very magnificence.' It is a vain pursuit, which, followed without regard to other considerations, must end in tragedy; but it is not ignoble. In *The Blessed Damozel* (written when he was eighteen), Rossetti pictures one of God's choristers as leaning out from the gold bar of heaven and longing for her earthly lover. To have more blessing than on earth, she does not desire, 'But to be as then we were,—being as then at peace.' As she gazes listening into the vast inane, she realizes that this is impossible.

> And then she cast her arms along
> The golden barriers,
> And laid her face between her hands,
> And wept. (I heard her tears.)

So, in a later poem, written after a bitter experience of the disappointments of life, he wrote:

> Look in my face; my name is Might-have-been,
> I am also called No-more, Too-late, Farewell;
> Unto thine ear I hold the dead-sea shell
> Cast up thy Life's foam-fretted feet between;
> Unto thine eyes the glass where that is seen
> Which had Life's form and Love's, but by my spell
> Is now a shaken shadow intolerable,
> Of ultimate things unuttered the frail screen.

CHRISTINA ROSSETTI
(*1830–1894*)

Of all the women poets of the nineteenth century, Christina Rossetti's reputation now stands the highest, not far below that of her gifted brother. The youngest of the four children of the Italian exile and philosopher, Gabriele Rossetti, she lived an uneventful life in London and her memory is still enshrined in the church on Woburn Square in Bloomsbury, which she attended with devout fidelity during her later years. The consolation which Dante Gabriel Rossetti sought in the worship of beauty, she found in Christian mysticism; and while her life was darkened by anxiety, bereavement, and much physical suffering, she met them with a religious resignation and looked forward with tranquil confidence to a future life:

> How can we say 'enough' on earth—
>   'Enough' with such a craving heart?
> I have not found it since my birth,
>   But still have bartered part for part.
> I have not held and hugged the whole,
>   But paid the old to gain the new:
>   Much have I paid, yet much is due,
> Till I am beggared sense and soul.
>
> Not in this world of hope deferred,
>   This world of perishable stuff;
> Eye hath not seen nor ear hath heard
>   Nor heart conceived that full 'enough':
> Here moans the separating sea;
>   Here harvests fail; here breaks the heart:
>   There God shall join and no man part,
> I full of Christ and Christ of me.

Of earthly lovers she had two: the first died before they were able to marry, the second she refused because of conscientious scruples as to his religious beliefs. Both appear to have been very ordinary mortals; but she found in them inspiration for exquisite and unforgettable elegies, of which one may be quoted:

> When I am dead, my dearest,
>   Sing no sad songs for me;
> Plant thou no roses at my head,
>   Nor shady cypress-tree;

Be the green grass above me
    With showers and dewdrops wet;
And if thou wilt remember,
    And if thou wilt, forget.

I shall not see the shadows,
    I shall not feel the rain;
I shall not hear the nightingale
    Sing on as if in pain;
And dreaming through the twilight
    That doth not rise or set,
Haply I may remember,
    And haply may forget.

The same spirit of Christian stoicism breathes in *Up-Hill:*

Does the road wind up hill all the way?
    Yes, to the very end.
Will the day's journey take the whole long day?
    From morn to night, my friend.

But is there for the night a resting-place?
    A roof for when the slow dark hours begin.
May not the darkness hide it from my face?
    You cannot miss that inn.

Shall I meet other wayfarers at night?
    Those who have gone before.
Then must I knock, or call when just in sight?
    They will not keep you standing at that door.

Shall I find comfort, travel-sore and weak?
    Of labor you shall find the sum.
Will there be beds for me and all who seek?
    Yea, beds for all who come.

<h2 style="text-align:center">COVENTRY PATMORE</h2>

(1823–1896)

Coventry Patmore combines Dante Gabriel Rossetti's worship of earthly love with Christina Rossetti's Christian mysticism, but he has not their distinction of spirit or their metrical facility. It is but rarely, as in the following *Farewell*, that he rises above the homely cadences of *The Angel in the House:*

With all my will, but much against my heart,
We two now part.
My Very Dear,
Our solace is, the sad road lies so clear.
It needs no art,
With faint, averted feet
And many a tear,
In our opposed paths to persevere.
Go thou to East, I West.
We will not say
There's any hope, it is so far away.
But, O, my Best,
When the one darling of our widowhead,
The nursling Grief,
Is dead,
And no dews blur our eyes
To see the peach-bloom come in evening skies,
Perchance we may,
Where now this night is day,
And even through faith of still averted feet,
Making full circle of our banishment,
Amazed meet;
The bitter journey to the bourne so sweet
Seasoning the termless feast of our content
With tears of recognition never dry.

ALGERNON CHARLES SWINBURNE
(1837–1909)

Swinburne's reputation has been more severely deflated than that of any other writer numbered among the 'Great Victorians.' His latest critic, W. J. Turner, dismisses him as 'one of the by-products of a general disintegration,' finds nothing shocking or immoral in *Poems and Ballads*, merely 'rhetoric whose virtues are essentially academic,' and will not even allow that he is a master of meter; on the contrary, he maintains that 'Swinburne, of all our poets of lyrical reputation, had the worst ear.' Harold Nicolson, commissioned, somewhat belatedly (1926), to give Swinburne a place in the English Men of Letters Series, endeavors to save a small part of the poet's product by jettisoning the bulk of the cargo and by setting up a theory that Swinburne was a victim of arrested development, that his emotional receptivity began to ossify in his twenty-first year, and that 'by the age of thirty-four, he became quite incapable of re-acting to the stimulus of any new experience.'

The son of a British admiral and brought up on the coast of the Isle of Wight, Swinburne early acquired the passionate love of the sea of which his most eloquent expression is *Thalassius*, published in 1880. At Eton College, where he arrived at the age of twelve with a huge volume of Shakespeare under his arm, he was variously regarded as a mad or inspired elf, though to his more matter of fact schoolfellows he appeared merely 'a horrid little boy with a big red head and a pasty complexion.' In spite of his delicate health and odd appearance, he was not persecuted, but was allowed to indulge his taste for reading the Elizabethan and Jacobean dramatists in the college library without molestation; another youthful infatuation, which continued to the end of his days, was Victor Hugo, whose novels and poems inspired in him 'a sort of rapturous and adoring despair.' At fourteen he wrote a versified welcome (after the manner of Pope's *Iliad*) to Queen Victoria on her visit to Eton, and about the same time received the blessing of the two surviving poets of the Romantic Revival, Wordsworth and Rogers. At Balliol College Swinburne passed for a brief space under the influence of the Oxford movement, but the controlling power, for good and evil, of his undergraduate days was an older student, John Nichol, from whom he acquired a passionate admiration for the Italian revolutionist, Mazzini, a fervent enthusiasm for republican principles in general, and an inclination for over-indulgence in alcoholic stimulants which was later to ruin his health and bring him in middle life to the edge of the grave. A more wholesome influence was that of the Pre-Raphaelites, Dante Gabriel Rossetti and William Morris, to be discerned in his juvenile dramas in the Elizabethan manner, *The Queen Mother and Rosamond* (1860). They fell absolutely unnoticed from the press, and Swinburne, having failed to win the university prize for English verse, left Oxford without a degree.

Swinburne's father was distressed by his son's behavior, especially by his refusal to train for any profession, but agreed to allow him a moderate income. For some time Swinburne kept house with the Rossettis in London, along with George Meredith, but there was too much genius for one roof to cover, and the literary household broke up, the reason alleged being that Dante Gabriel Rossetti offended his fellowcraftsmen by consuming an enormous breakfast every morning. Meredith was shortly afterwards visited by Swinburne in his Surrey cottage, where the younger poet arrived full of excitement over Fitzgerald's translation of Omar Khayyam, which he had picked up on a second-hand book stall. He was delirious with delight at the new meter, and dancing with joy there and then composed one of his most characteristic early poems, *Laus Veneris*. It is in the same measure as the *Rubaiyat*, but breathes the spirit of medieval diabolism rather than the Persian astronomer's combination of oriental fatalism with oriental sensuousness.

Swinburne passed on to a more serious undertaking, the composition of a tragedy in the Greek manner in which he had the encouragement and co-operation of Benjamin Jowett, Master of Balliol College and one of the leading classical scholars of his time. *Atalanta in Calydon* is severely classical in form, but its spirit and manner are modern. Matthew Arnold, whose *Merope* Swinburne hoped to outgo, thought *Atalanta* un-Greek, in that it contained 'too much beauty,' unaware perhaps that Swinburne's precise object was 'to do something original in English which might in some degree reproduce for English readers the likeness of a Greek tragedy, with possibly more of its true poetic life and charm than' had been achieved by previous efforts. For his subject he chose a classical legend which had been alluded to by Æschylus and Euripides; the latter wrote a tragedy founded on it which has come down to us only in fragments; the fullest and clearest version of the story is in the *Metamorphoses* of Ovid, which was probably Swinburne's source—unless it were merely the classical dictionary of Lemprière. The subject probably commended itself to him because it enabled him to represent the gods in a more unfavorable light than is usual in any of the Greek tragedians. Artemis, in resentment of the neglect of her rites by the King of Calydon, sends a wild boar which lays waste the country and terrifies the inhabitants. In Swinburne's play this situation is set forth in a brief prologue by the Chief Huntsman. The Chorus enter singing in seven stanzas the ode beginning:

> When the hounds of spring are on winter's traces
>   The mother of months in meadow or plain
> Fills the shadows and windy places
>   With lisp of leaves and ripple of rain;
> And the brown bright nightingale amorous
> Is half assuaged for Itylus,
> For the Thracian ships and the foreign faces,
>   The tongueless vigil, and all the pain.

Althæa, the Queen of Calydon, then tells of the gathering of heroes for the hunting of the boar, among them, the virgin huntress,

Atalanta, whom she fears on account of her young son, Meleager. Over him a strange fate hangs: he can live no longer than a brand, which Althæa had snatched from the burning, is kept unconsumed. Althæa has had a dream in which the brand burst into flames, and she is full of forboding, which the Chorus share:

> Before the beginning of years
> There came to the making of man
> Time, with a gift of tears;
> Grief, with a glass that ran;
> Pleasure, with pain for leaven;
> Summer, with flowers that fell;
> Remembrance fallen from heaven,
> And madness risen from hell;
> Strength without hands to smite;
> Love that endures for a breath:
> Night, the shadow of light,
> And life, the shadow of death.
>
> They gave him light in his ways,
> And love, and a space for delight,
> And beauty and length of days,
> And night, and sleep in the night.
> His speech is a burning fire;
> With his lips he travaileth;
> In his heart is a blind desire,
> In his eyes foreknowledge of death;
> He weaves, and is clothed with derision;
> Sows, and he shall not reap;
> His life is a watch or a vision,
> Between a sleep and a sleep.

Meleager comes in and receives from his mother counsels of prudence against falling in love with the Amazonian Atalanta:

> A woman armed makes war upon herself,
> Unwomanlike, and treads down use and wont
> And the sweet common honor that she hath,
> Love, and the cry of children, and the hand
> Trothplight and mutual mouth of marriages.
> This doth she, being unloved; whom if one love,
> Not fire nor iron and the wide-mouthed wars
> Are deadlier than her lips or braided hair.
> For of the one comes poison, and a curse
> Falls from the other and burns the lives of men.

But Meleager, himself virgin, cannot help admiring the maiden Atalanta, 'Most fair and fearful, feminine, a god, faultless.' The Chorus sing a hymn to Aphrodite:

> We have seen thee, O Love, thou art fair; thou are goodly, O Love;
> Thy wings make light in the air as the wings of a dove.
> Thy feet are as winds that divide the stream of the sea;
> Earth is thy covering to hide thee, the garment of thee.
> Thou art swift and subtle and blind as a flame of fire;
> Before thee the laughter, behind thee the tears of desire;
> And twain go forth beside thee, a man with a maid;
> Her eyes are the eyes of a bride whom delight makes afraid;
> As the breath in the buds that stir is her bridal breath:
> But Fate is the name of her; and his name is Death.

Then we have an account by a messenger of the slaughter of the boar by Atalanta and Meleager. His uncles are angry because he gives all the honors of the chase to Atalanta, and when they attack her, he defends her and slays them. Althæa, distraught by the death of her brothers, and driven by 'the bitter jealousy of God,' lights the fatal brand and brings her son's life to an end. Meleager dies, praying Atalanta to close his eyes.

> And now, for God's sake, kiss me once and twice
> And let me go; for the night gathers me,
> And in the night shall no man gather fruit.

But Atalanta, feeling herself merely 'a blast of the envy of God,' bids the dying Meleager a curt farewell:

> Hail thou: but I with heavy fate and feet
> Turn homeward and am gone out of thine eyes.

The Chorus close the play with reflections on the folly of contending against the gods, 'For the hands of their kingdom are strong.'

The play has not the restrained beauty of Greek tragedy, but it has a luscious beauty of its own, and it is noteworthy that when Professor Gilbert Murray, a generation later, undertook the translation of Euripides into English verse, it was the measures and manner of Swinburne that he adopted. The romantic spirit has entered so profoundly into English poetry that any close imitation of Greek tragedy seems bare and almost flat. Swinburne at any rate achieved a reproduction of something like the 'true poetic life and charm' of the original, and with the publication of *Atalanta* in 1865 he 'shot like a rocket into celebrity.' Professor Mackail, a leading classical scholar, spoke of it as 'something quite new, quite unexampled'; and Ruskin was equally enthusiastic.

It was Lord Houghton who asked Murray to publish *Poems and Ballads* and Murray indignantly refused on account of the sensual character of some of the poems. Moxon, having tried public feeling with a limited edition of *Laus Veneris*, which caused no explosion, launched *Poems and Ballads* in 1866; then the storm broke and Moxon promptly withdrew the edition; but the poems were issued by another publisher, and the outcry continued. John Morley in the Saturday Review described Swinburne as 'an unclean fiery imp from the pit' and the poems as 'the feverish carnality of a schoolboy.' Most readers of the poems to-day find in them mainly rhetoric and wonder what all the pother was about. But at the time they made considerable stir.

Before getting out the Second Series of *Poems and Ballads* in 1878, Swinburne achieved perhaps the highest mark of his poetical activity in *Songs before Sunrise* (1871). 'Of all I have done, I rate *Hertha* highest as a single piece, finding in it the most of lyric force and music combined with the most of condensed and clarified thought.' This was Swinburne's own opinion and it has been unanimously supported by critics and anthologists since.

> I am that which began
> Out of me the years roll;
> Out of me God and man;
> I am equal and whole;
> God changes, and man, and the form of them bodily; I am the soul.
>
> Before ever land was,
> Before ever the sea,
> Or soft hair of the grass,
> Or fair limbs of the tree,
> Or the flesh-colored fruit of my branches, I was, and thy soul was in me.
>
> First life on my sources
> First drifted and swam;
> Out of me are the forces
> That save it or damn;
> Out of me man and woman, and wild-beast and bird; before God was, I am.
>
> A creed is a rod,
> And a crown is of night;
> But this thing is God,
> To be man with thy might,
> To grow straight in the strength of thy spirit, and live out thy life as the
> light.

For truth only is living,
Truth only is whole,
And the love of his giving
Man's polestar and pole;
Man, pulse of my center, and fruit of my body, and seed of my soul.

Between the publication of *Atalanta in Calydon* (1865) and
Songs before Sunrise (1871) Swinburne enjoyed a burst of popularity which rather turned his head. He offended Tennyson and
alienated Lord Houghton, the most influential literary patron of
that time. Meredith, at first an enthusiastic admirer, made up
his mind that Swinburne had no 'central core.' Browning thought
even *Atalanta* a mere 'fuzz of words.' Morris 'never could really
sympathize with Swinburne's work; it always seemed to me to be
founded on literature and not on Nature. . . . The surroundings
of life are so stern and unplayful that nothing can take hold of
people which is not rooted in deepest reality and is quite at first
hand.' Rossetti, himself magnificently Bohemian, became hopeless of bringing Swinburne into contact with practical life. Walt
Whitman, whom Swinburne at first admired and then denounced
for 'Whitmanism,' when asked by Ernest Rhys for his opinion,
said with tremendous emphasis: 'Of all the damned simulacra
I have known, that man was the worst. He brought me to a table
spread with fair dishes, and when I lifted up the covers, behold,
there was *nothing there!*' After a final debauch in 1878 with John
Nichol, then a professor of Glasgow, Swinburne collapsed altogether, and was only saved from extinction by the intervention of
Walter Theodore Watts (afterwards Watts-Dunton), a London
lawyer of pronounced literary interests, who had looked after
Swinburne's business affairs and in 1879 carried him off to a house
at Putney (No. 2, The Pines) where the poet lived in seclusion for
the rest of his life.
   The Putney period, covering Swinburne's last thirty years,
was productive, but not distinguished. Swinburne followed a
regular *régime* and published a volume of verse or prose criticism
nearly every year. He rose at ten, walked on Wimbledon Common
at eleven; was back for luncheon at one and rested till four-thirty;
then he worked for two hours, and read aloud for an hour before
dinner; after dinner he returned to his study and worked till midnight. After his mother's death in 1896, Sir Edmund Gosse writes,
'he became even more gentle, more remote, more unupbraiding
than ever. He went on gliding over the commons of Wimbledon

with the old noiseless regularity, but it could hardly be said that he held a place any longer in the ordinary world around him. The thirteen last years of Swinburne's life were spent almost as if within a Leyden jar.' He published a great deal of verse—most of it mere echoes of his former greatness—but perhaps the most abiding result of this long period of hermitage was his critical work on Shakespeare and his contemporaries; he had a scholarly knowledge of the Elizabethan drama and brought to the task of interpretation boundless enthusiasm—and alas! an equally bound-less vocabulary of appreciation or vituperation.

WILLIAM MORRIS
(1834–1896)

William Morris put unusual energy into half a dozen activities, any one of which would have seemed a life work to a man of average gifts and ambition. He was in turn or simultaneously (1) a writer of narrative verse; (2) a writer of romantic prose; (3) an architect; (4) a painter; (5) an interior decorator; (6) a printer and book-binder; (7) a Socialist agitator; and in at least six out of these differ-ent fields he made a distinct mark on the life and work of his time.

Born of a middle-class family in a London suburb, he went to the newly organized public school of Marlborough and had his own way with his studies, so that when he went up to Exeter College, Oxford, he was in the unusual position of 'knowing most of what was to be known about English Gothic.' After taking a pass degree, he was for more than a year working in the office of the leading architect of English Gothic in Oxford and London, and extended his knowledge by a thorough study of Gothic in Northern France.

He had already passed through periods, first of Roman Catholic, and then of Anglican religious enthusiasm, of which all that re-mained was a keen sense of human brotherhood. Through his friendship with Burne-Jones and Dante Gabriel Rossetti, he came under the influence of the Pre-Raphaelites, and for the next five years was known as a painter. In 1858 he published his first narra-tive poem, *The Defence of Guinevere*, and during the same period built and decorated for himself a house in the country at Upton, Kent.

By this time, though he was still under thirty, Morris had made up his mind about life and what he wanted to do in it. The com-mercial life about him in the English metropolis seemed to him

ugly and aimless; lacking in beauty, it gave no joy, not even satisfaction. Looking back to the fourteenth century, before the
medieval system of craft guilds had begun to break up under the
impact of modern commercialism and mechanical industrialism,
he found there a delight in work and a pleasure in the results of
work done for its own sake, not for mere gain, that promised a
better way. He accordingly established in London a firm of
manufacturers and decorators, with workshops for the making of
things that were beautiful but simple and not expensive; he did
not want to paint pictures to hang in rich men's houses or build
churches for a faith that seemed to him outworn; he set himself
to make chairs that would be comfortable but well-shaped, fabrics
that would be well-woven and of good lasting color, schemes of
house decoration that would be simple but pleasing to the eye.
He soon found himself occupied with a large business and had to
give up his house in the country and live in London, near his
workshops.

At the same time he wished to cultivate his gift for telling stories
in verse. In 1867 he published a long narrative poem entitled
The Life and Death of Jason, followed in the next few years by *The
Earthly Paradise*. This is a story cycle after the manner of *The Canterbury Tales*. 'Certain gentlemen and mariners of Norway, having
considered all that they had heard of the Earthly Paradise, set
sail to find it: and after many troubles and the lapse of many years,
came old men to some Western land, of which they had never
before heard.' This is not the discovery of America by the Vikings,
but of the Atlantis of Plato, inhabited by descendants of the
ancient Greeks. The visitors are welcomed and thus saluted by
the chief priest:

> 'Dear guests, the year begins today;
> And fain are we, before it pass away,
> To hear some tales of that now altered world,
> Wherefrom our fathers in old time were hurled
> By the hard hands of fate and destiny.
> Nor would ye hear perchance unwillingly
> How we have dealt with stories of the land
> Wherein the tombs of our forefathers stand;
> Wherefore henceforth two solemn feasts shall be
> In every month, at which some history
> Shall crown our joyance.'

For a year, therefore, hosts and guests exchange stories month
by month, the inhabitants telling tales of classical legend, and the

visitors tales of Scandinavian saga and medieval romance—
twenty-four in all. Morris was a charming story-teller—not endowed with Chaucer's shrewd humor and keen eye for a dramatic
situation, but with a dreamy charm of his own:

> Of heaven or hell I have no power to sing;
> I cannot ease the burden of your fears,
> Or make quick-coming death a little thing,
> Or bring again the pleasure of past years,
> Nor for my words shall ye forget your tears,
> Or hope again for aught that I can say,
> The idle singer of an empty day.
>
> The heavy trouble, the bewildering care
> That weighs us down who live and earn our bread,
> These idle verses have no power to bear;
> So let me sing of names rememberèd,
> Because they, living not, can ne'er be dead,
> Or long time take their memory quite away
> From us poor singers of an idle day.
>
> Dreamer of dreams, born out of my due time,
> Why should I strive to set the crooked straight?
> Let it suffice me that my murmuring rhyme
> Beats with light wing against the ivory gate,
> Telling a tale not too importunate
> To those who in the sleepy region stay,
> Lulled by the singer of an empty day.

In pursuance of this plan Morris translated the *Æneid*, the
Odyssey, and many Icelandic sagas; but he was not content to
remain 'the idle singer of an empty day.' He saw, after twenty
years' experience, that the products of his workshop were bought
mainly by the well-to-do middle class, and that upon the domestic
life and everyday occupations of the working-class he was making
no impression. He began to take an active interest in politics and
soon lost satisfaction in the work of the party organizations. He
turned to the Socialists and allied himself in 1883 with the Democratic Federation, from which he withdrew the following year to
take the leading part in the organization of the Socialist League.
During these years he was actively engaged in Socialistic propaganda by tongue and pen, lecturing in various parts of the country, administering the affairs of the League and conducting its
organ, the Commonweal, writing pamphlets and books of which

the most important were *Signs of Change* and *A Dream of John Ball* (1888), and *News from Nowhere* (1890). In 1885 he was arrested but not brought to trial; he was present at the Trafalgar Square Riots of 1887, but was not even taken into custody—much to his chagrin. The ease with which a few hundred police scattered thousands of rioters on the latter occasion convinced Morris of the futility of any resort to force by the working-class and of the remoteness of the arrival of the Communistic Millennium. The policies of the Socialist League developed into ways of which he did not approve, and in 1890 he withdrew from it altogether. He went back to the writing and the manufacture of books, and issued from the Kelmscott Press some of the best printed and bound volumes that had been seen in England for centuries. The Kelmscott Chaucer (1896) was a triumph in the art of book-making, but its cost put it beyond the reach of the members of the Socialist League, even if they had wanted it.

Morris was in fact an artist, a story-teller, a dreamer, and he had no grasp of economics, theoretical or practical. *News from Nowhere* is a Utopian dream of the future, as *A Dream of John Ball* is a romantic vision of the past. The fourteenth century England of William Morris is a no man's land of his own imagination, not the medieval England of history. His England of the future is a fourteenth century England without robber barons, oppressive abbots, or greedy landowners, without self-seeking and without crime, and equally free from the mechanism and ugliness of modern industrialism. The bridges are of stone and wood—not of steel,—light and heat are obtained by candles and wood-fires, Manchester has disappeared altogether, and the population of London has been distributed into small communities scattered along the Thames Valley. But Morris never faces the fact that in Great Britain it is impossible to feed, clothe, and house forty million people by the methods which served—uncomfortably enough—for four million. In his Utopian London visitors go into the stores (tended by children) and obtain anything they like to ask for—and even things they do not ask for—as free gifts; but there is no explanation of how the warehouses and shops come to be filled with goods. Similarly, the houses are kept clean in the early hours of the morning by the labors of volunteer maids or the daughters of the house—even though the latter have sat up late to talk to the guests who are freely entertained wherever they go. They enjoy all the advantages of a well-to-do English middle-class family, with a staff of competent housemaids and waitresses, without any hint of the source from which all these material blessings flow. There are no factories, no tax-gatherers, no magistrates, lawyers, or police—in fact no government beyond very free and easy communal gatherings which never decide anything till practically everybody is of the same mind.

Morris himself described *News from Nowhere* as 'a Utopian Romance,' and the title itself says as much. The book is not valueless because it is a poet's dream, 'of imagination all compact.' It suggests an ideal to be hoped for and striven for, and it influenced many minds, not so much of the working-class, who did not buy or even read the handsome volumes of Morris's collected works, but of the more thoughtful members of the middle class who, comfortable enough themselves, began to be uneasy because their poorer fellow-citizens were less comfortable. The condition of the English working people has certainly improved since Morris died in 1896, and it is in part owing to the arousing of the conscience of England by Morris and his master, Ruskin. Neither of them was a competent economist, a political leader, or, on any large scale, a master of industry. But they were both prophets, denouncing obvious wrongs and abuses, and awakening the national consciousness to the need for improvement. Morris was, more than Ruskin, a man of practical ability and achievement, who did something to make Victorian England less repulsive in its household goods and less commercial in its outlook on life. In many ways he was a man looking forward to a better day.

PART III
LATE VICTORIANS
(1881–1901)

CHAPTER X

LATE VICTORIANS

(1881–1901)

THE last twenty years of the Victorian Era were at once the ending of an epoch and a striving towards a new and better state of things. The middle class still held firmly to Victorian standards and Victorian principles, but they were not so self-confident as they had been in the previous decades. They were uneasily conscious that their power was passing, and that their half-century of supremacy had not been so glorious as they had thought. The prophesyings of Carlyle and Ruskin, of John Stuart Mill, Matthew Arnold, and William Morris, had not been fruitless. The more conscientious and thoughtful members of the middle class felt that something must be done about the condition of the workers, though they were not either clear or unanimous as to what it was to be. The workers, having organized themselves in co-operative societies and trade unions, were becoming better educated and more self-reliant, more aware of the weapon put into their hands by the parliamentary and municipal suffrage. They were not aiming any longer at the reform of political machinery but at the exercise of political power for social and industrial advancement of a material kind. The main political campaigns of the period, though they seemed to aim at a reform of legislative and administrative machinery, were really directed at social and economic conditions which could be remedied only by legislative enactment. The agitations for Woman Suffrage and Irish Home Rule were based on claims for the redress of substantial grievances, not mere changes in the system of government. They were symptoms of a general and pressing desire for more fundamental and revolutionary changes than appeared on the surface—signs of profound unrest, not undiscerned by contemporary observers.

The Victorian historian, Frederic Harrison, writing in 1895, says: 'There is upon us also, both in England and in America, a social ferment that goes deeper than any mere constitutional struggle. It is the vague, profound, multiform, and mysterious upheaval that is loosely called Socialism,—not Socialism in any

255

definite formula but the universal yearning of the millions for power, consideration, material improvement, and social equality. The very vagueness, universality, and unbounded scope of the claim they make constitute its power. All orders and classes are concerned in it: all minds of whatever type are affected by it: every political, social, or industrial axiom has to be reconsidered in the light of it: it appeals to all men and it enters into life at every corner and pore. We are like men under the glamour of some great change impending. The spell of a new order holds us undecided and expectant. There is something in the air, and that something is a vague and indescribable sense that a new time is coming. Men felt it in France, and indeed all over Europe, from 1780 to 1790.' A more recent historian, G. M. Trevelyan, in a foreword to a composite picture of the period 1882–1932 made by twenty-seven contributors to the London Times, points out that 'the feet of clay of the Victorian giant was the condition of "the masses" in the industrial districts.' The condition of the Irish peasant was no less the real foundation for Irish discontent, not a mere cherishing of ancient antipathies, nor even of nationalistic aspirations. So, too, the heroine of Meredith's *Diana of the Crossways* (1884), speaking on behalf of her sex, says: 'Whenever I am distracted by existing circumstances, I lay my finger on the material conditions and I touch the secret. Individually, it *may* be moral with us; collectively, it is material—gross wrongs, gross hungers.' It is worth while to examine each of these positions in some detail.

THE STATUS QUO

In the first place one must realize that the vast majority of the middle class stood very much where they always did. Population was continuing to advance at a rapid rate, trade was expanding, wealth was increasing. The inroads of Socialistic or Radical opinion upon the minds of the mass of the bankers, stockbrokers, manufacturers, traders, shop-keepers, small professional people, and salaried clerks were very gradual. George Moore, in his realistic study of upper-middle-class life, *A Drama in Muslin* (1886) draws a picture of a London suburb as it remained, substantially unchanged, to the end of the century: 'In this suburb we find the ten-roomed house with all its special characteristics—a dining-room window looking upon a commodious area with dust and coal holes. The drawing-room has two windows, and the slender balcony is generally set with flower-boxes. Above that come the two windows of the best bedroom belonging to Mr. and Mrs., and above that again the windows of two small rooms, respectively inhabited by the eldest son and daughter; and these are topped by the mock-Elizabethan gable which enframes the tiny window of a servant's room. Each house has a pair of trim stone pillars, the crude green of the Venetian blinds jars the cultured eye, and even the tender green of the foliage in the crescent seems as cheap and as common as if it had been bought—as everything else is in Ashbourne Crescent—at the Stores. But how much does this crescent of shrubs mean to the neighborhood? Is it not there that the old ladies take their pugs for their constitutional walks, and is it not there that the young ladies play tennis with their gentleman acquaintances when they come home from the City on a Saturday afternoon? In Ashbourne Crescent there is neither Dissent nor Radicalism, but general aversion to all considerations which might disturb belief in all the routine of existence, in all its temporal and spiritual aspects, as it had come amongst them. The fathers and the brothers go to the City every day at nine, the young ladies play tennis, read novels, and beg to be taken to dances at the Kensington Town Hall. On Sunday the air is alive with the clanging of bells, and in orderly procession every family proceeds to church, the fathers in all the gravity of umbrellas and prayer books, the matrons in silk mantles and clumsy ready-made elastic sides; the girls in all the gaiety of their summer dresses with lively bustles bobbing, the young men in frock-coats which show off their broad shoulders—from time to time they pull their tawny moustaches. Each house keeps a cook and housemaid, and on Sunday after-noons, when the skies are flushed with sunset and the outlines of this human warren grow harshly distinct—black lines upon pale red—these are seen walking arm-in-arm away towards a distant park with their young men.'

THE AGRICULTURAL INTEREST

The decay of the agricultural interest, foreseen as the result of the repeal of the Corn Laws, began to operate in the last two dec-ades of the century. The county families, the farmers depending upon them, and the agricultural laborers the farmers employed were not immediately ruined by Repeal; the price of wheat (or 'corn' as the English call it) 'remained fairly steady for another generation, and with better times there was a greatly increased consumption of bread. The country-houses and farmsteads of England were never more wealthy, populous and happy than during the Mid-Victorian age,—the age of Trollope's novels and

John Leech's pictures. Indeed, the removal of all serious cause of bitterness between town and country left the "great houses" in a most enviable social position for another thirty years. Then, indeed, the development of trans-continental railways and great steamships enabled America to pour forth such quantities of food that, during Disraeli's Ministry in the late 'seventies, British corn-growing was at last very seriously affected. The world-wide organization of British commerce drew food to the island from every quarter, and the agricultural situation which we know today began to develop itself.' The proportion of the population engaged in agriculture, which had dropped by 1881 to about 12 per cent, continued to fall, but 'until the end of the Victorian Era there were still large numbers of persons in Great Britain born and bred as agriculturalists, and desiring no better than to obtain land of their own beyond the ocean.' (G. M. Trevelyan, *History of England*.)

Socially, however, the history of rural England in the later years of the nineteenth century is 'in many respects a chronicle of disaster.' As the price of wheat fell, thousands of acres of land went from tillage to pasturage, and the more enterprising agricultural laborers and small farmers left the country districts for the Western States, the Colonies, or the English manufacturing towns. Pasturage involved unemployment, lower prices meant lower rents, and a decreasing income meant that the county families could not maintain their estates or keep up their prestige; they were obliged to sell or let to successful manufacturers or traders—even to American millionaires—or to fight a losing battle in the attempt to keep up a large establishment on a diminishing income. The farmers were harassed on both sides—by the attempt to pay fixed rents on falling prices, and by the pressure of the laborers for higher wages, shorter hours, and more comfortable conditions of life. In an attempt to apply a legislative remedy to a sore which was essentially economic, the Liberal Government in 1884 enfranchised the agricultural laborer. The Conservative Government which came into power in 1886 followed this up by extending to the country districts by means of County Councils the privileges of self-government which had been given to the towns by the Municipal Corporations Act at the beginning of the Victorian Era. The succeeding Liberal Government, not to be outdone, localized the government of the country districts still further in 1894 by the establishment of Urban and Rural District Councils and Parish Councils. The result was to take local administration out of the hands of the local magnates and give it to popularly elected bodies, on which, it is true, the local magnates continued to serve as elected representatives, but subject to appeal to a democratic suffrage. The administration of justice and of liquor licenses was left to the county magistrates, but even the Bench was gradually democratized. The days were over when a great landowner could have a poacher on his preserves brought by his gamekeepers into his library and condemned to imprisonment offhand by himself in his own right as a county magistrate. The process continued under different forms—in open court, with lawyers and reporters present, and the prestige of the county magistrate was proportionately diminished. Walter Bagehot, who died in 1877, noted that even in his time the influence of the aristocracy was falling off. 'They have less means of standing out than they used to have. Their power is in their theatrical exhibition of their state. But society everywhere is becoming less stately. As our great satirist has observed, "The last Duke of St. David's used to cover the north road with his carriages; landladies and waiters bowed before him. The present Duke sneaks away from a railway station smoking a cigar in a brougham."' When the brougham gave place to an automobile the Duke became even less conspicuous.

THE IRISH QUESTION

At the general election of 1885 the Liberals were defeated in the towns but saved from utter rout by the newly enfranchised agricultural laborer to whom they had given the vote 'in the hope of obtaining some real improvement in his miserable lot.' Of all the agricultural laborers in the United Kingdom, the lot of the Irish peasant was the most miserable. George Moore, the son of an Irish landlord, draws a dreary picture of the state of the country in 1886, as seen by a young married couple of the upper middle class, driving away from an oppressed countryside in which it was impossible for them to win a tolerable living. 'Through the streaming glass they could see the strip of bog; and the half-naked woman, her soaked petticoat clinging about her red legs, piling the wet peat into the baskets thrown across the meager back of a starveling ass. And farther on there were low-lying, swampy fields, and between them and the road-side a few miserable poplars with cabins sunk below the dung-heaps, and the meager potato-plots lying about them; and then, as these are passed, there are green enclosures full of fattening kine, and here and there a dismantled cottage, one wall still black with the chimney's smoke, uttering to those who know the country a tale of eviction. Beyond these, beautiful plantations sweep along the crests of the hills, the pillars of a Georgian house showing at the end of a vista. The carriage turned up a narrow road, and our travelers came upon a dozen policemen grouped round a roadside cottage, out of which the furniture had just been thrown. The family had taken shelter from the rain under a hawthorn-tree, and the agents were consulting with their bailiffs if it would not be as well to throw down the walls of the cottage. "If we don't," one of the men said, "they will be back again as soon as our backs are turned, and our work will have to be begun all over again."'

It was with this background of poverty, and crime in the distance, that the Irish Nationalist leader, Parnell, and his united phalanx of devoted followers in the British House of Commons set themselves at Westminster to make not only the government of Ireland but the government of England impossible. When the general election of 1886 ended in a deadlock between the English Liberal and Conservative parties—each having the same number of members in the House of Commons and the Irish Nationalists holding the balance of power,—it was evident that something had to be done about it. Gladstone brought in a Home Rule Bill granting the Irish a considerable measure of self-government; the change of front was too sudden for the Whig wing of his party and their defection defeated the Bill. For the next half-dozen years the Conservatives held office with the support of the Liberal Unionists. Three years of Liberal government followed (1892–95): a Home Rule Bill was forced through the House of Commons and rejected by the House of Lords, whose judgment was confirmed by the electorate. The Liberals went into the political wilderness to the end of the century. The upshot was to delay the social and economic legislation of which England herself was in urgent need.

THE DECAY OF BEAUTY

The substitution of industrialism for agriculture and of democratic government for the authority of the landed aristocracy swept away some ancient oppressions and abuses, but it brought with it a loss apparently inevitable—a loss of beauty. Before the end of the eighteenth century, Cowper had written: 'God made the country and man made the town,' and had celebrated 'the grace of hedge-row beauties numberless, groves, heaths, and smoking villages remote.' In Lancashire and Yorkshire, in Derbyshire and

Staffordshire, these pleasant rural scenes and picturesque villages were transformed into scarred hill-sides disfigured by great heaps of coal and pottery-slag, polluted streams, masses of factory chimneys and long ugly streets of hideously monotonous cottages, so that the merry England of the Middle Ages became the 'black England' of the nineteenth century. Ruskin deplored the change which converted a lovely tree-shaded pool at Carshalton into a dismal and noisome swamp which was an offense to the eye and a danger to health, and reproached the Bradford manufacturers for the ugliness of their public buildings: 'Your railroad stations, vaster than the temple of Ephesus, and innumerable; your chimneys, how much more mighty and costly than cathedral spires! your harbor piers; your warehouses; your exchanges!—all these are built to your great Goddess of "Getting-on."'

It was not so much that the millowners and mineowners despised the element of beauty as that they were unaware of it. A writer in the London Times Literary Supplement remarks: 'The Nineteenth Century did not attack beauty. It simply trampled it under foot, with the result that our modern democracy is born atrophied, and has painfully to recover that love of significant form which has been one of the marks of civilized man from the Bronze Age until the Industrial Revolution temporarily destroyed it.' Arnold Bennett, who grew up in the pottery district of the English Midlands in the last dozen years of the century, said that his youth was passed 'in a world where beauty was not mentioned, seldom thought of. I believe I had scarcely heard the adjective "beautiful" applied to anything whatever, save confections like Gounod's "There is a green hill far away." Modern oak sideboards were called handsome, and Christmas cards were called pretty, and that was about all.' Nor can it be said that matters have been improved in the twentieth century by the advent of the motor-car, the charabanc, and the steady multiplication of means of transportation and communication, which has more than kept pace with the increase of the population. Professor Wallace Notestein, writing in 1931, while lamenting the growth of suburbia and the disappearance of the country-gentlemen, offers but little consolation for the disappearance of the quiet and beauty of the country-side. He says: 'What if county should disappear, what if the long lawns, the terraces, and the peacocks should go, what if the last enchantment of the Middle Ages should be broken, what if Magdalen Tower should fall? There will be less romance in the English setting, less poetry; the shires spread below Malvern's summit will look less fair on a summer's day; even the hedgerows and walls may vanish. But those who are concerned with utility as well as beauty, and have faith that out of utility may come new beauty, those who wish to see the fields productive and to see them the heritage of those who work them, those who suspect that feudalism is unsuited to our time, may face without too much misgiving the prospect of a middle-class England.'

Some consolation may be found in the fact that the town population, while manifestly lacking in physique, has improved in health; the prevalence of infectious diseases has decreased and the death rate has been greatly lowered, owing to better sanitation and superior medical care. Bird 'sanctuaries,' botanical gardens, and 'zoos' provide the urban populations with a few samples of the fauna and flora familiar to their ancestors, but country quiet, unbroken by anything but the sounds of wild life and agricultural toil, becomes rarer and more remote in England year by year.

THE INDUSTRIALIZED WORKERS

What have the toilers in mines and factories gained by removal from the fields, the moors, and the sequestered villages inhabited by their ancestors? As to the miners, we have the record of the personal experience of one of them, Thomas Jones, who contributed an article on 'The Life of the People' to the London Times record of the fifty years from 1882 to 1932. He writes: 'South Wales . . . is an area where the greatest natural wealth is found side by side with the greatest industrial unrest. And it had the usual features of a society founded on coal: male employment, boy labor at relatively high wages, early marriages, overworked mothers, high birth and death rates, high infant mortality, bad housing, a landscape scarred and smudged.' He gives us a picture of the mining town in which he grew up, a community of some 8,000 souls housed in a High Street, a mile or so in length, with less important streets branching at right angles or running parallel with it. Most of the houses belonged to the iron and coal company which provided employment, owned the local brewery and all the public-houses, paid the doctors and the clergymen, ran the 'company shop' (a large department store), and drew the workpeople from the rural counties of Wales, England, and Ireland, these last drawing wages amounting on an average to about three dollars a week. When Thomas Jones began to earn his own living as a timekeeper at fourteen years of age, his working-day lasted from

5.45 A.M. to 7 P.M., with three-quarters of an hour for breakfast, an hour for dinner. The directors of the company lived in London or in some place distant and unknown, and the chairman of the directors was a potentate in whose presence the leader of the largest union stood hat in hand, no matter how long their conference might last; to the miners, the chairman was 'remote, inscrutable, and fabulously rich.' It was a community of this kind that Carlyle described as 'like a vision of hell,' in a passage already quoted in Chapter III (see p. 50). In later years the situation has changed, both for better and for worse. Drunkenness declined, gambling increased, the birth rate fell by nearly 50 per cent and the death rate by rather more, wages, after a short-lived rise during the War, fell again, and unemployment became desperate. In the last census decade 250,000 people left the district, and it still has an unemployable surplus population of from 30,000 to 40,000 men.

As a young man Thomas Jones went to Glasgow to study, and saw from within the life of the workers in a great manufacturing city. 'It had one thing in common with our mining valleys—rain. Its housing was much worse. In my first year as a student I shared with a fellow-countryman a bed fixed on a shelf in a cupboard. Later, living at a university settlement in Cowcaddens it was one of my duties to visit the families in the neighborhood. I was allotted a "close" which had forty-four families on one staircase in forty-four rooms—the famous ticketed houses. My mission was to bring them evangelical comfort. I saw that what was needed was dynamite with which to blow up the whole street, after due notice to the occupants. The close is still standing. It is impossible to think of Glasgow, strenuous and serious city as it was when I first knew it, without thinking of its housing problem—the gloomy, giant tenements, the color of mud, built to last for ever, cut up into boxes, with a tap on the staircase. All water had to be carried in and the waste carried out. "A fifth of the population lives in one-room flats," declared the medical officer.' In the 'eighties barefooted women and children ran about the streets and 'closes,' the working-girls were ragged and untidy, the dressmaking, millinery, and tailoring trades were badly sweated. Boys were apprenticed at twelve for seven years and were paid a little more than a dollar for a week of fifty-one hours; skilled carpenters, masons, and bricklayers earned on an average from six to seven dollars a week.

From such misery and squalor the working people were to some extent redeemed, partly by their own exertions through organization in trade unions and co-operative societies, partly through education, not merely in books, but in self-respect and in standards of health and personal and domestic comfort, partly through legislation and improved municipal administration. Organization, education, legislation became the watchwords of the working classes, and under these ensigns they marched hopefully towards a moderate goal which seemed to them within measurable reach of attainment. In 1892 the founder of the Independent Labor party, Keir Hardie, took his seat in the House of Commons, and even before that date representative members of the working class, such as John Burns, had appeared in the House under the Liberal banner. In the last decade of the Victorian era, confidence in parliamentary methods was still firm, and, among the middle class and better paid workers, there was a general feeling that social progress was proceeding satisfactorily. As was pointed out in the section of our Introductory Chapter on 'The Condition of the People,' a review of social achievement at the second Victorian Jubilee in 1897 seemed to so competent a witness as George Gissing a legitimate ground for national congratulation. He noted an advance in cleanliness, sobriety, public order, freedom from oppression, education, a decrease of ignorance and a consequent diminution of disease and suffering—not merely material gains, but elements of progress on the intellectual and spiritual sides of life. With the improvement of the physical conditions under which people lived—more commodious and sanitary houses, better clothes, and more wholesome and varied food—their ambition for further progress was stimulated and encouraged. Conservative observers remarked with surprise that the workers were more restless and more eager than ever for the betterment of their conditions of labor and the extension of their opportunities to enjoy life. There were, as a matter of fact, still very substantial reasons for discontent. At the beginning of the twentieth century Sir Henry Campbell-Bannerman, who became Premier in 1905, declared that over twelve millions of the population of Great Britain were 'in the grip of perpetual poverty' and on the verge of hunger.

REVIEW

The spirit of unrest which manifested itself during the last years of the century in legislative reforms, a new status for woman, and the relaxation of parental authority and discipline was clearly reflected in the newspapers, periodicals, novels, and poetry of the time. There was no longer the prevailing conviction that English parliamentary institutions were perfect, and that the forces of industrial and commercial competition, if given free play, would work out justice and happiness for all. In the great commercial centers like London, Liverpool, and Bristol, and the manufacturing towns which spread like a network over the Midland counties, Lancashire, and Yorkshire, the spectacle of extreme poverty confronting excessive and unmanageable riches not only provoked bitter discontent among the depressed millions, but gave detached and disinterested observers cause for serious alarm and foreboding. Charles Booth's statistical survey of the condition of the London poor, published in the last decade of the century, put into concrete form, for everyone to read, facts which were already familiar to the clergy and other social workers in the slums of the richest metropolis of the world. The London dock strike (1889), which won for the casual laborer a pittance of sixpence an hour, drew public attention to the poverty and squalor in which many of the unskilled workers lived. The Salvation Army, founded in 1865, by its efforts to evangelize the brutalized and drink-sodden masses, made the condition of the poverty-stricken districts better known. Secularism, Socialism, Trade Unions, Co-operative Societies worked like a new leaven in the hitherto inert masses of English labor, and the main reforms for which the Chartist leaders had fought, and had been rewarded in their own day by public obloquy and imprisonment, were now carried into effect with comparatively little opposition.

In such a time of political conflict and social upheaval, there was no opportunity for the deep harmonious tones of a truly national literature: Tennyson's melodious accents and Browning's rhetorical dogmatism were felt to be inadequate as expressions of the restless self-questioning, inquiring, sceptical spirit of an age no longer either very confident of the present or very hopeful of the future. There were younger and more discordant voices—the humanistic transcendentalism of Meredith, the gentle yet grim pessimism of Hardy, the raucous imperialism of Kipling, the scientific scepticism of John Davidson, the classical stoicism of A. E. Housman, the religious faith of Francis Thompson, the Celtic mysticism of W. B. Yeats and 'A. E.'—but none of these, with the exception of Kipling's romantic and sentimental jingles and popular ballads, had any widespread influence or authority.

The novel was a more popular form of literature, but even in this field there were no writers who commanded the popular acclaim of Dickens and Thackeray among the Early Victorians, or even of George Eliot and Anthony Trollope—the characteristic writers of Mid-Victorian fiction. Meredith was at the height of his power and exerted considerable influence—but only among the intellectuals; Mark Pattison remarked in 1883: 'Meredith is well known, by name, to the widest circle of readers—the novel readers. By name, because his name is a label warning them not to touch'; and this remained true of Meredith's relation to the ordinary reader of fiction to the end of the century. Hardy's novels were in better case with the reading public—but even he gave up novel writing in 1896 for lack of intelligent appreciation and understanding of his work. Gissing, a consistent and conscientious realist in the realm of the ignobly decent, won the approval of critics and fellowcraftsmen, but had little popular success. R. L. Stevenson came nearer to achieving general popularity, but his romances always had an air of being addressed to youths in their teens. It was not until Conrad made his appearance, almost at the end of the century, that romance reached the atmosphere of reality and made an appeal to the mature intelligence. Kipling's stories, as well as his verses, were exceedingly popular for a time, but his mannerisms and his message went out of fashion almost as quickly as they had come in.

The novel in the hands of Dickens and Thackeray, of George Eliot and Anthony Trollope, had been thoroughly English—a domestic product, free from foreign influence. The novel of the last two decades of the century was more aware of what was being done abroad; French realism, or 'naturalism' as Zola called it, was known to Meredith only to be discarded as 'dirty drab,' along with the sentimental pink of popular English fiction. Gissing had a better understanding of Zola's methods and purposes, but his attitude towards the principles and practices of French realism was also one of avoidance rather than imitation. The actual introducer of the realistic spirit and manner, already long popular in France, was George Moore, whose *Esther Waters* (1894) is very obviously modeled on French examples. With Arnold Bennett the indebtedness to Flaubert and Maupassant becomes even clearer and more specific.

At the end of the century, in H. G. Wells and John Galsworthy come the heralds of a new day, in which poverty—its avoidance or cure—is the center of the picture. This is even more entirely true of Bernard Shaw, who in novel, pamphlet, or play never leaves out of mind as his ideal society a state in which the total income shall be divided equally among all its citizens. As James Agate, one of the acutest of contemporary dramatic critics, puts it: 'All roads in Mr. Shaw lead, and all roots dig down to, Communism.'

CHAPTER XI

LATE VICTORIAN NOVELISTS

GEORGE GISSING
(*1857–1903*)

Gissing's position in English literature is peculiar. His novels had no great circulation in his lifetime, and no collected edition of his works has been published since his death; though separate reprints of *New Grub Street* and *The Private Papers of Henry Ryecroft* have had a steady moderate sale, none of his books ever came anywhere near being a 'best seller.' Yet he has kept his place in literary history more securely and completely than almost any other Victorian novelist. The esteem he won as a conscientious artist and a veracious chronicler of the life of the humble poor has withstood the changes in literary standards, political opinions, social ideals, and religious views that have taken place since his death.

The continued interest in his work is due perhaps, at any rate in part, to a curious attractiveness about his personality and a touch of mystery about his career; the facts of his life are fairly well known; but it is not easy to harmonize them with what we know of his tastes and character. He came of a middle-class family in the North of England, the son of a druggist at Wakefield in Yorkshire. Owens College, which afterwards developed into the University of Manchester, was beginning to attract attention as a center of learning, and at fourteen Gissing won an entrance scholarship which enabled him to pursue his studies there. He was a diligent and gifted student, gaining prizes and scholarships both at Owens College and at the University of London, where he was first in the First Class at the B.A. Intermediate Examination of 1875. But a year or so later all these brilliant prospects were ruined by Gissing's own weakness and folly. A lonely boy, with a craving for companionship and little gift for the easy-going comradeship of college life, he formed a connection with a girl he picked up in the Manchester streets. As she wanted money and he had none to give her, he yielded to the temptation of helping himself from the pockets of fellow students who carelessly left loose cash in their overcoats in the college locker room. The money was missed, a detective was set on watch, and Gissing was caught in the act. Prosecution, conviction, and imprisonment followed; and the academic career to which Gissing might have looked forward with every assurance of success was forever closed to him.

Gissing's one interest in life was study. 'Now and then,' he wrote toward the end of his literary career, 'I have such a hunger for books that I loathe the work that forbids me to fall upon them.' It was not mere self-pity, for he was doing himself no more than justice when he added: 'With leisure and tranquillity of mind, I should have amassed learning. Within the walls of a college, I should have lived so happily, so harmlessly, my imagination ever busy with the Old World.' With this scholarly temperament he combined an incapacity for material interests which is not an uncommon accompaniment of a love of learning. But he had with his own hand closed the gates upon the college garden in which he might have passed the years in the quiet study of the classical authors of the Old World. It was not from choice, but from necessity, that he turned his face to the New World.

It was the year of the Centennial Exhibition at Philadelphia, and Gissing sought to bury his past and make a fresh start there. He found no opening and went on to Chicago, where he earned a precarious living by writing short stories for the Tribune. These have been disinterred from the newspaper files and re-published, but it cannot be said that they show any glint of genius or even great promise. They were, however, good enough to attract the attention of an editor at Troy, N. Y., who clipped them with his scissors and published them in his own paper. When Gissing grew sick of Chicago, he went on to Troy hoping to sell his wares to the appreciative editor; the latter, however, saw no point in paying for what he could easily steal, and Gissing was reduced to working as assistant to a commercial traveler who went round the country selling gasfittings—or photographic reproductions of old portraits. Gissing's own recollections of this time of stress were a little hazy in later years. The friends who had sent him out to America were appealed to for help to bring him back to Europe, and after a time of further exile in Germany Gissing made his way to London. With that odd mixture of a sense of duty and complete lack of judgment which was characteristic of him, Gissing married the Manchester girl who had ruined his career, and finding life with her impossible, provided her with a small income until she drank herself to death. He earned a poor pittance by private tuition and occasional writing, and lived in a garret from which, for the sake of saving a few cents a week, he moved to a cellar: 'The front cellar was stone-floored; its furniture was a table, a chair, a wash-stand, and a bed; the window, which of course had never been cleaned since it was put in, received light through a flat grating in the alley above. Here I lived; here I wrote.' His 'true home' was the Reading Room of the British Museum, where he pursued a prolonged course of study including the Greek and Latin classi-cal authors, ancient and modern philosophy, the history of the Christian Church from the Reformation, Dante, the field of medi-eval romance, German literature from Lessing to Heine—all subjects of interest to the scholar but having one characteristic in common, that they afforded little chance of making a living out of them. 'His money dwindled, and there came a winter dur-ing which he suffered much from cold and hunger. Friends in London he had none; but for an occasional conversation with his landlady he would scarcely have spoken a dozen words in a week. His disposition was the reverse of democratic, and he could not make acquaintances below his own intellectual level. Solitude fostered a sensitiveness which to begin with was extreme; the lack of stated occupation encouraged his natural tendency to dream and procrastinate and hope for the improbable. He was a recluse in the midst of millions, and viewed with dread the necessity of going forth to fight for daily food.'

There were days when even the 'blessed refuge' of the Museum Reading Room did not console him. Ordinarily 'its warmth en-wrapped him kindly; the peculiar odor of its atmosphere—at first a cause of headache—grew dear and delightful to him.' But sometimes even the smell of decaying book-bindings failed to charm. He fell into the mood of despondency he ascribes to one of the characters in *New Grub Street*, Marian Yule, a literary hack: 'One day at the end of the month she sat with books open before her, but by no effort could fix her attention upon them. It was gloomy, and one could scarcely see to read; a taste of fog grew per-ceptible in the warm, headachy air. Such profound discourage-ment possessed her that she could not even maintain the pretense of study; heedless whether anyone observed her, she let her hands fall and her head droop. She kept asking herself what was the use and purpose of such a life as she was condemned to lead. When already there was more good literature in the world than any mortal could cope with in his lifetime, here was she exhausting herself in the manufacture of printed stuff which no one even pretended to be more than a commodity for the day's market. What unspeakable folly! To write—was not that the joy and the privilege of one who had an urgent message for the world? Her father, she knew well, had no such message; he had abandoned all thought of original production, and only wrote about writing. She herself would throw away her pen with joy but for the need of earning money. And all these people about her, what aim had they save to make new books out of those already existing, that yet newer books might in turn be made out of theirs? This huge library, growing into unwieldiness, threatening to become a trackless desert of print—how intolerably it weighed upon the spirit!

'Oh, to go forth and labor with one's hands, to do any poorest, commonest work of which the world had truly need! It was ignoble to sit here and support the paltry pretense of intellectual dignity. A few days ago her startled eye had caught an advertisement in the newspaper, headed 'Literary Machine'; had it then been invented at last, some automaton to supply the place of such poor creatures as herself, to turn out books and articles? Alas! the machine was only one for holding volumes conveniently, that the work of literary manufacture might be physically lightened. But surely before long some Edison would make the true automaton; the problem must be comparatively such a simple one. Only to throw in a given number of old books, and have them reduced, blended, modernized into a single one for to-day's consumption.'

Gissing had 'no native impulse' for novel writing; but it offered the one chance of earning a living which did not involve the past he wished to obliterate. The alternative was private teaching, but in him the intellectual temper of the student, the scholar, was 'strongly blended with a love of independence which had always made him think with distaste of a teacher's life.' His life of squalid Bohemianism made him acquainted with the life of the London poor; but he had no love for it or them; in fact, he disliked them as much as the life he was compelled to lead among them: 'I could never feel myself at one with the native poor among whom I dwelt. . . . I came to know them too well.' And again: 'The London vulgar I abominate root and branch. . . . I know so much about them.' The current democratic and socialistic movements left him cold. 'I am no friend of the people,' he wrote. 'Every instinct of my being is anti-democratic.' He saw in the London poor just so much literary material which had not yet been adequately treated. But he 'thought nothing could be done' about the misery he represented, and he 'did not desire to do it.' He had none of the crusading zeal of a Zola or a Dickens. To him the roar of Demos was a phenomenon to be regarded with mingled hate and fear; 'there'll be a poor look-out for us if he gets what he wants.'

Gissing was aware that the stories he wrote were 'scraps of immature psychology—the last thing a magazine would accept from an unknown man,' but he had a natural desire to get what he had written into print. A legacy of five hundred dollars falling to him, he applied it to the expense of publishing his first novel *Workers in the Dawn* (1880). As it did not sell, he sent presentation copies to leading men of letters who might be able to help him, and one of these, a well-known writer and thinker of the time, Frederic Harrison, was induced to employ Gissing as tutor for his sons and endeavored to interest other persons of influence in the literary world. John Morley, then editor of the Pall Mall Gazette, offered Gissing regular work, but Gissing despised journalism. His solitary life of absorption in study had 'encouraged his natural tendency to dream and procrastinate and hope for the improbable.' He said to Mrs. Frederic Harrison in 1884: 'The conditions of my life are preposterous. There is only one consolation, that, if I live through it, I shall have materials for a darker and stronger work than any our time has seen. If I can hold out till I have written some three or four books, I shall at all events have the satisfaction of knowing that I have left something too individual in tone to be neglected.'

Gradually Gissing established his footing in the world of letters and put himself beyond the reach of actual want. In ten years he got out half a dozen novels and his receipts from them rose from two hundred and fifty dollars each to a thousand. One of them, *Demos*, went into a second edition, and with the unexpected payment thus obtained he indulged himself in a long-desired visit to Italy. 'There came into my hands a sum of money (such a poor little sum) for a book I had written. It was early autumn. I chanced to hear some one speak of Naples—and only death would have held me back.' He made friends and acquaintances—George Meredith, Grant Allen, Edward Clodd, H. G. Wells—but meanwhile he had involved himself in another complication with a woman. According to his friend Morley Roberts, Gissing's explanation was that he could stand the strain of loneliness no longer, 'so I rushed out and spoke to the very first woman I came across.' She was a woman of no natural attractiveness, intelligence, or education—and a bitter scold. H. G. Wells described her as a 'poor, tormented, miserable, angry servant girl'—but Gissing would not listen to the remonstrances of his friends. In *New Grub Street* (1891), published soon after his second marriage he puts his own answer to the plea that he was making 'an unpardonable fool of himself in marrying so much beneath him; that he might well have waited until his income improved': 'This was all very well, but they might just as reasonably have bidden him reject plain food because a few years hence he would be able to purchase luxuries; he could not do without nourishment of some sort, and the time had come when he could not do without a wife. Many a man with brains but no money has been compelled to the same step. Educated girls have a pronounced distaste for London garrets; not one in fifty thousand would share poverty with the brightest genius ever born. Seeing that marriage is so often indispensable to that very success which would enable a man of parts to mate equally, there is nothing for it but to look below one's own level, and be grateful to the untaught woman who has pity on one's loneliness.'

Gissing was grateful—for a while. The venture lasted long enough for two children to be born, but when the inevitable separation came, as Wells puts it, Gissing was 'no longer the glorious, indefatigable, impracticable youth of the London flat, but a damaged and ailing man, full of ill-advised precautions against the imaginary illnesses that were his interpretations of a general *malaise*.'

In the last few years of his life, with the pressure of need removed, Gissing was able to live quietly in the South of France in the congenial companionship of a French lady who translated some of his novels. To this period belongs some of his most popular work, including *The Private Papers of Henry Ryecroft*, which is pleasantly written but has not the grip and power of the novels of his prime.

He will probably be best and longest remembered by *New Grub Street*, into which he put all the bitterness of his personal experience as an author. Not only is the hero of the novel, Reardon, the scholar driven by circumstances to write fiction for money, obviously a reflex of his own fate, but some of the minor characters recall phases or incidents of his early career. Wheeldon tells the story of Gissing's American adventures, Biffen stands for the conscientious realism of Gissing's early novels, Alfred Yule is the unsuccessful author, burdened and irritated with an ignorant and ill-tempered wife. The following passage is clearly a plea in extenuation of his own incapacity to make his way, an *Apologia pro vita sua*: 'The chances are that you have neither understanding nor sympathy for men such as Edwin Reardon and Harold Biffen. They merely provoke you. They seem to you inert, flabby, weakly envious, foolishly obstinate, impiously mutinous, and many other things. You are made angrily contemptuous by their failure to get on; why don't they bestir themselves, push and bustle, welcome kicks so long as halfpence follow, make place in the world's eye—in short, take a leaf from the book of Mr. Jasper Milvain? But try to imagine a personality wholly unfitted for the rough and tumble of the world's labor-market. From the familiar point of view these men were worthless; view them in possible relation to a humane order of society, and they are admirable citizens. Nothing is easier than to condemn a type of character which is unequal to the coarse demands of life as it suits the average man. These two were richly endowed with the kindly and the imaginative virtues; if fate threw them amid incongruous circumstances, is their endowment of less value? You scorn their passivity; but it was their nature and their merit to be passive. Gifted with independent means, each of them would have taken quite a different aspect in your eyes. The sum of their faults was their inability to earn money; but, indeed, that inability does not call for unmingled disdain.'

To this personal note *New Grub Street* owes not only its defensive, self-justifying, almost plaintive tone, but also a vital force which Gissing's work often lacks. He defined art as 'an expression, satisfying and abiding, of the zest of life,' but he also held that 'art nowadays must be the mouthpiece of misery, for misery is the keynote of modern life.' In practice he inclined rather to the latter view, and the intensity of his work arises rather from a keen sense of suffering than from any sense of enjoyment. Yet theoretically he believed that 'the artist is moved and inspired by supreme enjoyment of some aspect of the world about him; an enjoyment in itself keener than that experienced by another man, and intensified, prolonged, by the power—which comes to him we know not how—of recording in visible or audible form that emotion of rare vitality.' This is curious, for it is precisely the lack of this sense of enjoyment in Gissing's novels that has led many readers to complain of their grayness of atmosphere, their general tone of pessimism and futility. He greatly admired Dickens and wrote an excellent book about him, but no writer could be further removed from the exuberant vitality of Dickens, and his ready sympathy with the simple humors and buoyant courage of the London poor as well as their sorrows and privations.

Gissing had nothing but contempt for the London mob, and for the populace of the provincial towns and the country districts, who were, in his view, sinking deeper and deeper into a vicious vulgarity. 'To flatter the proletariat is to fight against all the good that still characterizes educated England—against reverence for the beautiful, against magnanimity, against enthusiasm of mind, heart, and soul.' 'The people who earn enough for their needs, and whose spiritual guide is the Sunday newspaper—I knew them, because for a long time I was obliged to lodge in their houses. Only a consuming fire could purify the places where they dwell. Don't misunderstand me; I am not charging them with what are commonly held vices and crimes, but with the consistent love of everything that is ignoble, with utter deadness to generous impulse, with the fatal habit of low mockery. And these are the people who really direct the democratic movement. They set the tone in politics; they are debasing art and literature; even the homes of wealthy people begin to show the effects of their influence. One hears men and women of gentle birth using phrases which originate with shopboys; one sees them reading print which is addressed to the coarsest million. They crowd to entertainments which are deliberately adapted to the lowest order of mind. When commercial interest is supreme, how can the tastes of the majority fail to lead and control?'

These are the opinions of Godwin Peak, the hero of *Born in Exile*, and they are obviously the expression of Gissing's own views. Gissing, like his hero, felt himself 'an aristocrat *de jure*,' and Godwin Peak's attitude to the masses is his own. An incident in Hyde Park related in the novel is evidently a personal experience of the author's: 'He chanced once to be in Hyde Park, on the occasion of some public ceremony, and was brought to pause at the edge of a gaping plebeian crowd, drawn up to witness the passing of aristocratic vehicles. Close in front of him an open carriage came to a stop; in it sat, or rather reclined, two ladies, old and young. Upon this picture Godwin fixed his eyes with the intensity of fascination; his memory never lost the impress of these ladies' faces. Nothing very noteworthy about them; but to Godwin they conveyed a passionate perception of all that is implied in social superiority. Here he stood, one of the multitude, of the herd; shoulder to shoulder with boors and pickpockets; and within reach of his hand reposed those two ladies, in Olympian

calm, seeming unaware even of the existence of the throng. Now
they exchanged a word; now they smiled to each other. How
delicate was the moving of their lips! How fine must be their
enunciation! On the box sat an old coachman and a young footman; they too were splendidly impassive, scornful of the multitudinous gaze.—The block was relieved, and on the carriage
rolled.

'They were his equals, those ladies; merely his equals. With
such as they he should by right of nature associate.

'In his rebellion, he could not hate them. He hated the malo-
dorous rabble who stared insolently at them and who envied their
immeasurable remoteness. Of mere wealth he thought not; might
he only be recognized by the gentle of birth and breeding for what
he really was, and be rescued from the promiscuity of the vulgar!'

In spite of his dislike of the populace, Gissing accomplished
something on their behalf by his convincingly accurate pictures of
their misery. He was the first English novelist to show how the
poor lived and worked, to enable the middle class to realize the
squalor of the slums and the ignorance and degradation of their
inhabitants. In so doing he enlarged the scope of the English
novel, which had hitherto described the poor either with idyllic
sentimentalism or with grotesque humor. Gissing was acquainted
with the French realists and absorbed something of their spirit.
In the preface to his third novel, *Isabel Clarendon*, he sets forth
his theory of the novel in the following terms: 'He who is giving
these chapters of her history may not pretend to do much more
than exhibit facts and draw at times justifiable inference. He is
not a creator of human beings, with eyes to behold the very heart
of the machine he has himself pieced together; merely one who
takes trouble to trace certain lines of human experience, and,
working here on grounds of knowledge, there by aid of analogy,
here again in the way of colder speculation, spins his tale with
what skill he may till the threads are used up.'

This has much in common with Zola's theory of observation and
experiment, but Gissing was quick to perceive that Zola's practice
was far from consistent with his theory. Zola, he said, 'writes
deliberate tragedies; his vilest figures become heroic from the
place they fill in a strongly imagined drama.' Gissing's own practice, especially in his earlier novels, followed the maxims of the
French realist, although in the spirit and what might be called
the decorum of his stories he kept more closely to the example of
his immediate predecessors in the English novel—Thackeray,

George Eliot, and Anthony Trollope. He had nothing but contempt for the animal passion which had done so much to wreck his own life; he felt himself a free spirit only in his later years, when he was relieved 'from the temptations and harassings of sexual emotion. What we call love is mere turmoil,' he writes, and goes on to enter a vigorous protest against the practice of contemporary novelists in yielding to the popular demand for a love-story: 'If every novelist could be strangled and thrown into the sea we should have some chance of reforming women. The girl's nature was corrupted with sentimentality, like that of all but every woman who is intelligent enough to read what is called the best fiction, but not intelligent enough to understand its vice. Love—love—love; a sickening sameness of vulgarity. What is more vulgar than the ideal of novelists? They won't represent the actual world; it would be too dull for their readers. In real life, how many men and women fall in love? Not one in every ten thousand, I am convinced. Not one married pair in ten thousand have felt for each other as two or three couples do in every novel. There is the sexual instinct, of course, but that is quite a different thing; the novelist daren't talk about that. The paltry creatures daren't tell the one truth that would be profitable. The result is that women imagine themselves noble and glorious when they are most near the animals.'

Probably one of the reasons for the respect shown to Gissing by later novelists and critics is the dogged courage with which he refused, in spite of poverty and depression, to respond favorably to the popular cries of his own time. He declined to write romantic love-stories; but he refused also to feed the appetite for sensational realism in the treatment of sex. He despised the prevalent commercialism, but he expressed frankly his own opinions about the incapacities which made the English working class unable to achieve their own salvation. He had no respect—and showed none—for conventional religion, but he refused to bow the knee to the new deity of Science, which he denounced as 'the remorseless enemy of mankind.' His denunciation of Science has the tone of an ancient prophet foretelling the evil to come: 'I see it destroying all simplicity and gentleness of life, all the beauty of the world; I see it restoring barbarism under a mask of civilization; I see it darkening men's minds and hardening their hearts; I see it bringing a time of vast conflicts, which will pale into insignificance "the thousand wars of old," and, as likely as not, will whelm all the laborious advances of mankind in blood-drenched chaos.'

He was as unable to accept the assurances of a mechanistic evolutionary theory as he was to receive the consolations of orthodox Christianity, and much study of ancient and modern thinkers gave him no comfort beyond that of a vague agnosticism. He writes: 'That there is some order, some purpose, seems a certainty; my mind, at all events, refuses to grasp an idea of a Universe which means nothing at all. But just as unable am I to accept any of the solutions ever proposed. Above all it is the existence of natural beauty which haunts my thought. I can, for a time, forget the world's horrors; I can never forget the flower by the wayside and the sun falling in the west. These things have a meaning— but I doubt, I doubt—whether the mind of man will ever be permitted to know it.' His solitary communings and his experience of life led him to accept his lot in the end with a quiet resignation, a wistfulness which had enough courage to prevent him from ever becoming a whimperer. So he came to win the esteem of his fellows in the craft of writing and the respect of those who came after him to attempt to interpret life through the medium of fiction.

GEORGE MOORE
(1852–1933)

The long life of George Moore divides itself into four phases or periods: (1) his youth as an art student in Paris, which bore fruit in many magazine articles and his book, *Modern Painting* (1893); (2) coincident with this phase, or rather over-lapping it, is his more mature interest in French fiction, which found expression in the series of realistic novels from *A Modern Lover* (1883) to *Sister Teresa* (1901); (3) his alienation from England by the Boer war and his return to Ireland at the close of the nineteenth century, when, as he put it, 'the Englishman that was in me (he that wrote *Esther Waters*) had been overtaken and captured by the Irishman.' This was the period of his interest in the Irish drama and his autobiographical account of the Irish Renaissance entitled *Ave, Salve, Vale* (1911–14); (4) his settlement in London as a leading personage in the English literary world, revered for his mastery of style. The characteristic productions of this final period are *The Brook Kerith* (1916), *Héloise and Abelard* (1921), and *Aphrodite in Aulis* (1930). Only the first two periods fall within the Victorian Era and the scope of this book.

Moore spent his boyhood on the estate of his father, an Irish landowner, in County Mayo. But soon after his father's death in 1870 he left for the more congenial atmosphere of the Paris Quartier Latin. Here he plunged deep into French art, literature, and life, and in accordance with the French literary tradition began his career with two volumes of poetry written under the influence of Baudelaire and Verlaine—*Flowers of Passion* (1878) and *Pagan Poems* (1881). But his real interest was in French fiction, which was undergoing an important development under the leadership of Flaubert, the brothers Goncourt, and Zola. The influence of the first-named was directed against romanticism in life and art, but like the brothers Goncourt he attached the greatest importance to the problem of style. With Zola, however, the novel was a medium for the conveyance of truth ascertained by scientific investigation and more especially of moral truth; to enforce such truths, it was necessary that vice should be displayed in all its hideousness. 'Zola,' Moore said, 'was the beginning of me.' It was to arrange for the publication of a novel written in accordance with the Zola prescription that Moore left Paris for London in 1882. He at once sought out the publisher Tinsley, and explained that he had lived for years in France and had learned much from the French novelists, especially from Zola. He mentioned the title of his novel, *A Modern Lover*, to Tinsley and gave him a short account of the plot. Tinsley thought it 'a risky story,' but expressed willingness to undertake its publication if Moore guaranteed him from loss through the refusal of the subscription libraries to circulate it. He explained to Moore that while in France a novel sold for three and a half francs, in England the price was over ten times that amount owing to the system of publication in three volumes. This made any large sale over the counter impossible and put both publishers and authors at the mercy of the circulating libraries. The libraries distributed new novels by sending them to the homes of their subscribers, and were 'essentially domestic' in their tastes and standards; they had established a system of censorship, which prohibited the circulation of novels that parents might think unsuitable for their daughters to read.

'But you will break the censorship?' asked Moore, and Tinsley answered: 'I don't know, but it will be broken one day or another. Some two or three novelists, if they combined, would do it.' So Moore set out to break the censorship, and guaranteed Tinsley against loss on the publication of *A Modern Lover* to the extent of forty pounds, if the circulating libraries refused to take it. They did refuse, but Moore was saved from payment for the loss of cir-

culation by a fire which destroyed most of the edition and recouped
the publisher by the insurance.

With his second novel, *A Mummer's Wife*, Moore went to Vizitelly, already notorious as the publisher of the translations of
Zola's novels, for which he was later prosecuted at the instigation
of the Vigilance Society and sent to prison for three months.
Meanwhile Vizitelly published *A Mummer's Wife*, and made a
hundred pounds for Moore out of the sale, though it was again
banned by the circulating libraries. Moore gave Vizitelly an outline of the plot before he had written the novel—'the story of a
mummer, the head of an opera company, who lodges at a linen-
draper's shop and rescues the pretty draperess from selling reels
of cotton and pocket handkerchiefs.' 'And in what town does all
this happen?' asked Vizitelly. 'A great deal of the success of your
book depends upon the town and I hope you will make a significant choice. You must not rely on the luck of a chance thought,
you must go in search of everything.' This was sound doctrine
according to the Zola gospel, and Moore, who had not considered
the town, thinking of it merely as 'somewhere in the North of
England,' proceeded to make careful inquiries among the actors
who haunted the Gaiety Bar, near his lodgings in the Strand. He
heard many commonplace stories of the wooings of landladies in
provincial towns, but nothing to his purpose until an operatic
tenor said, 'I have had wooings, too, like any other man, but it
was not about singing on the staircase that we came to an understanding, but at the breakfast table when she said, "I think you
like fried eggs better than poached." "How do you know that?"
I asked. "Why, sir, when you were here a year ago you had fried
eggs," and marveling at the compliment she paid me I took her
hand and that was all.' The suggestion followed that Hanley was
the town Moore required, 'a town ugly and dull that would not
excite the imagination even of George Borrow.' Moore went to
Hanley and found it the place he wanted. He described it in
A Mummer's Wife to the admiration of Arnold Bennett, to whom it
revealed the fictional possibilities of the five towns he was afterwards to make famous. A quarter of a century later, when Bennett
was reading *A Mummer's Wife* for the third or the fourth time,
he entered in his *Journal* (September 7, 1910): 'This book really is
original and fine and beautiful. The Islington scenes are superb.
You have squalor and sordidness turned into poetry. And the
painter-like effects of visualization are splendid throughout.
Language a bit clumsy and coarse occasionally. "Booze" and

"boozed" are amazing words. There are others. But what an original and powerful work.' Even the contemporary critics, when the novel was first published, said that a new voice had come into literature, that nothing had been written with the same force as *A Mummer's Wife* for many a day.

Moore's third novel, *A Drama in Muslin* (1886) and his fourth, *Confessions of a Young Man* (1888), were also damned by the circulating libraries; according to Moore's *Communication to my Friends*, on which he was engaged at the time of his death, the first was a moderate success, and the second a real success. 'Everybody liked it.' But Moore did not yet feel that his effort to break down the censorship of the circulating libraries was a complete victory. 'Three more books,' said Henley, 'and the spell would be broken; but Moore realized that he had not the courage to write three more books as long as *A Mummer's Wife*. He determined, however, to write one more novel, and decided that the heroine of it should be a servant girl; long after, he said that the subject was suggested to him by an article in a newspaper, but he was probably influenced by French examples of the treatment of the same theme. He decided further that the girl should be a scullery-maid who has an illegitimate child, of which the footman is the father, though he thought there hardly seemed enough in that for a novel. 'But if the footman were carried off by one of the young ladies in the drawing-room and the unfortunate girl left to bring up her child on £18 a year. Such is the price of human flesh in our admirable city of London. My father bred and raced horses; a racing stable would make an admirable background in keeping with the subject of my story. I should have to draw portraits of jockeys and trainers, but they would be only accessories; the principal figure would be the indomitable mother who will sacrifice her life for her child.' Such was the story of *Esther Waters* as it shaped itself in Moore's mind; he aimed at outdoing George Eliot's treatment of a somewhat similar situation in *Adam Bede*, where Hetty Sorrel kills her child to save herself from shame; the 'true molding' of the subject would be the deserted mother living to save her child.

The death of Vizitelly after his imprisonment at the age of eighty left Moore without a publisher, but Walter Scott, who had bought the plates of his earlier novels, undertook to publish *Esther Waters* (1894). It was, and is, Moore's masterpiece, and met with immediate recognition. His own record of the fact reads: 'Every paper, high and low, literary and commercial, had the same tale to tell of *Esther Waters*—that a great novel had just been published;

illiterate and literate liked it.' When Macmillan asked Moore how many copies had been sold and learned that the number was 24,000, he remarked, 'A great sale indeed. I know of no other book that has sold as much except perhaps *Tom Brown's School-days.*' Mr. Gladstone approved of *Esther Waters* and the fact of his approval was reported in the Westminster Gazette. Moore took occasion to forward to the Smith Library an accountant's report that the firm had lost about £1,500 by refusing to circulate *Esther Waters*, and he heard with satisfaction that the firm sent word to their librarian that 'it would be well in the future to avoid heavy losses by banning books, especially books that Mr. Gladstone was likely to read and to express his approval of in the Westminster Gazette.' Moore felt that he had helped to bring the system of censorship by the libraries to an end, and congratulated himself on having served the cause of humanity.

No less important than Moore's victory over the strongholds of Victorian prudishness in the circulating libraries was the impetus *Esther Waters* gave to the new realistic movement in English fiction. The faithful and sympathetic portrayal of humble life in French fiction had been successfully achieved by the brothers Goncourt in *Germinie Lacerteux* (1865) and by Guy de Maupassant in *Histoire d'une Fille de Ferme* (1881) and *Une Vie* (1883), but in English fiction it was a novelty, except for the studies of Gissing, which were accurate but not sympathetic and had no popular appeal. After Moore's *Esther Waters* (1894), it was impossible to return to the treatment of the life of the English poor—half-sentimental, half-grotesque—which the genius of Dickens had established as the traditional method of the English novel. It was recognized as a necessity that the novelist should know the environment of his humbler characters, that he should represent it accurately, and that he should give a faithful, not a romantic or sentimentalized portrayal of their aspirations and struggles against untoward circumstances and their own inner weaknesses, their little triumphs, and their often magnificent and even tragic failures. Moore's heroine is 'a girl of twenty, firmly built with short strong arms and a plump neck that carried a well-turned head with dignity. Her well-formed nostrils redeemed her somewhat thick, fleshy nose, and it was a pleasure to see her grave, almost sullen, face light up with sunny humor; for when she laughed a line of almond-shaped teeth showed between red lips.' But Esther Waters is no radiant village beauty, like George Eliot's Hetty Sorrel; she is a not unusual type of the servant class of the

Victorian period, with very limited ideas and intelligence (she cannot read), an uncertain temper and an obstinate disposition. She has the religious notions of an obscure Protestant sect, and has left school as a child to earn a meager wage as a servant in London lodging-houses, some of them of an unsavory reputation. She is a good-hearted, ignorant girl, thrown by chance to earn her living as a kitchen-maid in the household of a county family, whose predominant interest is a racing stable. This is described in perhaps too meticulous detail because of Moore's intimate acquaintance since childhood with his father's racing stable; the detail, however, endows with convincing truthfulness the picture of life in the servants' hall and gives the novelist a sure touch in the use of his natural power of 'visualization,' as Arnold Bennett called it, his ability to make the reader see the scenes and persons as if they were before the eye with the rounded shape and pulsing vigor of actuality. Moore had quite unusual powers of vivid description and simple yet lively dialogue. The reader may know very little about racehorses and the life of the English racecourse, but he feels that the picture presented to him is true.

Esther's religious principles win the favor of her mistress and she is not unhappy in her unfamiliar surroundings. But the placid current of her life at Woodview is disturbed by a love-affair with the footman, William Latch, which results in her leaving her place and giving birth to a son in a lying-in hospital. It was the detailed description of this institution that determined the banning of *Esther Waters* by the circulating libraries, though it is completely void of offense to the modern reader. Esther undergoes many hardships in the struggle to earn her own living and bring up her boy. After some years she meets William again and consents to join him in the keeping of a public-house; though she finds that it is an illegal betting resort, which greatly offends her religious principles, she stands by William until he is reduced to poverty by a conviction in a police court, falls ill, and dies of consumption. At the end of the novel we find Esther back in service with her mistress at Woodview—a situation recalling that of Jeanne and her faithful maid Rosalie at the end of Maupassant's *Une Vie*— and the two ageing women comfort each other for the vicissitudes of their unhappy lives. Esther's boy, Jack, unable to find employment and unwilling to be a burden on his mother any longer, enlists, and our last glimpse of Esther is of her receiving a visit from him at Woodview: 'A tall soldier came through the gate. He wore a long red cloak, and a small cap jauntily set on the side of his close-clipped head. Esther uttered a little exclamation, and ran to meet him. He took his mother in his arms, kissed her, and they walked towards Mrs. Barfield together. All was forgotten in the happiness of the moment—the long fight for his life, and the possibility that any moment might declare him to be mere food for powder and shot. She was only conscious that she had accomplished her woman's work—she had brought him up to man's estate; and that was her sufficient reward. What a fine fellow he was! She did not know he was so handsome, and blushing with pleasure and pride she glanced shyly at him out of the corners of her eyes as she introduced him to her mistress.

"This is my son, Ma'am."

'Mrs. Barfield held out her hand to the young soldier.'

"I have heard a great deal about you from your mother."

"And I of you, ma'am. You've been very kind to my mother. I don't know how to thank you."

'And in silence they walked towards the house.'

By this time Moore had mastered a subtle and graceful style of extraordinary effectiveness which he was to use in a subsequent career of some forty years on the most diverse themes. His literary versatility was remarkable, and he lived to be the most distinguished stylist of the first three decades of the twentieth century. But none of the subjects which attracted his sometimes too ready wit and too facile pen enlisted the human sympathy of which he was capable to the same depth and to the same extent; and nothing that he wrote later made such an impact upon literary history as *Esther Waters*. It is the best study in English of the life of the racecourse and the betting ring—not unsympathetic, but so unflinching in its fidelity that it reveals the evils of that particular environment more effectively and impressively than any religious tract or parliamentary report could do. But its great virtue is that it tells an unfalteringly honest tale of the failures and triumphs of a sturdy, illiterate servant girl in her lifelong struggle against ignorance, poverty, misfortune, and adversity. She wins out, not by any lucky accident, but by sheer honesty of purpose and unfailing courage and determination to do her duty, as she sees it, in the most difficult and discouraging circumstances. In some of his later work Moore showed a waywardness and irresponsibility which won for him the epithet of 'the Puck of modern literature,' but he tells the story of Esther Waters in a way which entitles him to be recognized not only as a great stylist, but as a sincere and sympathetic moralist.

ROBERT LOUIS STEVENSON
(*1850–1894*)

It is difficult for young people to realize the popularity of R. L. Stevenson during the last few years of his life and the two decades after his death. The post-war generation sees in him only a graceful stylist with pleasing gifts for romantic narrative, travel sketches, and the occasional essay, a somewhat conventional moralist of no great insight or originality. His own contemporaries saw in him a gallant and charming personality, a romantic Bohemian rebellious against the trivial obligations of conventional society but sound on the fundamental principles of morality and order upon which life in the later years of Victoria's reign seemed to rest. Stevenson's life oscillated between the inclination to rebel against these fundamental principles, and the inclination to accept them. In his private life he rebelled; in his published work he accepted and even asserted them. The bonds of family tradition and a puritanical education were too strong for him to throw them off altogether.

His mother was a daughter of the Presbyterian manse, his father a successful engineer, President of the Royal Society of Edinburgh, a solid and well-to-do citizen who expected his son to follow the profession in which he and his ancestors had served with distinction since the organization of the Board of Northern Lighthouses in the eighteenth century. In deference to his father's wishes Louis went so far as to win a medal for an essay on *A New Form of Intermittent Light for Lighthouses*—a light which was highly praised but never used—but in the end the boy, whose interests were entirely literary, wore out his father's patience by his 'invincible triviality. The river was to me a pretty and various spectacle; I could not be made to see it otherwise. To my father it was a chequer-board of lively forces, which he traced from pool to shallow with enduring interest.'

The elder Stevenson was even more distressed by his son's unwillingness to tread in the godly steps of his Puritan ancestors. Louis not only rejected the stern Presbyterian faith of the Stevensons but was given to apparent idleness and low company. Again, the son's own account of his youthful Bohemianism is our best guide: 'I was always kept poor in my youth, to my great indignation at the time, but since then with my complete approval. Twelve pounds a year was my allowance up to twenty-three and though I amplified it by very consistent embezzlement from my mother, I never had enough to be lavish. My monthly pound was usually

spent before the evening of the day on which I received it; as often
as not, it was forstalled; and for the rest of the time I was in rare
fortune if I had five shillings at once in my possession. Hence my
acquaintance was of what would be called a very low order. Looking back upon it, I am surprised at the courage with which I first
ventured alone into the societies in which I moved; I was the companion of seamen, chimney sweeps and thieves; my circle was being
continually changed by the action of the police magistrate. I see
now the little sanded kitchen where Velvet Coat (for such was the
name I went by) has spent days together in silence and making
sonnets in a penny version book; and rough as the material may
appear, I do not believe these days were among the least happy I
have spent.'

Attempts have been made to prove that Stevenson's youth was
more dissolute than he was afterwards willing to admit, but there
is no convincing evidence that his dissipations went beyond the
usual outbreaks and indulgences of a boy in revolt against a parental authority which he regarded as tyrannical. His delicate
health forbad any violent excesses, and he worked hard at his
chosen craft of writing. He said in 1887: 'I imagine nobody had
ever such pains to learn a trade as I had; but I slogged at it day
in and day out; and I frankly believe (thanks to my dire industry)
I have done more with smaller gifts than almost any man of letters
in the world.' At sixteen he had written a historical sketch of the rebellion of the Covenanters, *The Pentland Rising*, which was printed
privately at the expense of an admiring aunt. At college he wrote
essays, plays, and stories, and edited the Edinburgh University
Magazine, which 'ran four months in undisturbed obscurity and
died without a gasp.' When his father saw that engineering was
hopeless as a profession for his wayward son, he accepted the
inevitable, but he urged the law as affording better prospects of
a livelihood than literature. Louis dutifully, though reluctantly,
submitted to his father's wishes; he passed the preliminary law
examination, entered the office of a legal firm to learn conveyanc-
ing, took his final examination in 1875, and was duly called to the
Scottish Bar; he appeared in court in four cases, but his heart
was not in the work, and it was clear that he would make nothing
of it. Small as was his father's faith in his son's literary ability
and indeed, in the desirability of writing as a profession for anyone,
he was obliged to allow Louis, who was now over 25 years of age,
to go his own way.

It was characteristic of Stevenson that, in spite of his acquiescence in his father's plans for his education, he was troubled with moral compunctions about the use he was making of his opportunities. Writing of himself in the third person about this time (though his confession was not published till after his death), he says: 'At college he met other lads more diligent than himself, who followed the plough in summer-time to pay their college fees in winter; and this inequality struck him with some force. He was at that age of a conversable temper, and insatiably curious in the aspects of life; and he spent much of his time scraping acquaintance with all classes of man- and womankind. In this way he came upon many depressed ambitions, and many intelligences stunted for want of opportunity; and this also struck him. He began to perceive that life was a handicap upon strange, wrong-sided principles; and not, as he had been told, a fair and equal race. He began to tremble that he himself had been unjustly favored, when he saw all the avenues of wealth and power and comfort closed against so many of his superiors and equals, and held unwearyingly open before so idle, so desultory, and so dissolute a being as himself. There sat a youth beside him on the college benches, who had only one shirt to his back, and, at intervals sufficiently far apart, must stay at home to have it washed. It was my friend's principle to stay away as often as he dared; for I fear he was no friend to learning. But there was something that came home to him sharply, in this fellow who had to give over study till his shirt was washed, and the scores of others who had never an opportunity at all. If one of these could take his place, he thought; and the thought tore away a bandage from his eyes. He was eaten by the shame of his discoveries, and despised himself as an unworthy favorite and a creature of the backstairs of Fortune. He could no longer see without confusion one of these brave young fellows battling up hill against adversity. Had he not filched that fellow's birthright? At best was he not coldly profiting by the injustice of society, and greedily devouring stolen goods? The money, indeed, belonged to his father, who had worked, and thought, and given up his liberty to earn it; but by what justice could the money belong to my friend, who had, as yet, done nothing but help to squander it.'

As Stevenson's scruples were written down for his own eye alone, we must accept them as genuine, and it is noteworthy that so long as he felt that he was incurring a debt to his father his failing health would not enable him to repay, he accepted as little from his father as possible. 'But so soon as he began to perceive a change for the better, he felt justified in spending more freely, to speed and brighten his return to health, and trusted in the future to lend a help to mankind, as mankind, out of its treasury, had lent a help to him.'

Stevenson's ill health began at the age of two, and it was throughout his life a factor that had to be reckoned with. At fourteen, after receiving the constant care required by a delicate child, he was still 'badly set up' in body, his limbs long, lean, and spidery, his chest flat, suggesting malnutrition. At twenty-three he had to consult a leading English specialist, Dr. Andrew Clark, who diagnosed his case as one of nervous exhaustion with a threat of consumption, and sent him off to spend the winter on the Riviera. From 1874 to 1879 he was compelled to spend some part of each year in France for the sake of his health, his favorite haunts being the artist colony of Barbizon and Grez in the forest of Fontainebleau. It was there that in 1876 he met Mrs. Fanny Osbourne, who had come with her two children to study art, leaving her husband behind in California. Stevenson fell deeply in love with her, and in 1878 she returned to California to obtain a divorce. Stevenson was still living on his father's bounty, as his literary efforts realized no more than five dollars a week. His published writings at this time were inconsiderable, consisting only of a few essays and travel sketches. He felt that his father would not approve of his marriage to a divorced woman, and decided to rely on his own slender financial resources to rejoin Mrs. Osbourne in San Francisco. He accordingly made the journey as an immigrant, and the hardships he had to endure proved too severe for his frail constitution. He arrived in San Francisco bankrupt in health and pocket, and only Mrs. Osbourne's devoted care saved him from death. A cablegram from his father assuring him of an income of £250 a year enabled the lovers to marry. This chapter in Stevenson's personal life found record in *The Amateur Emigrant, Across the Plains*, and *The Silverado Squatters*, the last an account of the honeymoon spent in a deserted mining camp in the mountains north of San Francisco. With his wife Stevenson returned to Europe, was reconciled to his family, and spent the next two years mainly in the Alpine consumptive resort of Davos Platz. There he gathered together two volumes of essays, *Virginibus Puerisque* and *Familiar Studies of Men and Books*, and one of short stories, *New Arabian Nights*, all published in 1881–82. They were favorably reviewed but made no great impression on the public. He wrote for a juvenile magazine a conventional romance of adventure, *Treasure Island*, which ran in Young Folks without attracting attention, but when published in book form (1883) made him at once well known. Encouraged by success, he settled down at Bournemouth in the South of England, wrote some long and short stories which made no particular impression, but again won public favor with *A Child's Garden of Verses* (1885) and *The Strange Case of Dr. Jekyll and Mr. Hyde* (1886).

In the following year the last illness of his father took Stevenson back to Edinburgh, where the climate added almost the finishing touch to the breakdown of his health, already seriously threatened by the strain involved in writing his romance *Kidnapped*, which he found himself unable to finish owing to physical weakness. He sought refuge at Saranac in the Adirondacks, and on landing at New York found himself already a literary celebrity owing to the success of *Dr. Jekyll and Mr. Hyde*, both in its original story form and in (unauthorized) versions on the stage, these being the days when English authors were still unprotected by international copyright.

The change in his financial fortunes was remarkable: his income from his writings jumped suddenly from a few hundred pounds to several thousand dollars. He refused an offer from the New York World of ten thousand dollars a year for a weekly article, but made an advantageous arrangement with Messrs. Scribner for the whole of his future work to appear in the United States—of which he was so forgetful that shortly afterwards he sold the serial rights of his next story to McClure. Saranac benefited his health, and his wife was able to leave him to visit her family in California. He was at Manasquan in New Jersey when he received a telegram that the yacht Casco might be hired for a trip in the South Seas, and while the telegraph boy waited, he wrote out a reply instructing her to accept the offer.

So opened the last chapter in Stevenson's adventurous career. He collaborated with his step-son, Lloyd Osbourne, in sea stories which added little to his fame, and wrote a series of descriptive letters about his travels in the South Seas which were equally unsuccessful. It was a visit to the leper island of Molokai that enabled him to write the one work of this period which had real distinction—a reply to an unworthy attack upon the character of the missionary Father Damien, who gave his life in devoted service to the lepers of the South Seas. This was in 1890, and the following year Stevenson was able to settle down on the estate he had bought near Apia on the island of Samoa. He called it Vailima, 'the five waters,' and entertained there many distinguished visitors, who sometimes failed to appreciate their host's simple fare and Bohemian habits. *The Vailima Letters*, published the year after his death, are the best record of his Samoan life and his efforts on behalf of the natives. He wrote also stories of the South Seas, was able to bring *Kidnapped* to a conclusion in a sequel entitled *Catriona*, and began two other novels, *St. Ives* (finished by Sir Arthur Quiller Couch), and *Weir of Hermiston*, which was left a fragment but a fragment of unusual promise, for it indicates a greater grip on life and character than had been shown in any of his previous work. He was buried on Vaea Mountain near by and the inscription on the tomb is his own *Requiem:*

> Under the wide and starry sky,
> Dig the grave and let me lie.
> Glad did I live and gladly die,
>   And I laid me down with a will.
>
> This be the verse you grave for me:
> *Here he lies where he longed to be;*
> *Home is the sailor, home from sea,*
>   *And the hunter home from the hill.*

The exaggerated praise given to Stevenson's work by his contemporaries provoked a natural reaction among the succeeding generation, and he has been unduly depreciated as well as overpraised. His 'invalidism,' which has been made a reproach to him by some of the objectors, was not his fault but his misfortune, and he can hardly be blamed for turning it to literary account. The year before his death he wrote to George Meredith: 'For fourteen years I have not had a day's real health; I have wakened sick and gone to bed weary; and I have done my work unflinchingly. I have written in bed, written out of it, written in hemorrhages, written in sickness, written torn by coughing, written when my head swam for weakness; and for so long, it seems to me I have won my wager and recovered my glove. I am better now, have been, rightly speaking, since first I came to the Pacific; and still few are the days when I am not in some physical distress. And the battle goes on—ill or well is a trifle; so as it goes. I was made for a contest, and the powers have so willed that my battlefield should be this dingy inglorious one of the bed and the physic bottle.'

This is a good example of the much discussed problem of Stevenson's style. It is a mannered style, for even in a personal letter the author does not hesitate to use such devices as repetition and inversion and a deliberately rhythmic cadence of phrasing. But it has ease, suppleness, limpidity, felicity—all the virtues except strength, naturalness, and simplicity. Its artifices offend many readers, but on those readers who do not notice these tricks of style or are able to overlook them it makes a distinctly agreeable impression, consonant with the charm of the writer's personality— a somewhat self-conscious charm, with an occasional touch of theatricality which has led to the condemnation of Stevenson as a poseur—but a real charm, nevertheless.

JOSEPH CONRAD
(1857-1924)

Within a year of Stevenson's death there came to the front a writer of romance who drew his material not from other books but from his own experience of life. He became known, first to the critics and then to the public on both sides of the Atlantic as Joseph Conrad, but his full name was Teodor Josef Konrad Nalecz Korzeniowski. He was born at Berdiczew in the Polish Province of Podolia, then under Russian rule. His parents were Polish aristocrats who died in exile after being driven from their estates by the Russian Government for revolutionary activities. This and the reading of his father's translation of Victor Hugo's *Travailleurs de la Mer* may be the explanation of the desire Conrad conceived in his boyhood for the free life of the open sea and his determination to seek service under the freer flags of France and England. However this may be, when he was seventeen and ready to matriculate at the University of Cracow, he persuaded his uncle to send him to Marseilles, where he entered the French merchant service. He made two voyages to the French West Indies, which included also gunrunning adventures in the Gulf of Mexico for the benefit of rebels in one of the Central American Republics. On Conrad's return, he tells us, his memory was full of these 'experiences, lawful and lawless, which had their charm and their thrill.' A gunrunning enterprise on behalf of the Carlist cause resulted in a shipwreck on the Spanish coast, after which Conrad found himself one evening 'entering Marseilles by way of the railway station, after many adventures, one more disagreeable than another, involving privations, great exertions, a lot of difficulties with all sorts of people who looked upon me evidently more as a discreditable vagabond deserving the attentions of gendarmes than a respectable (if crazy) young gentleman attended by a guardian angel of his own.' A youthful but hectic love-affair (Conrad was still under twenty-one) involved him in a duel in which he received a bullet wound, and the lady concerned having married her other suitor, Conrad left Marseilles on an English steamer, which after a voyage to Constantinople, landed him, still under twenty-one, at the English port of Lowestoft.

Conrad's fortunes after landing at Lowestoft are best related as he told them himself to his friend Sir Hugh Clifford, who reported them after Conrad's death as follows: 'At Lowestoft he made the casual acquaintance of an old fellow named Captain Cook who for untold years had been in command of a collier which plied regularly between that port and Cardiff. He was by then well stricken in years, but it was popularly reported of him that during the whole course of his sea service he had never been out of sight of land—a fact which, combined with the historic name he bore, caused him to be commonly known as "The Great Circumnavigator." By this old man was young Conrad befriended, and it was on board his collier that the latter, first as a common hand and later as an able seaman, made a succession of voyages between Lowestoft and Cardiff.

'Conrad had had a sound education, though the spirit of adventure in him had put a premature period to his studies. He had spoken Polish and French from infancy, and also knew, I think, some Russian and German, and he seems to have picked up a working knowledge of English with ease and rapidity. Meanwhile, during the long, uneventful days afloat, old Captain Cook, who had taken a fancy to the lad, coached him in navigation and seamanship, and when he believed his pupil to be ripe for the experiment, sent him up to London to sit for his examination for his second mate's certificate.' But before gaining an officer's certificate Conrad had to make voyages as a sailor before the mast, first on a sailing ship to Sydney, Australia, and then on a steamer to Mediterranean ports. It was not until two years after landing at Lowestoft that he made his first voyage as an officer, again on a sailing ship to Sydney, and back by Cape Horn. In 1881 he sailed as second mate with a salary of twenty dollars a month on the barque Palestine and underwent the adventures he afterwards related in *Youth* (1902). After misfortunes which kept them on the English coast for a year, the barque sailed for Bangkok and in the Indian Ocean caught fire and had to be abandoned; Conrad was put in command of one of the boats and made his way in it independently to Singapore. 'I remember nights and days of calm

when we pulled, we pulled, and the boat seemed to stand still.'
From Singapore he returned by steamer to London and passed his
examination as first officer. A dispute with his next captain led to
his leaving the ship at Madras and he took service on the sailing
ship Narcissus. His story *The Nigger of the Narcissus* gives an
accurate record of what happened on that voyage. He said so to
his biographer, G. Jean-Aubry, not long before his death: 'Most
of the personages I have portrayed actually belonged to the crew
of the real Narcissus, including the admirable Singleton (whose
real name was Sullivan), Archie, Belfast, and Donkin. I got the
two Scandinavians from associations with another ship. All this is
now old, but it was quite present before my mind when I wrote this
book. I remember, as if it had occurred but yesterday, the last
occasion I saw the Nigger. That morning I was quarter officer,
and about five o'clock I entered the double-bedded cabin where he
was lying full length. On the lower bunk, ropes, fids and pieces
of cloth had been deposited, so as not to have to take them down
into the sail-room if they should be wanted at once. I asked him
how he felt, but he hardly made me any answer. A little later a
man brought him some coffee in a cup provided with a hook to
suspend it on the edge of the bunk. At about six o'clock the
officer-in-charge came to tell me that he was dead. We had just
experienced an awful gale in the vicinity of the Needles, south
of the Cape, of which I have tried to give an impression in my
book.'

On his next voyage he was injured by a falling spar and found
himself in hospital at Singapore, emerging to become second mate
on the steamer Vidor which plied on a course of 1,600 miles among
the Malayan Islands. After making the round from and to Singapore some half-dozen times, the monotony of re-traversing the
same route and the lack of opportunity for advancement led Conrad to resign. It was, however, on these monotonous voyages that
he became acquainted with the characters and adventures which
make his earlier stories and in part his later ones. Almayer, the
hero, if such he may be called, of his first story, *Almayer's Folly*
(1895), and Willems, the villain of the second, *An Outcast of the
Islands* (1896), are taken from life and so is the Captain Tom
Lingard who not only figures in these earlier stories but is the
principal character in *The Rescue*, which was begun before the
end of the century but was not ready for publication until 1920.
Jim Lingard, in actual life the nephew of Captain Tom Lingard,
furnished some hints for the hero of *Lord Jim* (1900), though in

this instance the correspondence of character and circumstance between reality and romance is by no means so close.

Stranded at Singapore, Conrad thought himself fortunate to obtain the command of the sailing ship Otago, whose captain had died suddenly on the voyage to Bangkok. Conrad took the ship to Melbourne under conditions of peculiar difficulty and hardship which he has related exactly as they happened in *The Shadow Line* (1917).

Recalled to Europe by the illness of his uncle, Conrad was swept away by the current wave of enthusiasm for African exploration. It was not a new enthusiasm with him, for when he was a boy of twelve, he put his finger on the unexplored central region of a map of Africa and said, 'When I grow up, I shall go *there*.' In order to satisfy this ambition he sought and obtained service with the Belgian company for the development of the Congo and penetrated that river as far as Stanley Falls. 'Away in the middle of the stream, on a little island nestling all black in the foam of the broken water, a solitary little light glimmered feebly, and I said to myself with awe, "This is the very spot of my boyish boast." A great melancholy descended on me. Yes, this was the very spot. But there was no shadowy friend to stand by my side in the night of the enormous wilderness, no great haunting memory, but only the unholy recollection of a prosaic newspaper "stunt" and the distasteful knowledge of the vilest scramble for loot that ever disfigured the history of human conscience and geographical exploration.' Overwhelmed by the appalling hostility of Nature and the cruelty and cupidity of man, Conrad returned home with shattered health and a deep pessimism perhaps rooted in the Slavic melancholy of his disposition. His recollections of his African adventure are embodied in *Heart of Darkness* (1899).

Conrad took with him and brought back with him from the Congo the manuscript of *Almayer's Folly* which he had begun while waiting for his African appointment. He took it with him as mate on the sailing ship Torrens, on which he made two voyages from London to Adelaide and return. On the second voyage out, while talking about literature to a young Cambridge graduate named W. H. Jacques, Conrad showed him the manuscript of the first nine chapters of *Almayer's Folly* and asked him to read it. Next day Conrad asked Jacques, 'Is it worth finishing?' 'Distinctly,' was the answer. 'Were you interested?' Conrad inquired, and the Englishman laconically replied, 'Very much.' 'Now let me ask you one more thing: is the story quite clear to you as it stands?' 'Yes. Perfectly.' This was all Jacques said of it and they never spoke together of the book again. On the return voyage Conrad talked much with John Galsworthy, then a young man of twenty-five, but, as Galsworthy puts it, their talk was 'of life, not literature' and Conrad said no word of his literary ambitions. With the arrival of the Torrens at London in October, 1893, Conrad stepped out of his sea life altogether.

A timely legacy from his uncle enabled him to live in tolerable comfort for six months, during which he completed *Almayer's Folly* and dedicated it to his uncle's memory. Choosing a publisher at random, Conrad sent the manuscript to Unwin and it had the good fortune to fall into the hands of Edward Garnett, who was much impressed by it and recommended its publication. It was issued the same year, and with Garnett's encouragement Conrad went on with *An Outcast of the Islands*, which appeared in 1896. Both are stories of Malayan life and reveal Conrad's characteristic qualities.

His main quality was the power to make the reader *see*, to relate an incident or chain of incidents with such fidelity to fact and power of imagination as to convince the reader of their reality. He was a born story-teller and he had had remarkable experiences, but there was more in his genius than this natural gift and more in his success than the adventitious aid of the adventures through which he had passed. The Academy, in awarding him its prize for one of three of the most worthy literary productions of 1898 said of him: 'He blends human beings and nature. The puppet never fills the universe, as with certain other novelists. Everything is related and harmonized. This comprehensiveness of vision, this amplitude of outlook makes Mr. Conrad more than just a story-teller. He seems to have some of the attributes of the Greek tragic dramatists. He has their irony. He sees so much at once, and is so conscious of the infinitesimal place a man can fill. Hence his work belongs never to cheerful literature: it is sombre, melancholy, searching.'

These qualities in Conrad were recognized by the leading critics who brought them to the attention of the British government and procured for him a grant from the Civil List. This relieved, to some extent, the financial worries resulting from the insufficiency of his literary earnings and mitigated the suffering caused by his almost continuous ill health. But he had a severe struggle against adversity until, with the success of *Chance*, published in the New York Herald in 1912, he began the run of popularity which lasted up to

the time of his death. The success of *Chance* was somewhat surprising in view of the elaborate artistry with which the story is
presented by means of four narrators; Henry James noted it as a
supreme example of the 'way to do a thing that shall undergo most
doing.' Conrad had adopted this method of putting his story into
the mouth of an imagined narrator in *Lord Jim* (1900) and he used
it with acknowledged mastery, but this mode of presentation
involves a strain on the attention of the reader as well as on the
skill of the novelist. *Chance* will no doubt continue to be admired
by those able to appreciate the refinements of the novelist's art,
but it seems likely that Conrad's permanent fame will rest rather
upon simpler examples of romance, fortified by psychological
analysis and philosophical thought, such as *Victory* and *The Rescue*
in which the reader's interest is maintained by a straightforward
story.

RUDYARD KIPLING
(*1865-*   )

To those who can recall the ferments at work on the English
mind just before and during the decade of the two Jubilee Celebra-
tions (1887–97), Rudyard Kipling must appear a peculiarly Victorian product and a characteristic phenomenon of that period.
The transfer of all responsibility for the government of India from
the East India Company to the British Crown after the Indian
Mutiny of 1857, the purchase of the Suez Canal Shares in 1875,
and the proclamation of Queen Victoria as Empress of India in
1877 were important steps in the development of the new imperialism, but it commanded little popular support, as was made clear
by the decisive defeat of the chief exponent of that policy, Lord
Beaconsfield, and the recall of his great rival, Gladstone, to power
in 1880. Beaconsfield as early as 1872 had suggested the institution
of a representative council in London to bring the whole of the
Empire into continuous relation with the Home Government, and
in 1884 the Imperial Federation League, including leading members
of both the great political parties, was organized to discover some
plan of binding the Empire more closely together.

Sir John Seeley, who was appointed professor of modern history
at Cambridge in 1869, up to the time of his death in 1895 exercised
considerable influence upon the undergraduate mind by his lectures, which obtained a wider audience by their publication in book
form under the title *The Expansion of England* (1883). But all
these influences affected almost exclusively the governing and

intellectual classes; the first man to attempt to make imperialism popular, to bring it home to the people, not by argument, but by emotional appeals in song and story was Rudyard Kipling.

By birth and education, as well as by natural ability, he was well fitted for the task. Kipling's parents belonged to that Evangelical group of Anglo-Indian officials who believed that it was the will of God that they should rule India for the advantage of the Indians, in the interests of the British Government, and to their own profit; probably in most minds the supremacy of Great Britain was the predominant factor, but they believed that this conduced to the other aims they had in view. Born at Bombay and educated in England at a school for the children of Indian officials (United Services College, Westward Ho, Devon), young Kipling early showed the impress of imperialistic influences. Among his 'schoolboy lyrics' we find a poem, written when he was seventeen, under the title *Ave Imperatrix*, and addressed to Queen Victoria on the occasion of a foolish attempt upon her life in 1882. He sends from

> One school, of many made to make
> Men who shall hold it dearest right
> To battle for their ruler's sake,
> And stake their being in the fight,
>
> Such greeting as should come from those
> Whose fathers faced the Sepoy hordes,
> Or served You in the Russian snows,
> And dying, left their sons their swords.
>
> And all are bred to do Your will
> By land and sea—wherever flies
> The Flag, to fight and follow still,
> And work Your Empire's destinies.

Kipling returned to India the following year and joined the staff of the Civil and Military Gazette at Lahore, where his father was Principal of the Government school of art. Here he had a varied experience, bringing him into contact with all classes of the native and European population, for beside general reporting, he undertook the following list of duties: (1) to prepare for press all the telegrams of the day; (2) to provide all the extracts and paragraphs; (3) to make headed articles out of official reports, etc.; (4) to write such editorial notes as he might have time for; (5) to look generally after all sports, outstation, and local intelligence; (6) to read all proofs except the editorial matter. This opportunity for acquaintance with official and unofficial life in India was enlarged by the visit to the home of Kipling's parents of Queen Victoria's son, Prince Arthur, Duke of Connaught, then in military command of the North West District of India, to whom the youth was in due course presented. 'Well, young man, what can I do for you?' said the Duke, and the young hopeful promptly replied, 'I would like, sir, to live with the army for a time, and go to the frontier to write up Tommy Atkins.' So early was the way of destiny opened to the young aspirant for literary fame.

The Kiplings were a literary family and Rudyard before he was twenty was admitted to the honor of a place in family publications, but the real beginning of his literary career may be dated from the publication in 1886 of *Departmental Ditties* as 'a lean oblong docket, wire-stitched, to imitate a D. O. government envelope, printed on brown paper and secured with red tape.' The 'ditties' were easy rhymes, distinguished by youthful smartness and the no less youthful cynicism of an author under twenty-one. He had already published his first short story 'The Phantom Rickshaw' in an Indian magazine, and a number of others appeared in the columns of either the Civil and Military Gazette or the Allahabad Pioneer, to which he was transferred on leaving Lahore in 1887. In the following year he persuaded the Allahabad publishers, A. H. Wheeler & Co., to issue a small collection of his short stories, paper-bound, in their 'Indian Railway Library' under the title of *Plain Tales from the Hills*, and this small volume made a sufficient hit to justify the immediate issue of half a dozen others in the same series. These included 'certain passages in the lives and adventures of Privates Terence Mulvaney, Stanley Ortheris, and John Learoyd,' the 'soldiers three' who were afterwards to make Kipling famous; but for the time being he had to content himself with a success in his own Anglo-Indian community. Sir William Hunter in 1888 gave notice to the British public of 'a new literary star of no mean magnitude rising in the East,' but the British public paid no heed.

It was as a special correspondent for the Allahabad Pioneer that Kipling left India in 1889 to make for England by way of Japan and the United States. In San Francisco and New York he plied his journalistic pencil, securing an interview with Mark Twain which was published in the New York Herald, and he sent reports home regularly to the Pioneer of his travels and adventures, but he found no market for his short stories with the New York publishers, who were of the opinion that the American public took no

interest in stories of Indian life. He had no better success with the
London publishers until an enterprising journalist, Edmund Yates
of the World, had a lucky inspiration to seek out Kipling in his
obscure London lodgings and published an account of a new Anglo-
Indian writer, whose name was up to then unknown to the British
public. This caught the eye of a Times reviewer who remembered
that he had on his desk the Allahabad editions of some stories
by Kipling, and a Times review gave the new author the necessary send-off. In one issue of Macmillan's Magazine in 1890
there appeared two Kipling contributions—'The Incarnation of
Krishna Mulvaney'—one of his best stories, and 'A Ballad
of East and West'—one of his best poems. Kipling was only
twenty-five, but the doors of the temple of fame lay wide open
before him.

In spite of his youth, Kipling was fully prepared to accept the
opportunity to become the popular apostle of the new imperialism,
and was well equipped for the task. He added a dozen new stories
to those he had already published and brought the whole collection
out in a new London edition under the title, which had already done
good service in India, *Plain Tales from the Hills*. Assuming the
imperial poet's robes with the jauntiness of youth, he promptly
issued *Barrack-Room Ballads*, in which the atmosphere and language of the barrack-room were reproduced with appalling but
magnificent fidelity. The ear of the least poetical of the readers of
verse was caught by the brassy insistence of the rhymes and the
startling vivacity of the vocabulary. Not only in barrack-rooms
and tap-rooms, but by peaceful firesides wherever the English
tongue was spoken, people sung or recited *Mandalay*, or *Fuzzy
Wuzzy*, or *Gunga Din* as long and as often as their hearers would
submit to it. Not only were the soldiers' joys of loot and painful
recollections of cells realized, and the adventures and misadventures of recent campaigns recalled, but the critics of imperialism
were rebuked and a warning addressed to those who think the
Empire 'still, is the Strand and Holborn Hill.' 'What should they
know of England who only England know?' Queen Victoria herself was irreverently described as 'The Widow at Windsor,' and
foreign nations were bidden:

> Hands off o' the sons o' the Widow,
>   Hands off o' the goods in 'er shop,
> For the Kings must come down an' the Emperors frown
>   When the Widow at Windsor says 'Stop!'

As Kipling grew older, the accents of his Muse became more sedate and her tone more dignified. He used the language of the Council Chamber more and the language of the barrack-room less:

> A Nation spoke to a Nation,
>   A Throne sent word to a Throne:
> 'Daughter am I in my Mother's house,
>   But mistress in my own!
> The gates are mine to open,
>   As the gates are mine to close,
> And I abide by my Mother's house,'
>   Said our Lady of the Snows.

In these terms Kipling hymned the offer of a preferential tariff by Canada to the Mother Country in 1897, and his *Recessional* for the Second Jubilee Celebration the same year adopted the words and attitude of the Hebrew Psalmist:

> The tumult and the shouting dies;
>   The captains and the kings depart:
> Still stands thine ancient sacrifice,
>   An humble and a contrite heart.
> Lord God of Hosts, be with us yet,
> Lest we forget—lest we forget!
>
> If, drunk with sight of power, we loose
>   Wild tongues that have not thee in awe—
> Such boasting as the Gentiles use,
>   Or lesser breeds without the Law—
> Lord God of Hosts, be with us yet,
> Lest we forget—lest we forget!

The plan to cement the union of hearts by preferential tariffs within the bounds of the Empire was supported by statesman after statesman—Chamberlain, Balfour, Baldwin, in turn staked their political fortunes upon it and lost—but it still holds the field as the hope of the future, and the Imperial Conference of 1932 saw it put, at any rate tentatively and partially, into actual operation. So, when Kipling in 1933 published his collected verse, extending over nearly half a century, Basil de Selincourt gave to it the distinctive praise that 'it has fulfilled and steadily goes on fulfilling the ends for which it was written. . . . Many gifts combined to establish so remarkable an achievement: an unfailing eloquence, a riotous love of careering rhythm, a high dramatic sense of the points of an argument or a story, an ever-watchful and controlling spirit of craftsmanship by which words, tune, and the very life and substance of a song were mastered to the mold. But, over and above all these, continually informing them, was the working human sympathy which bound him to all sorts and conditions of men in all they had to do and suffer.'

In the restricted field of the short story Kipling has no equal in English literature; and in other tongues there are few who can match him in skill to create an atmosphere, to present a situation, and to produce from it the utmost possible effect by a few dashing, brilliant strokes. His scope indeed is limited: he deals best with primitive peoples and primitive emotions, perhaps best of all with children and with the wild beasts to whom the impulses of children and savages can most readily be ascribed. His *Jungle Books* and *Just So Stories* show these powers at their height. When he has to deal with the more complex natures of intelligent men and women he is less successful, and he sometimes gives the impression of admiration not merely for strength but for its degeneration into an almost ferocious brutality. But in his inculcation of the principles of obedience to law, fair-play, discipline, and order he is excellent, and he has an extraordinary power for releasing the universal emotions which lie at the basis of our common humanity. All this was recognized in the award of the Nobel Prize for Literature in 1907.

A later generation came to regard Kipling mainly as a reactionary, and perhaps he was, in the sense of believing that 'they should rule who have the power and they should keep who can'; but it must be remembered that the forces against which he was re-acting when he began his literary career in England were forces of disintegration rather than of reform, of decadence, as the French called it, and even of degeneration. There was little inspiration for youth in the fashionable creed of disdainful estheticism and cloistered intellectualism preached by the Oxford don, Walter Pater, 'a lover of words for their own sake,' who in 1888 (*Studies in the History of the Renaissance*) had proclaimed as the modern gospel: 'A counted number of pulses only is given to us of a variegated, dramatic life. How may we see in them all that is to be seen in them by the finest senses? How shall we pass most swiftly from point to point, and be present always at the focus where the great number of vital forces unite in their purest energy? To burn always with this hard, gem-like flame, to maintain this ecstasy, is success in life.' The last decade of the century, in which Kipling won his

popularity, was the decade of the Yellow Book, of Aubrey Beards-
ley and Oscar Wilde, whose flashy epigrams in fiction, drama, and
conversation enjoyed a temporary vogue. 'The first duty of life
is to be as artificial as possible; what the second duty is no one has
as yet discovered.' For such paltry intellectual fare as this Kipling's
contagious enthusiasm for strenuous exertion and heroic sacrifice
was at any rate a wholesome corrective.

CHAPTER XII

LATE VICTORIAN POETS

THERE was an increasing store of Victorian poetry piled up for the reader in the last two decades of the nineteenth century, but few new poets put in a convincing and continuing claim on public notice during that period. The great Victorian poets were still the Victorians of the past—Tennyson, Browning, Swinburne, Meredith, Hardy, Rossetti, William Morris, Matthew Arnold. A new name would for a time attract general attention, but only to lose it again. There were minor poets such as William Watson, Stephen Phillips and Robert Bridges, who followed in the traditional path with enough originality to merit recognition by those who took special interest in poetry as an art, but not enough to win general acclaim or permanent attention. Francis Thompson's *The Hound of Heaven* (1893) for a time aroused the expectations of lovers of devotional poetry whose sympathies went out to a writer of true lyrical gift overwhelmed by sickness and poverty. From the degradations of the London slums Thompson was rescued by an older poet, Alice Meynell (1848-1922), whose delicate and subtle verse was much admired. More responsive to the stresses of modern thought was John Davidson, whose *Fleet Street Eclogues* (1893) presented in the staccato rhythms Kipling had made popular the problems of science and industrialism as they offered themselves for solution to a London clerk endeavoring to keep a wife and family on about a dollar a day ('Thirty Bob a Week'):

> And it's this way that I make it out to be
>   No fathers, mothers, countries, climates—none;
> Not Adam was responsible for me,
>   Nor society, nor systems, nary one:
> A little sleeping seed, I woke—I did, indeed—
>   A million years before the blooming sun.
>
> I woke because I thought the time had come;
>   Beyond my will there was no other cause;
> And everywhere I found myself at home,
>   Because I chose to be the thing I was;
> And in whatever shape of mollusc or of ape
>   I always went according to the laws.

Davidson's sympathy with the London poor was genuine, for he had himself experienced their hardships. Historical plays, novels, and even popular songs and ballads won him no substantial recognition beyond a civil list pension of a hundred pounds, and soon after he was fifty he gave up the struggle and admitted defeat by suicide. There was much talk in the last decade of the Victorian Era of the decline of poetry under the growing influence of science, but what really happened was a decline in the appreciation of poetry.

ALFRED EDWARD HOUSMAN
(1859-   )

A further illustration of this lack of general appreciation is the case of Alfred Edward Housman, who practised poetry from the safe seclusion of a classical professorship, and whose total productivity up to the age of seventy amounted to about a hundred short poems, included in two slim volumes, issued with an interval of over a quarter of a century—*A Shropshire Lad* (1896) and *Last Poems of a Shropshire Lad* (1922). An Oxford graduate, he obtained a clerkship in the civil service (Patent Office) which he held for some ten years, and gave up to become Professor of Latin, first at University College, London, and then at Cambridge University, for the next forty years.

In form Housman attains a compression of thought and a classical perfection of finished expression which are extremely rare; his spirit is one of stoical acceptance of the facts of life. His favorite themes are the inconstancy of man and woman, the transience of human joys and sorrows, the inevitable and unending oblivion of death. Variations on these themes are composed with an almost invariable simplicity and directness of manner, but in tones ranging from ingenuous humor to ironical cynicism. A characteristic stanza runs:

> Think no more, lad; laugh, be jolly:
>   Why should men make haste to die?
> Empty heads and tongues a-talking
> Make the rough road easy walking,
> And the feather pate of folly
>   Bears the falling sky.
> Oh, 't is jesting, dancing, drinking
>   Spins the heavy world around.
> If young hearts were not so clever,
> Oh, they would be young forever:
> Think no more; 't is only thinking
>   Lays lads underground.

Sudden death, especially death by hanging, which in English executions always takes place at 8 A.M. has an odd fascination for his Muse. He pictures the condemned man on the scaffold, listening to the town clock as it strikes the four quarters of his last hour:

> Strapped, noosed, nighing his hour,
>   He stood and counted them and cursed his luck;
> And then the clock collected in the tower
>   Its strength, and struck.

With something of the same almost cynical realism Housman recently analyzed, in an address to the University of Cambridge, the nature of poetry. An American editor had asked him for a definition of poetry, and he had answered that he could no more define poetry than a terrier could define a rat, but he thought they could both recognize the object by the symptoms it provoked in them. The symptoms were physical and not altogether pleasant. The first he described as a bristling of the hairs on the head, accompanied by a shiver down the spine; another consisted in a constriction of the throat and a precipitation of water to the eyes; a third was a sensation in the pit of the stomach best described in the words of Keats, it 'goes through me like a spear.' The production of poetry, he said, is less an active than a passive and involuntary process, comparing it to a morbid secretion, like that of the pearl in the oyster. 'I have seldom written poetry unless I was rather out of health, and the experience, though pleasurable, was generally agitating and exhausting.' As an example he instanced the composition of the following poem:

> I hoed and trenched and weeded,
>   And took the flowers to fair:
> I brought them home unheeded;
>   The hue was not the wear.
>
> So up and down I sow them
>   For lads like me to find,
> When I shall lie below them,
>   A dead man out of mind.
>
> Some seed the birds devour,
>   And some the season mars,
> But here and there will flower
>   The solitary stars,

And fields will yearly bear them
As light-leaved spring comes on,
And luckless lads will wear them
When I am dead and gone.

Two of the stanzas came into the poet's head exactly as they
stand, during an afternoon walk on Hampstead Heath, a third
came with a little coaxing after tea. But the fourth was a laborious
business. 'I wrote it thirteen times, and it was more than a twelve-
month before I got it right.' The English critics have puzzled
their brains in choosing which were the two stanzas first composed,
and which the one that gave so much trouble, but the poet has
kept his own secret so that the reader is left to make his own choice.

WILLIAM BUTLER YEATS
(*1865–*)

W. B. Yeats is perhaps best known as the moving spirit in the
Irish Literary Renaissance and the organizer of the Abbey Theatre
Company which made his own plays and those of J. M. Synge
known throughout the English-speaking world. But he was first
recognized by the public as a lyric poet with a mystical turn of
thought and a haunting charm of expression. He came of an
Irish Protestant family, 'very well-bred and very religious in the
Evangelical way,' but the chief influence of his childhood was the
companionship of his father, who was an artist and an unbeliever,
and told him stories from Homer and Walter Scott and Balzac.
Later his heroes were Byron's Manfred and Shelley's Alastor,
and when he began to write poetry, his verses were imitations of
Spenser or Shelley. He early became conscious of the spell of the
romantic coast of Sligo, where the home of his ancestors was
situated, and his dreams centered particularly about a little
island in Lough Gill called Innisfree, partly because of its beauty,
partly because of a local story identifying it with the Island of the
Hesperides. Thoreau's *Walden* inspired him with the ambition to
conquer bodily desire and his natural inclination to women and
love, and to live there, as Thoreau lived, seeking wisdom. He was
twenty-two or three before he gave up this dream, and it was of
this little island that he wrote one of his best remembered lyrics:

I will arise and go now, and go to Innisfree,
And a small cabin build there, of clay and wattles made;
Nine bean rows will I have there, a hive for the honey bee,
And live alone in the bee-loud glade. . .

I will arise and go now, for always night and day
I hear lake water lapping with low sounds by the shore;
While I stand on the roadway, or on the pavements gray,
I hear it in the deep heart's core.

'Innisfree' was regarded by Yeats as 'my first lyric with anything in its rhythm of my own music. I had begun to loosen
rhythm as an escape from rhetoric and from that emotion of the
crowd that rhetoric brings.' The impulse to its composition came
from the sudden remembrance of lake water suggested to the poet
when, 'walking through Fleet Street very homesick,' he 'heard a
little tinkle of water and saw a fountain in a shop-window which
balanced a little ball upon its jet.'

The longing of Yeats was always to escape from life and from
the haunts of men. Victorian Science he hated 'with a monkish
hate' and thought that 'only ancient things and the stuff of dreams
were beautiful'; he did not care for 'mere reality.' Protestant
Ireland seemed to him to think of nothing but getting on, and he
sought consolation in a Young Ireland Society, whose President
was John O'Leary the Fenian. 'From these debates, from O'Leary's
conversation, and from the Irish books he lent or gave me has
come all I have set my hand to since.' Yeats hoped to bring the
two halves of Ireland together by means of 'a national literature
that made Ireland beautiful in the memory and yet had been
freed from provincialism by an exacting criticism.' The mystical
side he nurtured by studies of spiritualism, esoteric Buddhism, and
Brahminism; he and his friends even persuaded a Brahmin philosopher to come from London and stay for a few days with the
only one among them who had rooms of his own in Dublin. 'It
was my first meeting with a philosophy that confirmed my vague
speculations and seemed at once logical and boundless.' But he
received most spiritual sustenance from renewed contact with the
fairy lore of the countryside which was part of the recollections
of his childhood. This was the inspiration of two Sligo stories,
and of his first poem drawn from Irish legend, *The Wanderings
of Oisin* (1889). He also edited about the same time *Poems and
Ballads of Young Ireland, Fairy and Folk Tales of the Irish Peasantry, Stories from Carleton*, and two volumes of *Representative Irish
Tales*. In 1892 he helped in the foundation of the Irish National
Literary Society at Dublin, as he had helped the year before in
the organization of the London Irish Literary Society. In the
inaugural lecture of the latter Society the Reverend Stopford

Brooke took it for granted that the work already done to preserve
and edit old Irish MSS. would be continued and urged:—(1) that
the pieces of the finest quality should be accurately translated
'with as much of a poetic movement as is compatible with fine
prose, and done by men who have the love of noble form and the
power of shaping it'; (2) that Irishmen of formative genius should
take, one by one, the various cycles of Irish tales, and grouping
each of them round one central figure, supply to each a dominant
human interest to which every event in the whole should converge
after the manner of Malory's *Morte d'Arthur;* (3) that suitable
episodes in these imaginative tales should be treated in verse, re-
taining the color and spirit of the original; (4) that the folk-stories
of Ireland should be collected. As examples of the kind of work
that had been done already he mentioned Douglas Hyde's *Beside
the Fire* and *The Wanderings of Oisin* by William Butler Yeats—a
young Irish poet at that time very little known.

The subsequent life of Yeats was to be divided between these
two impulses—(1) the impulse to reverie and the study of mystical
lore; (2) the impulse to organization. The latter found scope in the
Irish Literary Societies of London and Dublin, founded in the
early 'nineties, and the subsequent campaign, along with Lady
Gregory and George Moore, for an Irish Literary Theatre, which
resulted in the foundation of the Irish National Theatre Society
with Yeats as President. Thus Yeats's lyric drama *The Countess
Cathleen,* printed in 1892, made its way to a Dublin stage in 1899,
and early in the present century the Abbey Theatre Company,
still under Yeats's direction, began its distinguished career, with
Synge, whose genius Yeats had discovered and directed, as its
principal dramatist. These efforts, combined with political activities which culminated in the election of Yeats as a Senator of
the Irish Free State, somewhat distracted him from his original
aims and ambitions, which were purely literary. His original
purpose was to provide the public with a substitute for the commercial theater of the day, with its cheap melodrama and costume
plays, appealing only to the love of sensationalism, sentimentalism,
and stage effects, and 'to make the theater a place of intellectual
excitement.' The plays he wrote in the nineteenth century were
lyric dramas of which the scene was set in the Ireland of legend and
were without political intention, with the possible exception of
Cathleen ni Hoolihan (acted in 1902), which deals with the Irish
rebellion of 1798, and speaks prophetically of those who will lay
down their lives for the Ireland of the future: 'It is hard service

they take that help me. Many that are red-cheeked now will be pale-cheeked; many that have been free to walk the hills and the bogs and the rushes will be sent to walk hard streets in far countries; many a good plan will be broken; many that have gathered money will not stay to spend it; many a child will be born, and there will be no father at its christening to give it a name. They that had red cheeks will have pale cheeks for my sake; and for all that they will think they are well paid.'

In Yeats's mysticism, as in his dramatic activities, the original center of his imagination was in Irish folk lore, of which he said 'I have been at no pains to separate my own beliefs from those of the peasantry.' Not being a Catholic, he found the religious tradition of Catholic Ireland not always sympathetic to his mood, but he discovered a 'more universal and more ancient' tradition in Celtic mythology. In his first long poem, *The Wanderings of Oisin*, Oisin or Usheen (the Ossian of the Celtic revival of the eighteenth century) rejects the rosary and the 'milk-pale face under a crown of thorns and dark with blood.' St. Patrick's threats of hell and promises of the joys of the Christian heaven alike fail to move him; he prefers to join the heroes of Old Ireland after death 'And dwell in the house of the Fenians, be they in flames or at feast.' *The Countess Cathleen*, the first play by Yeats to be put on a Dublin stage, gave similar offense to Catholic sentiment. The Countess seeks to relieve the famine-stricken peasantry, who are dependent upon her for help, by selling her soul to the devil for gold to buy them food, and obtains at the end of the play the divine approval for her self-sacrifice. This heretical view roused the ire of some Dublin Catholics, who wished to show their orthodoxy by an attempt to break up the performance and had to be quelled by the police. The mood of the next play Yeats wrote, *The Land of Heart's Desire*, (1894) is, as Dr. H. S. Krans has pointed out, 'purely pagan,' and so is that of *The Shadowy Waters* (1900). Forgael, the Celtic hero, in a characteristic passage, says:

> All would be well
> Could we but give us wholly to the dreams
> And get into their world that to the sense
> Is shadow, and not linger wretchedly
> Among substantial things; for it is dreams
> That lift us to the flowing, changing world
> That the heart longs for. What is love itself,
> Even though it be the lightest of light love,
> But dreams that hurry from beyond the world

To make low laughter more than meat and drink,
Though it but set us sighing? Fellow-wanderer
Could we but mix ourselves into a dream
Not in its image on the mirror!

While the kernel of Yeats's mystical faith was the pre-Christian Celtic mythology and folk lore, he mixed with these many other and strange ingredients. He wrote in 1917: 'I have always sought to bring my mind close to the mind of Indian and Japanese poets, old women in Connaught, mediums in Soho, lay brothers whom I imagine dreaming in some medieval monastery the dreams of their village, learned authors who refer all to antiquity; to immerse it in the general mind where that mind is scarce separable from what we have begun to call "the sub-conscious"; to liberate it from all that comes of councils and committees, from the world as it is seen from universities or from populous towns.' His dislike of modern democracy and industrialism was increased by his removal to England at the end of the 'eighties with his father, who was a disciple of the Pre-Raphaelite Brotherhood, and brought his son under the influence of Ruskin and William Morris. Yeats saw nothing good in London: 'Certain old women's faces filled me with horror, faces that are no longer there, or if they are, pass before me unnoticed: the fat, blotched faces, rising above double chins, of women who have drunk too much beer and eaten much meat. In Dublin I had often seen old women walking with erect heads and gaunt bodies, talking to themselves with loud voices, mad with drink and poverty, but they were different, they belonged to romance.' As an expression of his revolt against Victorianism he founded with Ernest Rhys the Rhymers' Club, which met nightly in an upper room with a sanded floor in an ancient eating-house in the Strand called the Cheshire Cheese. Lionel Johnson, John Davidson, Ernest Dowson and other poets of the Yellow Book group were members. William Watson joined but never came; Francis Thompson came once but never joined. Oscar Wilde, with whom Yeats was on friendly terms, came occasionally if the Club met in a private house; but he would not come to the Cheshire Cheese, for he hated Bohemia. When he was told that the East End was the only place where people did not wear masks upon their faces, he retorted that he lived in the West End 'because nothing in life interests me but the mask.' These young poets read their verses to one another and encouraged each other in their quarrel with the great Victorians, holding that Swinburne in one way, Browning in another, and Tennyson in a third, had filled their work with what Yeats called 'impurities, curiosities about politics, about science, about history, about religion; and that we must create once more the pure work.'

In his antagonism to established institutions and beliefs Yeats went further than his fellows. Lionel Johnson and Francis Thompson were devout Catholics; John Davidson had faith in science. Yeats detested Huxley and Tyndall, who had robbed him of the simple-minded religion of his childhood, and he had no love for the materialistic philosophy of Karl Marx. At a Socialistic meeting presided over by William Morris, Yeats asked heatedly, 'What is the use of talking about some new revolution putting all things right, when the change must come, if come it does, with astronomical slowness, like the cooling of the sun?' Getting no answer to his question, he repeated it, and had to be rung down by the chairman's bell. He was pleased when Oscar Wilde said to him, 'Bernard Shaw has no enemies but is intensely disliked by all his friends,' and felt revenged upon a notorious hater of romance. At that time he failed to recognize his fellow Irishman's generosity and courage.

Yeats and Shaw were at one in their scorn of the English middle class and its bourgeois morality, but while Shaw believed in realism and rationalism, Yeats clung to romance in its most mystical sense. He was greatly affected by the study of William Blake, whose works he edited during his residence in England in the early 'nineties; he began to set forth his own ideas about the same time in his earliest important prose work *The Celtic Twilight* (1893), followed by *The Secret Rose* (1897). In the twentieth century he developed his mystical theories further in *Ideas of Good and Evil* (1903), a volume of essays entitled *Discoveries*, and a series of autobiographical works extending in publication from 1915 to 1922. Yeats has a distinguished prose style, but he is much more poet than philosopher, and it seems likely that he will be chiefly remembered for the charm and freshness of his early lyrics. He may be right in his view that what the Western World wants is a new religion; but the mind of the modern man must be fed on more substantial fare than vague theories about the world-soul and the complementary daimon or anti-self. Still, there will probably always be readers who will be glad to be transported in imagination to the 'Land of Heart's Desire' where

The fairies dance in a place apart,
Shaking their milk-white feet in a ring,
Tossing their milk-white arms in the air;
For they hear the wind laugh and murmur and sing
Of a land where even the old are fair,
And even the wise are merry of tongue.

CHAPTER XIII

VICTORIAN DRAMA

THE early Victorian theater, to quote a modern dramatic critic, was 'so lacking in ideas, so ephemeral, so paltry and jejune that it is impossible to think of it without a yawn.' But we must form at least a nodding acquaintance with it if we are to realize the pit from which modern English drama was dug out. When Queen Victoria came to the throne London had only two theaters at which regular drama could be legally performed—Drury Lane and Covent Garden—and when the young Queen ordered two performances 'by royal command' at the former house, it was to see the special attraction of a famous lion-tamer in combination with tight-rope dancers. But Victoria, hardly yet out of her teens must not be too harshly blamed for her girlish preference for a circus show at Drury Lane to Lord Lytton's sentimental melo-drama, *The Lady of Lyons*, at Covent Garden, although the latter was the best known modern play on the London boards almost to the end of her reign. Until 1843, when the monopoly of the two 'patent' houses was abolished by Act of Parliament, the Queen had the further choice between 'legitimate' drama and 'aquatic' drama at Sadler's Wells, where the heroine fell into real water to be rescued by a Newfoundland dog, or 'equestrian' drama at Astley's, where the famous circus master Ducrow exemplified his famous instruction to his actors, 'Cut the cackle and come to the 'osses,'—a maxim which passed into a proverb in other arenas of English public life.

Even when the London theaters all enjoyed the privilege of reviving Shakespeare's plays or the only two dramatic master-pieces which had survived from the eighteenth century,—Gold-smith's *She Stoops to Conquer* and Sheridan's *School for Scandal*,—they were slow to take advantage of the enlarged opportunity. Professor Henry Morley, in the prologue to his *Journal of a London Playgoer from 1851 to 1866*, gives a woeful account of the state of the English drama in that period: 'The great want of the stage in our day is an educated public that will care for its successes, honestly inquire into its failures, and make managers and actors feel that they are not dependent for appreciation of their efforts on the verdict that comes of the one mind divided into fragments between Mr. Dapperwit in the stalls, Lord Froth in the side-boxes, and Pompey Doodle in the gallery. . . . But what if Doodle, Dapperwit and Froth do clap their hands at pieces which are all leg and no brains; in which the male actor's highest ambition is to caper, slide, and stamp with the energy of a street-boy on a cellar-flap, the actress shows plenty of thigh, and the dialogue, running entirely on the sound of words, hardly admits that they have any use at all as signs of thought? Whose fault is it that the applauders of these dismal antics sit so frequently as umpires in the judgment of dramatic literature?'

The fault, as Morley points out, was that of the public, who, both in England and America, now had a choice between Lytton's sentimental melodrama and the sensationalism of the prolific Irish playwright, Dion Boucicault. In the later 'sixties and 'seventies another diligent theatergoer, George Henry Lewes, noted that 'The Drama is everywhere in Europe and America rapidly passing from an Art into an Amusement; just as of old it passed from a religious ceremony into an Art. Those who love the Drama cannot but regret the change, but all must fear that it is inevitable when they reflect that the stage is no longer the amusement of the cultured few, but the amusement of the uncultured and miscultured masses, and has to provide larger and lower appetites with food. For one playgoer who can appreciate the beauty of a verse, the delicate humor of a conception, or the exquisite adaptation of means to ends which give ease and harmony to a work of art, there are hundreds, who, insensible to such delights, can appreciate a parody, detect a pun, applaud a claptrap phrase of sentiment, and be exhilarated by a jingle and a dance; for one who can recognize, and recognizing, can receive exquisite pleasure from fine acting, thousands can appreciate costumes, bare necks, and "powerful" grimace; thus the mass, easily pleased, and liberally paying for the pleasure, rules the hour.'

Matthew Arnold, writing a little later (1879), says: 'In England we have no drama at all. Our vast society is not homogeneous enough, not sufficiently united, even any large portion of it, in a common view of life, a common ideal capable of serving as basis for a modern English Drama.' There was, as a matter of fact, a promise of better things in the 'cup and saucer' drama of T. W. Robertson, whose *Caste* (1867) not only brought the drama back to modern life, but in spite of its stilted diction, sentimentalism, and forced humor, made some attempt at realism in presentation. It was a distinct achievement to supplant the tawdry scenery, shabby furniture, absurd dresses, and rhetorical diction of the romantic 'costume' plays by comedies which in their speech and setting made some attempt to reproduce the conditions of modern life. It made the theater a place in which actors could appear on the stage and intelligent people in the audience without loss of self-respect. The comic operas of Gilbert and Sullivan in the 'eighties made a further advance in the same direction. Half a dozen actors received knighthoods, and Oxford graduates and fashionable ladies began to take to the stage as a profession. But the plays themselves (aside from Shakespearean revivals and imitations) were still on a low intellectual level until the influence of Ibsen began to make itself felt through the translations of William Archer in the early 'eighties. Looking back to that period at the end of his life, he confessed that he was puzzled to conceive how anyone with the smallest pretension to intelligence could in those years seriously occupy himself with the English theater; but he did so occupy himself, as a translator, a dramatic critic, and collaborator with Bernard Shaw in the latter's first play. It was the production of Ibsen's *Ghosts* in London in 1891 that encouraged Arthur Pinero in 1893 to compose for the London stage a modern play *The Second Mrs. Tanqueray*, which was at once hailed as opening a new era in the history of British drama.

If we judge this epoch-making play according to modern standards, we shall probably be as disappointed as with *Caste*. Forty years ago it was described as a problem play, but to the theater-goer or student of to-day it would not present much of a problem. Was it prudent for a man of the world with a grown-up daughter, living in a conventional 'county' society, to take as his second wife a mistress who brought to him as her only marriage portion a catalogue of the names of the men with whom she has previously had irregular relations? Obviously not, especially as she turned out to have neither good manners, nor good temper, nor common sense. Even in the more liberal times in which we live, such a marriage would be almost certain to end in social disaster. Still, the British public of 1893 was sufficiently interested and stirred by *The Second Mrs. Tanqueray* and its successor, *The Case of Rebellious Susan*, by Henry Arthur Jones, to realize that a little more intellectual content would do the British drama no harm, and the way was thus opened for an appreciation of the more revolutionary dramatic experiments of Bernard Shaw, whose first play to command the attention of the British and the American public, *Arms and the Man*, was put on in 1894.

GEORGE BERNARD SHAW
(*1856-*   )

In Bernard Shaw the rebellion against Victorian ideas and institutions reached its climax. His successful career as a dramatist
did not really begin till the twentieth century, but all the multi-
farious activities of his youth and early middle age fell within the
Victorian Era. In order to get a clear idea of what these activities
were it will be convenient to divide his Victorian career into four
or five periods: (1) His youth in Ireland up to 1876. (2) Four
Bohemian years as a free lance in London, 1876-79. (3) Four years
of novel writing, 1879-83. (4) Fifteen years of journalism and
pamphleteering, 1884-98. (5) The years of playwriting overlap
the last period, beginning with *Widowers' Houses,* completed and
produced in 1892 and printed in 1893. *Plays Pleasant and Unpleasant* (published in 1898) included also *The Philanderer* and
Mrs. Warren's Profession, both written 1893-94, but not put on
the stage till the twentieth century; these were the 'unpleasant'
plays. The 'pleasant' plays were *Arms and the Man, Candida,
The Man of Destiny,* and *You Never Can Tell,* all written 1894-96
and produced in the nineteenth century, which also saw the production of *The Devil's Disciple, Cæsar and Cleopatra,* and *Captain
Brassbound's Conversion,* written in 1897-99 and published in 1901
as *Three Plays for Puritans.*

Bernard Shaw came of an aristocratic but impecunious Irish
Protestant family. His father had a Government sinecure which
resolved itself into a pension; he then set up in a wholesale business
which proved unprofitable. All through Bernard's childhood and
youth his parents were in financial distress, aggravated by his
father's drinking habits. He had a desultory education and at
fourteen went to work as a clerk in a Dublin real estate office. His
mother fled from a home that had become intolerable to teach
singing in London, taking her only daughter with her; and before
Bernard was twenty-one, he also became a member of the London
household, whose only resources were Mrs. Shaw's earnings, supplemented by an allowance of five dollars a week from her husband
and a maternal legacy on which she could draw in an emergency.

For some years Bernard Shaw contributed very little to the family exchequer. He had a temporary job with Edison Telephone
Company and earned twenty-five dollars by writing an advertisement for a patent medicine; but that was about all. He described himself as 'an ablebodied pauper in fact if not in law'

until 1885, when he succeeded in making about ten dollars a week.

In 1879 Shaw took to novel writing, penning laboriously five pages a day; if the five pages ended in the middle of a sentence, he did not finish it till next day; if he missed a day, he made up for it next day by writing ten pages. In this fashion he produced in the next five years five novels, which he afterwards recalled as 'five heavy brown-paper parcels, which were always coming back to me from some publisher, and raising the very serious financial question of the sixpence to be paid to Messrs. Carter, Paterson & Company, the carriers, for passing them on to the next publisher.' He sent them to all the publishers in London and some in America; but they always came back. As a professional writer he acknowledged that he was a complete failure, and abandoned the novel, recognizing his own incompetence for popular fiction. 'I had no taste for what is called "popular art," no respect for popular morality, no belief in popular religion, no admiration for popular heroics. As an Irishman, I could pretend to patriotism neither for the country I had abandoned nor the country that had ruined it. As a humane person I detested violence and slaughter, whether in war, sport, or the butcher's yard. I was a Socialist, detesting our anarchical scramble for money, and believing in equality as the only possible permanent basis of social organization, discipline, subordination, good manners, and selection of fit persons for high functions. Fashionable life, open on indulgent terms to unencumbered "brilliant" persons, I could not endure.' *The Irrational Knot, Love among the Artists, Cashel Byron's Profession,* and *An Unsocial Socialist* found their way to serial publication in a Socialist review. The first novel written, 'with merciless fitness' entitled *Immaturity,* stayed with its author for over fifty years as a pile of manuscript partially devoured by mice, 'but even they had been unable to finish it.' In the preface to the collected edition of his works (in which it was first published, 1930) he tells the reader, 'You will not lose very much by skipping it.'

Shaw 'ladled out' his novels to the Socialist Magazine editors in inverse order of composition—*An Unsocial Socialist* came first as a serial, followed by *Cashel Byron's Profession.* The publisher of the latter was so pleased with it as a novel about prize-fighting that he used the stereo magazine plates of the story to bring out a 'misshapen' edition in book form. This elicited complimentary notices from William Archer, W. E. Henley, and others; R. L. Stevenson wrote a half-flattering letter, in which he analyzed the literary content of the novel into five parts, $1\frac{1}{2}$ of original talent, 1 gaseous folly, and the rest imitation of Charles Reade, Henry James, and Disraeli. Shaw afterwards congratulated himself (with a shudder) on his narrow escape from becoming a successful novelist at the age of twenty-six, but by this time he had acquired a new interest which was absorbing a large part of his energies. His practical experience of the problem of poverty made him take a keen interest in Henry George's *Progress and Poverty* published in 1880 in New York and in 1881 in London, where it met with 'astonishing success,' two cheap paper editions appearing in England in 1882. Acquaintance with Henry George's doctrines led Shaw to a study of Karl Marx's *Capital* and for a time he fell under the spell of Marx's theory of 'surplus value,' absorbed by the employer and capitalist, though he rejected the necessity for a class war. In an address to the Economic Section of the British Association for the Advancement of Science in 1888, when he had arrived at more moderate views, Shaw ridiculed the extravagance of the expectations of the young British Socialists when he first became interested in the movement: 'Numbers of young men, pupils of Mill, Spencer, Comte, and Darwin, roused by Mr. Henry George's *Progress and Poverty*, left aside evolution and free thought; took to insurrectionary economics; studied Karl Marx; and were so convinced that Socialism had only to be put clearly before the working-classes to concentrate the power of their immense numbers in one irresistible organization, that the Revolution was fixed for 1889—the anniversary of the French Revolution—at latest. I remember being asked satirically and publicly at that time how long I thought it would take to get Socialism into working order if I had my way. I replied, with a spirited modesty, that a fortnight would be ample for the purpose. When I add that I was frequently complimented on being one of the more reasonable Socialists, you will be able to appreciate the fervor of our conviction, and the extravagant levity of our ideas.' He followed this up by further ridicule of the revolutionary Socialists in a magazine article in which he spoke of the extremists as 'romantic amateurs who represent nobody but their silly selves.'

By this time Shaw was already recognized as a leader in the moderate Socialist group of young intellectuals who organized themselves in 1884 as the Fabian Society. Their motto was: 'For the right moment you must wait, as Fabius did most patiently when warring against Hannibal, though many censured his delays. But when the time comes you must strike hard, as Fabius did, or your waiting will be in vain, and pointless.' He wrote the Manifesto of the Society published in 1884, which set forth its aims and principles in the following propositions: '(1) That it is the duty of each member of the State to provide for his or her wants by his or her own Labor. (2) That a life-interest in the Land and Capital of the nation is the birthright of every individual born within its confines; and that access to this birthright should not depend upon the will of any private person other than the person seeking it. (3) That the State should compete with private individuals—especially with parents—in providing happy homes for children, so that every child may have a refuge from the tyranny or neglect of its natural custodians. (4) That the State should secure a liberal education and an equal share in the National Industry to each of its units. (5) That the established Government has no more right to call itself the State than the smoke of London has to call itself the weather. (6) That we had rather face a Civil War than such another century of suffering as the present one has been.' Nos. 5 and 6 soon appeared mere rhetoric as the more moderate wing, led by Sidney Webb (afterwards a Labor Minister and Lord Passfield) obtained control of the organization. In a pitched battle, the more advanced section, led by H. G. Wells, who was in favor of the endowment of motherhood and a more active policy generally, was easily vanquished by Shaw's greater argumentative skill and tactical sagacity. Wells withdrew and fought in a long series of pamphlets, novels, and treatises, for his own hand. Shaw emphasized his more moderate position in papers entitled *The Impossibilities of Anarchism* (1891) and *The Illusions of Socialism* (1896), and used his six years' experience of municipal administration as a member of St. Pancras Vestry and Borough Council in a pamphlet, severely practical and moderate in tone, entitled *The Common Sense of Municipal Trading* (1904). Long before this, however, Shaw's intellectual interests and activities had been turned in other directions.

During the nine years Shaw was subsisting on his mother's bounty and writing unsaleable novels and articles he was really engaged in completing his neglected education, by reading in the British Museum Library, visiting the London Art Galleries (on free days), and attending the best concerts (in the cheapest seats). He joined a debating club called the Zetetical Society in 1879, and, by hard practice on its platform and on soap boxes at Hyde Park and on street corners, developed himself from a shy and embarrassed, halting speaker into one of the readiest and most effective impromptu debaters of the day—no one quicker at an apt retort to a heckler than Bernard Shaw. He became a recognizable figure in London literary and journalistic circles as a combination of 'all the appropriate eccentricities of a conscientious intellectual revolutionary: Atheism, vegetarianism, Jaegerism and malnutrition—having a dead-white complexion and orange patches of whisker about his cheek and chin, but being extraordinarily witty and entertaining.'

William Archer, already a reviewer and dramatic critic of established reputation, noticed this lank, fiery-haired Irishman with a face 'like an unskilfully poached egg,' at the British Museum Library, engaged in reading a French translation of Marx's *Capital* and the score of a Wagner opera, apparently both at the same time, and wondered who he was. He met Shaw later at the house of a friend and was very much attracted by his intellectual brilliance and personal charm. He saw that Shaw was a young man with unusual ability who did not know how to make it marketable, and as a practised journalist he undertook to show the budding genius the ropes. He put Shaw in the way of doing book reviewing for the Pall Mall Gazette and art criticism for the London World, for which the pay was ten cents a line. By these makeshifts Shaw was tided over three difficult years 1885–88. In this last year T. P. O'Connor founded the London Star, a Liberal evening paper, and on Archer's recommendation a position on the editorial staff was given to Bernard Shaw, whose name, O'Connor remarked later, 'neither I nor indeed anybody else had ever heard of before.' Shaw soon, however, became known to O'Connor from his propensity for getting the paper into trouble. He was a militant Socialist and in his editorial criticism did not spare the Liberal leaders in whose interests the paper had been started. An attack upon John Morley brought matters to a crisis, and O'Connor felt an end must be put to this fire of hostile criticism from within the party lines. But, as he had himself experienced the precariousness of London journalism, he did not like to set Shaw adrift to resume his poverty-stricken struggles as a free-lance writer. So he promoted Shaw from leader writing to musical criticism, with an advance in salary from twelve to fifteen dollars a week. Over the pen name 'Corno de Bassetto' Shaw contributed to the Star 'a mixture of triviality, vulgarity, farce and tomfoolery with genuine criticism' for about a year, and was then promoted to be musical critic for the World at nearly double the salary. In 1894, with a further advance of salary he became dramatic critic to the Saturday

Review which had been bought by Frank Harris; again the appointment was made on the suggestion of Archer, to whom the position
was first offered. In May, 1898, Shaw was enabled, by the success
of his plays on the American stage, to give up regular journalism,
and to settle down to his career as a professional playwright.
Forthwith, he married, in June, 1898, Charlotte Payne Townshend,
a 'charming Irish millionairess with green eyes,' who was an ardent
Socialist and his devoted admirer. She carried Shaw off from the
almost squalid Bohemianism of his mother's home to her own comfortable quarters in Adelphi Terrace, where he continued to live
for thirty years.

Shaw was never in any sense ashamed of his career in journalism,
which, he said 'can claim to be the highest form of literature, for
all the highest literature is journalism. . . . I also am a journalist,
proud of it, deliberately cutting out of my works all that is not
journalism, convinced that nothing that is not journalism will live
long as literature, or be of any use whilst it does live.—And so,
let others cultivate what they call literature: journalism for me!'
This is from the Preface to *The Sanity of Art*, first published in
1895 in a New York magazine called 'Liberty.' Shaw's immediate
purpose was to answer Max Nordau's superficial essay, which was
then enjoying a fleeting popularity, on the degeneracy of modern
art; but it enabled Shaw to set forth, in all seriousness, his conception of the purpose of art in general: 'Art should refine our sense of
character and conduct, of justice and sympathy, greatly height-
ening our self-knowledge, self-control, precision of action, and
considerateness, and making us intolerant of baseness, cruelty,
injustice, and intellectual superficiality or vulgarity. The worthy
artist or craftsman is he who serves the physical and moral senses
by feeding them with pictures, musical compositions, pleasant
houses and gardens, good clothes and fine implements, poems,
fictions, essays, and dramas which call the heightened senses and
ennobled faculties into pleasurable activity. The great artist is he
who goes a step beyond the demand, and, by supplying works of
a higher beauty and a higher interest than have yet been perceived,
succeeds, after a brief struggle with its strangeness, in adding this
fresh extension of sense to the heritage of the race.'

Shaw's journalistic activities were supplemented by the production of two books which may be fairly described as journalism—
The Quintessence of Ibsenism (1891) and *The Perfect Wagnerite*
(1898). In both the personal opinions of the critic give a decided
bias to his interpretation of his subject, in accordance with his

declared conviction that 'the way to get at the merits of a case is not to listen to the fool who imagines himself impartial, but to get it argued with reckless bias for and against.' Accordingly every one of Ibsen's plays is interpreted against the romantic idealism which was the particular bogey in Shaw's mind at this particular stage of his career. He wrote in 1898 'Idealism, which is only a flattering name for romance in politics and morals, is as obnoxious to me as romance in ethics or religion. In spite of a Liberal Revolution or two, I can no longer be satisfied with fictitious morals and fictitious good conduct, shedding fictitious glory on robbery, starvation, disease, crime, drink, war, cruelty, cupidity, and all the other commonplaces of civilization which drive men to the theater to make foolish pretences that such things are progress, science, morals, religion, patriotism, imperial supremacy, national greatness and all the other names the newspapers call them.'

In *The Perfect Wagnerite* Shaw's other predominant interest— Socialism—is made use of to explain the significance of the Nibelung cycle. The dwarf Alberich, who makes an instrument of oppression out of the gold which to the Rhine Maidens was merely a pretty plaything, is identified with the 'vulgar factory-owner portrayed in Friedrich Engels' *Condition of the Working Classes*, and the liberating hero Siegfried becomes a born Anarchist 'upsetting religion, law and order in all directions, and establishing in their place the unfettered action of Humanity doing exactly what it likes, and producing order instead of confusion thereby, because it likes to do what is necessary for the good of the race.' Shaw ingenuously admits that Wagner may not have had these ideas in his own mind, but being a genius, he expressed the 'most inevitable dramatic conception' of the nineteenth century without being himself conscious of it. In spite of—or perhaps because of— the peculiar twists given by Shaw to his interpretation of Ibsen's and Wagner's thought, both books proved acceptable enough to go into later editions, *The Quintessence of Ibsenism*, 'now completed to the death of Ibsen,' in 1913 and *The Perfect Wagnerite* in Chicago, New York, and Leipzig, as well as in England.

Shaw's newspaper contributions to musical criticism were not republished until the limited edition of his complete works was issued in 1930, but his *Dramatic Opinions and Essays* selected from the Saturday Review by James Huneker, a New York critic, appeared in 1906, and are still regarded as the most important criticisms of the modern theater in the English language. When Shaw began to write dramatic criticism for the Saturday Review in 1894, the battle between the partisans of the ancients and the moderns on the English stage was at its height, and the verbal war was being waged with a storm of vituperation going beyond the excesses of political acrimony. Ibsen, whose *Doll's House* was put on the London stage in 1889, followed by *Ghosts* in 1891, was assailed with a violence of opprobrious adjectives which can only be described as literary Billingsgate. Shaw's first play, *Widowers' Houses*, was produced in 1892, and was greeted by an audience prepared to hoot or to applaud in accordance with their personal prejudices. 'It made a sensation out of all proportion to its merits and even its demerits; and I at once became infamous as a dramatist.' When Shaw obtained a weekly forum in the columns of the Saturday Review, he went into the fight with a joyous ardor and an intemperance of expression equal to that of his adversaries. The stronghold of the dramatic reactionaries was the worship of Shakespeare, whose plays were reproduced with mutilated texts, but with a lavishness of expense on scenery and setting that commanded almost universal admiration. The principal temple for this kind of worship was the London Lyceum Theater with Sir Henry Irving as its great High Priest. The production of *Cymbeline* in 1896 gave Shaw, as he thought, an opportunity for an attack in force, and he wrote a sensational article; the first sentence describes the play as 'for the most part stagey trash of the lowest melodramatic order, in parts abominably written, throughout intellectually vulgar, and, judged in point of thought by modern intellectual standards, vulgar, foolish, indecent, offensive, and exasperating beyond all tolerance.' In reading these and other outbursts one must bear in mind Shaw's apology prefixed to the collection of his dramatic criticisms in book form: 'I must warn the reader that what he is about to study is not a series of judgments aiming at impartiality, but a siege laid to the theater of the nineteenth century by an author who had to cut his own way into it at the point of the pen and throw some of its defenders into the moat.' Elsewhere, Shaw acknowledged that *Othello*, *Lear*, and *Macbeth* are masterpieces and that Shakespeare is 'unsurpassed as poet, story-teller, character draughtsman, humorist, and rhetorician.' It was Shakespeare's philosophy of life and his skill as a dramatist that he criticized, not his power as a poet. Shaw's judgments of his contemporaries, though not free from prejudice or even personal feeling, are more temperately expressed, but always with the wit, liveliness, and acumen characteristic of him in his best years.

It was in 1892, when Shaw was still engaged in musical criticism for the London World, that Ellen Terry, the leading romantic actress of the time, wrote to him with reference to a musical prodigy in whom she was interested. The resulting correspondence (which was not published till 1931) is a remarkable interchange of wit and sentiment between two very distinguished minds. Shaw, fascinated by the popular (though not financial) success of *Arms and the Man* in 1894, was eager to detach Ellen Terry from the romantic drama, which (he thought) did not give sufficient scope for her powers, and to enlist her talents in the service of the modern drama (particularly his own comedies). But in addition to this professional interest, there was a strong personal friendship between them, although, except for some casual meetings in connection with the stage, their communications were entirely through the post office. When the correspondence began Ellen Terry was forty-four years of age and Shaw was eight years her junior; it continued till she was seventy-four and had almost ceased to write letters to anyone. She stood by Shaw when he was out of public favor during the War, and expressed, not long before her death at the age of eighty, her constant affection for him. In answer to the criticism that 'it was all on paper,' Shaw rejoined that 'only on paper has humanity yet achieved glory, beauty, truth, knowledge, virtue, and abiding love.' He wrote in the stage directions of *The Man of Destiny* a personal description of the Strange Lady which is 'an obvious pen portrait of Ellen Terry' as he saw her in 1895. 'She is tall and extraordinarily graceful, with a delicately intelligent, apprehensive, questioning face: perception in the brow, sensitiveness in the nostrils, character in the chin: all keen, refined, and original. She is very feminine, but by no means weak: the lithe tender figure is hung on a strong frame: the hands and feet, neck and shoulders, are useful vigorous members, of full size in proportion to her stature. . . . Only, her elegance and radiant charm keep the secret of her size and strength. . . . She is fair, with golden brown hair and gray eyes.'

The correspondence between these two remarkable personalities had just begun when Shaw put on the stage his first play, *Widowers' Houses*. Its performance was part of that dramatic revival of which the enterprises of the Théâtre Libre in Paris (1887), the Freie Bühne in Berlin (1889), and the Independent Theater in London (1891) were important manifestations. But before any of these, in 1885, when, as Shaw says, he had just reached the close of his novel-writing period, he and his friend Archer had under-

324 LEADERS OF THE VICTORIAN REVOLUTION

taken to collaborate on a new play of which the theme was to be
the power of money in modern society. The arrangement was
that Archer was to supply the plot and Shaw was to do the dialogue,
and it was agreed that the general framework might be adapted
from a French comedy by Augier, *La Ceinture Dorée*. Archer
accordingly wrote out a scenario and gave it to Shaw to work over.
Shaw went at it with such a will that at the end of two acts he
had used up all the material and came back to Archer for more.
Laying violent hands on Archer's plan for a 'well-made play'
after the Paris type then in fashion, Shaw, as he himself confessed,
had 'perversely distorted it into a grotesquely realistic exposure of
slum landlordism, municipal jobbery, and the pecuniary and
matrimonial ties between them and the pleasant people with
"independent" incomes who imagine that such sordid matters
do not touch their own lives.' At the end of the first act Archer was
outraged to find that what he had intended as a sympathetically
romantic play had been turned into a piece of grotesque propaganda in which the chief spokesmen were one of the worse slum
landlords in London, 'a husband-hunting virago,' who is his
daughter, and her lover, a raw young doctor who holds a mortgage
on some of the slum property and is the nephew of the owner of
the groundrent from the land. Archer wanted to hear no more
than the first act; but Shaw persisted in going on with the second.
Archer then took advantage of a resource he had acquired by long
practice as a dramatic critic and went to sleep! This was enough
to convince Shaw of the folly of the undertaking (especially as
Archer firmly refused to have anything more to do with it), and
the manuscript was cast aside. Half a dozen years later, when the
Independent Theater was on the look-out for new dramatists and
new plays, Shaw bethought himself of his discarded effort, raked
it out from his dustiest pile of rejected manuscripts, added a third
act of his own invention, and gave it the mock-scriptural title of
Widowers' Houses. The performance did not achieve a success,
but it provoked an uproar, for the crude socialistic sallies of the
dialogue were furiously applauded by Shaw's personal friends,
and frantically hooted by the ordinary playgoers. If the play
did not achieve fame, it at least brought its author notoriety.
For a week after its fleeting appearance on the stage it was being
discussed in the London press, not only by the critics, but editorially in leading articles. Shaw was delighted at the publicity
and quite convinced of his ability as a writer for the stage.

The Philanderer, Shaw's next play in order of composition, was an attempt at a high society comedy, exposing the follies and extravagances of the Ibsenite craze just then affected by advanced intellectuals in London. The characters include, beside the philanderer who gives the play its title, and the two women in love with him, a blustering elderly colonel; a sentimental idealist, who is also a dramatic critic, and a doctor who, by means of vivisection, has discovered a fatal disease which turns out to have no existence. Before Shaw finished the play, he realized that its demands on the most expert and delicate sort of high comedy acting went beyond the resources of the Independent Theater, for which it was written, and J. T. Grein, the manager, came to the same conclusion. When it was put on the stage in New York about fifteen years later, it proved to be not only beyond the capacity of the actors but beyond the comprehension of the audience and the critics, who even in the twentieth century continued to regard it as an enigma. In writing a preface for its inclusion in his complete works in 1930, Shaw hazarded the opinion that it was still thirty-six years ahead of the public, so that the ordinary reader must not expect to understand it till 1966—and by that time he probably will not be inclined to make the effort.

Shaw himself agreed that it would not do for 1893, and he returned to his first idea of the propaganda play with an attack upon contemporary institutions in *Mrs. Warren's Profession*. Thirty years later, Shaw described it as a terrible play, written when he was 'a young tiger, fearing neither God nor man'; and of the three 'unpleasant' plays he had yet done, it was certainly the unpleasantest. Although Shaw protests that 'Society, and not any individual, is the villain of the piece,' Mrs. Warren's occupation as procuress and manager for a white slave syndicate posing as the conductors of an international chain of 'private hotels' is not redeemed by anything sympathetic in her personality, and her business associates are even more repulsive than herself. The plot, such as it is, turns on the uncertain paternity of Mrs. Warren's illegitimate daughter, which adds another element of unpleasantness almost justifying the remark of William Archer that Shaw could not 'touch pitch without wallowing in it.' It was not surprising that the dramatic censor interdicted the performance of the play as 'immoral and otherwise improper for the stage,' and thus secured for Shaw an amount of publicity almost as large as if the play had been put on. It was printed in 1898 and given a private performance by the London Stage Society in 1902. Attempts to act the play in New York in 1905 and later in Kansas

City met with police interference, and the drama had to wait till 1926 for public performance in London. It had a warm welcome from the critics and the public, and had a long run (eighty-six performances). The Censor withdrew his ban, insisting only on the omission of the incidental reference to Lord Beaufort as the owner of Tintern Abbey; Shaw substituted Carnarvon Castle and an unnamed Duke as its owner and the proprieties were satisfied. Times do change even in the office of the British Censor. As an acting play, *Mrs. Warren's Profession* was shown to have decided merits, indicating a considerable advance on Shaw's part in dramatic construction and effective dialogue.

But in 1894 it was evident that Shaw had to make further concessions to the play-going public if he were to secure their attention; the dose of propaganda had to be decreased, and the sugarcoating of the pill by an envelope of comedy had to be done more skilfully and generously. An opportunity was offered by the subsidizing of the Avenue Theater for the production of modern plays under the direction of Florence Farr, who had made a success of Ibsen on the London stage. Since Shaw had as yet nothing but 'unpleasant' plays in his repertoire, he hastily constructed a pleasant one for the occasion. It was an amusing trifle in three acts, called (in burlesque of the first line of Virgil's *Æneid*) *Arms and the Man*. It is a light-hearted satire of the romance of war, its hero being a Swiss mercenary soldier, who carries chocolate in his cartridge boxes and regards the military profession as merely a matter of business. The period is 1885 and the scene Bulgaria, which had no friends among London theatergoers so that the witty author had a free field for satire on the conventions of a Balkan semi-civilization of half a century ago. Goodnatured fooling about pacifism, patriotism, and the youthful romanticism which likes to chatter sentimental idealism found a ready hearing, and the play ran for nearly three months. It made its way to the comic opera stage as *The Chocolate Soldier* and gave Shaw his first taste of the sweets of dramatic popularity. The leading American actor of the day, Richard Mansfield, saw *Arms and the Man* in London, liked it, and gave New York the first American production of a play by Shaw at the Herald Square Theater on September 17, 1894. 'They think more of me in America than in England,' Shaw wrote sardonically to Ellen Terry, 'thanks to *Arms and the Man*.'

The American production of *Arms and the Man* was Shaw's first box-office success. The English production brought a loss of $25,000 to its anonymous 'angel' (afterwards revealed as Miss

Horniman, later the benefactress of the Abbey Theater in Dublin and the Gaiety in Manchester). With the royalties, Shaw records, 'I opened a very modest bank account, and became comparatively Conservative in my political opinions.' By this time he was earning a reasonable salary as dramatic critic of the Saturday Review, but he was still far from any assured access to the London commercial stage. Sir William Rothenstein in his *Men and Memories* recalls the Bernard Shaw of this period as 'a wild man in public, violent, aggressive, and paradoxical; in private he was the instinctive gentleman, ever on the side of the oppressed and unpopular, tender-hearted and generous, though he had little enough in those days to be generous with. . . . He was a figure apart—brilliant, genial, wholesome, a great wit, a gallant foe and a staunch friend, a Swift without bitterness, sharer and castigator of the follies of mankind, whose cap, though of Jaeger, was worn as gaily as motley.'

Candida, Shaw's second attempt at a 'pleasant' play, had great difficulty in making its way to the stage. The chief characters are a Christian Socialist clergyman—more clergyman than Socialist; his wife, Candida, who, according to Shaw, is the 'Virgin Mother,' a charming incarnation of the spirit of motherhood in the likeness of Ellen Terry; and her young lover, a boyish Shelley, who lies on the hearthrug in a state of ecstacy and reads or recites poetry. Shaw's first idea was to get Ellen Terry to persuade Sir Henry Irving to produce *Candida* at the Lyceum Theater, but Irving did not see a part for him in either the clergyman or the poet. Richard Mansfield rejected it for the same reason; and ultimately, for purposes of copyright, it made an occasional appearance on a provincial tour of the Independent Theater, 'to the great astonishment of its audiences.' Irving wrote, after reading it, 'When I got to the end, I had no more idea what you meant by it than a tom cat.' Yet when it was produced by Arnold Daly in New York in 1903–04, it laid the foundation of Shaw's supremacy of the twentieth century stage.

Shaw made a further attempt to please the Lyceum management with a one-act play, *The Man of Destiny*, in which Irving was to appear as Napoleon, and Ellen Terry as 'a Strange Lady'— a wondrous idealization of her own charm and intelligence as she appeared to Shaw's fond imagination. She liked it, but Irving, after long consideration and hesitation, turned it down.

Cyril Maude, then manager of the Haymarket Theater, hearing of the tribulations of *Candida*, asked to see the manuscript, suggesting that it might suit the Haymarket; Shaw, realizing better than its manager the requirements of a fashionable West End theater, firmly replied that it would not, but he undertook to write one that would. This was *You Never Can Tell*, on which, indeed, Shaw had been at work for some time; it was intended to satisfy 'the popular demand for fun, for fashionable dresses, for a pretty scene or two, a little music, and even for a great ordering of drinks by people with an expensive air from an—if possible—comic waiter.' The play has all these attractive ingredients, with only a dash here and there of Shavian propaganda, but it was evidently beyond the comprehension of the Haymarket Company, accustomed only to a very different medium. Shaw had terrible times at rehearsals and swore nothing could induce him to witness its performance. He was spared the ordeal, for at the last moment the play was withdrawn. Shaw accepted the disappointment heroically, and wrote a comic account of the catastrophe, putting the story into the mouth of Cyril Maude, who printed the tale as his own in his book *The Haymarket Theatre:* 'Mr. Shaw was one of those persons who use a certain superficial reasonableness and dexterity of manner to cover an invincible obstinacy in their own opinion. We had engaged for the leading part (I myself having accepted an insignificant part as a mere waiter) no less an artist than Mr. Allan Aynesworth, whose reputation and subsequent achievements make it unnecessary for me to justify our choice. Mr. Shaw had from the first contended that one of the scenes lay outside Mr. Aynesworth's peculiar province. There can be no doubt now that Mr. Shaw deliberately used his hypnotic power at rehearsal to compel Mr. Aynesworth to fulfil his prediction. In every other scene Mr. Aynesworth surpassed himself. In this he became conscious and confused; his high spirits were suddenly extinguished; even his good-humor left him. He was like a man under a spell—as no doubt he actually was—and his embarrassment communicated itself most painfully to my dear wife, who had to sit on the stage whilst Svengali deliberately tortured his victim.

'At the same time I must say that Mrs. Maude's conduct was not all I could have desired. I greatly dreaded an open rupture between her and the author; and the fiend somehow divined this, and used it as a means of annoying me. Sometimes, when he had cynically watched one of her scenes without any symptom of pleasure, I would venture to ask him his opinion of it. On such occasions he invariably rose with every appearance of angry disapproval, informed me that he would give his opinion to Miss

Emery herself, and stalked up the stage to her in a threatening manner, leaving me in a state of apprehension that my over-strained nerves were ill able to bear. Not until afterwards did I learn that on these occasions he flattered my wife disgracefully, and actually made her a party to his systematic attempt to drive me out of my senses. I have never reproached her with it, and I never shall. I mention it here only because it is the truth; and truth has always been with me the first consideration.

'At last Aynesworth broke down under the torture. Mr. Shaw, with that perfidious air of making the best of everything which never deserted him, hypnotized him into complaining of the number of speeches he had to deliver, whereupon Mr. Shaw cut out no less than seventeen of them. This naturally disabled the artist totally. On the question of cutting, Mr. Shaw's attitude was nothing less than Satanic. When I suggested cutting he handed me the play, begged me to cut it freely, and then hypnotized me so that I could not collect my thoughts sufficiently to cut a single line. On the other hand, if I showed the least pleasure in a scene at rehearsal he at once cut it out on the ground that the play was too long. What I suffered from that man at that time will never be fully known. The heart alone knoweth its own bitterness.

'The end came suddenly and unexpectedly. We had made a special effort to fulfil our unfortunate contract, of which even Harrison was now beginning to have his doubts. We had brought back Miss Kate Bishop from Australia to replace Miss Coleman. Mr. Valentine had taken the part repudiated by Mr. Barnes. The scenery had been modeled, and a real dentist's chair obtained for the first act. Harrison, whose folly was responsible for the whole wretched business, came down to the rehearsal. We were honestly anxious to retrieve the situation by a great effort, and save our dear little theater from the disgrace of a failure.

'Suddenly the author entered, in a new suit of clothes!!'

What really happened was told long after by John Harwood, then stage-manager of the Haymarket, in a letter to the New York Times (April 12, 1922): 'The members of the company had not the faintest idea of what they were talking about, and I suppose Shaw was either too lazy or too pained to tell them, and the climax came when Allan Aynesworth and Winifred Emery said to Shaw, "Why don't you cut these parts?" "Right!" replied Shaw. "A rehearsal for cuts at 11 o'clock tomorrow." The next morning Allan Aynesworth walked on to the stage with the largest blue pencil I have ever seen. God knows where he had got it, but it was about eighteen inches long and about three in circumference. With a beatific smile on his face, he strolled down to Shaw and, handing him his part, said, "You said you would cut my part, Mr. Shaw; here is a pencil." Shaw took the part, glanced at the pencil and without batting an eye took the pencil with a "Thanks, very much, I've left mine at home" and deliberately made a downward stroke on every page of the part. There were snickers and muttered conversation all round. Rehearsal was dismissed. Harrison, Maude, and Shaw retired to the office. One hour after Cyril Maude said to me with great glee: "We're not going to produce the play; ain't that a bit of luck!" Just about three weeks after that I met Ailsa Craig (daughter of Ellen Terry) on the street. She said: "Hello: your management has turned down the best play written for years!"'

Meanwhile Shaw had been busy with many other things. He was preparing for the press *Plays Pleasant and Unpleasant*—the seven plays discussed above, only two of them as yet put on the stage for regular performance. He was engaged to be married; he was elected a member of the St. Pancras Vestry; and he was writing a new play, *The Devil's Disciple*, a curious combination of intellectual burlesque and historical melodrama, set in the period of the American Revolutionary War. Produced by Richard Mansfield at the Fifth Avenue Theater, New York, in October, 1897, it had a long and successful run, bringing in a handsome toll of royalties to its author, who wrote to Ellen Terry: 'I roll in gold. I am a man of wealth and consideration.' In May, 1898, Shaw was able to give up regular journalism and the following month was married to Miss Payne Townshend. The publication of *Plays Pleasant and Unpleasant* increased the respect of the critics and gave him a hold upon a larger public, but he had still to conquer the London stage.

The London theater managers were impressed by Shaw's American success, but they still regarded him as an impossibility for commercial production. He wrote *Cæsar and Cleopatra* for Johnston Forbes-Robertson, who felt unable to 'run the risk of such a heavy production,' and still another play, *Captain Brassbound's Conversion*, for Ellen Terry, who gave a single performance for copyright at Liverpool before she sailed for her last American tour with Sir Henry Irving. Richard Mansfield declined *Cæsar and Cleopatra*, and Shaw wrote for him no more. In 1901 he published *Three Plays for Puritans*, of which only *The Devil's Disciple* had yet achieved success on the boards. But it was really the darkest hour before the dawn for Shaw and the London stage. The Stage Society put on private performances of *You Never Can Tell, Candida,* and *Captain Brassbound's Conversion* in the last two years of the nineteenth century, and the success of these performances showed that commercial production of Shaw on the London stage need not prove a financial failure. In three seasons, beginning in 1904, the Royal Court Theater gave over seven hundred performances of Shaw plays, and Shaw's popular success in the United States, begun by Richard Mansfield with *Arms and the Man* and *The Devil's Disciple,* was continued by Arnold Daly with *Candida, The Man of Destiny,* and *You Never Can Tell.*

Shaw's greatest stage triumphs and the establishment of his world-wide dramatic supremacy (recognized in 1926 by the award of the Nobel Prize) were reserved for the twentieth century and lie beyond the scope of this volume; but it must always be remembered that the greater part of his life was passed in the Victorian Era and that the development of his genius was a distinctly Victorian phenomenon. As a poverty-stricken Don Quixote fighting with intellectual weapons for power and influence, he is a more sympathetic figure than as the successful international dramatist, enriched by enormous royalties and preaching his old doctrine of equality of income amid universal applause. He was a characteristic Victorian in that the ideas he conceived and propounded in the nineteenth century were so generally accepted in the twentieth as to become almost commonplace. He had not a little of the Victorian inconsistency: he girded at the folly of unattainable ideals and himself held up the ideal of equality of income when he must have been paying large amounts of super-tax to the Government on an income to which every one of the big nations was contributing; he preached the gospel of a free-for-all marriage and was himself the devoted husband of one wife; he expressed contempt in public for the virtues of the Puritan middle class, and illustrated them magnificently in private. He scoffed at clergymen in *Mrs. Warren's Profession* and *Candida,* yet did more preaching than any other man of his time. With all this, jester or prophet, he became the most popular and distinguished of international celebrities, welcomed with equal enthusiasm by the leaders of the Soviet Government at Moscow and by the bankers of New York. His doctrinaire Communism, proclaimed with the same courage in the days of his impecunious youth and his extremely wealthy old age, gave the less offense because he never made any serious effort to put it into effect. Under his leadership the Fabian

Society became an organization whose main efforts seemed to be directed to giving sound advice in principle and in practice letting things alone. Yet, first and last, he was a gallant fighter and a brilliant expositor of his own peculiar heresies. He made it not only permissible but popular to deny the established dogmas in economics, in science, in religion, in politics. To the young people of the turn of the century he was an inspiration and a hope; and if the crusade for which they enlisted under his banner led precisely nowhere, they had at least the exhilaration of not acquiescing in states of thought and life which were evidently coming to an end. If the later Victorians had to choose a representative champion, there would be none likely to cut a better figure in history than Bernard Shaw.

INDEX

In accordance with the practice of the Congressional Library Catalogue, initial A *and* The *are omitted in book titles.*

333

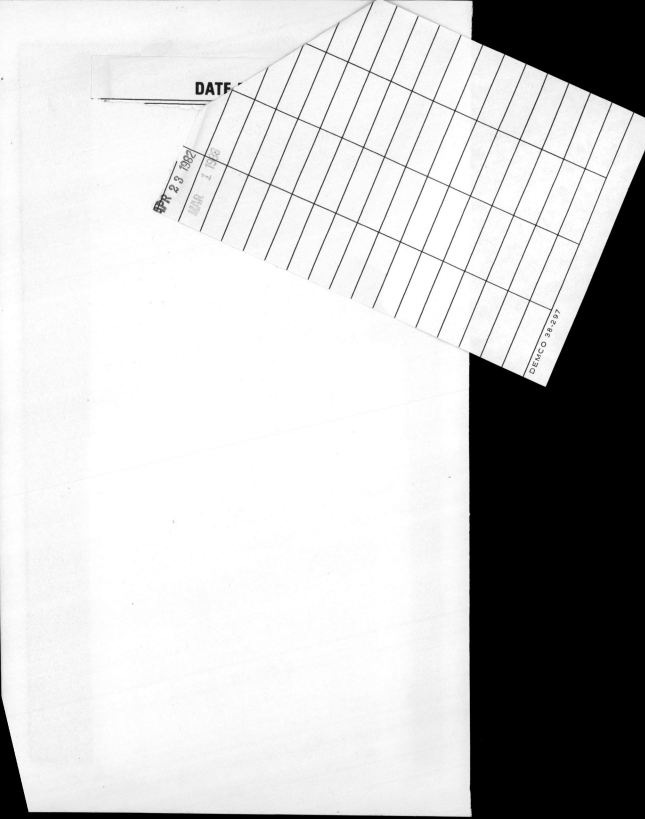